Second Edition

Twenty Studies That Revolutionized Child Psychology

Wallace E. Dixon, Jr.

East Tennessee State University

PEARSON

Boston   Columbus   Indianapolis   New York   San Francisco   Hoboken
Amsterdam   Cape Town   Dubai   London   Madrid   Milan   Munich   Paris   Montréal   Toronto
Delhi   Mexico City   São Paulo   Sydney   Hong Kong   Seoul   Singapore   Taipei   Tokyo

VP, Product Development: Dickson Musslewhite
Senior Acquisitions Editor: Amber Chow
Editorial Assistant: Luke Robbins
Executive Field Marketer: Kate Stewart
Senior Product Marketer: Lindsay Prudhomme Gill
Marketing Assistant: Frank Alarcon
Director, Project Management Services: Lisa Iarkowski
Project Team Lead: Linda Behrens
Project Manager: Shelly Kupperman
Program Manager: Diane Szulecki

Procurement Manager: Mary Fischer
Procurement Specialist: Diane Peirano
Cover Design: Lumina Datamatics, Inc.
Full-Service Project Management: Anju Joshi, Lumina Datamatics, Inc.
Printer/Binder: STP Courier
Cover Printer: STP Courier
Cover Image: viperagp/Fotolia
Text Font: 10/12 point Minion

Credits and acknowledgments borrowed from other sources and reproduced, with permission, in this textbook appear on pages 268–270.

Library of Congress Cataloging-in-Publication Data

Dixon, Wallace E.
  Twenty studies that revolutionized child psychology / Wallace E. Dixon, Jr., East Tennessee State University.—
Second Edition.
        pages cm
  ISBN 978-0-205-94803-1—ISBN 0-205-94803-0 1. Child psychology. 2. Infant psychology. 3. Child development.
  4. Child rearing. I. Title.
  BF721.D59 2015
  155.4—dc23

                                                                                    2014044732

10 9 8 7 6 5 4 3 2 1

ISBN-10:   0-205-94803-0
ISBN-13: 978-0-205-94803-1

This book is dedicated to my academic mother, Peg Smith.
May I ever be so fortunate to inspire my students
as you have inspired me.

CONTENTS

Part III Four Studies That Revolutionized Social Development

Part IV   Seven Studies That Revolutionized Parenting and Clinical Child Psychology

PREFACE

I don't claim to have any special knowledge of how the field of child psychology operates. I'm just an average Joe trying to make a living doing what child psychologists do. One of the most important things they do is read the work of other child psychologists. Over the three decades or so that I've been reading these works, I've developed an impromptu, but fairly comprehensive classification scheme for what I think are the most important research topics, who are the most influential child psychologists, and which are the most revolutionary scientific publications. I've gotten to the point that whenever I read the work of another child psychologist, the second thing I do is look over the References section (the first thing I do is read the title and abstract). The reason I turn to the references first is that I can get a good sense of the tone, the purpose, and the outcome of the article, just by seeing who gets cited in it.

But as I first started thinking about the first edition of this text, I began to wonder whether other child psychologists developed their own mental classification schemes too, and whether their schemes were similar to mine. For example, I wondered whether other researchers considered the works of Robert Fantz and Renée Baillargeon as revolutionary as I did. So in the summer of 2000, I launched a research project of my own in an attempt to uncover the major child psychology research projects published in the second half of the twentieth century. I asked child psychologists from all walks of life to nominate and vote on the studies they believed were the Most Important, Most Revolutionary, Most Controversial, and Most Fascinating. The first edition of this book described those 20 studies that fell into the category of "Most Revolutionary."

Now, some 10–13 years later, depending on how you count, I thought it would be fun to take another look at the field to see how things have changed. The increased technology has allowed for a larger and more comprehensive study, including tapping into a broader range of research communities and constituencies; and using Survey Monkey to make it much easier for participants to add their contributions. By polling members of three different professional societies, including the Society for Research in Child Development, the Cognitive Development Society, and the International Society on Infant Studies, I found I had a built-in cross-checking system to see if certain studies were more preferred by certain kinds of child psychologists than others. It turns out that at the top end of the rankings, they generally weren't. Ainsworth's work, for example, was rated number one by all three societies; and Bandura's work was rated in the top four by all three societies. When there were major differences between the societies, they tended to be at the lower end of the rankings. In these cases, members of one society may have ranked a study as very revolutionary, while members of another may not have done so.

My friend and colleague Karen Adolph once wrote that a classic paradigm in science includes three earmarks: sensational and memorable images, a simple yet elegant design, and common sense appeal. For the most part, the studies described in this edition have all three. There are a few studies in which the common sense appeal is buried a couple of levels down, but a little digging goes a long way. There are also a few studies in which the methodology seems complicated at first, but that emerges in full glory upon further reflection. Sometimes experimental procedures are a lot easier to understand in the mind's eye than through retelling in mere words.

The project was a major undertaking, and I would be remiss if I didn't acknowledge the contributions of a number of generous individuals. I would like to re-acknowledge the overwhelming effort put forth by Debbie Hoffman during the development of the first edition. Deb was crucial in making the success of that first edition possible. Thanks also go to Chuck Moon,

Matt McBee, and Stacey Williams, who guided me in developing a research design to identify the most revolutionary studies in child psychology. Thanks are due to a number of individuals who read, commented on, or otherwise provided guidance for how I might approach individual chapters, including Cynthia Anderson, Tim Anderson, Daniel Cruikshanks, Brian Haley, Farrah Hughes, Elizabeth McRae, Michele Moser, Matt Palmatier, and Ken Porada. Relatedly I thank a number of people who provided useful adjunctive information for me to use in my book, including: Bob Berg, Sarah Dixon, Xiaoming Huang, Muthoni Kimemia, Steve Velazquez, Ayako Tabusa, and Hendrix and Julia Price (one of whom apparently really is literally the most annoying person on the planet). Very special thanks go to Nadège Dufort, whose diligent translations, and Jean-Jacques Ducret and the Jean Piaget Foundation, whose facilitated permissions, made inclusion of Piaget's original 1945 French text in Chapter 3 possible. Finally, I wish to acknowledge a number of the top 20 authors or their close acquaintances for giving me direction and suggestions for ways to approach the text; especially Karen Adolph, Dick Aslin, Renée Baillargeon, Joe Fagan, Andrew Meltzoff, Jenny Saffran, Beverly Ulrich, and Janet Werker.

A number of people deserve special mention for providing me with the mental fortitude to pursue the project: Esther Strahan for telling me my book-writing future was inevitable, Peg Smith for telling me it was about time I wrote a book, Wallace Dixon, Sr., for telling me book writing is where the real money is, and Tim Lawson for trying to outdo and write more books than me. Finally, special thanks with sugar on top to my wife, Michele Moser, and my kids, Aiden and Sarah, for putting up with me as I stressed out while meeting my personal deadlines.

Wallace E. Dixon, Jr.

1

Introduction

Congratulations! You've taken your first step into the exhilarating world of child psychology. Of course, I may be a little biased. After all, I've been doing child psychology for nearly 30 years, and my livelihood depends on getting others to believe what I do is important. (If my employers didn't think so, I'd be out of a job!) Still, the reason I got involved in this field in the first place was partly because it was so exciting and partly because new scientific findings in child psychology seemed to occur more rapidly than a firing neuron. In fact, I remember in my college days being puzzled that everyone else wasn't majoring in child psychology. After all, in what other profession can you get paid to play with toys and cute little babies (without the stinky diapers)? Who would want to do anything else?

But as I took upper-level child psychology courses, the drawbacks of the field became more apparent. I found that not all of child psychology is balloons and rainbows. Clinical and applied child psychologists have to deal with supremely frustrating elements of children's development. They work on problems such as repairing children who've been damaged by physical abuse and neglect, and improving the quality of life of children born with Down syndrome or autism. These developmental disabilities can be devastating, and to work with them every day must require an emotional constitution of steel. Still, the work needs to be done, and the fact that I'm part of a field that addresses these overwhelming challenges makes me proud.

Despite my own excitement about child psychology, I'm willing to concede that other folks may not see things the same way I do. Over the years I've also found that a lot of people don't like to play golf, most people don't like to play chess, and very few people besides marine biologists and saltwater aquarists care about the difference between a soft and a stony coral. So it's not surprising that from time to time I've come across a few individuals who find the topic of child psychology an invitation to snooze, although it's still completely beyond me.

After giving the matter some thought, I think part of the reason that some people aren't exhilarated by the field can be traced to how most child psychology textbooks are written. Let's face it, child psychology texts don't exactly read like *Twilight*. If the truth be told, I've yet to find a child psychology textbook as absorbing as the field it describes. This is not to blame the textbook authors—quite the contrary. Child psychology textbook authors are extraordinarily competent professionals who've taken upon themselves the colossal task of summarizing an entire field in less than 700 pages. Now you might think 700 pages is a lot. But Piaget wrote over 700 pages in just

2 of his 100+ manuscripts, and Piaget is just one of several thousand child psychology researchers who've actively published in the field in the last 50 years. To me, at least, it's easy to understand the impossibility of the task confronted by the child psychology textbook author. Just for a moment, imagine yourself in her position. On the one hand, you'd want to be as complete in your coverage as possible; but on the other hand, you'd have some serious space limitations. Would any nondelusional person expect to sell a 5,000-page textbook? So, through some sort of a textbook version of Darwinian natural selection, textbooks have evolved into a dense collection of research findings held together by the organizational glue provided by the creative talents of the authors.

The problem can also be traced to the plight of the child psychology instructor. Now, trust me when I say, without any bias whatsoever, that you can't find better people on a college campus anywhere. Child psychology professors are wonderfully talented individuals. They work hard. They study hard. But they also get caught up in a couple of inescapable binds. First, as with textbook authors, instructors have the daunting task of covering a virtually infinite range of information in a conspicuously finite amount of time. At the completion of every semester, I'm amazed at how little I actually accomplished in my 45 hours of class time. Instructors are further obligated to meet the needs of a wide variety of students. If an instructor deviates too much from the textbook material, she risks dissatisfaction from students who fume over spending $190 on a textbook the professor didn't use. Yet if she deviates too little from the textbook, she offends a different group of students who are fuming over having spent $1,000 on a course when all they needed to do was read the textbook. It's a no-win situation.

Even if students actually read the textbooks, and even if they actually pay attention during class, it's no trivial matter that many theories and findings in child psychology are simply beyond a normal student's grasp. For one thing, students have to overcome the "common sense" hurdle. Many people come to a child psychology course confident in their expectation that the course will confirm what they already know. After all, they were kids themselves once. Some students even have their own children. Obviously, parents must know a lot about child psychology, right? The obstacle presents itself when many findings in child psychology contradict commonsense beliefs and child-rearing folklore. I'll never forget the middle-aged woman who came up to me after class one day (back in my youthful days when I still got carded when buying beer) just to tell me that I didn't need to feel intimidated by her extensive personal child-rearing experience.

On top of all this, child psychology theories undergo considerable refinement and revision from year to year. Understanding contemporary child psychology theory is like hitting a clay pigeon with a blunt arrow at a hundred paces. Some theories have gotten so complicated and so far removed from the children they describe that they're not even recognizable as child psychology theories anymore. I remember covering one such theory in class several years ago. This theory, which child psychologists call "information processing theory," is a modern approach that uses the computer as a metaphor for thinking about children's thinking. One day, to get my students to grapple with how this theory might be relevant to children's thinking, I gave them a schematic drawing of the general parts of a computer, including a keyboard, a printer, the RAM, and a hard drive. I broke the class into groups and had each group trace the path on the diagram, from input to output, that they thought best described how information moves through a computer. Most of the duty-bound students engaged the task eagerly. However, after about 10 minutes, in front of the whole class, an exasperated student burst out, "What does this crap have to do with kids?" I was stunned by the question, not because of its boldness, but because the connection was completely obvious to me. I thought students would surely see that computers process information in ways that parallel children's thinking. But this connection was completely lost on this student. The connection between information processing theory and real live children was so remote, so disconnected from how the students thought children thought, that they missed the point entirely. These days I realize that child psychology instructors must take a few steps backward from their intensely passionate immersion in child psychology if they're going to have any hope of being effective instructors. Followers of Piaget would describe this as becoming less egocentric.

In order to be effective, child psychology instructors really have to work hard at making connections between the unfamiliar, sometimes even bizarre theories and facts in the discipline and the children who are the objects of study. I think instructors would spend their time much more wisely if they tried to construct bridges to reach the minds of students rather than expecting students to build bridges to reach the minds of instructors. Unfortunately, as we've just seen, such a task can be exceptionally challenging. There's just too much information in child psychology to share effectively.

Now, left in the wake of the frontline child psychology instructors, the hardworking textbook authors, and the confused students, are the unsung heroes of child psychology, the sources of all those tidbits and factoids that fill the pages of child psychology textbooks: the research studies themselves. Here are some of the most ingenious innovations ever constructed in all of psychology, if not all of science. With them, the revolutionary advancements in our understanding of child development that have taken place in the last 50 years are unparalleled in all of human history. Yet, for whatever reason, the beauty of the studies, coupled with the ingenuity and driving motivations of the researchers who created them, are often left behind like clippings on the editing room floor. Instead, instructors sometimes get caught in the rut of asking students to memorize facts and findings, the stages, ages, and phases (SAPs) of research investigations. I admit to doing so myself on many occasions. But this focus places disproportionate value on the outcomes of child psychology research, at the cost of ignoring everything that went into producing it. I think we could excite students of child psychology about the field a lot more if instead of pelting them with trivia, we bathed them in the ingenuity of a few of the most powerful studies. It seems to me that students whose interest is piqued through this method will pick up the trivia on their own.

Oh sure, sometimes individual studies are covered in great detail. For example, many child psychology students remember that Piaget's research on cognitive development was prompted by detailed observations of his own three children. And no doubt, somewhere on the planet, students' eyes are glazing over as they recite Piaget's four main stages of cognitive development. But I wonder if students would find Piaget a more interesting figure if they knew he initially had no interest in studying children. He was actually more interested in mollusks. And although he eventually tripped over a career opportunity involving the observation of children, even then he really didn't find his job all that interesting, at least not at first. I also wonder if students would be fascinated to find out that Piaget coauthored his first professional article, not as a psychologist, but as a biologist, before he entered puberty. And in fact, as a result of the popularity he obtained from that article, he was put in the unfortunate position of having to turn down a job as a curator of the mollusk collection at the Museum of Natural History in Geneva, Switzerland, at age 15 (because he had to finish high school). My notion is that this kind of background information places Piaget's accomplishments in a much more interesting light, and that by providing child psychology students with this kind of "gossipy" background information, we might just find that they view the rest of what Piaget had to say much more interesting. And, if all goes well, they might remember it better to boot.

I'm willing to bet that once students have a fuller understanding of the person or studies behind the theory, they'll feel more immersed and more involved. They'll begin taking the issues more seriously because they're connecting with them. You can tell when students are connecting when they say things like, "How can a theory of all children be based on observations of only three children?" Or, with regard to Sigmund Freud, "How can we trust the theory of a coke-head?"

(referring to Freud's cocaine habit). And of course this is my point. By inviting students backstage, child psychology instructors can hope to show students the motivating forces behind child psychology research. When students understand these motivations, they can better place the field in a broader context against which they can evaluate, embrace, and experience its parts.

In writing this book, I hope to spread my enthusiasm for child psychology by laying out the field in the context of 20 studies that have revolutionized our way of thinking about children. My objective is to give you something of the child psychologist's perspective on doing child psychology, after which I think it'll be hard for you *not* to share my enthusiasm. In the process of gaining this perspective, you'll have to learn something about the various histories of the field. You'll have to know what things were like in the old days before we knew about babies' newfound superpowers, before we knew that even newborns could understand, organize, and think about things. If I can get you to appreciate the methodologies of these research studies as well as their historical contexts, I think it will be impossible for you not to apply the term *exhilarating* to the field of child psychology yourself. All I ask is that you read this book, think about what I say, and raise questions about this stuff in the classroom. If you do all this, I won't guarantee it, but I think you'll have a pretty good chance of getting an A in the course.

Before we begin, there are a few things we should discuss and a few assumptions we should reveal about the field of child psychology. First, I feel I have to point out that child psychology, like psychology more generally, and like biology, chemistry, astronomy, and physics, is above all else a science. It is a *true* science in every possible sense of the word. Saying this is in some ways saying very little and in some ways saying a great deal. It says very little because it only points out that child psychology follows the scientific method. That is, child psychology obeys the rules of scientific questioning, reasoning, procedures for data collection, data analysis, and theory revision. Child psychology does all the things you've heard science does ever since your eighth-grade science class. However, saying child psychology is a science can also seem heretical. Many people in our society question the wisdom of analyzing children, as if doing so will expose some secret, confidential plan. Others argue that child psychology isn't a science at all because human beings aren't subject to the same kind of scientific laws and scientific scrutiny that nematodes, chemical reactions, and meteor showers are. To this attitude I respond, "Hogwash!" The scientific method is a procedure, a way of inquiring about the world, and knows nothing of the content of its application. So you can apply the scientific method to just about any topic of study. Predicting the direction and velocity of a 10-kilogram child toddling down a garden path may not be as precise as predicting the direction and velocity of a 50-gram sphere on a 20° plane, but child psychology is just as much a science as any other method of inquiry that obeys the scientific method. The important thing is that, because child psychology is a science, we can't make our beliefs about children true just by thinking them. Facts about child psychology have to be well supported by sound reasoning and strong evidence. Students in my classes know very well, after hearing me recite it countless times, that opinions about children in the absence of systematically obtained data are scientifically worthless. Claims about what children do, think, know, and feel have to be backed up by scientific data.

Another erroneous belief is that findings in child psychology can't be valid unless they apply to every child. But this belief also reveals ignorance about the way science works. It would probably be most accurate to say that child psychology applies to all of the children some of the time, some of the children all of the time, but never to all of the children all of the time. Because children are so different from one another, and because their life circumstances are so varied, child psychologists don't realistically believe that their scientific findings will always apply to all kids. They merely do their best to explain as much about children as they can for as many children as they can under as many circumstances as they can. So when child psychologists conduct scientific investigations with children, they strive to include as many children as possible. However, many laypeople don't seem to appreciate the need for a large sample size. In fact, some laypeople seem to believe that one encounter is sufficient for a comprehensive understanding of some aspect of psychology. Their argument goes something like this: "Psychology is about people. I've been around people; therefore, I know about psychology." Now sometimes this approach is okay, but sometimes it can get you into trouble. For example, if you knew someone who snorted cocaine and then became a successful business executive, would you conclude that all people who snort cocaine will become successful business executives? I doubt it. Just because you might be aware of someone or some case that violates some child psychology finding somewhere, doesn't mean that you can dismiss the scientific finding as untrue. There are going to be exceptions.

THE WAY IT WORKS

It wasn't until I was a sophomore in college that it finally occurred to me that the "studies" being referred to by news anchors when they said, "Recent studies have shown . . ." were often studies conducted by psychologists. This discovery was very exciting to me. As a psychology major, it meant that I might one day conduct a study that could make the evening news. Of course, not every study rates a mention on the evening news. The study has to be a good one, and it has to be exciting to people outside the field. But most importantly, when a study finally makes the news, it has usually undergone a very long and excruciating period of development and evaluation beforehand.

Conducting a scientific study involves a lot more than meets the eye. First, a scientist has an idea about how something works. At this point it's just an idea, and the scientist's idea is no better or more valid than anybody else's. However, unlike nonscientists, the scientist goes on to test the accuracy of the idea by collecting information from the world that has some bearing on it. This is called data collection. The scientist's original idea is usually framed in such a way as to ask a specific question. And data are collected so as to answer the question. Once the question is answered, the idea that generated the question is either proven wrong or not. The researcher might then go on to test additional questions generated by the idea. As this idea→question→data collection process cycles through a few times, a more fully elaborated idea develops. At this more sophisticated level, the idea can be called a theory. Most textbook authors define a theory as a set of statements that accounts well for an existing set of data. A good theory should also make accurate and specific predictions about the future.

But finding a desirable answer to the initial question isn't the last step. The last step is called "dissemination." Dissemination is the way scientists get their work known by their peers and colleagues in the scientific community. The dissemination step itself has several procedures that have to be followed. First, the study and its results have to be "written up." The document that gets written up is called a manuscript. The scientist then submits her manuscript to the editor of a professional scientific journal for publication. However, before publishing the manuscript, the journal editor sends the article out to be reviewed by other people who know a lot about the scientist's field. These people are called reviewers. The reviewers read the manuscript, find everything wrong with it that they possibly can, then summarize the manuscript's faults in a letter back to the journal editor. If there aren't too many problems with either the study or the manuscript describing it, the journal editor may decide to publish the manuscript in the journal (after the scientist revises it once or twice). Once the manuscript gets published in the journal, all the scientists in the world can read about the study and its findings. Some textbook authors may even wish to include the results of the study in the latest editions of their textbooks.

ARTICLE STRUCTURE

Articles that get published in scientific journals have a fairly standardized look. Psychology articles might have a slightly different appearance than articles published in other disciplines, but the general structure is the same. First, there is an introduction section, followed by a method section, followed by a results section, and ending in a discussion or conclusion section. Each of these four sections has a specific purpose in the article. Because journal articles are so standardized, readers know just where to look if they have a specific question about the article.

Introduction Section

The introduction section of an article is the place where the scientist, now the author, describes the reason for doing his scientific study in the first place. This section is where the author tells his readers why they should be interested in the study he's describing. The scientist also tells the readership what work has already been done on that topic, what the limitations are of that previous work, what work has yet to be done, and how her own study will make a contribution to the existing body of child psychology knowledge.

Method Section

To use a dessert metaphor, the method section can be likened to the recipe used for baking a cake. Here the author gets down to the nitty-gritty of specifying how the actual study was conducted. Here is where the author can describe the organisms studied: how many there were, what age they were, their gender distribution, their ethnicity (if they're human), their species, and how they were recruited to participate. (Human animals are usually recruited. Other animals are usually, shall we say, strongly encouraged.) In the old days we used to call the subjects of psychological research simply "subjects," but these days we call them "participants," especially if they're human. This change in phraseology reflects psychology's discipline-wide efforts toward treating people as people, rather than only as objects of study. But no matter what you call human participants in a psychological investigation, they're still the objects of study in the investigation.

The method section is also the place for the author to explain how she "operationally defined" all the abstract psychological concepts that she studied. The idea of an **operational definition** is essential for scientists because it allows them to state in clear, unambiguous terms how they measured an otherwise abstract concept. If you wanted to study the intellectual development of first-graders, for example, you couldn't just look at a group of first-graders and know how intelligent they were. You would have to *measure* their intelligence in some way. Typically, you might use an IQ test of some sort. An IQ test score in this example would be the operational definition of intelligence. When a scientist operationally defines an abstract concept, she isn't implying that her way is the best way to measure the concept; she's only declaring that it is her way. Other scientists can use other ways to measure the same abstract concepts if they want. The point of the method section is to let the reader know how *this* scientist measured *this* abstract concept on *this* occasion.

The method section describes not only the ingredients the scientist used (the participants and the operational definitions) but also how she mixed them together (the methodological procedure). Here the author specifies things like how the measurements were taken, when they were taken, the various conditions under which they were taken, how many times they were taken, and the order in which they were taken. If you've ever baked a cake, you know that the order of procedures makes all the difference. You wouldn't put the cake pan in the oven before mixing the ingredients, for example. Well, in specifying her experimental procedure, the researcher is telling the reader how and in what order she mixed together her ingredients. Because the author divulges this information, any reader who doesn't like the taste of the cake (the outcome of the study) can at least attempt to bake his own, making modifications to the ingredients or the mixing procedures wherever he wishes. The fact that such recipes are so public and so open to scrutiny is one of the best features of science. Scientists don't walk around in secret societies conspiring to overthrow all that is good and sincere. Science is exquisitely public, which makes it open to public scrutiny, to public criticism, and to people who think they can do it better. The result of such openness is continued scientific progress.

Results Section

If the participants, operational definitions, and procedures of a study can be likened to the ingredients for baking a cake, then the results can be likened to its taste. In the results section of a journal article, the scientist presents a detailed account of the data she collected from the participants using the operational definitions and the procedures that she described in the method section. Usually, you'll see a lot of statistics here. Even advanced psychology majors are overwhelmed at the mathematicality of journal articles; and there are all those weird F, t, and p thingies throughout results sections too. Well, it's no coincidence that psychology majors usually have to take at least one statistics course as part of their major. The results sections of psychology journal articles are loaded with descriptive statistics, inferential statistics, p-values, F-ratios, degrees of freedom, and betas, etas, lambdas, and deltas. It takes at least one, but usually many more, courses in statistics to begin to understand the statistics presented in results sections of journal articles.

Of course, I can't go into much detail here in explaining what all the various kinds of statistics mean; but I can say that most researchers don't include statistics in their journal articles just for the fun of it. There is in fact a very important goal in presenting all those statistics: They are meant to demonstrate to the reader that the findings obtained were unlikely to have happened by accident. In sum, the job of the scientist in writing up the results section is to review each of the initial research questions, to present statistics that guide her in answering each of her questions, and to determine whether any of the correlations or differences that she found for each of the questions was accidental. The scientist then describes to the reader her interpretations of the statistics in light of the initial research questions.

Discussion

Continuing along with our cake-baking metaphor, the discussion section provides a venue for the scientist to reflect on how good the cake tasted and how good a job she did in baking it. Here she can describe what ingredients she wished she'd used instead, how she might like to focus next time on baking a chocolate cake instead of another yellow one, whether she would like to bake the thing at a different temperature, or even whether she would prefer to use a completely different oven. The scientist also uses this section to describe to the reader how her findings can be integrated into the field as a whole, and to make suggestions for future studies that might help fill in the gaps in understanding left empty or even created by her study. My graduate adviser told me to think of the discussion section as a place to "ride off into the sunset." I think what she meant is that every study has a silver lining, and the discussion section should act like a happy ending for the story of the research study. I know, it may sound corny, but the author who publishes a scientific study really is telling a story. It's a story with a beginning, a middle, and an end. There are characters and props. There is a narrative leading up to some goal (the introduction), a means set up to achieve the goal (the method section), a climax (the results section), and a denouement (the discussion section). Viewed in this way, the discussion section really should leave the reader with a sense of accomplishment and a sense of success. The reader should walk away feeling happy.

MY TACK

The purpose of my book is to share the field of child psychology with you by presenting 20 of the most revolutionary studies ever published in the field. In reviewing each of these 20 studies, where possible, I will take some time to familiarize you with each study by reviewing the four major areas with you. That is, I will review why the authors wanted to do the study, what the authors hoped to accomplish, how the study was conducted, what was found, and how the findings revolutionized the field. Where possible, I'll indicate how the findings from the original study are still relevant to the field of child psychology today or to modern society more generally.

Now, because I believe so strongly in the role of science in producing new knowledge, I didn't want to be a hypocrite by relying on my own intuition in deciding which studies to include in this book. I think I have a pretty good sense of the field of child psychology, and I think I could do a pretty good job of selecting most of the revolutionary studies on my own. But I thought a far more accurate list of the revolutionary studies could be determined by taking a scientific poll of professional scholars in the field. So I undertook a scientific investigation of my own. I began by surveying the memberships of three of the leading organizations in child psychology: the Society for Research in Child Development (SRCD), the International Society on Infant Studies (ISIS), and the Cognitive Development Society (CDS). The study took place in two phases. In the first phase, I simply asked people to nominate the studies they thought had revolutionized the field of child psychology. This was the "open-ended" portion of my survey. Many, many dozens of studies were nominated in this phase. Because such a wide variety of studies were nominated in Phase I, I conducted Phase II to narrow down the list. This time, I redistributed a list of the 30 most frequently nominated studies to the same three organizations. In this "closed-ended" version of the survey, I asked respondents to rank order what they believed were the top 10 most revolutionary studies. These results allowed me to narrow the list down to the 20 you'll read about in this book.

THEMES

Many traditional child psychology textbook authors make a point of highlighting common themes that operate throughout the whole of child psychology. You'll note a number of common themes that run through the revolutionary studies described in this book as well. Some of these themes are no doubt the same as described in other child psychology textbooks, but there are also a few that are probably unique to our revolutionary studies. The prominent themes running through these 20 studies include:

THE THEME OF NATURE VERSUS NURTURE   Perhaps the most popular theme running throughout these 20 revolutionary studies is that of "nature versus nurture." As you're probably aware, the nature/nurture issue has to do with the extent that children are the product of their own genes versus being a product of their unique environments. Researchers no longer ask whether genes or environment are more responsible for human behavior. Instead, they ask how they are responsible. The authors differ quite a bit in how much time they spend dealing with the nature/nurture issue, at least in terms of the works presented in this book, but most address the theme to some degree. Researchers who tend to fall on the nature side of things include Fantz (Chapter 8), Baillargeon,

Spelke, & Wasserman (Chapter 5), Harlow and Harlow (Chapter 16), Bowlby (Chapter 17), and Ainsworth (Chapter 18). Researchers who tend to fall on the nurture side of things include Vygotsky (Chapter 4), Bronfenbrenner (Chapter 14), Baumrind (Chapter 20), Saffran, Aslin, and Newport (Chapter 11), and Bandura, Ross, and Ross (Chapter 14). Researchers who place greatest focus on the interaction between nature and nurture include Piaget (Chapters 2 and 3), Gibson & Walk (Chapter 7), Thomas, Chess, and Birch (Chapter 16), Thelen & Ulrich (Chapter 6), and Hubel and Wiesel (Chapter 9).

THE THEME OF THE ACTIVE CHILD   It's also a common theme in child psychology textbooks to point out that children play an active role in their own development. Piaget (Chapters 2 and 3), for example, talks about how children are endowed by biology with certain starting points for knowledge and how they build on this knowledge by virtue of their own sensorimotor activity. And Gibson and Walk (Chapter 7) address the issue of how experience with locomotion impacts the extent that children are willing to cross over the visual cliff. Other studies that address how children play an active role in their own development include Bowlby (Chapter 11), Thomas, Chess, and Birch (Chapter 16), Hubel and Wiesel (Chapter 9), and Bronfenbrenner (Chapter 14).

THE THEME OF EVOLUTIONARY THEORY   One theme that may be less emphasized in standard child psychology textbooks is the extent that theories and research are based on Darwin's theory of evolution. In a number of studies reported here, however, Darwin's theory of evolution played a central role. It becomes very clear in Chapter 1, for example, that Piaget's entire theory of cognitive development was based on his application of evolutionary theory to children's intellectual development. Bowlby's entire attachment theory (Chapter 17), as well as Ainsworth's adaptation of it (Chapter 18), is similarly deeply rooted in evolutionary theory. And Fantz (Chapter 8) suggested that babies might be "built" by evolution to prefer to look at human faces.

THE THEME OF PERSPECTIVE   It appears that a number of studies were revolutionary because they brought a new or different perspective to the field of child psychology. For example, Piaget (Chapters 2 and 3) made great progress in child psychology largely because he approached the field from the perspective of a biologist. The same was true of Thelen (Chapter 6), whose doctoral dissertation in the biological sciences attracted her to the behavior patterns of animals in their natural environments. Vygotsky's (Chapter 4) claim to fame had a great deal to do with the fact that he applied Marxist ideologies to the cognitive and language development of children. And Bandura (Chapter 12) was a social psychologist, and so he explored children's aggression as a socially learned phenomenon.

THE THEME OF REBELLION   If there's a theme that's particularly conspicuous among studies that revolutionized a field, it's the theme of rebellion. Many of the studies described in this book had a revolutionary impact on child psychology precisely because they were rebelling against the status quo. Behavioral psychology was a common target of many of these revolutionary researchers. For example, the works of Fantz (Chapter 8); Harlow and Harlow (Chapter 16); Bandura, Ross, and Ross (Chapter 12); and Thomas, Chess, and Birch (Chapter 19) were all inspired by a common rejection of mainstream behavioral psychology.

Other revolutionary researchers were more idiosyncratic in whom they rebelled against. For example, Baillargeon (Chapter 5) set out to disprove Piaget. In contrast, the Harlows (Chapter 16); Bowlby (Chapter 17); and Thomas, Chess, and Birch (Chapter 19) all had Freudian theory in their crosshairs, whereas Thelen and Ulrich's Dynamic Systems theory (Chapter 6) was bent on showing that fixed action patterns weren't really all that fixed.

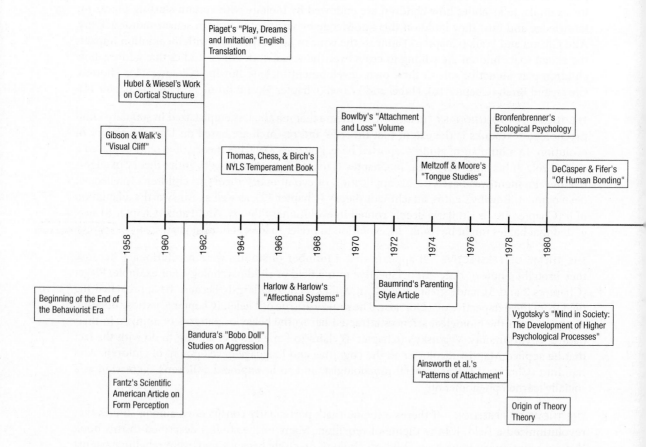

Piaget's "Play, Dreams and Imitation" English Translation

Hubel & Wiesel's Work on Cortical Structure

Gibson & Walk's "Visual Cliff"

Bowlby's "Attachment and Loss" Volume

Bronfenbrenner's Ecological Psychology

Thomas, Chess, & Birch's NYLS Temperament Book

Meltzoff & Moore's "Tongue Studies"

DeCasper & Fifer's "Of Human Bonding"

1958 1960 1962 1964 1966 1968 1970 1972 1974 1976 1978 1980

Beginning of the End of the Behaviorist Era

Harlow & Harlow's "Affectional Systems"

Baumrind's Parenting Style Article

Bandura's "Bobo Doll" Studies on Aggression

Vygotsky's "Mind in Society: The Development of Higher Psychological Processes"

Fantz's Scientific American Article on Form Perception

Ainsworth et al.'s "Patterns of Attachment"

Origin of Theory Theory

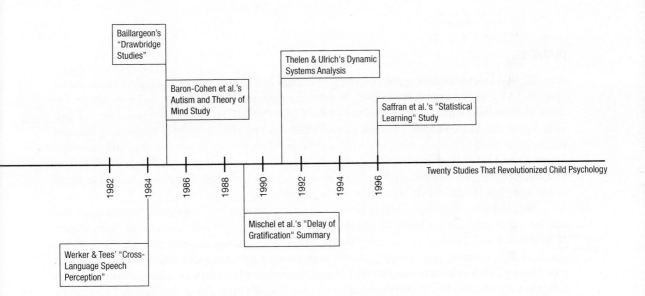

Baillargeon's "Drawbridge Studies"

Baron-Cohen et al.'s Autism and Theory of Mind Study

Thelen & Ulrich's Dynamic Systems Analysis

Saffran et al.'s "Statistical Learning" Study

1982 1984 1986 1988 1990 1992 1994 1996

Twenty Studies That Revolutionized Child Psychology

Mischel et al.'s "Delay of Gratification" Summary

Werker & Tees' "Cross-Language Speech Perception"

2

From Mollusks to Rugrats
Biological Principles and Psychological Ideas

(RANK 3)

Anyone who knows anything about child psychology has heard the name Piaget (pronounced "pee-ah-JAY," with a very soft j sound). In fact, the first question I ask my students besides "Is there anyone here who's not scheduled to take Child Psychology 206?" is "How many of you have heard the name Piaget?" Almost all the hands go up! This in itself is interesting because the students have obviously not completed a child psychology course yet, but they still recall his name. Then I ask, "How many of you with your hands up remember what Piaget did?" Just as quickly, all the hands go down! After about 10 seconds or so of silence, someone raises her hand feebly and says, "Didn't he do something with stages?"

Stages. Ugh. Of the hundreds of books and articles written by Piaget and his colleagues, the one item that students are likely to recollect is that the old codger did "something" with stages. Now this is ironic because if you ask me, his stages were among his least interesting developments. Yet high school and college students nationwide learn that according to Piaget, children pass through four qualitatively different stages, stepwise, from birth to adolescence, at which time they apparently stop. If you're going to say that Piaget's main thing was "stages," you might as well call Michelangelo's Sistine Chapel "a painting." You see, Piaget's contributions to science were much, much further reaching. I would even argue that the total of Piaget's work amounted to perhaps the single most intensive, coherent, sweeping theoretical integration of all the life sciences the world had yet seen. (But also see Thelen and Ulrich in Chapter 6, who's Dynamic Systems Theory may have the same potential.)

I can still understand why students only remember Piaget's stages. For one thing, stages are easy to remember; and Piaget offered only four of them. It's a lot easier for child psychology teachers to teach about four stages than it is for them to lecture about a comprehensive integration of all the life sciences. Second, Piaget's writings are so dense and so complex that they bring even the most able-minded doctorate-level child psychology scholar to his knees. In graduate school I used to think that Piaget's books were so difficult to read because they were translated from their French originals, until I learned that people who read the French originals found them just as difficult. A comprehensive effort to communicate Piaget's ideas to child psychology classes would probably take months. Since the typical child psychology text usually allots just a single chapter to Piaget, which translates into about three 50-minute class periods, full coverage of the man's ideas is obviously impractical. Given such space limitations, reviewing Piaget's four stages seems a more reasonable goal. But then the essence of Piaget's genius is missed; and students' understanding of Piaget as a brilliant integrator is replaced with an understanding of Piaget as "that stage guy."

What I propose to do in the next few pages is to provide a middle ground. In this chapter and the next, I'll review two courses of the full Piagetian feast. First I will outline Piaget's purposes and goals in doing research on the psychological development of children. This will be the theoretical Piaget; you know, the kind of stuff that describes what Piaget was all about. Here you'll get a sense of what made Piaget tick, where he was coming from, and why his ideas were so comprehensively integrating. Then in Chapter 3 I will deal more directly with some of Piaget's observations and findings excerpted from his 1962 book *Play, Dreams and Imitation*. It was this book that was voted into my list of the top 20 studies that revolutionized child psychology. This chapter will be more typical of the sort of pattern I'll be following throughout the remainder of the book—that of presenting a single study and describing its revolutionary impact on the field of child psychology. Given the depth and breadth of Piaget's impact on the field as a whole, I think it's only proper that Piaget gets two whole chapters to himself.

PIAGET: THE CHILD BIOLOGIST

Let me go back to my assertion that Piaget's efforts were really aimed at integrating the whole of the life sciences. Partially underlying this claim was the fact that Piaget was first and foremost a biologist. His childhood interests were in biology, his professional training was in biology, and most of his early scientific publications dealt with biological organisms of the nonhuman sort. And when I say "early" work, I mean *really, really* early. As a young child in turn-of-the-century Neuchâtel, Switzerland, Piaget published his first professional paper—on the topic of a partially albino sparrow he once saw while playing in a local park—when he was only 10! At 12 years of age he developed an intense interest in collecting mollusks, and by the ripe old age of 13 Piaget was working as an assistant to Paul Godet, the director of a nearby natural history museum. In exchange for being his assistant, Godet gave Piaget various mollusk specimens to add to his own collection. Godet befriended Piaget, and shared with him the excitement of science as well as the hard work of cataloging the museum's massive collection of mollusks and shells. So Piaget spent many of his childhood days measuring, recording, and categorizing. Now you might think it incredibly nerdy that any young child would spend his spare time staring at and categorizing mollusk shells. But there were at least two driving forces behind Piaget's motivations.

First, as Piaget himself described it, he had a troubling childhood, primarily as a result of having to deal with a profoundly religious, and mentally ill, mother. Given Piaget's prodigious experiences in doing science, coupled with his admiration for his historian father who was devoutly nonreligious, it was probably not a bad idea for family harmony for him to steer clear of intellectual battles with his mother. For Piaget, collecting mollusks and working at the museum was an escape from this otherwise difficult life. And I suspect that, all things considered, Piaget's form of escape was probably a lot less dysfunctional than other forms of escapism he could have chosen.

Even so, it's probably not fair to call Piaget a nerd. His interests in categorizing mollusks really reflect nothing more than a natural tendency of all living organisms to categorize their surroundings. You yourself have been categorizing things since you were a baby. Babies put things in their mouths all the time. When babies put things in their mouths, it's as if they have a primitive little category of "things you suck on." Ask your parents how many different things you put in your mouth when you were little. Would you classify yourself as an infant nerd because you spent your time categorizing the world into suckable things? Older children also like to categorize stuff. When my daughter Rachel was 3, she got the interesting idea in her head that she should gather up all her yellow toys and put them together in one tidy little pile. Red and blue toys weren't permitted to join the party. She ran up and down the stairs, and in and out of her play areas, gathering everything she could find that was yellow. When she was done, she sat back and admired her golden gathering. Yes, categorizing things is definitely natural, it's fundamental, and we do it throughout our lifetime. And if we do it objectively and systematically, we call it science. Why shouldn't a young boy like Piaget enjoy doing his own science?

Very soon afterward, in his early adolescence, and after looking over a lot of mollusk shells, Piaget began making his own scientific discoveries. Now here I'm not really sure that Piaget showed any particularly unique genius. I imagine that anyone who looked over enough shells for a long enough time might start noticing patterns of similarity and difference. But, with the encouragement of Godet, Piaget ran with his observations. He presented his work at various learned societies of the times (ones Godet took him to), and before long, Piaget's reputation was so well known around the world that he was offered a job as curator of the mollusk collection at the Natural History Museum of Geneva. I guess they didn't know Piaget was only 15 years old. Piaget probably figured he'd better finish puberty, so he turned down the position. Anyway, as you can see, Piaget was well entrenched in the biological sciences long before he attended college, and not surprisingly, the major tenets of the field of biology became infused into Piaget's personal outlook on the meaning of life.

PIAGET CARRIES THE TORCH FOR EVOLUTIONARY THEORY

Now, if you recall from your eighth-grade science class, a central guiding focus of the biological sciences is the theory of evolution through natural selection. And so it was that Piaget brought this notion full force into his conceptions of the psychological development of children. He held these beliefs very strongly. To Piaget, it made no sense to think that some parts of the natural world would develop according to one set of laws, while other parts would develop according to other laws. To him, all life must follow the same developmental laws, including the lowly mollusk and the intelligent human. It also made no sense for him to think that intellectual development would take place any differently than physical development. Again, he believed that all biological development must proceed according to the same set of rules, period.

For Piaget, then, any distinctions between biology and psychology were in many ways arbitrary and trivial. To him, the theory of evolution through natural selection was an equal opportunity employer; and studying the psychological development of children reflected nothing more than his continuing interest in the biological sciences. But this still doesn't explain why Piaget gave up on his study of mollusks. Personally, it wouldn't surprise me if he just got bored with the whole mollusk thing. But why was he so interested in studying the psychological development of children? Of all the things that he could've chosen as his next topic of study, why children? It wasn't because he marveled at his own children, because when he first entered the field of psychology he was childless. The trigger for Piaget's shift of interest seems to have come from his godfather, who thought Piaget was just too narrowly focused. After all, is it normal for a child to obsess over mollusk shells exclusively? So to broaden Piaget's horizons, his godfather, Samuel Cornut, gave him a philosophy book by a guy named Bergson. The rippling effect of this relatively innocent act was to change the science of children's psychological development forever.

The book that got Piaget so fired up dealt with the topic of **epistemology**. Okay. Whoa. Back the train up. What is epistemology? Well, epistemology is a branch of philosophy that deals with the meaning and origins of knowledge. Epistemologists deal with deep questions like "What is knowledge? Where does knowledge come from? What can be known, and can known things be known for sure? Is knowledge constant or changing?" Apparently, Bergson got Piaget thinking about whether the development of human knowledge conformed to the principles of biological development, especially to the principles of evolution through natural selection. Piaget's logic might've gone something like this: If evolution through natural selection is fundamental to biology, and if humans are biological organisms, and if the development of knowledge is a product of those biological organisms, then knowledge development itself should be subject to the principle of evolution through natural selection. There's no reason to believe that the mental would be any different from the biological.

Now, the reason organisms evolve at all is that it helps them fit into their surrounding environments better than their ancestors did. If you pull a fish out of water and drop it into your boat, it'll flop around for a while and eventually suffocate. Of course, the reason for the fish's death is simply that fish have evolved to extract oxygen from water, and they don't fare so well when asked to extract it from air. Fish have adapted to survive in watery environments. Presumably, human intelligence evolved for much the same reason: to allow humans to better fit into their environments.

The problem confronting Piaget in studying the evolution of human intelligence was rather large. Evolution takes place over hundreds of thousands of generations, and more complex species such as *Homo sapiens* take especially large numbers of generations to evolve. Although Piaget was a great scientist, he was mortal. He couldn't very well follow human evolution for a few million years. So he had only one lifetime to address the matter of the evolution of intelligence. To remedy this quandary, he adopted the old adage "Ontogeny recapitulates phylogeny." Although it sounds fancy, all this phrase really means is that the development of the individual **(ontogeny)** mirrors the development of the species **(phylogeny)**. So Piaget believed that to study the development of intelligence in the human species he only needed to study the development of intelligence in the human individual. Moreover, because intelligence begins in infancy, or maybe even before birth, it made sense to study psychological development in children. Indeed, children represented the ideal starting point to understand the evolution of intelligence. The primitive intellectual functioning of modern human children probably mirrors the primitive thinking of archaic human adults. Anyway, I hope you can get a sense of why Piaget's interests shifted from mollusks to children. To him, both types of organisms, mollusks and children, served as vehicles for studying the same general principles of evolution that were so central to his view of the world.

EVOLUTION IN CHILDREN'S INTELLECTUAL DEVELOPMENT

Now we can focus on Piaget's interests in intellectual development more specifically. Recall that a key outcome of evolution is adaptation. If a species or an individual is to survive in an environment, it must be able to adapt to changes in that environment. A species that can't adapt will become an extinct one. If environments change slowly, say over thousands or millions of years, then evolution through natural selection has a chance to work. But if environments change very rapidly or very drastically, then there is a good chance that whole groups of species could be wiped out. One popular theory for the extinction of the dinosaurs is that a huge meteor smashed into the Earth and kicked up the biggest dust storm the planet had ever seen. Because dinosaurs weren't prepared to extract oxygen from dust particles, they died out; and apparently they did so rather suddenly. However, sometimes environments can change rapidly but not drastically. When this happens, some members of a species might die, and others might survive. The members of the species that survive live to see another day and, importantly, reproduce. If the offspring of these individuals possess the same characteristics as their parents, they too may be capable of surviving in the changed environment. This is why they call it natural selection: Some natural catastrophe happens, and the surviving organisms are more or less "selected" to survive.

Humans are pretty successful at being able to survive fairly radical shifts in surrounding environments. How many other species of plants or animals can live and reproduce in the +120 °F heat of Kenya, the −90 °F cold of Antarctica, the atmosphere-less outer space, and the airless underseas? Of course, the reason humans can adapt to such diverse settings is because of their intelligence. The intelligence of humans permits them to create tools. They use these tools, and a little more intelligence, to infuse buildings and other support structures with life preserving technology. And they can use these buildings and other structures, along with still more intelligence, to create whatever climate-controlled environments they need. Of course, modern infant humans are incapable of creating climate-controlled environments. So how could they ever develop into modern adults capable of such great feats of intellectual sophistication? For Piaget the answer was simple: **intellectual adaptation**.

Piaget's idea of intellectual adaptation can be thought of as a sort of sped-up version of evolution through natural selection. However, instead of the species as a whole evolving, it is the intelligence of the individual that evolves. The parallels between intellectual evolution and species evolution are enormous. Just as poorly adapted members of a species might die off when confronted with environmental adversity, so might poorly adapted ideas in one's intellect die off when confronted with logical inconsistency. So for Piaget, the task of explaining children's intellectual development really amounted to observing the conditions under which ideas die off, as well as the conditions under which they survive.

Piaget believed that almost all of a person's intelligence resulted from that person's unique history of interacting with a wide variety of environments. He thought that over the course of an individual's lifetime, particularly during early childhood, ideas that were goofy or unadaptive would become "extinct," whereas ideas that proved adaptive and helped the individual negotiate a variety of environments would remain "alive." In infancy, the idea that the mother's breast should be sucked is a good one because it results in the baby getting fed when she's hungry. So the baby would no doubt find breast sucking adaptive, and would likely maintain the breast-sucking idea among her collection of viable ideas—at least for a while. But if the baby kept this idea too long, say into late childhood, she would probably get teased by her friends and would eventually abandon this idea.

The process of keeping good ideas and getting rid of bad ones is the essence of what Piaget meant by the adaptation of intelligence. Piaget thought of intellectual adaptation as an *equilibrium* between the action of the organism on the environment and the effects of the environment on the organism. (*Equilibrium* means that a system is in balance.) Thus, to be truly intelligent, humans should strive to make sure their intelligence is in balance with their surrounding environment. Breast sucking in infancy provides a good source of nutrition, and so with this idea the child is in balance with the environment. Breast sucking in late childhood is potentially odd and could result in the child receiving a certain amount of antagonism from the environment, perhaps in the form of teasing, and so reflects an imbalance between the child and the environment.

Still, not all intelligence can be acquired through experience. Piaget believed there must be some important inborn characteristics as well, some kind of biological stage for the environment to build on. After all, other biological systems are in place and working at birth, so why should intelligence be any different? For Piaget, the starting point for intellectual development was no different than the starting points for other biological things that develop. Piaget was especially known for drawing out the parallels between intellectual structures and processes and biological structures and processes. Let's consider the biological activity of digestion, for example. There are many *structures* in place at birth to aid a baby in extracting and using nutrients from the environment. Let's see, we have a mouth, a stomach, a large and small intestine, and a whole series of fluid-secreting glands. There are also a whole bunch of *processes* in place that encourage the extraction of nutrition from the environment. Just a few of the processes that come to mind include swallowing, peristalsis (moving food along the digestive tract), and enzyme secretion. These digestive *processes* use the preexisting digestive *structures* (like the stomach and the glands) for the adaptive purpose of extracting nutritional elements from the surrounding environment and infusing them into the biological functioning of the individual organism. Of course, digestion isn't the only biological thing happening. As another example, the biological act of breathing involves preexisting *structures* (lungs, diaphragm) and preexisting *processes* (muscular contractions of the diaphragm, extraction of oxygen from the pulmonary capillaries). Did you notice the words *structure* and *process* in the last few sentences? I've used them frequently and even italicized them because understanding both structure and process, as well as knowing the difference between them, is crucial for getting a grip on Piaget's theory.

Piaget believed that the same kind of preexisting processes that act in concert with preexisting structures in biological adaptation to the environment must also underlie intellectual adaptation to the environment. Remember, Piaget's goal was to show that intellectual development is just another manifestation of the basic principles underlying all of biology. However, there was one major difference between intellectual adaptation and other kinds of biological adaptations. Although you can easily see and measure basic structures and processes for biological activities such as digestion and breathing, you can't very easily see or measure the basic structures and processes for the biological activity of intelligence. So Piaget had to more or less "invent" them. (Well, he didn't actually invent them, he sort of borrowed them from an American psychologist, James Mark Baldwin, but this fact tends to get lost in popular accounts of Piaget's theory.) The concept that Piaget ended up adopting as the most fundamental *structure* for intellectual development was the **schema**, and the fundamental *processes* for intellectual development were **assimilation** and **accommodation**. Piaget's notion of a schema is rather abstract and kind of difficult to follow; but that's primarily because you don't yet have a schema for the concept of the schema! So let's develop one, shall we?

SCHEMAS, ASSIMILATION, AND ACCOMMODATION

In some ways, the schema is to intelligence as the stomach is to digestion. Just as the goal of eating is to put food into your stomach so that digestion can take place, the goal of learning is to put information into your schema so that intelligence can take place. And in both digestion and intelligence, the stomach and schema are present even before birth. But here the similarities end. For example, in digestion you have only one stomach, but in intellectual development you have hundreds and thousands of schemas. And while your basic digestive structures pretty much stay the same over your entire lifetime (except that they may get bigger), your basic intellectual structures are changing continually. Schemas do get bigger, but they may also get smaller. They may subdivide like body cells, they may aggregate like Cheerios dancing on the surface of the milk in your morning bowl of cereal, or they may subsume each other like so many Pac-Men chomping down power pills through a video maze. A schema may be a reflex, such as sneezing or blinking; or it may be a highly complex understanding of subatomic particles of quarks and neutrinos. But no matter how you look at it, intellectual development happens when the basic, primitive schemas that are present even before birth, evolve toward the very complex and highly interrelated schema network found in the adult. The question Piaget addressed, and it took pretty much the rest of his lifetime, was how this evolution took place.

THE DEVELOPMENT OF BABY INTELLIGENCE

Piaget began by assuming that there had to be some basic knowledge schemas in place before any new learning could happen. Without these basic schemas, there would be no "place" for an organism to put its very first information. It would be like a baby eating, but not having a stomach to hold the food. So Piaget had to come up with some idea of what the first schemas probably looked like. Piaget found the answer to his dilemma in basic reflexes. I'm quite sure you know what **reflexes** are, especially if you've ever coughed, sneezed, or startled in your lifetime. But to be a bit more technical, we can define reflexes as more or less genetically determined, hardwired, organized patterns of behavior that usually occur in response to some environmental event. The sucking reflex, the grasping reflex, and the orienting reflex are just a few of the dozens of reflexes that human babies bring to the world with them. And it is through these basic reflexes that babies first understand the world.

So babies' first understanding of the world isn't a "blooming, buzzing confusion" as psychologist William James once suggested. Rather, babies are prepared by nature to understand the world in terms of how their reflexes can act on it. Remember earlier when I talked about how babies seem naturally predisposed to categorize the world into things that are suckable and unsuckable? This is the essence of what Piaget was going for! Reflexes are babies' first schemas. Although they don't do it intentionally, babies spend much of their time reflexively responding to events going on around them. And it doesn't take long for babies to start modifying their reflexes either. Once a baby figures out that a reflexive schema doesn't fit particularly well here or there, she begins to modify the schema slightly. Sucking car keys takes slightly different lip formations than sucking nipples, and both of these acts require different tongue action and lip formation than sucking a finger. Even though these differences are very slight, the process of adjusting existing schemas to be more consistent with the demands of the surrounding environment is the very essence of intellectual development, according to Piaget. Adjusting one's schemas to fit the environment is also a reflection of the very kind of evolutionary adaptation that Piaget thought made intellectual development completely consistent with the general principles of biology.

The next step, then, is to explain how schemas get adjusted. The key to understanding this kind of intellectual adaptation is in understanding the complementary processes of assimilation and accommodation. These processes work as a team, and their common goal is to ensure that an individual's internal schemas about the external world are *in balance* with the actual external world. Unfortunately, the terms *assimilation* and *accommodation* are very easily confused. They are closely related to each other in meaning, and they describe highly abstract concepts that you can rarely see in real life and that you really can't even imagine all that well. In a feeble attempt at illustrating the difference between assimilation and accommodation, let me go back to my favorite type of analogy: food.

Imagine that you want to make a peanut butter sandwich (which as a 3-year-old was my daughter Sarah's favorite!). The first step is to spread peanut butter on a slice of bread. Now notice three things about this very mundane activity. First, you are spreading the peanut butter on the bread—not on your nose, not on a banana, not on your television screen. The very concept of making a peanut butter sandwich requires that the peanut butter be put on the bread. If it were put on something else, you would no longer have a peanut butter sandwich. Instead you'd have something like "peanut butter nose" or "peanut butter TV." Second, after you spread the peanut butter on a slice of bread, the bread really isn't just bread anymore—it's bread with peanut butter on it. The very essence of that piece of bread has changed forever. Sure, the bread is still there, but it's not the same bread that was there without the peanut butter. The peanut butter has permanently changed the essence of that piece of bread. The bread is no longer just bread; it has become part of a peanut butter sandwich. Third, notice that you can't put the peanut butter on the bread without the bread also having some peanut butter put on it.

If you're following my wacky train of thought here, then you understand the basic concepts of assimilation and accommodation. But let me try to explain them in the sense of how they can be applied to intellectual development. Assimilation and accommodation are the processes responsible for making sure that a baby's understanding of the world is consistent with what he experiences in the world. And remember that a baby's first understanding of the world is through the basic schemas he possesses. Well, every time that a baby attempts to understand new parts of the world, he first tries to understand them in terms of the schemas he already has in place. For a very young baby, who maybe only has a sucking schema, this might mean trying to suck everything. If the baby tries to suck something he has never sucked before, say a dog biscuit, then we would say he is assimilating the dog biscuit into his sucking schema. But by the very act of sucking the dog biscuit, he is in a very real sense learning about the dog biscuit, and he is learning about it by assimilating it into his sucking schema (and not to any other schema). Had he attempted to assimilate the dog biscuit into any other schema, then he wouldn't have been sucking on it. Notice that this is similar to the requirement that to make a peanut butter sandwich, you have to put peanut butter on bread. If you put peanut butter on something else, you wouldn't be making a peanut butter sandwich. To make a peanut butter sandwich, the peanut butter has to be more or less assimilated to the bread.

But when the baby starts sucking the dog biscuit, the sucking schema itself gets permanently changed. It is no longer a sucking schema that has never encountered a dog biscuit before; it is a sucking schema that has now had experience with dog biscuits. This experience converts the sucking schema into a dog-biscuit-sucking veteran. A baby who has experienced dog biscuit sucking has a sucking schema that is more sophisticated than the sucking schema of a baby who is a dog-biscuit-sucking newbie. The fact that the schema changes in some way every time it encounters some new experience demonstrates the idea of accommodation. When a baby sucks a dog biscuit, he is assimilating the biscuit to his sucking schema (and not his grasping schema); but at the same time, the sucking schema accommodates the new information about the world that the dog biscuit provides. The fact that an existing schema gets permanently changed by every piece of new information that is assimilated into it is in some ways similar to how the bread in a peanut butter sandwich gets permanently changed by the peanut butter that is spread on it.

To restate these ideas more succinctly, assimilation happens when new information is forced into existing schemas, and accommodation happens when existing schemas are adjusted to allow for the new information. To make a peanut butter sandwich, you have to put peanut butter on bread, but the very act of putting peanut butter on the bread changes the bread from being just bread to being part of something larger than itself—being part of a peanut butter sandwich.

DEVELOPMENT FROM HERE ONWARD

Now all this talk about primitive reflex schemas, assimilation, and accommodation is just the starting point. To say that babies have intellectual structures like schemas and have intellectual adaptive processes like assimilation and accommodation is only to say that babies are biologically prepared to learn about the world from the very beginning. And even then, saying that babies are biologically prepared doesn't really say much about how babies develop. Here is where the idea of stages is often introduced. Stages are a way of describing how far along babies are in the development of their schemas.

Now, before going any further, let me ask those of you who remembered that Piaget had "something to do with stages," don't you find it interesting that you've spent a whole chapter reading about Piaget with almost no discussion about stages? Obviously, stages aren't the most interesting part of Piaget's theory. Far more interesting is how Piaget ties intellectual development to basic biological functioning and evolutionary theory.

Still, I suppose I should say a few words about stages since most college textbooks spend so much time describing them. Let me start by saying that stages are really overrated. A stage is really just a shorthand way of describing a single point in time, but as you might imagine, it's not particularly useful to talk about a single point in time unless you know what happened before and what's going to happen afterward.

Let me give you an example by having you recite the alphabet to yourself. Now when you get to K, let me know. Are you there yet? Okay, now stop reciting. I hereby declare that you are in the "K-stage" of reciting the alphabet. Aren't you excited? No? The K-stage doesn't really do much for you, does it? What's useful about the alphabet is not that there is a K somewhere along the line, but that the alphabet can be used in highly productive ways for communicating with others through writing. Similarly, what's useful about children's intellectual development is not that there are points along the line where you can stop counting and say that a child is in a particular stage. Rather, what's useful is that intellectual development as a whole can be used in an attempt to explain how a child is able to learn about and survive in the world.

Still, as child scientists we have a tendency to try to pigeonhole children into one of Piaget's main stages—the Sensorimotor, the Preoperational, the Concrete Operational, or the Formal Operational—or even more finely into one of his substages. (Remember my point earlier about our natural tendency to categorize?) But whether we need to talk about stages in order for the science of child psychology to make progress is questionable. Yes, Piaget talked about stages and substages. But how important they were is arguable. It seems that we Americans are the ones hung up on stages. In fact, I've even heard the debate about the importance of stages called "the American problem." Piaget's followers who studied under him in the Genevan tradition (i.e., people who worked with him in his own lab in Geneva, Switzerland) seem to think that the stages themselves are far less important than the structures and processes that contribute to intellectual development. Nevertheless, it is entirely true that if you take a snapshot of intellectual development at any particular point of time, it will appear that a child is at a specific stage of development. I guess that places you at the "end of Chapter 2" stage of this book.

Bibliography

Beilin, H. (1992). Piaget's enduring contribution to developmental psychology. *Developmental Psychology, 28,* 191–204.

Cairns, R. B. (1992). The making of a developmental science: The contributions and intellectual heritage of James Mark Baldwin. *Developmental Psychology, 28,* 17–24.

Ginsburg, H. P., & Opper, S. (1988). *Piaget's theory of intellectual development.* Englewood Cliffs, NJ: Prentice Hall.

Messerly, J. G. (1996). *Piaget's conception of evolution.* Lanham, MD: Rowman & Littlefield.

Piaget, J. (1950). *The psychology of intelligence.* London: Routledge & Kegan Paul.

Piaget, J. (1952). "Piaget." In E. G. Boring, H. S. Langfeld, H. Werner, & R. M. Yerkes (Eds.), *A history of psychology in autobiography.* Worcester, MA: Clark University Press.

Vidal, F. (1994). *Piaget before Piaget.* Cambridge, MA: Harvard University Press.

Questions for Discussion

1. Would Piaget's impact on the field of child psychology have differed had he not been trained as a biologist?

2. Would child psychology look different today if Piaget had gotten along better with his mother? Why or why not?

3. Why is it important for the laws of psychology to correspond to the laws of biology? In general, how important is it for laws to correspond across any group of scientific fields?

4. No one has ever seen a mental schema, and it's unlikely that anyone ever will. Given this fact, can the notion of a schema have any scientific usefulness?

3

When Thinking Begins

Play, Dreams and Imitation

Piaget, J. (1945). *Permission granted by the Jean Piaget Foundation.* (RANK 3)

I must admit at the outset that by including Piaget's 1962 book in my list of 20 studies that revolutionized child psychology, I embrace a certain amount of chronological dishonesty. Now it's not like I robbed the campus bookstore or anything. But keep in mind that the whole premise of my book is to showcase revolutionary child psychology research that's taken place since 1960. Although *Play, Dreams and Imitation* (hereafter simply called *Play*) really was published in its English version in 1962, the book was originally published in French in 1945. In fact, the data presented in *Play* were originally collected in the 1920s!

So why include *Play* in this post-1960 list? Well, there are at least three reasons; feel free to choose whichever one you like best. First, this is my book, and I can handle it any way I want to, so there. Second, I'm an American elitist and as far as I'm concerned, science really isn't science until it's translated into English (just kidding). Or third, *Play* was one of the most frequently nominated studies in my empirical survey. Indeed, *Play* is so popular that according to Google Scholar it's been cited 6769 times! Obviously members of the child psychology research community view the book as really important.

Okay, but why? In speculation, I think much of the popularity of *Play* comes from its expansion on some significant theoretical points about early intellectual development that Piaget had been working on in other recently published work. You see, *Play* was the third in the series of three books, a "trilogy" if you will, that collectively served as a compendium of Piaget's core theoretical ideas. The first two books, *The Origins of Intelligence in Children* and *The Construction of*

Reality in the Child, were published in English the decade prior (1952 and 1954, respectively). So *Play* took foundational ideas from those works, and built upon them to show how psychological structures available in infancy could be transformed into psychological structures available for later childhood and eventually adulthood.

And as always, Piaget was a master storyteller in linking his theoretical claims with real-life observations that helped create and support them. Unlike other epistemologists of the time, many of whom were mere armchair philosophers, Piaget, eminent scientist that he was, was very aware of the need to present scientific data in defense of his positions. I think the book's popularity—or indeed that of the entire trilogy—also came from the fact that it exploded onto the American scene right at a time when American developmental psychologists were trying to escape from the twin asphyxiating grips of Freudian psychosexual theory and Watson's/Skinner's behaviorism. For many scholars Piaget's general biological approach, which was captured in the publication of the trilogy, was truly a breath of fresh air.

INTRODUCTION

Because I was able to use much of the preceding chapter to describe the forces driving Piaget's theory, along with many of its central tenets, I have, in essence, already given you the introduction to this study. And so I also have much greater latitude in dealing with Piaget's findings in *Play*. Still, let's review very briefly the main points of the previous chapter in a rough logical order. (1) Piaget was an evolutionary biologist. (2) Therefore, he believed that all organisms must adapt to survive. (3) Adaptation takes place at the species level *phylogenetically*. (4) Adaptation also takes place at the individual level *ontogenetically*. (5) Intelligence happens in biological organisms. (6) Therefore, intelligence is a biological process. (7) Therefore, intelligence adapts. (8) Because intelligence adapts ontogenetically, we should be able to observe it in the development of children. (9) The ontogenetic adaptation of intelligence in children might give a good approximation of the phylogenetic adaptation of intelligence that took place in the human species since at least 300,000 years ago.

So Piaget's grand theoretical framework was pretty much laid out. But the busy work of compiling the evidence to support his notions was still in progress. All he had to do was present his data convincingly. In the first volume of his trilogy, *The Origins of Intelligence in Children*, Piaget laid out the development of intelligence during the first two years of children's lives. Here, he also laid out his evidence for the first major stage of cognitive development, the *sensorimotor* stage, by charting children's progress through each of six substages. In the second volume, *The Construction of Reality in the Child*, Piaget described how children use their intelligence to form a basic understanding of the concepts of objects, space, causality, and time. In *Play*, Piaget undertakes an account of how children transition from sensorimotor intelligence, the kind of intelligence that dominates the first two years of psychological life, to true operational (i.e., logical) thinking, the kind of intelligence dominating more developed periods of life. For Piaget, the transition from sensorimotor intelligence to logical intelligence was woven by the ribbon of "mental representation" and so the developmental emergence of mental representation formed the subject of study for *Play*.

Mental representation, or the use of internal, mental symbols to represent things in the real world, was a fundamental component of human intelligence for Piaget, and something that he believed separated humans from other species. Can you imagine what it would be like to live a life without being able to think about the real world using images and pictures, or words and phrases? As humans, at least adult ones, we spend almost all of our waking time thinking about things that we aren't currently experiencing. We think about the morning's breakfast, or our recreational plans for the upcoming weekend. We think about previous conversations we've had and especially how we could've said something in a better or wittier way. But every one of our thoughts depends on our ability to represent external reality in our minds, and we mentally represent that external reality using symbols like words and images.

In Piaget's view, children first become *capable* of using mental representation at the end of the sensorimotor stage (about 2 years of age), but they don't fully realize the power of mental representations until the beginning of the concrete operational stage (about 7 years of age), when they start thinking logically. There is, then, this entire 5-year period from 2 to 7 years of age during which children convert their early illogical symbolic thinking into a more advanced, and logical, symbolic kind of thinking.

To chart the emergence of mental representation, Piaget tracks the development of two abilities that he argues form the foundation for mental representation. As the title of the book foretells, these two component consist of play and imitation. Why these two abilities? Well, let's digress for a moment. You'll recall from Chapter 2 that assimilation and accommodation serve as two foundational intellectual processes. For Piaget, assimilation and accommodation work together to allow children to adapt their *understanding* of the world to the *actual realities* of the world. Through assimilation, children incorporate new information into existing knowledge, which allows them to categorize things they've never seen before. Through accommodation, children modify existing knowledge to allow for new information, which allows them to form new categories. For Piaget, the concepts of play and imitation map perfectly onto assimilation and accommodation. For him, play is almost pure assimilation. Through play, children make the entire world conform to their own understanding of reality. Imitation, on the other hand, is almost pure accommodation. Through imitation, children force themselves to conform completely to the external world. By tracking the joint ontogenetic development of play and imitation, Piaget believed he was also tracking the ontogeny of assimilation and accommodation, in the context of the emergence of mental representation.

It proves tricky to describe Piaget's account of the development of play and imitation in this third book of his trilogy, because so much of it depends on the six sensorimotor substages he introduced in his first book. So you have to kind of know the first book in order to understand the lessons from the third book. Since I reckon there is almost zero probability that you have actually read the first book, what I'll do here is *very* briefly review each of Piaget's sensorimotor substages, and then describe how they impact the ontogeny of play and imitation.

METHOD

Participants

The participants that Piaget observed for his study were two girls and one boy, all siblings, and all Piaget's own children. The children were observed several times a day, probably every day, essentially from the moments of their births. Jacqueline was born in 1925, Lucienne was born in 1927, and Laurent was born in 1931. So from Jacqueline's birth until the time of Laurent's 4th birthday, Piaget made detailed recordings of at least one kid pretty much constantly for 10 years. Although this would be a Herculean effort for anybody, Piaget's challenge was obviously reduced because at least the three research participants were his own children. Plus, even Mrs. Piaget helped out on occasion. It's been said that she used to carry a small notebook attached to her necklace so that she could record Piaget's observations as requested.

Procedure

Because Piaget was a pioneer in the scientific investigation of children's development, and because he was dealing with very, very young babies, there really weren't many existing methodologies at his disposal to use in measuring babies' thinking abilities. Compounding the problem further was the fact that 1-week-old babies are notoriously difficult to carry on a conversation with. This means that almost every method Piaget used to measure the thinking of babies was of his own creation. You've heard of the phrase, "Necessity is the mother of invention"? Well, Piaget invented dozens of methods to test out his various hypotheses, many of which are still used to this day. Among the most famous are his *means-ends* test, and his *a-not-b* test. But for most of the observations he describes in *Play*, Piaget doesn't use any standardized techniques or laboratory tests. He mostly just describes what he sees his children do on their own, with both objects and people, and then ad-libs in the moment to see how the children respond to his creative interventions. Hey, nobody ever said doing experiments with babies had to be fancy. As the great philosopher and baseball coach Yogi Berra once said, "You can observe a lot just by watchin'."

RESULTS

Piaget's results in *Play* were not neatly summarized into a single, concise "Results" section, as would be typical of professional journal articles. Instead, they were pretty much scattered throughout the book in various sections and subsections, brought to the reader's attention as Piaget needed them to make some theoretical point about play or imitation. It took him 291 pages to tell the entire story. What I will attempt to do in my much shorter redescription of his results is to profile his major findings as they pertain to play and imitation. At the conclusion, I will also talk about how Piaget believed play and imitation contributed to the emergence of mental representation.

As noted earlier in this text, the first thing we have to do is lift some of Piaget's ideas from the first book in his trilogy, and bring them to the forefront in our discussion of this third book. Referring back to that first book, *The Origins of Intelligence in Children* (let's call it *Origins* for short), Piaget investigated intellectual development in babies from birth to about 2 years of age. His results were pretty much presented in chronological order, starting with the intellectual adaptations of newborns and ending with the intellectual adaptations of 2-year-olds. But he also subdivided the 2-year time frame into six sequential, but unequally spaced, substages. In progressing through his description of each of the substages, Piaget focused on one or more of the major developmental breakthroughs demonstrated by his children during the sensorimotor stage. Let me just reiterate from Chapter 1 that in my opinion the interesting feature of the developmental story is not that children achieve each of these substages, but that their intellectual functioning represents a kind of adaptation through natural selection just as in all other aspects of biology.

In the pages that follow, I will run through each of the six substages that Piaget proposed. Then I will characterize how play and imitation becomes manifest in these substages. I would also like to give you a flavor of Piaget's writing style, so I will reproduce excerpts from the observations he made of his own children. This is something ordinary child psychology textbooks don't do, but I think you will get a better sense of the way that Piaget thought about things. Throughout these excerpts, you will see references to the children's ages that look something like this: 1;4 (14). This is Piaget's shorthand for noting that the child was 1 year, 4 months, and 14 days old. Obviously, Piaget was quite a stickler for detail. And many times he would make observations of exactly the same behaviors on several days in a row.

Let me also provide you some guidance about what to look for. As noted earlier in this text, both play and imitation are special instances of human intelligence in which there is either pure assimilation (as in play), or pure accommodation (as in imitation). In "normal" intelligent acts, assimilation and accommodation work together in a harmonious chorus of mutual and recipro- cal engagement. But in the special conditions of play and imitation, assimilation and accommo- dation *do NOT* work together as a team. Instead, one dominates the other. So in the examples that follow, you should keep an eye out for when assimilation works without accommodation, and when accommodation works without assimilation. For these are the very special cases that provide a glimpse into the unique functioning of the individual component abilities, uncontami- nated by the functioning of the other.

THE FIRST SUBSTAGE: THE USE OF REFLEXES   In many ways, the believability of Piaget's entire theory comes down to how well he can account for children's thinking in the very first days of life. It's one thing to say that an advanced level of thinking comes from an earlier level of thinking, but it's an altogether different thing to say where the very first thinking comes from. The roots of adult thinking, for example, can be traced to childhood thinking; but this just takes a difficult problem at one level (understanding adult thinking) and makes it a difficult problem at another level (understanding child thinking). And as much as one might wish to keep moving the problem to earlier and earlier periods in human development, for example from late childhood to early childhood, then from early childhood to toddlerhood and so on, eventually someone has to pay the piper. At some point, we have to account for the very first thinking. But this is like a chicken-and-egg problem. As the old conundrum goes, you can't have a chicken without an egg, but it takes a chicken to lay the first egg. In just the same way, you can't have thinking without the first thought, but you can't have the first thought without having thinking. So Piaget carried quite an intellectual burden in trying to explain the very first thinking. Let's see how he dealt with it.

If you remember from the previous chapter, Piaget's problem really amounted to explain- ing where children got their first schemas. Schemas are the knowledge structures that underlie all thinking, and so what he had to do was account for the very first ones. Undoubtedly, one important breakthrough took place when Piaget realized that early schemas didn't need to look much like adult ones at all. In fact, the earliest schemas could look quite different from later ones. The key similarities between the first schemas and later schemas were to be found not in their structures, but in their function, in what they allowed the baby to do. Remember, thinking is a biological process that helps the organism adapt to the world. All Piaget had to do was figure out what babies brought with them into the world that would allow them to adapt to it. Piaget's solu- tion to the problem was simple: *REFLEXES!*

Although reflexes are often regarded as "hardwired" in the brain, they aren't impervious to environmental experience. Indeed, the fact that reflexes become modified as a result of inter- acting with the world is what made them ideal candidates for children's first schemas. Take the sucking reflex for instance. Babies will reflexively suck on a nipple, on a finger, on a pencil, and on a set of car keys. But because each object is slightly different than the other, successful sucking requires the baby to modify his "sucking schema" to accommodate the differences between the objects. Sucking car keys, for example, requires slightly different sets of mouth and tongue move- ments than sucking a nipple.

These first schemas are found in sensorimotor Substage 1, which is why Substage 1 is also where the earliest precursors to play and imitation are found. But true forms of neither are yet present. According to Piaget, the most advanced thing a child in Substage 1 can do is continue a reflex beyond the removal of the stimulus. For example, a 1-month-old might continue sucking even after removing a nipple. But this behavior gives evidence of neither pure assimilation nor pure accommodation.

PLAY   In Substage 1, there is no play proper. But there is something that looks a lot like play. Piaget writes that almost all children's behaviors are susceptible to becoming play as soon as they are repeated purely for functional pleasure, but there is no evidence it happens in Substage 1. The closest we come here is the baby who continues to suck after the removal of the stimulus. But even in this case, Piaget writes, "However, it seems very difficult to consider reflex exercises as real games when they simply extend the pleasure of breastfeeding-time and consolidate the functioning of the hereditary set up."

IMITATION   In Substage 1, there is also no imitation proper. However, the reflex mechanisms that are exercised in this substage do set the stage for later imitation. To understand why, let's back-up a little bit. Piaget defines imitation as, "the reproduction of a model." Furthermore, the reproduction of a model involves "an element acquired by experience." Therefore, if a child is ever going to become capable of imitation, she will have to eventually become proficient at responding to external stimuli. Thus, even though sucking on a nipple is almost pure assimilation, the fact that it involves forcing the nipple (an external stimulus, or an "element acquired by experience") into the sucking schema, means that the child will have to modify the sucking schema to accommodate the nipple. In other words, exercising the sucking schema through external stimulation gives the child some preliminary practice with "elements acquired by experience." This practice will lay the groundwork for eventual imitation. Piaget writes, "Insofar that the reflex leads to repetition which lasts long after the initial stimulus has been removed (cf. suction in the void, etc.), it implies that it is being practiced through functional assimilation." It is this functional assimilation that will make later "conditioning through accommodation" possible.

THE SECOND SUBSTAGE: THE FIRST ACQUIRED ADAPTATIONS AND THE PRIMARY CIRCULAR REACTIONS   The first substage is very short-lived—about a month—because babies' reflexes so quickly start adapting to the surrounding environment. Once a reflex changes as a result of coming into contact with the environment, in even the tiniest way, then the reflex is no longer exactly the same as it was. We can say the reflex has adapted. In watching his kids, Piaget noticed that sometimes, beginning in about the second month, they would exercise their schemas apparently merely for the enjoyment of the activity. These kinds of repetitions of activity indicated that the actions were no longer purely reflexive, because there was nothing around that stimulated them. Instead, it was as if the activity was self-generated. Sucking, for example, could often be seen even in the absence of any reflex-causing trigger—that is, without anything actually touching the lips.

At about this time, Piaget also noticed that his children would often try to activate their own reflex schemas by stimulating them with other parts of their own body. At first, they usually did so accidentally. For example, as their arms flailed about randomly, their hands would sometimes smack into their face and accidentally make contact with the lips. Their fingers would then slip into their mouths and then get sucked. Of course, in this case, sucking was initially being activated reflexively as the fingers rushed in uninvited. But if the fingers fell back out, the babies seemed to try to "coordinate" the sucking reflex with the movements of the arm as if trying to repeat the chance occurrence. Clearly, you can see that the sucking schema is no longer a reflexive island, passively responding to environmental stimulation, but is instead being coordinated with other activities of the child's own body. And the fact that the child frequently reinstated the initial chance encounter showed that there was a certain amount of circularity involved. That is to say, an action happened by accident, the baby seemed to find it interesting, so he tried to make it happen again. Piaget called this kind of coordination between existing schemas and body activity a "circular reaction." But because the next substage also involved these kinds of circular activities, Piaget wanted to make a distinction between the kinds of circular reactions that involved only the child's own body and those that involved other objects. Therefore, the kinds of circular reactions that take place on the child's own body, Piaget called "primary"; and so putting all these terms together, we get Piaget's term **primary circular reaction**. The primary circular reactions are most common from about the 1st month to the 4th month. But afterward, their frequency dies down and kids start showing **secondary circular reactions** (see Substage 3 as described in the next section).

PLAY   Play clearly begins for Piaget in Substage 2. He writes, "We realize, in fact . . . that the child, after demonstrating by his seriousness that he is making a real effort at accommodation, later reproduces these behaviors merely for pleasure, followed by mimicking smiles or even laughter without the expectation of results characteristic of (regular) circular induced-learning reactions." Observation 59: "One needs to remember that T (abbreviation for "Laurent"), at 0;2 (21) adopted the habit of throwing his head back to look at familiar frames from this new position. However, at 0;2 (23 or 24), he seemed to repeat this movement with an ever-growing sense of joy and ever-declining interest in the external result: he brought his head back to the upright position and then threw it back again several time, laughing loudly. In other words, the circular reaction ceased to be 'serious' or instructive, if we can say so for a baby of less than three months, and became a game. At 0;3, T played with his voice, not only for (the) sound appeal, but also for 'functional pleasure,' laughing at his own power. At 0;2 (19) and (20), he smiled at his hands and at 0;2 (25) at objects that he shook with his hand, while in other occasions he gazed at them with deep seriousness."

IMITATION   Piaget wrote that Substage 2 is characterized by the fact that reflex schemas are broadened to include additional elements, as a result of experience, into "differentiated" circular reactions. For example, the child's sucking schema is differentiated enough to be able to suck either a nipple or a finger. He goes on to say that, "Two conditions are, therefore, necessary for imitation to occur. The schema must be capable of differentiation . . . and the model must be perceived by the child to be analogous to results he obtained by himself." In other words, if a child doesn't already have a schema for something, he won't be able to imitate anything using that schema. With his daughter Jacqueline, Piaget noticed that she started imitating her mother's voice, an activity he called "vocal contagion." In J's case [abbreviation for Jacqueline], vocal contagion appeared to begin only during the second half of the second month. At 0;1 (20) and 0;1 (27), for instance, I noticed some bursts of sound as vocal responses to her mother's voice. At 0;2 (3), she replied about twenty times in similar circumstances, stopping after each burst, and at 0;2 (4) she reproduced certain specific sounds which she had made spontaneously a short time before."

THE THIRD SUBSTAGE: THE SECONDARY CIRCULAR REACTIONS AND THE PROCEDURES DESTINED TO MAKE INTERESTING SIGHTS LAST   As his children moved past about the 4th month, Piaget observed that they not only tried to reenact interesting experiences that took place on their own body, but that they often tried to incorporate external objects into their schemas as well. If you think about it, there's little difference in *how* you can apply your basic schemas either to your own body or to other things. Does your sucking reflex really care whether it's activated by your own fingers or a set of car keys? So we would say that the sucking schema is **functionally invariant**; that is, it works the same no matter whether the baby is sucking on his fingers or a Barbie Doll. But by and large, as Piaget found, babies' efforts to incorporate external objects into existing schemas tended to occur later in time. This is the main change that happens in the third substage, it is pretty much the same as the second except that external objects are now the focus of the schemas.

Although I've been focusing on the sucking schema as a primary means that babies learn about the world around them, this schema was only one among many that Piaget talked about. Another major player among infants' first knowledge schemas involved vision, or as we called it in the previous chapter, the orienting reflex. Regardless of which schema we are talking about, Piaget's goal was to provide evidence that schemas are present at birth in the form of reflexes, and that they slowly but surely get incorporated into grander and grander patterns of behavior that will give babies a fuller and better understanding of the world. Development isn't all-or-none. It takes place gradually—as later schemas build on earlier ones—with each passing experience the child has.

PLAY   Play in Substage 3 is essentially the same as in Substage 2, except that the schemas that are repeated involve the incorporation of external objects instead of the child's own body. An example can be found in Observation 60: "L [abbreviation for Lucienne] discovered the possibility of making objects hanging from the top of her cot swing. At first, between 0;3 (6) and 0;3 (16), she studied the phenomenon without smiling, or smiling a little, but with what seemed to be a deep interest as if she was studying the phenomenon. In the following years, however, from about 0;4 she never indulged in this activity which lasted up to about 0;8 and even beyond without showing exhilarant joy and power. In other words assimilation was no longer accompanied by current accommodation and therefore was no longer an effort at comprehension: there was merely assimilation to the activity itself meaning use of the phenomenon for the pleasure of the activity, and that is what play is all about."

IMITATION   Piaget writes that, "With the co-ordination of vision and prehension . . . new circular reactions through which influence can be exerted on objects make their appearance . . . the imitation of the third stage is still essentially conservative, showing no indication of efforts at accommodation to new models such as will be observable in the following stages. . . . The child learns at this stage to imitate other people's movements which are analogous to the familiar, visible movements he himself makes." Piaget notes that many imitations involve speech sounds the child has heard others make, but only if the child already has those sounds in his own repertoire. But children also begin demonstrating imitations of others' actions, as in Observation 12: "At 0;8 (13), I observed that J alternatively opened and closed her right hand while watching it with close attention as if this movement, as an isolated schema, was new for her. I didn't try any new experiment at that point but, the same evening I showed her my hand as I opened and closed it repeatedly. She imitated the movement soon after, rather awkwardly but in a quite distinctive way. She was lying on her stomach and not looking at her hand, but there was an obvious correlation between her movements and mine (she was not making this movement just before)."

THE FOURTH SUBSTAGE: THE COORDINATION OF THE SECONDARY SCHEMAS AND THEIR APPLICATION TO NEW SITUATIONS   In Substage 4, which Piaget thought began at about 8 or 9 months of age, babies take a major intellectual leap forward. All along they've been developing individual, isolated schemas that have been informed by environmental feedback. They have schemas for seeing things, hearing things, sucking things, grabbing things, shaking things, pulling things, and hitting things. But before now, babies haven't coordinated two or more schemas in order to carry out some planned action. Before now, babies pretty much just reacted to things. But in Substage 4, instead of being mostly reactive, babies start being proactive. They start acting on the world, *intentionally*, in order to achieve some overarching goal. The coordination of schemas also permits the emergence of new levels of play and imitation.

PLAY   Beginning in Substage 4, Piaget begins talking about "ludic behaviors." The term *ludic* in this context, really just means that the action was playful, reproduced for its own sake, and not performed to accomplish any particular goal. A good example of Laurent's ludic Substage 4 play can be found in Observation 61: "After learning how to remove an obstacle to reach his objective at 0;7 (13), T began to enjoy this type of exercise around 0;8 (15)–0;9. When several time in a row I put my hand or a piece of cardboard between him and the toy he discovered, he reached the stage when he forgot momentarily the toy and pushed the obstacle aside while bursting into laughter. What had been intelligent adaptation thus became play, through transfer of interest to the action itself, independently of its goal." In this example, you can see that the play emerges in the context of a coordination of secondary circular reactions, because Laurent coordinates a grasping schema with an obstacle-removing schema. That is, Laurent has to remove the obstacle before he can grasp the toy. But after mastering the coordination of the two schemas, Laurent then bursts into a bout of play, and begins playing around with only the first of the two inter-coordinated schemas.

IMITATION   A major advance for imitation in this substage results from the fact that infants can imitate activities that they cannot see. They can accomplish this kind of imitation because their visual schemas have become coordinated with schemas from other domains, such as the schemas for grasping or making other bodily movements. For example, Observation 20: "At 0;8 (9), I stuck out my tongue in front of J, thus resuming the experiment interrupted at 0;8 (3) which up till then had given only negative results. . . . At the beginning, J watched me without reacting, but around the eighth attempt, she started biting her lips as before, and at the ninth and tenth attempt, she became more daring and reacted each time in the same way afterwards. The same evening her reaction was immediate: as soon as I stuck out my tongue she bit her lips. . . . Subsequently, the act of biting the lips appeared to be for her the adequate response to every movement of someone else's mouth." A similar behavior can be observed in Observation 26: "At 0;11 (8), J had her left forefinger in her ear and she was exploring the inside tactually. I then put my finger in my ear as I stood in front of her. She watched me closely and stopped what she was doing. I stopped, too. When I did it again, she looked at me again with great interest and then put her finger back into her ear. The same thing occurred five or six times, but with no guarantee that there was real imitation. However, after a few minutes break, during which J was doing something quite different (crumpling up a newspaper), I raised my finger closer to my ear. Then, while she was looking at me, she clearly brought her finger closer to her ear and put hers in shortly after I put in mine."

THE FIFTH SUBSTAGE: THE TERTIARY CIRCULAR REACTION AND THE DISCOVERY OF NEW MEANS THROUGH ACTIVE EXPERIMENTS   The progress of intelligence through the first four substages has more or less involved the application of familiar schemas to new situations. In Substage 2, reflexive schemas are applied to accidental encounters with one's own body and are reproduced to make them last. In Substage 3, the same schemas are applied to accidental encounters with outside objects, but they are still reproduced to make them last. In Substage 4, familiar schemas are coordinated with one another to achieve some new ends. But in Substage 5, there is a new push to use old knowledge to achieve novel results, at an even higher level. This time, existing schemas are used in the pursuit of novelty itself. These are called **tertiary circular reactions**. The tertiary circular reactions of Substage 5 have much the same flavor of the circular reactions of Substages 2 and 3 in that they're repeated over and over. But in the more primitive Substages 2 and 3, the circular reactions pretty much just reproduced the *same* interesting effect each time. Substage 5 circular reactions, on the other hand, are aimed at producing different interesting effects each time. Here an old schema is applied—dropping things, for instance—but the schema is not reproduced just to get the same effect that has just occurred. Rather the goal is to produce a series of novel effects. True, the same *general* schema is enacted over and over, but the specific details vary.

It seems as if the baby's goal in Substage 5, then, is to learn about how the object interacts with the world, and to learn about *relationships* between objects. And a good way to find out how the object interacts with a variety of aspects of the world is to vary the ways in which the object is *given the opportunity* to interact with various aspects of the world. In this substage, the baby is a little scientist. He drops an object from a variety of locales, noting the different behaviors of the object each time it is dropped. Not only is he learning about the behavior of the object with respect to the world, he is learning about the world with respect to the object. In so doing, the baby is learning about gravity (when an object falls), friction (when an object slides down another object), solidity (when one object collides into another object), bounciness (when one object bounces off another), mass (when a big object comes into contact with a smaller object), and so on.

PLAY   Tertiary circular reactions in the domain of play maintain the repetition of schemas of the earlier substages, but they result in novel ways for implementing schemas, which Piaget indicates "become games almost immediately." Consider Observation 63: "At 1;0 (5), J was holding her hair with her right hand while taking her bath. The hand, which was wet, slipped and struck the water. Then, J repeated the action right away, first by delicately putting her hand on her hair then quickly bringing it down on to the water. She varied the height and position, and one might have thought it was a tertiary circular reaction but the child's attitude demonstrated that it was nothing but a question of ludic combinations. However, on the following days, during each bath session, the game was repeated with the regularity of a ritual. For instance, at 1;0 (11) she struck the water as soon as she was in the bath, but later she stopped as if something was missing; she then raised her hand up to her hair and found her game again."

IMITATION   As applied to imitation, Substage 5 behaviors maintain the quality of varying the outcomes, but they do so in the capacity of imitating something just observed by the child. Observation 40: At 1;1 (10), "J was in front of me. I rubbed my thigh with my right hand. She watched me, laughed, and rubbed first her cheek then her chest. At 1;2 (12), when I struck my abdomen, she hit the table, then her knees (she was sitting down). At 1;3 (30), she hit her knees without hesitation when I did it, and then when I rubbed my stomach, she hit first her knees then her thigh. . . . She only reached her stomach at 1;4 (15). Also at 1;3 (30), I lifted up my waistcoat and slid my finger underneath, at waist level. She then put her forefinger on her knee, felt round about, and finally slid it into her sock."

THE SIXTH SUBSTAGE: THE INVENTION OF NEW MEANS THROUGH MENTAL COMBINATIONS   Arguably, the most important achievement of the entire sensorimotor stage is the *internalization* of schemas that previously had to be enacted physically. These internalizations take place in Substage 6, usually between 18 and 24 months of age. In other words, schemas go mental. This achievement provides some serious adaptive advantages over previous behaviors. For one thing, babies don't have to actually perform an action in order to know something about the world. Instead, they can more or less anticipate what will happen by imagining it. Piaget called this "pre-vision." Through pre-vision, babies can figure out how to solve some kinds of problems without the consequences of trial and error. But as a result of the availability of internalized mental symbols, both play and imitation take on a new significance in the child's life. In the domain of play, the child begins to apply old schemas to completely inappropriate objects and situations that have heretofore not been associated with the old schemas; in other words, the child can now pretend. In the domain of imitation, the child begins to acquire and store for later use, behaviors previously witnessed in a different place and time. Piaget called this ability "deferred imitation."

PLAY   Without a doubt, the most famous example of Substage 6 play, which involves completely internalized mental combinations, or "true ludic symbols," comes from Jacqueline. Observation 64: At 1;3 (12), "She saw a cloth whose fringed edges vaguely reminded her of those of her pillow; she seized it, held one of its folds in her right hand, sucked the thumb of the same hand and lay down on her side, laughing hard. She kept her eyes open, but blinked from time to time as if she was mimicking closed eyes. Finally, while laughing more and more, she cried 'Néné' (Nono). The same cloth triggered the same game on the following days. At 1;3 (13) she treated the collar of her mother's coat the same way. At 1;3 (30), it was the tail of her rubber donkey which played the role of the pillow. And from 1;5 onwards, she also made her animals, a bear and a plush dog also do 'nono.'"

IMITATION   Jacqueline also provides the most famous example of Substage 6 imitation, which, because it takes place some time after observing the original event, Piaget called "deferred imitation." Observation 52: "At 1;4 (3), J had a visit from a little boy of 1;6 whom she used to see from time to time, and who, in the course of the afternoon had a temper tantrum. He screamed while trying to get out of a playpen and pushed it backwards, stamping his feet. J, who had never witnessed such a scene before, looks stunned and motionless. The next day however, she was the one screaming in her playpen and trying to move it by stamping her foot lightly several time in a row. The imitation of the whole scene was striking. Had it been immediate, it would naturally not have involved representation, but since it happened after an interval of more than twelve hours, it must have involved some representative or pre-representative element."

To summarize, by the end of the sensorimotor period, just as intelligence is no longer bound to the child's actions on the world in conjunction with the sensory feedback those actions produce, neither are play and imitation bound to the sensory-motor domain. The most adaptive schemas at this point are those that are capable of being represented mentally—freed from the here and now. Because schemas can be invoked mentally without needing real-world objects to act upon, children in the sixth substage have some serious intellectual advantages over children in the more primitive substages. For one thing, they don't have to actually do things in order to gain knowledge. Instead, they can gain knowledge just by imagining things. Does it make for an adaptive advantage to be able to use your imagination? Heavens yes! Consider, for example, how long it would take you to learn about weight differences if you had to physically lift a watermelon and an orange in order to know which was heavier. A second advantage of having your schemas go mental is that they allow you to invent solutions to problems that wouldn't have occurred otherwise. This is where Piaget's phrase "invention of new means through mental combinations" comes into play. Mentally, schemas can be combined with each other in ways that could never happen in reality. For example, imagine flying a Honda Accord to Lake Erie to go fishing for whales and sharks. Of course, none of this could happen in reality, but it could happen very easily in mentality! Obviously, once schemas go mental there's a whole new range of possibilities for intellectual adaptation to the world. Piaget believed that once schemas become mentally represented, they can assimilate one another not only rapidly, but spontaneously—almost automatically.

AND ONWARD TO MENTAL REPRESENTATION

Piaget tells his substage-by-substage story of the development of play and imitation to get to the main point of his exposition, which is to explain the child's construction of mental representation. To add a couple of new terms to the mix, and similar to Vygotsky's terminology (Chapter 4), Piaget characterizes mental representation as requiring two elements: a *signifier* and a *signified*. A signifier is something that is used to stand for, or mean, some other thing. It can be a word, such as when the word *box* stands for the thing *box*; it can be a gesture, such as when you make a "V" sign with your first two fingers (which means "peace" in the United States); and it can be an image, such as when the golden arches stands for a McDonalds restaurant. In contrast, a *signified* is the thing that is being referenced by the signifier. In the three examples above, the *signified* includes 1) the concept of a box, 2) the abstract concept of peace, and 3) everything that a McDonald's restaurant means to you.

Thus, for Piaget, mental representation emerges when the child internalizes, and uses, both a bunch of signifiers and a bunch of signifieds. The child uses the signifiers to stand for the things that are signified. But importantly, and not coincidentally, the child constructs these two pieces of the mental representation puzzle through the processes of imitation (pure accommodation) and play (pure assimilation), respectively. How does this happen, you ask? Well let's see if I can do justice to Piaget's explanation.

ACQUISITION OF THE SIGNIFIERS   Piaget explains that the signifier, "appears to be the product of accommodation since it is continued as imitation, therefore, as images or interiorized imitations." What he really means by this rather cryptic claim, is that the only way we can acquire signifiers, or at least ones that make sense to ourselves and people in our culture, is by imitating the signifiers we see other people use. If you think about it, this makes sense. Every word, gesture, or image we know, we copied into our memories from our day-to-day experiences. English speaking children pick up English words from their English-speaking caregivers. And we use the gestures we know according to the conventions of our culture. Indeed, if a gesturer were to use a gesture outside of cultural conventions, she could find herself in trouble. For example, did you know the "ok" hand-gesture as used in the United States can be interpreted by some people in Mediterranean countries as referring to a particular body orifice located where the sun doesn't shine? So you might not want to flash the "ok" sign at a recent French immigrant. Through imitation, then, we acquire all the signifiers that we will ever use in our acts of mental representation. Of course, the signifiers don't have any meaning until they are eventually linked up with the signified; but this process at least explains one half of the process.

ACQUISITION OF THE THINGS THAT ARE SIGNIFIED   The other half of the process explains how we acquire the signified. In Piaget's account, "'The signified' is obviously the product of assimilation, which, by integrating the object into earlier established schemas, thereby provides it with a meaning." Again, in typical Piagetianese, this is very cryptic. But what it means is that for a signified to be meaningful to us, it has to be linked to something we already know. Imagine you see a strange pattern that looks like this: ♑. Initially you may not know what it is, and so it doesn't mean anything to you. But suppose you learn it is the symbol for the astrological sign of Capricorn. Once you learn this fact, then you can assimilate the symbol into your Capricorn schema. The symbol becomes the signifier through accommodation, and everything you already know about the astrological sign of Capricorn becomes what is signified. As Piaget summarizes succinctly, "Representation is thus the union of a 'signifier' that allows a recall with a 'signified' supplied by thought."

SUMMARY

Piaget's single goal in his trilogy was to present data that showed that intelligent adaptation as a result of experience takes place, and that it takes place in a manner consistent with the basic tenets of evolutionary theory. In achieving this goal, Piaget developed a framework for describing how the intelligence of babies adapts to reality, and it was a framework that applied equally well across all six substages of infancy; from the earliest, most primitive reflexive schemas of newborns to the most advanced mental combinations of 2-year-olds. The keys to his theory were the "functionally invariant" roles played by the adaptive processes of assimilation and accommodation. By "functionally invariant" adaptive processes, I mean that although the specific items that are assimilated and accommodated to, will change over time, the processes themselves work the same way no matter what the items are or how old the child is. It doesn't matter if you're assimilating a car key to your sucking schema or a matchbox opening to your mouth-opening schema, assimilation is assimilation is assimilation. *Play* extends this line of thinking to the stage of mental representation.

CONCLUSIONS

As I mentioned previously, Piaget gets so much space in this book because he was so important to the field of psychology for so long. Piaget laid his cards down for everyone to see, and by doing so, he set the standard that everyone else would have to live up to. And, as a matter of fact, the 1960s and 1970s represented a Piagetian golden age. Everybody was testing this or that hypothesis generated by Piagetian theory. And the old master himself was still alive and kicking and doing as much as he could to further our understanding of children's cognitive development.

But as you might imagine, when you're the leader of a major revolution of any sort, it doesn't take long before other people start having second thoughts about your leadership. And so it was that a number of anti-Piagetian movements started to rise and gain momentum. The behaviorists, who, throughout the 1950s and 1960s, remained strong vocal opponents of the notion of internal mental development Piaget so clearly articulated, took potshots whenever possible. And nativists like Renee Baillargeon and Elizabeth Spelke gained considerable scientific momentum in the 1990s and 2000s with their suggestion that babies probably already know most of the basic concepts of reality at birth.

In the four decades since Piaget's death in 1980, the influence of his theory has waned, but still his theory remains subject to continual criticism by child psychologists. We will see in Chapter 5, for example, that Renee Baillargeon took a huge bite out of Piaget's argument that the mental representation of objects doesn't fully develop until 18–24 months of age. But the result of attacks like these has often been only to show that Piaget might have been wrong about the specific cognitive mechanisms and timing underlying a particular behavior, not about *whether the behavior* existed. In the end, it's a tribute to Piaget's vision, ingenuity, and comprehensiveness that his theory essentially founded contemporary child psychology theory. While it may be true that his theory no longer commands the attention of the entire field as it once did, his ideas remain so central to modern child psychology as to be almost invisible.

Bibliography

Piaget, J. (1952). *The origins of intelligence in children*. New York: International University Press.
Piaget, J. (1954). *The construction of reality in the child*. New York: Basic Books.

Questions for Discussion

1. What might be some limitations of basing an entire theory of cognitive development on observations of only three children?
2. Compare and contrast the concept of development with the concept of differentiation, as they apply to basic reflexive schemas.
3. Why is the concept of functional invariance important for a developmental theory?

4

A Marxist Revolution in Psychology

Mind in Society: The Development of Higher Psychological Processes

Vygotsky, L. S. (1978). *Cambridge, MA: Harvard University Press.*
(RANK 8)

And now, finishing in eighth place among the most revolutionary studies in child psychology published since 1960, the famous work of the Russian psychologist we all know and love, Lev Semenovich Vygotsky! Wait, what? You've never heard of Vygotsky? Ok, maybe you're not alone. Vygotsky (pronounced "vih-GOT-skee") tends not to get a lot of coverage in child psychology textbooks. I wonder if some psychologists might not even recognize the name. So in some ways it might be surprising that Vygotsky's work was regarded by so many child psychologists as so revolutionary. On the other hand, he does rank among the three most influential child psychology theoreticians in the last 50 years (alongside Piaget and Bowlby), which is really quite an accomplishment given that Vygotsky died more than 80 years ago. It's not like he's been able to hobnob with the intellectual elite or anything. Whereas Piaget lived to the ripe old age of 84 and got the chance to revise and refine his theories until 1980, Vygotsky lived only to see his 37th birthday, and had to have his theoretical juggernauts in place by 1934. No, whatever revolutionary fires Vygotsky ignited, he did so with about half as many matches as Piaget. Nevertheless, in recent years Vygotsky has exploded onto the scene.

Like Piaget, Vygotsky's interests actually extended far beyond the world of child psychology. In his doctoral work, he was especially interested in law and literature. In fact, before he even began his studies of children, he earned a law degree and went on to write a doctoral dissertation on William Shakespeare's famous work *Hamlet*. Vygotsky was a well-read man. But even when he began his investigations of children's mental development, he was always working from within the philosophical-political framework of Karl Marx's theories on government and labor. Marx's writings consistently emphasized the importance of people within a community working together toward a greater, common good. Marx believed that the common good could be obtained through cooperative labor, including the use of tools. The idea was that if everyone worked together toward achieving the values of a society then the society as a whole would be far better off than if individual members of the society competed with one another in promoting their self-interests. Vygotsky believed that Marx's ideas should be applied to the science of psychology as well. Unfortunately, the mainstream psychology of Vygotsky's time—that which was taking place in Western Europe and the United States—tended to focus on the individual. So he set out to revolutionize psychology by creating a science in which the development of the individual was always considered in the context of the individual's surrounding physical and social environments (a la Bronfenbrenner, Chapter 14).

COMPARISONS BETWEEN VYGOTSKY AND PIAGET

Before diving into Vygotsky's work more deeply, I'd like to point out a number of similarities between him and Piaget. I think by understanding their commonalities, we can better appreciate what it takes to achieve greatness in the field of child psychology. First off, both Vygotsky and Piaget were juvenile geniuses. Vygotsky scholar James Wertsch writes that when Vygotsky was an adolescent, he and his teenage buddies used to act out fictional debates between historical figures of great intellectual prominence, such as Aristotle and Napoleon. Given these kinds of antics, it seems to me that if Vygotsky and Piaget had met each other on the playground, which was physically possible since they were born in the same year (1896), they might have developed a great friendship. Both of them seemed to enjoy doing odd, nerdy things. It's also noteworthy that Vygotsky, like Piaget, worked tirelessly and published massively at a very young age. By the time of his premature death of tuberculosis at the age of 37, Vygotsky had already published or written over 180 scientific works. Amazingly, many of his writings continued appearing in the press long after his death. Unfortunately for the rest of the world, however, many of Vygotsky's writings remained hidden from the English-speaking public for many decades, primarily as a result of the long arms of Stalin's communist regime. Only in the last 35 years or so has the collection of Vygotsky's writings become generally accessible, including the release of a multivolume series published in the mid-1980s.

A second and perhaps more important similarity was that both Vygotsky and Piaget were struggling with issues that exceeded the scope of child psychology. Whereas Piaget was coming from the point of view of Darwin's theory of evolution, Vygotsky was coming from the point of view of Karl Marx's theory of government and labor. Still I find it ironic that although Vygotsky and Piaget were rated as two of the most revolutionary scientists in child psychology, neither one of them had child psychology as their primary interest. Both scientists viewed child psychology as a small piece of the much larger puzzles they were working on.

A third similarity is that Vygotsky's *Mind in Society*, like Piaget's *Play*, was first written in various forms many years before 1950. It wasn't until Vygotsky's writings were translated into English, making them available to the vast American psychological community, that his ideas began taking the American field of child psychology by storm. And since then, Vygotsky's works have attracted as much attention as an ice cream vendor on a hot summer day.

It's important to point out that *Mind in Society* wasn't a direct translation of a Russian version of the same book. Rather, as noted by its editors, the book was more of a compendium of a number of different chunks of Vygotsky's writings. They were masterfully interwoven by the editors to tell the story of Vygotsky's psychology to the rest of the world. And like Piaget, Vygotsky apparently had a very difficult style, so the editors admitted to taking liberties with pieces of his work so as to best represent his intention without misrepresenting his meaning. So what's all the excitement about? Let's take a look.

INTRODUCTION

In the beginning of the book, Vygotsky indicates that the purpose of any psychology should be to explain the relationship between humans and their surrounding environments. Right away, you can see Marx's influence. There are two types of environments that humans (and the psychologists who study them) have to deal with. First, there is the physical environment. The physical environment consists of all the stuff humans come into contact with: trees, rocks, ponds, chairs, screwdrivers, and so on. Second, and far more importantly, there is the social environment. By their very nature, humans are social creatures. Vygotsky believed that this fact had to be acknowledged as a basic tenet of psychology. Any psychology that failed to recognize the social nature of humans was doomed. Understanding the nature of humans without taking into account their socialness is like playing baseball without the bases. And language was one aspect of the social environment that played an especially important role for Vygotsky, particularly in terms of the development of what he called the *higher psychological processes.*

Now, keep in mind that when Vygotsky was doing his psychology thing in the early 1900s, the science of psychology was still pretty young. Psychologists around the globe were still trying to figure out what psychology should do and how it should do it. So there were lots of different opinions about the best way to do psychology. According to Vygotsky, there was at least one way *not* to do psychology. The way *not* to do psychology was to start by isolating a research subject from his or her natural surroundings. In other words, you should never bring anyone into the laboratory.

Unfortunately, this was exactly how much of the rest of the field of child psychology chose to proceed. These psychologists wanted to study kids in the laboratory because they thought human environments were too rich, too complex, and too varied to be able to make much sense about how kids behaved in them. They believed that doing psychology was like looking for a needle in a haystack, where the human behavior was the needle and the environment was the haystack. Vygotsky would've called these psychologists "artificialist psychologists," because they seemed to be focusing on constructing artificial environments in the laboratory, and pulling children out of their natural surroundings. He believed that it was precisely those rich, complex, and varied environments that should be the focus of psychological study.

Still, the goals of the artificialist psychologists made some sense. For example, have you ever tried to listen to a weak AM radio station? Sometimes it's hard to even hear what song is playing unless the radio station's signal is relatively strong compared to the amount of noisy static in the background. Well, the goal of the artificialist psychologists was to reduce the "noisy static" of children's surrounding environments by bringing the children into laboratories. These psychologists reasoned that by using a laboratory, they would be able to reduce the noisy static of the environment, and increase the signal of human behavior. As a result, artificialist psychologists believed, true human nature would be much easier to detect. And in fact, this logic is standard practice among scientists in all other scientific disciplines as well. Consider the biologist who cultures bacteria in a petri dish. Although bacteria can grow in lots of other places, it's easy to culture specific bacteria under the artificial, highly controlled conditions that are found in a petri dish. Doesn't it make sense that psychology should adopt such tried-and-true methods too?

But as I said, Vygotsky completely rejected this approach. He believed that any psychology that artificially removed its subject of study from its natural surroundings was bound to be wrong. For psychology to be right, he argued, it would have to take into account not only the people themselves, but where they lived, what they ate, whom they dated, and how they talked to one another. People simply must be studied within their natural surroundings before a valid psychology could even become possible.

Tool and Symbol in Child Development

Vygotsky began his Marxist-based psychology by trying to identify the kinds of things that were uniquely and truly human, and that were responsible for promoting the welfare of human society. One of these things was the relationship between tool use and speech. By "tool use," Vygotsky meant the ability to use some part of the environment to solve a problem. By "speech," he meant the symbols and signs humans use to communicate with each other about ideas as well as about objects and events in the world. Vygotsky believed that tool use and speech were essential to the development of human societies as a whole, and so he sought to investigate their influence on the development of the individual.

Vygotsky was fascinated by the work of some of his contemporaries with chimpanzees. He believed that chimps provided psychology with a very interesting, and essential, comparison group. On the one hand, chimps, like humans, are capable of using tools to do certain kinds of things. For example, chimps have long been known to poke skinny tree limbs into termite mounds in order to pull out gobs of deliciously tasty termites. On the other hand, chimps lack speech. So as similar as chimps and humans are to one another in tool use, humans are still the champs as a result of their speech-using capability. So Vygotsky believed that an analysis of the similarities and differences between chimpanzees and human children (before and after the onset of speech) could shed some powerful light on truly and uniquely human forms of intelligence.

Of course, human babies don't pop out of the womb speaking or using tools. Rather, these capacities develop only after several months of postnatal experience—after the child matures a bit physically, and after he accumulates a good deal of learning about his physical and social worlds. Babies use tools? Absolutely. In Piaget's means-ends task, infants are able to pull one object (like a pillow) to get at another object sitting on top of it (like a bell). In this case, the pillow is being used as a tool.

Vygotsky believed that although the capacities for tool use and speech followed relatively separate ontogenetic paths in human babies, when a child became capable of doing both, something very magical happened: the tool-using infant developed into the speech-using preschooler. For Vygotsky, this achievement catapulted the child into a whole new level of intellectual functioning. Vygotsky called this whole new level of intellectual functioning a **higher psychological process**. A higher psychological process is simply something that can be accomplished only by humans. He noted: "[T]he most significant moment in the course of intellectual development, which gives birth to the purely human forms of practical and abstract intelligence, occurs when speech and [tool use], two previously completely independent lines of development, converge."

Vygotsky spent a lot of time studying how children's problem-solving abilities improved as they gained proficiency at speech. In fact, he believed that the problem-solving abilities of pre-speech children were more or less like those of chimpanzees. It wasn't until children became good at speech that they left the world of the lowly chimp to enter the world of higher psychological functioning. Why was speech so important? For one thing, according to Vygotsky, it gives rise to a whole new level of intellectual freedom. With speech, whether they speak aloud or not, children can talk about things that don't exist, they can make plans about the future, and they can recall mistakes they made in the past. Because words are internal devices used to signify external things in the world, children can use words to think about the things they signify in the absence of the actual things themselves. Pre-speech children, like chimps, can't think about things in the abstract, they can think about them only when acting on them directly. Notice here the striking similarity with Piaget's notion of representation, which includes a signifier and a signified (Chapter 3). Speech also gives children the means to "talk through" a problem before implementing the specific strategies necessary to solve it. Creatures without speech are more or less stuck in the here and now. They are imprisoned by the limited information provided to them by their senses in the immediate situation, and so they can pretty much solve problems only through trial and error.

Vygotsky found that one of the first ways that speech helps children use tools is when, after failing to solve a problem on their own, they seek outside assistance. To get help from somebody else, children often have to describe the problem verbally. This is what Vygotsky called the **interpersonal function of speech**, which means that speech between two people is needed to solve a problem. But as children gain lots of experience speaking with others, they eventually become capable of speaking to themselves. Then they can use their *own* speech to help themselves through the problem. Vygotsky called this the **intrapersonal function** of speech; and at this point, speech is said to be internalized. With this so-called **inner voice**, children have a whole new level of psychological awareness available to them; and they become capable of the higher psychological functions available only to humans. To recap using Vygotsky's own words: "Signs and words serve children first and foremost as a means of social contact with other people. The cognitive and communicative functions of language then become the basis of a new and superior form of activity in children, distinguishing them from animals."

Speech and Signs

The intrapersonal function of speech has extremely powerful effects on a number of psychological abilities. For example, a child's inner voice improves her perception of the surrounding environment, her memory for past experiences, and her ability to pay attention. But when you get down to the nitty-gritty, the reason internalized speech transforms children's intellectual functioning isn't so much because of the specific speech that is used, it's because of the *signifying function* that individual words and sentences serve. In Vygotsky's terms, words are a type of sign. And the importance of signs is that they signify things. Indeed, the astute among you will even notice that the word *sign* makes up the word *signify*.

I remember when my youngest child was very little. I was driving down the road in our minivan, with Sarah buckled snugly in the back seat. We caught a red light at an intersection next to a local police station, and after several seconds of apparently detailed environmental scanning, Sarah said, "Look, Daddy, she has a fuzzy driving center." Of course, I didn't know what Sarah meant, nor who "she" was, but I began scanning all four corners of the intersection to see if I could catch a glimpse of exactly how fuzzy the driving center was. Obviously, Sarah was trying to share an idea with me, although I had no clue what she meant. Eventually I caught Sarah's line of visual regard, and noticed that she was looking at the driver in the car next to us. After scanning the interior of that car, I realized that Sarah was using the signs "fuzzy driving center" to signify the fuzzy steering wheel cover being used by the female driver. Of course, it helps when one person uses a sign that's understandable by the other person, but it's the fact that children can use signs in the first place that matters.

Vygotsky believed that when children become capable of using words to signify, the important thing is not that they are using specific words, but that they are using arbitrary symbols to stand for other things. If you think about it, when we say a word, we are really just producing a certain pattern of sounds. This pattern of sounds signifies the underlying idea. The specific sound pattern really doesn't matter. Take the word *car*, for example. The sounds we make when we say "car" have no necessary connection with the meaning of the word *car*. Different languages use different patterns of sounds to signify the meaning of "car." In Spanish we would say "auto" (pronounced something like "OW-toe"), in German we'd say "Wagen" (pronounced "VAHG-n"), in Japanese we'd say "kuruma" (pronounced "kuh-roo-MA"), and in Swahili we'd say "gari" (pronounced "GA-ree"). The fact that speaking children are speaking is important because it means that they have reached the point where they can use an arbitrary pattern of sounds to stand for something else. If something as simple as a pattern of sounds can stand for an idea, then other things can stand for an idea too. Right now while you are reading these words, you may be seeing patterns of black ink on a white background. Clearly, these patterns of black ink, like the sound patterns we just talked about, signify things. There is no special meaning in the black lines, curves, and dots, it's all in the fact that they are used to signify. In sum, when children start using signs to stand for things, they are entering the world of higher psychological processes.

Probably more so than his experimental work, Vygotsky's major contribution to the field of child psychology lies in his theoretical work. Still, in an effort to demonstrate how he translated his theoretical model into scientific practice, it's worthwhile to consider one of his experiments as a case in point. In one such experiment, Vygotsky set out to explore just how well arbitrary signs can help children function in the world, particularly in the domain of basic memory. Now here Vygotsky talks about two different types of memory: natural (or immediate) memory and sign-assisted (or mediated) memory. The distinction is a difficult one to grasp, but I'll do my best to explain it.

First is natural memory. Natural memory is a very basic, even primordial, type of memory that is pretty much driven exclusively by our senses. Vygotsky described it as "very close to perception, because it arises out of the direct influence of external stimuli upon human beings." I think the kinds of memories Vygotsky is talking about here are the kinds I get when on certain occasions I get a whiff of a particular type of perfume. Whenever I smell one certain perfume, I get an immediate flashback, sort of a mental photograph, of my old girlfriend from high school. Come to think of it, there's another type of perfume, but one I rarely encounter anymore, that brings up an image of a girl I used to have a crush on in junior high. These kinds of memories pop up automatically, they are immediate, and they even appear as visual images of the kind I might have had when looking right at these people.

The other kind of memory is mediated memory. Mediated memory is so-called because it occurs when memories are mediated by signs. What this means is that sometimes our memories can be aided by something external to the memory itself. Vygotsky uses the example of how even primitive peoples put notches in sticks to help them remember quantities of things. Another example, commonly seen in movies, is when a prisoner makes marks on a prison or dungeon wall to remind him of how many days he has been incarcerated. Vygotsky points out that no other animal, not even the higher primates, have ever given any evidence of using this kind of sign-enhanced memory. Therefore, it must be a uniquely human process. And as a uniquely human process, it results from humans' essentially social nature. The following experiment, conducted under the leadership of A. N. Leontiev in Vygotsky's lab, sought to investigate children's use of signs to enhance memory. In the experiment, the investigators played a version of the popular parlor game "Taboo." If you've never played the game before, the goal is to get partners on your team to say a particular word. The catch is that there are certain words that you are not allowed to say when prompting your partner. If you were supposed to get your partner to say "key," for example, you might not be permitted to say "lock" or "ignition switch." The version of this game used in Vygotsky's lab was only slightly different. The experimenters asked children a series of questions, some of which would have color words as their answer. A sample question was "What color is the floor?" The children were expected to provide an answer even though sometimes they were told that certain color words could not be used. Of course, if the floor was green, and the child used the taboo word "green" to answer the experimenter's question, an error would be recorded for this child's response. Vygotsky and Leontiev wondered whether giving children cards with colors on them would help reduce the number of oral errors they ended up making. In essence their question was, "Would children use color cards as external signs to help them answer questions correctly?"

METHOD

Participants

Vygotsky doesn't give us much detail about the participants involved in this study. But we know that at least four age groups participated. There were 7 participants in the 5–6-year-old age range, 7 in the 8–9-year-old age range, 8 in the 10–13-year-old age range, and 8 in the adult category (ranging in age from 22 to 27 years).

Materials

The only materials needed for this experiment were a series of nine color cards. The colors on the cards were black, white, red, blue, yellow, green, lilac, brown, and gray.

Procedure

The procedure was pretty straightforward. Children were presented with groups of questions that they were expected to answer, but they were placed under increasingly strict restrictions regarding how they could answer. For example, consistent with the game Taboo, children were supposed to answer some questions without using specific words. Early on, children were asked a series of questions about the colors of various objects and they were allowed to answer using single-word responses. But then more restrictive rules were imposed. In the second set of questions, for example, "there were two color names the child was forbidden to use, and no color name could be used twice." The third set of questions included the rules from the second set, but this time children were give nine color cards, and told "these cards can help you to win."

Here are the kinds of questions Vygotsky posed to children (with the caveat that saying "green" or "yellow" was not allowed): (1) Have you a playmate? (2) What color is your shirt? (3) Did you ever go on a train? (4) What color are the railway carriages? (5) Do you want to be big? (6) Were you ever at the theater? (7) Do you like to play in the room? (8) What color is the floor? (9) And the walls? (10) Can you write? (11) Have you seen lilac? (12) What color is lilac? (13) Do you like sweet things? (14) Were you ever in the country? (15) What colors can leaves be? (16) Can you swim? (17) What is your favorite color? (18) What does one do with a pencil?"

TABLE 4.1 Average Number of Errors in Answering the Questions with and without the Availability of Color Cards

Age	Number of Participants	Question Set 2	Question Set 3	Difference
5–6	7	3.9	3.6	0.3
8–9	7	3.3	1.5	1.8
10–13	8	3.1	0.3	2.8
22–27	8	1.4	0.6	0.8

RESULTS

The actual results from the study can be found in Table 4.1. In that table, you'll notice that the individual age groups are listed on the left side of the table. Then, to the right of the age group-ings, you can see the average number of errors for the second and third groups of questions. Comparing the errors on only these two tasks is important because they stand for the participants' scores on the trial when the color cards weren't used and the scores on the trial when the color cards were used. Remember, the research question was whether the availability of signs (the color cards) would improve children's ability to answer the questions. On the far right side of the table you can see the difference between the scores when the color cards were or weren't used. Notice that for all age groups, having the color cards in hand helped the participants make fewer errors than not having the color cards.

Pay special attention to the difference scores in the right-most column. Although all the groups did better with the cards than without them, notice that the cards had the largest effect on the memories of 10- to 13-year-old children. In contrast, the cards really didn't improve memory very much for the adults, nor for the 5- to 6-year-olds. We'll return to this point momentarily.

DISCUSSION

According to Vygotsky, the results of this study show that there are three basic stages in the de-velopment of mediated memory. Among the youngest children, having the color cards simply did not improve memory. (Although there is a 0.3-point improvement in the memories of the young-est children, the difference was apparently not important to Vygotsky.) At this stage, external signs aren't used profitably to aid memory. However, in the second stage of development, when children were between 8 and 13 years old, having the cards improved memory tremendously. Specifically, the errors dropped by 1.8 points for 8- to 9-year-olds, and by 2.8 points for 10- to 13-year-olds. The reason for the improvement was that the children at this age were able to use the color cards as external signs. Finally, look at the scores of the adults. Having the cards really didn't help them perform any better than not having the cards. Why would this be? Apparently, it was because the adults' performance was so high to begin with, that they made very few errors even without the cards. It's as if they were using their own internal "mental" signs from the outset. Because they already had their own internalized mental signs, having the color cards didn't give the adults any special advantage. Vygotsky wrote, "The external sign that school children require has been transformed into an internal sign produced by the adult as a means of remembering."

This experiment supported Vygotsky's idea that the development of higher psychologi-cal processes in children results from the progressive internalization of signs that are originally available only externally, through social communication. Of course, one limitation of this study is that we can't be sure the adults were actually using internal signs. Still, the outcome of the experiment was consistent with what we would predict if adults were capable of using internal signs to assist, or mediate, memory.

Something Else That Vygotsky Was Famous for (or Practical Everyday Applications of Vygotsky's Theory)

The experiment I just described was focused on only a very small part of Vygotsky's grander theory of the development of the individual within the larger societal context. Something else which Vygotsky talks about in the book, and which also earned him quite a bit of fame, was his notion of the **zone of proximal development**. The zone of proximal development directly reflects Vygotsky's driving interest in applying his theoretical ideas to real-life situations. Modern educators still spend considerable effort incorporating the zone of proximal development idea into their educational systems.

So what is this zone thing? It's basically the gap between what you can do on your own and what you can do with the help of a social partner, teacher, or mentor. We already mentioned this idea briefly when we talked about how young children may seek out adults to help them solve problems they can't solve on their own. In this way, the zone of proximal development is an *inter*psychological process. But let's explore some of the ramifications of the zone of proximal development.

Suppose we have two 8-year-old children who are just learning how to skateboard. Zachary and Joshua have never really skateboarded before, but they've played lots of skateboarding video games on their Xbox Ones, and they're ready to give it a try in real life. Suppose you catch a glimpse of them trying out some skateboard moves in the parking lot at the local library after you've just returned your latest copy of *Hunger Games*. You notice that neither one seems to be having much success in completing the tricks he's attempting. Although they seem to be getting the hang of standing and balancing on their boards, and they do fairly well at pushing off the ground to get the boards moving, neither one seems to come close to doing a 360 or an Ollie, and neither can "grind" the fence-rail along the wheelchair ramp (all typical skateboard moves). As far as you can tell, both children seem to be performing age-appropriately, and about equally well, but neither is particularly impressive at doing any tricks.

Now imagine another boy comes along who looks to be about twice the age of Zachary and Joshua. Aiden is also carrying a skateboard, but you get the impression that he has a little more experience than the other two boys. Sure enough, Aiden thrills and amazes the two younger ones with all sorts of tricks, jumps, and spins. He seems to be interested in helping the younger boys learn one simple trick, and so starts to teach them some basic strategies for learning how to grind the edge of one of the library's landscaping walls. In very short order, Joshua seems to get the hang of grinding, and he starts grinding practically everything that has an edge. Zachary, on the other hand, has much less success. He gains slightly better balance, and so stays on his board longer. But whenever he tries to grind something, he falls down. Zachary never quite demonstrates the same skill at grinding that Joshua does. Then Zachary skins his knee and goes home.

This example demonstrates one of the fundamental features of the Zone. First, at the beginning both boys were pretty much at the same level of functioning. They both could get on their boards and ride, but neither could do much else. Vygotsky would call these initial abilities their "actual developmental level." The actual developmental level is the level of performance a child is capable of on his own, without the help of adults or more capable peers. Second, notice that

Zachary and Joshua performed better under the guidance of the 16-year-old. Vygotsky would call this their "potential levels," which is the level of performance a child can achieve under the guidance of another person. Vygotsky calls this boost in ability an *inter*psychic process (because it involves the interactions between two people). The gap between what children do on their own and what they do with somebody else's help, or the distance between their actual level and their potential level, is what Vygotsky called the zone of proximal development. The larger the child's zone, the more prepared he is to move on to higher levels of performance. "What is in the zone of proximal development today will be the actual developmental level tomorrow." In our example, Joshua's zone was much larger than Zachary's, and so he is poised to move at a faster pace than Zachary, at least in the area of skateboarding. So even though you'd probably guess that Joshua and Zachary were at the same actual developmental level, based on observing them without the help of the older peer, there is something appreciably different about them in terms of their developmental potential. Wouldn't you say?

Now the zone of proximal development sounds like a pretty basic, intuitive idea. But it raised some important issues in its time, and it still raises some important concerns for educators today. Consider standardized testing. In American education policy there seems to be an obsession with inflicting standardized testing on American schoolchildren. Politicians seem to believe that if children are given standardized tests on a regular basis, then American taxpayers can be sure that children are being given the education they deserve. This movement started under Republican President George W. Bush back in the early 2000s, and it has continued throughout both terms of Democratic President Barack Obama. I must say that it's pretty disappointing indeed when a policy opposed by so many educators, psychologists, and social scientists, actually gains the support of both political parties, who otherwise fight and argue about everything else.

What's so wrong with standardized testing? Well, even 70 years ago, Vygotsky had a number of reasons to oppose it. For one thing, standardized testing places far too much emphasis on the achievements already made by children. When we use standardized testing we are really only measuring children's *actual developmental levels*. We're measuring their past achievements. And when schools are preparing their students to take standardized tests, their focus is on getting the kids to memorize content that is likely to be on the test. But the question we should be asking is not, "What are American children's actual developmental levels?" Rather, it should be, "What are American children's potentials for success?" The zone of proximal development, which is a concept rejected by proponents of standardized testing, represents an intellectual preparedness that is real, that is important, and that has greater implications for the successful adaptation of children to their environments than the actual developmental levels measured by standardized tests. Yet, we still reward teachers for cramming information into children's heads, rather than rewarding them for encouraging children to think creatively, productively, and flexibly. It would make far more sense, as we saw in the case of Zachary and Joshua, to measure children's intellectual potential.

Of course, educating children according to Vygotsky's notion of the zone of proximal development would require a different educational approach and philosophy. Instead of working to maximize children's *actual* developmental levels, teachers would work to maximize children's *potential* developmental levels. They would work within each child's zone, so to speak, trying to make it bigger. Have you ever had the experience of taking an exam in one of your classes, only to find out that you didn't understand something as well as you thought you did? This frustrating encounter demonstrates your own personal experience with the zone of proximal development. What you understood perfectly well in class with your teacher by your side, you understood rather poorly when she wasn't there to guide you. This phenomenon often happens in undergraduate statistics courses. I frequently give homework assignments to my students when I teach statistics. Yet, without fail, on the day the homework is due, some students will hand in an incomplete homework assignment, saying that they understood what I was talking about in class, but got completely lost when trying to do it on their own.

Clearly, people can perform better when working with other people, which was Marx's, and consequently Vygotsky's, central point. And the American educational system could benefit significantly by revising its educational practices accordingly. Rather than focusing on competitive, individualized academic achievement, perhaps we should focus on cooperative group-based learning. But as a nation, the United States can't seem to decide what to do. For a while in the middle 2000s, educational practices began moving away from a teacher-centered approach in which the teacher knows and tells all and the student copies down everything the teacher says, toward a student-centered approach, in which students discover knowledge on their own while working with their teachers or with groups of their peers. Grade schools, junior highs, and high schools showed a surge in this kind of discovery-based learning. But beginning in the 2010s, there seemed to be an about-face in state legislatures throughout the country, who once again began mandating a focus on students' achievement of learning outcomes. In Tennessee, which is my current state of residence, legislators even passed a law linking teachers' licensure to how well their students performed on standardized tests.

CONCLUSION

Vygotsky made a significant impact on the field of child psychology, to be sure. He was at least as important for giving the field a new way to think about doing psychology as he was for producing the specific scientific findings themselves. He introduced the world to a Marxist-flavored alternative to standard European and American ways of doing psychology. And importantly, his emphasis on considering human behavior in its natural context foreshadowed the theoretical viewpoints put forth by a number of other authors described in this book.

For example, Vygotsky would've loved the work of John Bowlby (Chapter 17). Bowlby's research focus was on mother–infant relationships. He was well known for his belief that mother–infant relationships were best understood in terms of the environments in which they were embedded. Bowlby argued that even though mothers and their babies were designed by thousands of years of evolution to be attracted to one another, the strength of their mutual attraction depended on their environments. Bowlby pointed out that attachment disorders are more likely now than ever before because the prehistoric environments in which attachment relationships originally evolved didn't have much in common with the kinds of environments in which today's mothers and children find themselves. Consequently, when mothers and infants find themselves in unusual or strange environments, such as the hospital or the prison, and when mothers are prevented from responding to their babies' signals in some way, attachment disorders become very real possibilities.

Vygotsky also would have been tickled by Urie Bronfenbrenner's theory (Chapter 14). Like Vygotsky, Bronfenbrenner believed it was silly to do research on children without simultaneously taking into account the environmental influences on those children. But, he went one step further than Vygotsky. He suggested that there were several different, interacting layers of environment, and therefore several different levels of influence of the environment on children. For example, children's behavior is influenced not only by whether they have a lot of toys to play with, but also by whether or not they live in a free, democratic society. So Bronfenbrenner suggested that environmental influences ranged from direct, immediate impacts to indirect, long-term impacts.

It is unfortunate that Vygotsky didn't live long enough to see the explosion in child psychology that took place in the latter half of his century. So many provocative and fascinating findings about the capabilities of infants and children have come out since Vygotsky's death, one can only wonder about what Vygotsky could have done had he known about them.

Bibliography

Miller, P. H. (1993). *Theories of developmental psychology.* New York: W. H. Freeman and Company.

Newman, F., & Holzman, L. (1993). *Lev Vygotsky: Revolutionary scientist.* London: Routledge.

Wertsch, J. V. (1985). *Vygotsky and the social formation of mind.* Cambridge, MA: Harvard University Press.

Questions for Discussion

1. What role does government play in the kinds of scientific research that get done? What role does science play in the kinds of government work that get done?
2. In what fundamental way does Vygotsky's approach to child psychology differ from Piaget's? How are the two approaches similar?
3. If we are going to insist on using standardized tests as a way to assess our children, how might we modify the procedure to make it more compatible with Vygotsky's approach (particularly his notion of the zone of proximal development)?
4. Do you think it's possible for chimpanzees to enter the domain of higher psychological processes? Why or why not? What would be the limiting factor, according to Vygotsky? Could that limiting factor be overcome through other means than vocal speech?

5

The Drawbridge Studies

"Object Permanence in Five-Month-Old Infants"

Baillargeon, R., Spelke, E. S., & Wasserman, S. (1985). *Cognition, 20*, 191–208. (RANK 5)

Every now and then a scientific study comes along that defies description in ordinary scientific terms. Such a study goes beyond the mere production and reporting of empirical data and actually penetrates the social and political milieu of the scientific community itself. To capture the spirit of such a study, we sometimes have to turn to other academic fields such as the humanities and fine arts to find the right labels. Renée Baillargeon's (pronounced "by-er-JOHN," with a soft *j* sound) 1985 study is one such work. This now famous study is at once an allegory of the classic biblical tale of David and Goliath (but without the bloodshed) and an embodiment of a French Impressionist painting.

It's an allegory of the David and Goliath story because in her labors Baillargeon was like the young, wet-behind-the-ears shepherd boy whose strong convictions were sufficient to bring down the stout, dominant, and overbearing force of the Philistine giant Goliath. Baillargeon's Goliath was Piaget. The work was like a French Impressionist painting because to fully appreciate it you have to take a few steps backward and embrace the piece as a whole. If you look too closely at the detail, the essence of the piece loses coherence. But also, being of French Canadian descent, Dr. Baillargeon has a marvelous French accent that makes a wonderful impression on those who hear her speak English. (Get it? She makes a French impression.)

PIAGETIAN OBJECT PERMANENCE   To understand where Baillargeon is coming from in this study, you first have to understand a bit about Piaget's concept of object permanence. It was Piaget's concept of object permanence that was the target of her attack. Although we spent considerable time reviewing Piaget's work in Chapters 2 and 3, we didn't spend much time on object permanence. So I'll review it briefly here.

Object permanence refers to the basic understanding that objects continue to exist even when they're no longer available to the senses. As adults, we have no problem with this concept. When I put a Butterfinger candy bar in my desk drawer, I know it'll be there the next time I need a sugar rush. And if it's not there when I go for it, I'll know it's because one of my children snuck it out when I wasn't looking. According to Piaget, we're not born with object permanence. An understanding of object permanence develops over time, and usually isn't fully available until about 18 months, although the beginnings of object permanence can be seen at around 9 months. Object permanence is essential for survival in the world, for without it we wouldn't be able to make plans about the future and remember the past. We wouldn't even remember what food we have in our refrigerator.

Piaget based his reasoning about object permanence on some innovative experiments he employed with his own children. He invented various techniques where he would hide one object behind another and look to see what his children would do, at different ages. As an example, he might take a rubber ducky and cover it up with his monogrammed handkerchief. If his kid failed to search for the ducky, he might pull the hanky just enough to reveal the ducky's tiny little tail, and so on. When his kids failed to search for the hidden objects, he saw it as an indication that they lacked object permanence. According to Piaget, babies younger than about 9 months don't search for hidden objects because they don't yet realize (1) that objects have separate identities, and (2) that objects continue to exist when they're outside of sensory awareness. Piaget marked 9 months as an important age because it was then that babies first began searching for objects that were hidden from view. This was pretty much the point of departure for Baillargeon's revolutionary study.

INTRODUCTION

Baillargeon and colleagues begin their article by telling the reader the same thing I just told you—that Piaget thought object permanence didn't begin until about 9 months of age. But they go on to point out that other researchers have also questioned Piaget's interpretation of his children's performance on the object permanence tasks. The central criticism is usually that Piaget's object permanence task actually requires two abilities, instead of just one. Imagine you are a subject in one of Piaget's object permanence experiments. You are given an attractive toy to play with, say a Fisher-Price Little People figure. You look at it, you bang it on the table, and then you put it in your mouth (because you're only 6 months old). Now imagine Piaget takes it from you and hides it under a cloth handkerchief in the middle of the table in front of you. In order to get the object back, what do you have to do? Of course, you must first realize that the object continues to exist. If you do, you have object permanence. But if all you do is remain sitting there quietly in your high chair, no one actually knows that you have object permanence, do they? You have to do something else to prove that you have object permanence. Specifically, you have to reach out and lift the cloth hanky off the Fisher-Price Little People figure. Now, whether or not you really had object permanence, Piaget couldn't be sure you had it until you reached out and grabbed the cloth. So, to the outside world, your ability to demonstrate object permanence depends on your ability to reach out and grab the cloth. If you don't have the capacity for removing the cloth and grabbing the toy, no one will have the slightest clue that you actually *have* object permanence.

Herein lies Baillargeon's major objection to Piaget's task. He required children to have two abilities (object permanence and the ability to reveal and grab a hidden object) before he was willing to give them credit for just one (object permanence). In Baillargeon's mind, Piaget's test of object permanence was just too hard. And because it was too hard, it was unfair. In sum, she believed it didn't permit the accurate measurement of object permanence.

According to Baillargeon, Piaget failed to detect "real" object permanence in children because his object permanence test required them to be capable of means-ends sequencing. Means-ends sequencing happens when one action is needed in order to allow another action to take place. You remove the cap from your Pepsi bottle *in order to* drink the Pepsi. That's means-ends sequencing. Thus, when Piaget required his children to remove the cloth in order to grab the hidden toy, he was requiring them to engage in means-ends sequencing. Baillargeon reasoned that means-ends sequencing might be a more sophisticated ability than object permanence. If so, then requiring a child to demonstrate means-ends sequencing in order to demonstrate object permanence would result in a serious underestimation of children's object permanence abilities.

Baillargeon's goal was to develop a simpler object permanence task to find out when children *really* understand object permanence. She would at least need a task that didn't require means-ends sequencing. But Baillargeon was confronted with one small problem: There was no other object permanence task available. So like all good little revolutionaries, she invented one. And it was ingenious. Taking advantage of the well-known measure of infant looking behavior (see Chapter 8 on Robert Fantz's work), she fashioned a method for measuring object permanence that would require little more than having children look at stuff. It was from children's looking behavior that Baillargeon purported to detect their emerging understanding of object permanence. She believed it was a much simpler task, and at least it didn't require children to engage in means-ends sequencing.

Now I am going to perpetrate a little "bait-and-switch" in my narrative. Although it was Baillargeon's 1985 article, coauthored by colleagues Elizabeth Spelke and Stanley Wasserman, that was voted the fifth most revolutionary article published since 1960, I am going to describe a slightly more recent 1987 article instead, because it focused on even younger babies, and included an even more thorough investigation. Don't worry, you won't miss out on anything. The content is the same, the rationales are the same, and the procedures are the same. It's just that in the 1987 article, Baillargeon extended her 1985 findings with 5-month-olds down to 4½- and even 3½-month-olds. This was a research tactic that would foreshadow much of Baillargeon's subsequent career, and seemed to be founded on the principle of identifying an effect in a population of babies of a certain age, and then tracing the effect to earlier and earlier points and time, with a view to seeing just how early the effect could be observed. Thus, in the 1987 article, Baillargeon conducted three related experiments. Experiment 1 looked at whether 4½-month-olds could show object permanence. Experiment 2 looked at whether 3¾-month-olds could show it, and Experiment 3 looked at whether 3½-month-olds could show it.

Experiment 1

METHOD

Participants

Twenty-four full-term infants ranging in age from 4 months, 2 days to 5 months, 2 days participated. Half of the infants were assigned to an experimental condition; half were assigned to a control condition. An additional 5 infants were excluded from the experiment because they were fussy (3 babies), they were drowsy (1 baby), or the equipment failed (1 baby). Parents of babies who participated were offered reimbursement for their travel expenses.

Materials

APPARATUS   Baillargeon used a specially designed experimental apparatus to conduct her experiments. Now describing the setup is a bit tricky since I can only use words. But you can find a depiction of the study on YouTube at:

- https://www.youtube.com/watch?v=u2ovHFt5YXc.

Or you can Google the terms: baillargeon, violation of expectation, drawbridge. If you don't have access to the Internet at the moment, we'll have to rely on the next best thing—your imagination.

Baillargeon's apparatus looked a little bit like the stage for a puppet show. From a distance, it looked like a large wooden box roughly the size of a kitchen stove, with a hole cut out of the middle of the front wall for viewing the "show." If you have a viewing window in your oven door, you can get a good idea of what Baillargeon's device looked like, only Baillargeon's viewing window was larger.

If you were to look through the viewing window of Baillargeon's device, you would see a silver cardboard screen that was affixed to a metal axle. What was special about this screen was that it could be rotated on its axle toward and away from the observer, through an arc of 180°. If you were to watch the screen go through its entire 180° range of motion, you would see it start out lying flat (let's say it was lying toward you), then begin to rise until it was eventually standing straight upright, and then begin to fall backward, away from you, until it became completely flat again. As an example, if you laid this book flat on a hard surface and turned a page, you would be turning the page in a 180° arc. And if you kept flipping the page back and forth, you'd pretty much be mimicking the motions of the silver cardboard screen in Baillargeon's apparatus. Although I know some of you "don't do numbers," I will use the term "180°" throughout the rest of the chapter to refer to the times when the screen in Baillargeon's apparatus rotated from one flat position all the way over to the other flat position.

Baillargeon also used a little wooden box in her apparatus, which was roughly the size of a Nerf football. The box was painted yellow, it had a little clown face painted on it, and it was placed behind the silver screen so that if the screen were leaning toward you, you would be able to see the box in the background, but if the screen were leaning away from you, the box would be hidden from your view. As you might imagine, if the screen tried to go through its full range of motion when the box was present, it would stop whenever it made contact with the box. At least this is what you would expect to happen. However, Baillargeon also fashioned a tricky little trap door under the box that would allow it to fall below the level of the surface whenever the screen contacted it. So rather than stopping when it contacted the box, the screen could be made to go through its full 180° range of motion. But if the screen did stop upon contact with the box, it would rotate through only part of its full range of motion. Specifically, Baillargeon calculated that the screen rotated through only a 112° arc.

THREE DIFFERENT EVENTS   All together, three different "events" could be created using this apparatus. First, babies could just watch the screen rotate back and forth through its entire range of motion, with the little clown box nowhere to be seen. Baillargeon called this event the *familiarization event* because it served to familiarize babies with how the screen was capable of moving. When the box was present, and located "behind" the screen, one of two additional events could happen. On the one hand, the screen could rotate back and forth, "contacting" the box each time. In this event, which Baillargeon called the *possible event*, the screen would rotate through only the 112° arc and would stop whenever it made contact with the box; then it would begin to rotate back in the other direction. In the third kind of event, the screen could be made to rotate through its full 180° range of motion, making it seem to rotate magically right through the box. Baillargeon called this the *impossible event*, because normally, solid objects can't pass through other solid objects. Of course, the impossible was made possible in this case because of the little trap door in the floor that allowed the box to be secretly removed whenever the screen passed by.

Procedure

Babies who participated in Baillargeon's study sat on their mothers' laps in front of the apparatus, with a perfect view of the events taking place. Mothers were asked not to talk to their babies during the experiment. Before each "show," the babies were allowed to hold and play with the little wooden clown box. This allowed them to see for themselves what the box was like. I think the most important thing was that they learned the box was made out of a hard material rather than some spongy substance.

Two observers looked through little peepholes in the apparatus and watched where the babies looked. It's important to have two observers watch where the baby looks to improve the accuracy of their observations. If Baillargeon had used only one observer, she could never be sure that that observer was observing accurately. By having two observers, she could calculate the percentage of the time the two observers agreed. If the percentage agreement was high, then she could be assured that the observations they were making were accurate. In this study, agreement between the observers was high (about 88%).

EXPERIMENTAL CONDITION   Each baby in the experimental condition first saw the familiarization event. Remember, this event was designed simply to familiarize babies with the 180° range of motion of the silver screen. The babies saw the familiarization event over and over until they became bored with it. How did Baillargeon know the babies were bored? That's easy. They just stopped watching the show. Once the babies were bored, Baillargeon began showing them the two other events: the possible event and the impossible event. She alternated her presentation of the possible and impossible events so that babies would see first one event, then the other, then back to the first. In the possible event, the little wooden clown box was present. The screen rotated to the point where it bumped into the box, it stopped, and then it rotated back the other way (112° arc of motion). In the impossible event, the box was also present, but the screen rotated all the way through its range of motion—right through where the box was supposed to be. When it rotated all the way down, it stopped and began rotating back in the other direction (180° arc of motion).

CONTROL CONDITION   Babies in the control condition saw exactly the same sequence of events as the experimental babies, but with one major difference—the box was never present during any of the screen rotations. So these babies first saw the familiarization event until they were bored with it. Then Baillargeon alternately showed them the two other events, but because no little wooden clown box was present she couldn't call these events possible and impossible. Both of these events were possible. So instead, she just called them the *180° event* and the *112° event*. If you've been paying attention, you'll realize that the 180° event was really the same as the familiarization event.

PREDICTIONS   Before moving on to the results of Baillargeon's Experiment 1, I think it would help you to understand the spirit of Baillargeon's study if we were to entertain a couple of predictions about what might happen in the experimental and control conditions. The key dependent variable here is looking time. Baillargeon was primarily interested in what would happen to babies' looking times when they saw the impossible event. She reasoned that if babies are like grown-ups, when they see an impossible event they should be surprised. And just like grown-ups, when they show surprise at the impossible event, they should look at it for a relatively long period of time. At least they should look longer at the impossible event than at the possible one. But notice what it would take for these babies to be able to be surprised in the first place— they would have to recognize that the impossible event was, in fact, impossible. According to Baillargeon, to recognize that the impossible event was impossible babies would have to (1) realize that the little wooden clown box continued to exist even when they could no longer see it behind the silver screen, and (2) realize that two solid objects can't occupy the same physical space at the same time. In other words, to show surprise at the impossible event babies must have an understanding of object permanence.

On the other hand, if babies didn't recognize the impossible event as impossible, they would show no special inclination to look at it. If anything, babies might be inclined *not* to look at the impossible event because in that event the screen is rotating in a 180° arc. Remember, 180° is the same amount of rotation that they just got bored with during the familiarization period. After observing the 180° rotation event during the familiarization period, babies should show a preference for the possible event, in which the screen rotated only 112°. From the babies' point of view, the 112° rotation would be more interesting because it was new.

EXPERIMENT 1: RESULTS AND DISCUSSION

As you might have guessed, Baillargeon found that 4½-month-old babies did indeed look longer at the impossible event than the possible event. Specifically, after they became familiarized with the familiarization event, as reflected by a decrease in looking time to the familiarization event, the babies showed a significant increase in looking time to the impossible event. But they showed no increase in looking time to the possible event.

Now, the fact that babies showed an increase in looking time to the impossible event was interesting enough. It supported Baillargeon's expectation that these babies expected the wooden clown box to continue to exist even though it was hidden from view by the silver screen. But the fact that they showed *no* increase in looking time to the possible event was also interesting. Consider why. Previously we predicted that babies would prefer the 112° rotation because it was different from the 180° rotation they saw in the familiarization event. But they preferred the 180° rotation they saw in the impossible event, despite the fact that they had just been observing a 180° rotation in the familiarization event. It was as if their preference for the impossible event outweighed any preference for looking at a different rotation distance.

Based on these data, Baillargeon concluded, "contrary to Piaget's claims, infants as young as 4½ months of age understand that an object continues to exist when occluded." The word *occluded* is just another word for *hidden*.

Experiment 2

METHOD

Experiment 2 was designed to examine whether children even younger than 4½ months were capable of demonstrating object permanence. Experiment 2 was exactly the same as Experiment 1, except that younger babies were used. In this experiment, the babies were about 3¾ months of age.

Participants

Participants in this study ranged in age from 3 months, 15 days to 4 months, 3 days. Forty babies partook. As before, half the babies were assigned to the experimental condition, and half were assigned to the control condition. An additional 6 babies were excluded from the experiment because of fussiness (5) or drowsiness (1). Baillargeon wrote that she needed more babies in this experiment because the younger babies were a lot more variable in their looking behavior. Some babies consistently were short-lookers, while others consistently were long-lookers.

Materials and Procedure

The apparatus and procedure were exactly the same as in Experiment 1.

EXPERIMENT 2: RESULTS AND DISCUSSION

In contrast to the babies in Experiment 1, babies in Experiment 2 did *not* look longer overall at the impossible than at the possible event. While it would have been easy enough for Baillargeon to give up and conclude that object permanence didn't exist this early, she looked a little deeper into the data and made an interesting discovery. She noticed that babies who got bored with the familiarization event very quickly mirrored the pattern of the older babies. That is, they looked longer at the impossible event than at the possible event. But the babies who took longer to become bored with the familiarization event didn't look longer at the impossible event compared with the possible event. She called the short-looking babies (those who got bored with the familiarization event rapidly) **short-habituators**, whereas she called the babies who didn't get bored with the familiarization event rapidly, **long-habituators**. For some reason, the rate at which babies got bored with the familiarization event had something to do with whether they showed surprise at the impossible event.

Experiment 3

METHOD

The fact that Baillargeon decided to run a third experiment was interesting. In part, she wanted to push the envelope further to see whether even younger babies could demonstrate object permanence. But in reading her explanation, one also gets the sense that maybe she was surprised at her own results and wanted to be sure she could replicate her findings. She wrote, "Given the unexpected nature and potential significance of the results obtained in the experimental condition of Experiment 2, it seemed important that they be confirmed. Experiment 3 attempted to do so with 3½-month-olds."

Participants

The participants in this experiment were 24 babies ranging in age from 3 months, 6 days to 3 months, 25 days. The average age was 3 months, 15 days.

Materials and Procedure

The apparatus and procedure were pretty much exactly the same as in the previous two experiments, with one very interesting difference. Rather than using the small, wooden, clown-faced box as the object, she used a Mr. Potato Head doll. Mr. Potato Head was smaller than the wooden box that was used in the previous two experiments, so the silver screen rotated further down than in the previous two experiments. More specifically, the screen rotated 135° before it made contact with the object, rather than the previous 112°.

EXPERIMENT 3: RESULTS AND DISCUSSION

Just as in Experiment 2 with the 3¾-month-olds, Baillargeon found that, as a group, 3½-month-olds did not show longer looking times at the impossible event than at the possible event. But also just like in Experiment 2, she found that there were differences between long-habituating and short-habituating babies. Short-habituating babies did look longer at the impossible event than at the possible event, again suggesting that they were surprised to see the silver screen pass right through good ol' Mr. Potato Head.

GENERAL DISCUSSION

The general finding from all three experiments was that babies as young as 4½, 3¾, and 3½ months of age looked reliably longer at the impossible event than at the possible event. Baillargeon viewed this as evidence that babies show both an awareness that an object continues to exist when they can no longer see it and an awareness that two objects can't exist in the same place at the same time. Of course, there is an alternative interpretation of these findings. It could be that babies just liked to watch the silver screen move through the full 180° rotation in the impossible event rather than the 112° (Experiments 1 and 2) or a 135° (Experiment 3) rotation found in the possible event. But this interpretation isn't a very good one, according to Baillargeon, because of the fact that the babies in the control group did *not* look reliably longer at the 180° event compared to either the 112° or 135° rotations.

Based on these findings, Baillargeon takes on Goliath, er, Piaget, on a couple of different levels. First, she challenges Piaget's claim about the age when object permanence begins. Remember Piaget believed that the first signs of object permanence began at about 9 months at the earliest. But Baillargeon's data indicated the existence of object permanence as early as 3½ months of age, at least for the short-looking babies. In her view, the reason she observed object permanence in babies this young was that she didn't require them to do a fairly complicated behavior in order to demonstrate their object permanence abilities. Therefore, she also challenged the validity of Piaget's object permanence task. By challenging the validity of the *task*, Baillargeon made a very important distinction between children's *knowledge* of hidden objects and their ability to *search for hidden* objects. Why should we force children to go through all the trouble of searching for hidden objects, she reasoned, if all we want to know is whether they know about hidden objects?

The answer to this question is, "It depends on whom you ask." Piaget didn't believe you could separate knowing about something from acting on it. In fact, he had a whole theory that said children gain knowledge about the world by acting on the world. So it's not so surprising that he used a task that required babies to search for a hidden object in order to demonstrate they knew about the hidden object. His theory didn't allow for the possibility that babies could know about a hidden object without searching for it.

The Emergence of Nativism

Now Baillargeon wasn't limited by Piaget's theory, so she wasn't tied to the belief that you had to act on something to know about it. But what is the alternative? If you don't have to act on something to know about it, how else can you learn about it? Or more specifically, if babies don't learn about the permanence of objects by searching for hidden ones, how do they learn about them instead? Baillargeon suggested two possibilities. Both suggestions were so radical that Baillargeon might have been safer poking a stick into a hornet's nest.

Baillargeon's first suggestion was a simple one: Maybe object permanence is inborn. The belief that children's knowledge is inborn is called *nativism*, and so her suggestion could be called a nativist one. If this suggestion was right, then the reason Baillargeon was able to detect object permanence in babies as young as 3½ months old was because these babies had an understanding of the permanence of objects from birth. Notice that from this point of view, object permanence isn't something that develops from experience. It's something that's there from the outset.

Baillargeon's second suggestion was a little more complicated, but it still had a nativist flavor. If object permanence isn't present from birth, she thought, maybe babies are born instead with a special learning ability that allows them to create an understanding of object permanence very quickly, with relatively little experience. We might call this special learning ability an object permanence acquisition device. To support this possibility, Baillargeon called attention to research done by other child psychologists, which showed that babies younger than 4 months of age often perform arm extensions in the presence of objects. These arm extensions are thought to be precursors to more mature reaching and grasping abilities that are in the process of emerging. Baillargeon argued that when babies extend their arms in the presence of objects, they gain experience seeing objects hidden by their own arms and hands and will also gain experience seeing their own arms and hands hidden by objects. These experiences may be all that's necessary for the object permanence acquisition device to kick in and establish an understanding of object permanence within the baby.

CONCLUSIONS: POKING A HORNET'S NEST

In the original David and Goliath story, once David took out Goliath, Goliath's army put its tail between its legs and ran away. And David, well, he eventually became king. But the story wasn't quite the same for Baillargeon in her efforts to dethrone Piaget. Challenging even this one small part of Piaget's theory agitated the child development research community into a frenzy. Attack after attack was leveled at both Baillargeon's methodology and her interpretations. Of course, the attacks weren't directed so much at Baillargeon herself as they were at the nativist claims she was making. And to be sure, Baillargeon had a number of allies on her side as well. But because Baillargeon's study was so prominent (after all, it was voted the fifth most revolutionary study published in the last 50 years), it may have taken on a disproportionate burden of criticism.

Attacks on Baillargeon's claims have been at two levels. At the level of theory, Baillargeon was criticized for her suggestion that object permanence could be innate. At the level of methodology, Baillargeon was criticized for overlooking some minor perceptual details when she developed her rotating-screen procedure. Let's consider each level of criticism in turn.

The Problem with Innateness

It's a good bet that anyone who's criticized Baillargeon's nativist speculations would be equally critical of any other nativist explanations about how knowledge gets into children's heads. It's not that these kinds of critics believe nothing is present at birth, it's just that they think there are far too many claims for things that are. Anti-nativists view nativist explanations for children's thinking as at best unhelpful and at worst deceptive and misleading. "Where does Baillargeon get off claiming object permanence is inborn," they might rant, "when every kid she's looked at has already had 3 months of experience?" As critic Elizabeth Bates pointed out, 3-month-olds "have had 90 days, approximately 900 waking hours and 54,000 minutes, of visual and auditory experience." By the time these kids participate in Baillargeon's experiments, they're not newborns anymore, and therefore claims of innateness aren't justified.

But what if Baillargeon is right? What if object permanence really is present from birth? Then could we say that object permanence is innate? Well, maybe. But critics of nativism would still argue that calling object permanence innate doesn't do anything to advance science. In fact, they would argue that explaining object permanence by calling it innate isn't an explanation at all. At best, it only moves the explanation of object permanence from one level to another, from a postbirth phenomenon to a prebirth one. But nothing is explained by calling it innate. Critic Linda Smith wrote, "Stopping at only one level of analysis—no matter how well motivated—just is not good enough if we want to understand how change really works, if we want to understand it well enough that we can alter the causal chain to a good end. Stopping short of real causes is not 'good enough' for developmental psychology either." So even if object permanence really does turn out to exist before birth, developmental psychologists will simply have to try harder to explain it, even if it means they have to start looking at it prenatally.

Overturning the Drawbridge Studies: Drawing on the Principle of Parsimony

Additional attacks have been levied at Baillargeon's methodology, especially her rotating-screen experiments and the interpretations she made of babies' looking behaviors. The problem amounts to her interpretations being at odds with the **Principle of Parsimony**. In science, the principle of parsimony states that if two different theories are equally good at accounting for children's behavior, then the simpler theory is preferred. But object permanence in infancy is not a very simple thing to explain in newborns, because there is no accounting for how it gets there. So researchers soon began testing whether babies in Baillargeon's experiments might've looked longer at the impossible event for reasons other than having object permanence. "Could there be something else," they wondered, "that would make babies look longer at the 180° rotating screen than at the 112° rotating screen?" Maybe there was just something about the 180° rotating screen that attracted babies' interest, and maybe it had nothing to do with object permanence.

In one famous critical study, Thomas Schilling tested this possibility. He started out by giving Baillargeon the benefit of the doubt and assumed that her data were not flawed. He was willing to accept that her babies really did look longer at the impossible event than at the possible event, but he wasn't willing to assume it was because the babies had object permanence. Instead, he thought, their looking behavior probably just had to do with the way babies look at things, the way they *visually process information*. To fully understand what Schilling was saying, we need to back up a bit and introduce the concept of **information processing**.

Whenever you and I look at something, we need to "process it" in order to understand it. The way we use the term in psychology, information processing something simply means that we take in information from the thing; maybe to recognize it, to encode its shape or colors, or even to realize that we've never seen anything like it before. But everything we pay attention to gets some level of processing. Sometimes we process things a lot; sometimes we process things very little.

To illustrate the process of information processing, suppose you go out for an evening of dining and dancing in mid to late December. At Alta Cucina Italian restaurant, the hostess seats you at a table where you get a clear view of a largish white man seated across the room from you. He has a full white beard and moustache, a velvety red coat hemmed in white fur, plump rosy cheeks, and a belly that jiggles like a bowl full of jelly when he laughs. How interested would you be in looking at this man? Especially if you were dining on Christmas Eve? You'd probably be so fascinated by this man's wardrobe that you'd have to force yourself not to stare. But truth be told, you'd probably be fascinated by the way this man was dressed any other day of the year too. Now suppose instead that the situation was exactly the same, except that the man you saw was normal in size, was wearing a sweater typical for an early winter evening, had no rosy cheeks, and had a belly that didn't jiggle. How interested would you be in looking at this man? My guess is that this second man would appear so normal (at least in the United States) that you wouldn't even notice him, unless he was the only other person in the restaurant.

Now the question is, why did the St. Nick look-alike attract your interest? And why were you inclined to look at him longer than at the more typical man? Was it because you recognized the man in the velvety red coat as Santa Claus? Or was it simply because he wore clothes and facial hair that were unusual? A Baillargeon-type explanation might be that the man attracted your interest because you recognized him as looking like Santa Claus. But a more parsimonious (simpler) explanation would be that your interest in looking at the man was based on his unusual clothes and facial hair. Why is this a more parsimonious explanation? Well, people who knew nothing about Santa Claus might also find this man interesting to look at based on his visual appearance alone. Knowing about Santa Claus requires an additional level of knowledge, and so represents a more complicated explanation.

Now back to Schilling's experiment. Schilling thought that Baillargeon's 3½-month-olds preferred to look at the impossible event more than the possible event not because of the impossibility of the event, but because of the 180° rotation of the screen. If you remember her procedure, Baillargeon first showed all her babies a rotation event where the screen rotated 180° without the box. She familiarized them with this event *prior* to showing them the rotation events with the box. Although exposing babies to this event may very well have familiarized them with the motion of a 180° rotating screen, they may not have had enough time to *fully* process the motion of the 180° rotating screen. Schilling argued that if a baby is given too brief an exposure to something, she will prefer to look at it again the next time she gets a chance—probably to finish processing it. However, if a baby is given a long enough exposure to something the first time, she won't need to look at it a second time to finish processing it. Schilling suspected that Baillargeon's babies preferred to look at the impossible event, not because it was impossible, but because they didn't get a chance to fully process the 180° rotating event during the familiarization period. By exposing babies to the impossible event, in which the screen was again rotating 180°, Baillargeon gave the babies a chance to finish processing the event. And it was for *this* reason that babies looked longer at the impossible event.

To test his hypothesis, Schilling replicated Baillargeon's experiment exactly, except that he varied how many familiarization rotations the babies saw. Baillargeon had babies observe the familiarization period only until the babies began looking away, and her babies might have differed from one another in how many familiarization rotations they observed. Schilling, however, exerted much more control over the specific number of familiarization rotations babies watched. In his experiment, half the babies saw the screen rotate 180° exactly 6 times, while half the babies saw the screen rotate 180° exactly 12 times. His results were also fascinating. Babies with the short familiarization periods were the only ones who looked longer at the impossible event (when the screen also rotated 180°, but through a wooden box). But babies who received the longer familiarization period actually looked longer at the possible event! Schilling reasoned that babies who were familiarized with the 180° rotating event 12 times had fully processed it, and so wanted to move on to something new. Therefore, the 112° rotation event (the possible event) was more interesting to them. Babies who observed the 180° rotation only 6 times didn't process the event fully, and so preferred to look at the impossible event so that they could finish processing the 180° rotation.

If Schilling is right, then Baillargeon's conclusions about the existence of object permanence in 3½-month-olds become questionable, because her findings could be an artifact of the procedure she used. Babies' interests in the impossible event could be due, not to object permanence, but simply to how far the screen rotates. Is this yet another example of the David and Goliath story, only this time with Baillargeon starring as Goliath? Well, Baillargeon hasn't given up the ship yet.

In an article published in the same journal and issue as Schilling's, Baillargeon defended her position strongly by pointing out a number of shortcomings with Schilling's "replication." For one thing, she noted that she gave her babies a chance to touch and explore the box prior to the experiment. Schilling didn't. This finding alone could've been enough to account for their different results. As a result of this difference, maybe Schilling's babies didn't realize his box was a solid, three-dimensional box and that it was capable of stopping the screen from rotating. But there were other differences too. Baillargeon's box had a big clown face painted on it, whereas Schilling's didn't. Baillargeon's box was also bigger. These two differences could've drawn more attention to Baillargeon's box than to Schilling's, resulting in babies' being more attuned to the impossibility of the screen passing through the box in Baillargeon's version of the experiment. The bottom line is that the differences between the two studies were sufficient to call into question Schilling's questioning of Baillargeon's results.

Based in large part on the reception her study received, controversial or otherwise, Renée Baillargeon has assumed a leadership role alongside Piaget within the child development research community. She did so by taking Piaget's object permanence task to task. It was a bold move for her to take on Piaget, given that when her study was published she was only 4 years out of graduate school and hadn't even been promoted to associate professor yet. But take him on she did. And the consequence was that she revolutionized child psychology.

Reference

https://www.youtube.com/watch?v=u2ovHFt5YXc

Bibliography

Baillargeon, R. (2000). Reply to Bogartz, Shinskey, and Schilling; Schilling; and Cashon and Cohen. *Infancy, 1*, 447–462.

Bates, E. (1999). Nativism versus development: Comments on Baillargeon and Smith. *Developmental Science, 2*, 148–149.

Schilling, T. H. (2000). Infants' looking at possible and impossible screen rotations: The role of familiarization. *Infancy, 1*, 389–402.

Smith, L. (1999). Do infants possess innate knowledge structures? The con side. *Developmental Science, 2*, 133–144.

Questions for Discussion

1. Is it more important to demonstrate that children *have* an ability or that children can *demonstrate* an ability? Why? What's the difference between the two?

2. What's an advantage of claiming that an ability or behavior is innate? Does calling something innate contribute to scientific progress?

3. Piaget claimed that object permanence emerged in full bloom at about 18–24 months of age. Baillargeon argued that it was more like 3½ months of age, or even earlier. Why does it matter how early object permanence exists?

4. Baillargeon had a scientific "coming out party" at an extraordinarily early point in her career. However, other scientists never achieved Baillargeon's success. What kinds of factors do you think influence the notoriety and stature of individual scientists?

6

Children in Chaos

"Hidden Skills: A Dynamic Systems Analysis of Treadmill Stepping During the First Year"

Thelen, E., & Ulrich, B. D. (1991). *Monographs of the Society for Research in Child Development, 56*, (1, Serial No. 223).   (RANK 18)

As an academic psychologist, and especially as the chair of an academic psychology department, one of my pet peeves is when people make a sharp, but false, distinction between the "social sciences" and the "natural sciences." Or they describe the difference as between the "soft sciences" and the "hard sciences." The reason I am peevish on this point is that psychology is usually lumped into the soft, social science category, rather than the hard, natural science category. There is an implied prestige drop when psychology is relegated to second-class, messy, social-science status. Why, even my dean makes regular snarky remarks about the messiness of psychology's subject of study. But that isn't what really irks me. What really irks me is that because the discipline of psychology doesn't go with the other "natural sciences," it's somehow focused on something unnatural. I mean, how else can you interpret a statement like, "Psychology isn't a natural science"? Does anyone seriously believe that human behavior is *not* a natural system?

On the other hand, psychology has to take some of the blame for failing to assert itself aggressively among the natural sciences. As I talk about in Chapter 14, many psychologists either have an inferiority complex relative to other "real" scientists, or they have a chip on their shoulder because they aren't regarded as "real" scientists by everyone else. Because of these disconnects, psychology has a long history of not playing well with others.

The revolutionary study I describe in this chapter, by Esther Thelen and Beverly Ulrich, goes a long way in reducing the gap between psychology as a natural science and all the other natural sciences. Their ostensible objective was to present the results of a study on infant tread-mill stepping. The results are interesting, but not especially revolutionary. Far more impactful and truly revolutionary, was the new theory of child psychology they introduced in order to account for those findings. The theory, variously known as *Dynamic Systems Theory* or in more recent versions, *Dynamic Field Theory*, combines concepts from physics, chemistry, biology, robotics, kinetics, and meteorology, among many others, with everything we already know, or thought we knew, about child psychology.

In this chapter I will begin with a description of the Thelen and Ulrich study proper. In the context of describing the study, I will introduce some of the more basic concepts of the new theory, expanding upon some of the more intriguing ideas. I will close with some observations about where Dynamic Systems Theory stands today, as well as how it fits in with other popular child psychology theories.

HIDDEN SKILLS: BABIES ON THE TREADMILL

It's often said that the beginning of any major journey, such as introducing an innovative new theory of child psychology, starts with baby steps. So it is fitting that Thelen and Ulrich's revolutionary study was on that very topic. The study of baby steps, or infant self-locomotion more generally, is part of a much broader study of infant motor development. As a student of children's cognitive development, I must say that I've never been especially intrigued by studies on motor development. They've always seemed rather boring to me. Much more interesting have been topics such as how children learn to talk and think. But in admitting to this bias, I am also admitting to an ignorance, maybe even a prejudice, against some of the most foundational aspects of cognitive development. It turns out that the study of children's motor development has profound implications for the study of cognitive development, if for no other reason than that both systems reflect the development of the central nervous system (CNS). After all, does it make any sense that core principles of the CNS would differ as a function of the domain of study?

But much more than this, as argued so forcefully by dynamic systems theorists, cognitive development and motor development are strongly and mutually intertwined. Developments in one system inform, and are informed by, developments in the other. A new field of *developmental embodied cognition* has even emerged. From a dynamic systems perspective, to focus on cognitive development at the exclusion of motor development would be akin to studying the architecture of a submarine with no conception of the sea. No, the two go hand-in-hand, and cognitive de-velopmentalists really must learn from motor developmentalists. They should even go to lunch sometimes.

Thelen and Ulrich were interested in the factors that contribute to children's earliest "walk-ing" behavior. I have *walking* in quotes because the earliest walking behavior really doesn't in-volve walking at all. Rather, it involves stepping; and infants can be observed to engage in reflex-ive stepping behavior as soon as they are born. True walking is something that emerges much later, usually around 12 months of age, although there are substantial differences in the age of walking onset between children. Historically, the explanation for why infant walking occurs so late in the developmental progression, when stepping occurs so early, has been that infants need time for the strength, agility, and balance necessary for bipedal locomotion to mature. But in Thelen and Ulrich's minds, the fact that such other factors are necessary for walking, means that they should be seen as central to the capacity for walking, and not simply as unrelated developing abilities. Even the considerable differences in the onset of walking between babies are something that a truly scientific theory must be able to explain. Rather than sweeping under the rug such individual differences as noise in the system, the differences themselves contain crucially valuable information that shouldn't be overlooked by any reasonably comprehensive and defensible theory.

INTRODUCTION

In their article, which actually conforms to a much longer "monograph"-style format than is typical of other journal articles, Thelen and Ulrich set up the rationale for their study by taking a closer look at some of the historical explanations for the onset of infant walking. Some of the most strongly entrenched theories of infant walking, they point out, have been those based on "maturational" explanations. As a group, maturational explanations suggest that changes in behavior, in this case the emergence of walking, are based on an increasingly mature CNS. In other words, as the brain matures, grows, and develops, so does the complexity of the behaviors that result from the brain's activity—which are all of them of course. But according to Thelen and Ulrich, this kind of explanation is relatively useless; something hardly worth mentioning. They wrote, "*It goes without question* that the nervous system changes dramatically during postnatal development and that a complete understanding of behavioral development must include its neural basis" (emphasis added). The question isn't *whether*, but *how*.

The problem with a maturational explanation, then, is that it really isn't an explanation at all. To say that children transition from a stepping reflex in early infancy to a period of no stepping in later infancy, to real walking in toddlerhood, all because the brain is maturing, simply moves the question from one level (how do babies learn to walk?) to another level (how does the brain develop to allow babies to learn to walk?). In science, it's not enough to say that A explains B, because then you still have to explain A. Otherwise you're just begging off, or passing the buck, or something. It's rather like cheating. The goal of science has to be to explain, not merely to push explanation from an observable level to an unobservable one. The same criticism can be applied to genetic explanations of walking.

In the case of walking then, what have to be explained are *all* the components of walking that collectively make walking possible. And with walking, there are apparently lots of components! Consider Thelen and Ulrich's summary,

> *First, a walker must generate a synchronized ensemble of muscle contractions to produce the locomotor movement. This usually involves muscles spanning many joints and body segments: the legs alternate in a pattern of swing and stance, the pelvis rotates and tilts, and the arms and shoulders swing forward and back in phase with the opposite leg . . . For a biped to move forward, at least one foot must be airborne some of the time . . . the leg that is not airborne must bear all the body weight, and the weight bearing must alternate between the legs. The support leg needs to be strong and stable to support the body weight, and the [walker] must compensate for these alternating shifts of weight and remain balanced. This, in turn, requires the continual monitoring of the sensory messages of balance received from the visual system, the vestibular apparatus, and the soles of the feet to make the appropriate corrections within the changing biomechanical demands. Upright walkers must also be able to compensate very quickly for unexpected perturbations in paths, such as obstacles, uneven surfaces, and changes in direction.*

And this doesn't even take into account infants' motivation to walk in the first place.

Thelen and Ulrich contend that the only adequate way to explain the confluence of so many different factors in a single behavior of interest is to consider it a *dynamic* system. Every one of the component systems involved in walking, which include balance, support, vision, the sense of touch, error detection and correction, and motivation to move through space, are all independently developing systems that have their own developmental histories and trajectories. Walking happens when all of these subsystems come together in one hierarchically organized overarching system.

Of course, these subsystems aren't only used in the service of walking. They also come together in other hierarchically organized overarching systems that serve other infant behaviors, such as sitting and crawling. Some subsystems will eventually participate in very different kinds of behaviors altogether. Error correction and detection will eventually become involved in learning arithmetic and spelling. Motivation to move through space will eventually be involved in learning to drive a car or traveling on an airplane. The general point is that child psychological development depends upon the interactions of many different systems, which break apart and come together, as needed and appropriate, to allow the child to accomplish whatever developmental tasks are relevant at the time.

The fact that so many component systems are called upon in the service of children's achievements of developmental tasks also explains the considerable differences between children. Rather than thinking of the differences between children as messiness or noise to be ignored or overlooked, Thelen and Ulrich suggest that such differences should be regarded as a major source of crucial information to be used in helping explain the phenomenon under investigation. By understanding the component systems that are involved in a hierarchically organized behavior system, one can make more accurate predictions about a child's progress toward achievement of the behavior.

Prelude to Thelen & Ulrich (1991)

With these basic ideas in mind, we can turn now to the core experiments presented in the 18th most revolutionary study published in child psychology since 1960. The experiments described in the monograph were designed to follow on the heels of an interesting set of preliminary findings that Thelen, Ulrich, and other colleagues had uncovered in a couple of earlier studies involving infant treadmill stepping. In one of these studies, Thelen found that when 7-month-old babies were supported on a treadmill, the treadmill elicited walking-like behavior from the babies. Now, at only 7 months of age, these babies weren't even able to stand on their own, let alone walk. Yet, when supported on the treadmill, 7-month-olds didn't just stand there and move backward as if standing on a conveyor belt, they alternated their leg movements in a walking-like fashion. When one foot was drawn back by the treadmill, the other foot appeared to lift and move forward. Then, when that leg was pulled back far enough, the first foot started its own motion forward.

This apparent walking wasn't just a reflex. For one thing, the neonatal stepping reflex had already disappeared by this age. Moreover, Thelen found that when the treadmill speed was increased, the rate of stepping increased. If stepping were just a matter of reflex activity, the stepping rate of the babies would remain constant, and be insensitive to the speed of the treadmill. Instead, as the speed of the treadmill increased, babies "walked" faster. They decreased the length of time each foot stayed in contact with the treadmill, in inverse proportion to the speed of the treadmill. The faster the treadmill, the less time each baby-foot stayed in contact with the belt. In contrast, stepping didn't happen when babies were supported on the treadmill when turned off.

In the second earlier study, Thelen and her colleagues used a "split-belt treadmill." This apparatus allowed each of two little treadmill halves to operate at different speeds. When placed on this device, babies adjusted their "walking speed" mid-cycle, depending on the speed of the belt each foot made contact with. The foot that made contact with the fast belt stepped quickly, while the foot that made contact with the slow belt stepped slowly. Obviously, something about the different speeds of the belts activated different speeds of stepping activity in the children.

Based on these two sets of findings, Thelen and Ulrich raised the provocative possibility that 7-month-olds have "a 'hidden' ability of considerable complexity." Simple contact with the treadmill when the treadmill wasn't in motion didn't elicit stepping, so the sense of touch on the bottom of the feet alone was insufficient to explain the behavior. The babies weren't moving through space, so motion cues provided by the visual system also couldn't explain the stepping. And of course, maturation had almost nothing to do with it, because non-walking babies clearly *could* "walk," when provided the appropriate environmental "control parameters" (i.e., the treadmill).

Thelen and Ulrich concluded that, "A sophisticated perception-action system for locomotion is in place, therefore, long in advance of the normally performed behavior. The perception system is tuned to the dynamic context, and the motor system coordinates the contraction of muscles in both legs in a very precise way. The fundamental unit in this system is a two-leg synergy, which is context sensitive as a functional ensemble." The discovery of this "hidden skill" was an important one, and led to a whole series of follow up questions. When did it emerge, or was it always there? Does it follow the same trajectory across different babies? How stable is it? How easily can it be perturbed (i.e., disrupted)? Is it correlated with other abilities?

These were the questions that formed the impetus for the 1991 revolutionary study. To begin to address them, Thelen and Ulrich decided to conduct a longitudinal study (remember that a longitudinal study involves measuring the same children repeatedly over a period of time). They brought babies into the lab twice per month, starting at Month 1, and then again every month afterward until their 7-month birthday. Each pair of lab visits occurred within 2–3 days of each other, and were always held within 1 week of the babies' monthly birthdays.

METHOD

Participants

Thelen and Ulrich started out with 13 babies, but because some didn't complete the study, they ended up with a sample of 9 babies who participated at least through Month 7. All babies were white, and full-term.

Apparatus

The main apparatus used by Thelen and Ulrich was their split-belt, variable speed treadmill. Each of the belts was driven by a separate motor that could be adjusted independently of the other, and which allowed the two belts to move either at the same or different speeds. The researchers also attached infrared light emitting diodes at two locations on each foot: the pointy part of the outside ankle bone (malleosus) and the outside edge of the little toe (metatarsophalangeal joint). The purpose of these infrared diodes was to allow Thelen and Ulrich to use very sophisticated video recording technology to monitor finely detailed movements of each foot during treadmill testing.

Each baby was also measured each month on a number of "anthropometric" parameters, including: "weight, length from crown to heel and crown to rump, circumference of thigh and calf, and skinfold thickness at subscapula, triceps, and umbilicus."

Procedure

At each of the 14 visits (2 visits @ each of 7 months), each baby was given 11 individual trials. Each trial was designed to test a different aspect of treadmill-elicited stepping. On most of the trials, the belts moved in unison, but at incrementally faster speeds. On two of the trials, however, the split belts moved at different speeds, resulting in either the right foot or the left foot needing to step at a faster rate. Here is a brief description of what happened on each trial:

- Trial 1: Baseline, infants supported on the treadmill, but the treadmill was turned off.
- Trial 2: Belts moved in unison, at about .11 meters/second (roughly 1/4 mile per hour).
- Trial 3: Belts moved in unison, at about .14 meters/second.
- Trial 4: Belts moved in unison, at about .17 meters/second.
- Trial 5: Belts moved in unison, at about .20 meters/second.
- Trial 6: Belts moved in unison, at about .23 meters/second.
- Trial 7: Belts moved in unison, at about .26 meters/second.
- Trial 8: Belts moved in unison, at about .29 meters/second (roughly 2/3 mile per hour).
- Trial 9: Baseline again, infants supported on the treadmill, but the treadmill was turned off.
- Trial 10: Belts moved at different speeds, right belt moved at .11 meters/second, left belt moved at .23 meters/second.
- Trial 11: Belts moved at different speeds, right belt moved at .23 meters/second, left belt moved at .11 meters/second.

Because these babies couldn't stand on the treadmill under their own power, support was provided by a human research assistant. Specifically, "A research assistant supported the infants under their arms and in an upright position so that the infants' feet rested on the belts of the treadmill and they supported an apparently comfortable amount of their own weight." Use of a human support device, rather than some sort of mechanical device, allowed for a more sensitive accommodation of the postural uniqueness of each of the babies.

RESULTS

DEFINING A "STEP"   One of Thelen and Ulrich's first steps in analyzing their data (no pun intended) was to define what they meant by a "step." You might think it pretty easy to know when you see a baby step. But research with babies is often messy, or "noisy." Babies rarely exhibit precise, cleanly identified behaviors of interest. Measuring baby steps is apparently no different. Thus, it was important for Thelen and Ulrich to provide an operational definition of a step, so they could distinguish true "alternating steps" from other kinds of possible steps, or even random foot movements. As a result, Thelen and Ulrich identified and tracked four different kinds of baby steps. These included true alternating steps, but also three kinds of nonalternating steps. Among the nonalternating steps were those that involved one foot taking a step without the other foot also taking a step (this was called a "single step"), taking two steps with the same foot (this was called a "double step"), and both feet stepping in the same direction at the same time (this was called a "parallel step").

But of the kinds of steps that were possible, the most interesting were the alternating ones, because, "alternation requires an informational link between the legs such that the dynamic condition of one leg is used to regulate the initiation and trajectory of the second leg . . . thus, selecting alternating steps as a dependent variable captures the cooperative ability of the system to respond to the imposed task." And of course, alternating steps are needed for mature walking. Here you can see how Thelen and Ulrich conceptualize the interaction of subsystems in the service of the overarching hierarchical walking system. In this case, they are focusing on the subsystems of the individual legs themselves. The movement of each leg independently, provides information to the other leg, and collectively the information contributes to the higher-level system responsible for "walking." In Thelen and Ulrich's terms, walking becomes an "emergent property." Walking is not *in* the child, either in terms of gene combinations or in terms of a maturing brain. Instead it *emerges* at the confluence of subsystems, each with its own developmental history and trajectory. Among these subsystems is something of an inter-leg communication system in which information from one leg is used to regulate the activity of the other leg.

This would be a good time to introduce one of the core concepts of Dynamic Systems Theory. Because "walking," or alternating stepping as the case may be, represents the collective efforts of all of the subsystems that contribute to its emergence, Thelen and Ulrich characterize "walking" as a **collective variable**. As a concept, a collective variable occupies a very important place in Dynamic Systems Theory. For every collective variable that can be identified, there are dozens if not hundreds of contributing subsystems that are responsible for producing the behavior. Accordingly, collective variables provide a way to simplify what would otherwise be exceedingly complex. As a collective variable, walking has relatively few parameters. For simplicity let's say there are four parameters, namely speed, quality, direction, and stability. But by studying walking as a four-parameter system, you are still, nevertheless, studying the collective contributions of the dozens of subsystems that contribute to each of the four parameters. And each of these dozens of subsystems that contribute to walking probably has its own large set of parameters. Thus, characterizing walking as a collective variable is a way of funneling hundreds of parameters into something with only a few parameters, which ultimately has the effect of simplifying otherwise exceedingly complex systems. For Thelen and Ulrich, walking is the main collective variable of interest in their 1991 monograph. But it's easy to imagine other collective variables in child psychology, including talking, object permanence, or even IQ.

With walking as the main collective variable of interest, the alternating stepping histories of the nine babies form the basis for the vast majority of Thelen and Ulrich's data analyses. Unfortunately (or maybe *fortunately*, depending on your perspective), a complete review of their analyses far exceeds the scope of this chapter. After all, they spend 28 pages, 15 figures, and 5 tables on displaying their findings. So I'll focus instead on the main findings, particularly as they relate to Dynamic Systems Theory.

FINDING 1: AGE AND SPEED EFFECTS   It was generally the case that babies increased their frequency of alternating steps as the treadmill got faster, and as they themselves got older. Many babies showed alternating stepping during even the first month, with three babies averaging as many as five alternating steps on Trials 2 through 8 (i.e., when the treadmill was moving and the belts were in unison). But while all the babies stepped more frequently as they got older, there was also a period of time when each baby's rate of alternating stepping declined for a short period, before increasing again with age. In all cases, there was almost no stepping on the treadmill on the baseline trials (Trials 1 & 9).

FINDING 2: DEVELOPMENTAL CHANGES IN STEP-TYPE REPERTOIRE   It's important to remember that babies were under no obligation to engage in any stepping behavior no matter what the treadmill speed. Yet they did step, and they stepped more as they got older and as the treadmill got faster. The kinds of steps babies took also changed. With the exception of one baby named DG, who was an alternating stepper from the very beginning, all of the babies had a mixture of stepping types early on, followed by an almost exclusive reliance on alternating stepping later. The most frequent type of first-steps babies took on the treadmill was single stepping. Remember, these were steps in which only one leg took a step on the treadmill while the other leg did nothing. I fancy it looked a bit like one-legged hopping.

But there were also differences between babies in the variety of stepping patterns they employed. At 3 months, for example, baby SL was an equal opportunity employer; with about 26% of SL's steps being single, about 37% being parallel, and about 37% being alternating. Similarly, baby JF at 3 months, was using about 42% single steps, 20% parallel, and 38% alternating. But other babies were more restrictive in their step selection. At 3 months, baby ES was employing about 90% single steps; while babies DG, CH, and TS were all upwards of 80% reliant on alternating steps. Baby SL was especially interesting, because over time SL had a hard time choosing a stepping style and sticking with it. Over the 6 month period, SL's stepping preference went from single, to parallel, to alternating, back to single, back to parallel, and finally by 7 months, back to alternating.

FINDING 3: QUALITY OF ALTERNATING STEPS   So far we have seen that as babies got older, and as the treadmill got faster, babies were more inclined to employ alternating steps. But we haven't said much about the quality of those alternating steps. In mature walking, each leg is perfectly out of phase with the other. When one leg is all the way to the front, the other leg is all the way to the back. As the front leg starts backward, the back leg starts forward. There is a certain biomechanical music to the synchrony that results from mature walking. But with babies, the music can be fairly far out of tune.

To analyze the quality of infants' alternating steps, Thelen and Ulrich computed a measure they called a "phase lag." A perfect phase lag score, reflecting mature walking, would be .5, and would indicate that one leg starts moving when the other leg is half way through its cycle. To understand how this works, let's define the start of the "right leg cycle" when the right leg is in front. Halfway through the right leg cycle, the right leg would be in the back. Completion of the right leg cycle would happen when the right leg moves back to the front again. To generate a .5 phase lag, then, the left leg should be in the front when the right leg is in the back; meaning that the left leg is perfectly out of phase with the right leg. In other words, the left leg should move to the front when the right leg is 50% through its cycle.

Using their phase lag measure, Thelen and Ulrich found that babies' leg phases were not quite up to snuff. Even the most advanced alternating steppers tended to have phase lags of less than .5. Their trailing legs started moving forward too soon, at least as compared with fully mature walkers. But Thelen and Ulrich also made two additional discoveries. First, perhaps not surprisingly, they found that babies more closely approximated the ideal .5 phase lag as they got older. Second, maybe somewhat surprisingly, babies also tended to approach the ideal, mature .5 phase lag with faster treadmill speeds. In other words, faster treadmill speeds seemed to "attract" babies' phase lags closer toward the ideal alternating stepping pattern.

FINDING 4: MANAGING PERTURBATIONS AND A BRIEF DIGRESSION INTO DYNAMIC SYSTEMS THEORY   Before getting to the last set of findings reported by Thelen and Ulrich, those that relate to their efforts to perturb infants' walking systems, it will be useful to introduce a couple more core concepts of Dynamic Systems Theory. A basic understanding of these core concepts will make it easier to make sense of Thelen and Ulrich's perturbation data.

Up till now, we have characterized infant walking as reflecting a hierarchically organized system, which results from the coming together of a number of component subsystems. We have also characterized walking as a collective variable, which, from the point of view of the observing scientist, reflects the degree to which a very large number of subsystems that make walking possible are collectively represented in one measure. But I haven't yet described how walking works as a *dynamic system*. According to Dynamic Systems Theory, walking is but one example of many dynamic behavioral systems that spontaneously self-organize at the confluence of many other subsystems. The idea here is that when you put specific component subsystems together for the first time, they can cooperate in new ways, and so give rise to new systems. When walking first emerges in infancy, for example, it is because the conditions are right, and the subsystems are sufficiently developed to function in ways that enable walking. But just because systems *can* self-organize into new systems doesn't mean they'll necessarily do so, so what is the "incentive" for the component subsystems to self-organize? The answer is that systems self-organize into new systems because there is value inherent in the new organization. As a form of self-locomotion, for example, walking provides a far more efficient solution to the problem of getting from point A to point B, than crawling.

To explain systems' tendencies to act in one way or another, either when transitioning to new systems or when transitioning between old systems, Thelen and Ulrich use the concept of an **attractor**, or an attractor state. According to Thelen and Ulrich, the attractor concept, "says that complex systems (and we include developing organisms) autonomously prefer certain patterns of behavior strictly as a result of the cooperativeness of the participating elements in a particular context. Although the dynamic history of the system is important, the attractor states are not encoded or programmed beforehand. Nowhere in the water of the faucet is there a rule or a scheme that produces the elaborate patterns of drip sequences."

But how can a system "prefer" anything? Do systems have their own minds? No, of course not. Thelen and Ulrich are simply using the term *prefer* as a metaphor; perhaps in the same way that you might say water prefers to flow downhill, or that light prefers to reflect off glass. By "prefer," Thelen and Ulrich simply mean that systems are attracted toward behaving one way or another under particular conditions. Water tends to flow downhill, but only when there is gravity. When there is no gravity, such as in the International Space Station, water tends to particulate into individual free-floating droplets.

The concept of the attractor state is especially useful for explaining "discontinuous, non-linear" development. Discontinuous, non-linear development can happen either when a new ability suddenly seems to emerge out of nowhere, such as when 7-month-olds "walk" on the treadmill, or when development appears to involve reorganization in kind or quality. A developmental reorganization in kind or quality happens, for example, when an acorn becomes an oak tree, or when a caterpillar becomes a butterfly. In each case there is both an early state and a later state in the same biological system, but the later state doesn't look anything like the early state. Nonlinear discontinuity is apparent in these cases because the oak tree is different from (and more than) a big acorn, and a butterfly is different from (and more than) a big caterpillar. Yet in each case, the former is the mature form of the latter.

In addition to developmental transitions over long time frames, Dynamic Systems Theory can also explain transitions from one system to another in the here-and-now. In both cases, the dynamic principles are the same; transitions from one system to another are the product of the current state of the biological system (e.g., component subsystems within the child) in collaboration with the current parameters of the environment. To clarify this phenomenon, Thelen and colleague Linda Smith use the very nice example of the gait of a horse.

You may already know that when a horse locomotes at faster and faster speeds, it transitions from a simple walk, to a trot, and then ultimately to a gallop. The shifts from gait to gait (or "system to system" if you prefer) are discontinuous and nonlinear. If you're not familiar with the differences between these three kinds of gaits, here are some descriptions borrowed from the website: http://plus.maths.org/content/walk-trot-gallop.

- Walk: The walk is a regular four-beat movement, e.g., back left, front left, back right, front right. Leg movement takes place at regular intervals. One leg is always in the air. Speed is about 4 miles per hour.

- Trot: The trot is a two-beat movement. Diagonally opposite legs move in unison, and hit the ground together. Two legs are always in the air. Speed is about 8 miles per hour.
- Gallop: The gallop takes the horse back to a four-beat movement, but the beat is irregular. The two back legs hit the ground almost together, and then the two front legs hit the ground almost together. In each case, though, the two legs on one side of the body hit the ground slightly before the two legs on the other side of the body. All four legs are simultaneously in the air at least part of the time. Speed is about 25–30 miles per hour.

Notice that each gait is not just a sped-up version of the gait that emerged before, which means that the three gaits are discontinuously and nonlinearly related to one another. According to Dynamic Systems Theory, the reason horses use these different gaits at different speeds is not because they are genetically programmed to do so, an explanation that doesn't really do any explaining, but because each of the gaits maximizes the efficient use of energy under the control parameters of the situation. If the horse wants to escape from a predator, then using a really fast walking gait would be extremely clumsy and difficult to maintain. It would also be pretty ineffective. A far more efficient use of energy would be to launch into a full-out gallop. But if a horse wanted to move slowly, then a gallop would be very hard to maintain because all four legs would have to be in the air some of the time. In this case, the horse risks losing its balance. Each gait is matched to a particular set of needs under a particular set of conditions. In dynamic systems terms, there is an attractor state for each gait system.

The forces that are acting on the horse at any point in time are the result of systems *within* the horse (including many of the same ones present in infants, such as balance, strength, coordination, vision, energy preservation, motivation) in combination with systems acting on the horse from the outside (environmental threats, incentives, surface conditions). All of these internal and external systems function conjointly to produce the behavior that results. The behavior that results, then, is an *emergent* system that derives from all the contributing component systems. Generally speaking, an attractor state is the preferred state of a system under a specified set of conditions. When a horse wants to locomote fast, then the locomotion system is attracted to the galloping gait. Similarly, when a baby is placed on a treadmill, the attractor state is one of stepping with alternating legs (at least for 7-month-olds, the attractor state for many younger babies seems to be one of single-stepping).

The attractor state is a useful concept because it can explain a system's tendency to return to a particular state when it is disrupted in some way. In fact, the strength of the attractor state is actually defined as the system's ability to return to the attractor state despite perturbations to the system. Perturb any component system, and the resulting emergent system will be affected. For example, a frightened horse, no matter his degree of motivation, cannot easily gallop over an ice-covered lake or an overgrown swamp.

Using the terminology we've just learned, Thelen and Ulrich were interested in introducing perturbations into infants' stepping behavior to see whether infants would return to a preferred attractor state, namely, an alternating leg movement pattern, despite the perturbation. The perturbations offered by Thelen and Ulrich were of two types: increasing the speed of the treadmill, and exposing babies to a split-belt treadmill.

As we have already discussed, the results showed that simply increasing the speed of the treadmill seemed to have the result of increasing the likelihood of infants using the alternating stepping pattern. In dynamic systems terms, increasing the speed of the belt had the effect of increasing the attractor strength for alternating stepping. However, Thelen and Ulrich also found that even during split-belt trials (Trials 10 & 11), alternating stepping served as an attractor state for infants, especially as infants got older. So instead of disrupting the alternating stepping system, both types of perturbations introduced by Thelen and Ulrich actually had the effect of strengthening the system's commitment to alternating stepping.

DISCUSSION

As a result of their study of infant treadmill stepping behavior, Thelen and Ulrich not only had data in their hands that could be interpreted in the context of Dynamic Systems Theory, but they also had data that could be used to demonstrate the power of Dynamic Systems Theory. Against a backdrop of the dynamic systems perspective, they produced evidence that walking was not *in* the child, but that it was an emergent property resulting from the coming together of a variety of biological and physical systems. They concluded that the fact "that infants can perform treadmill stepping in the first months of life yet do not walk alone until nearly a year later is strong presumptive evidence that even a fundamental skill such as locomotion is multiply determined and that the component elements do not mature synchronously." They go on to suggest that,

> when human infants who are awake and not distressed are placed on the treadmill, the regular alternating step configuration of their legs becomes an attractor state at some point in the infants' first few months of life. As defined by dynamic systems theory, this pattern was stable over a wide range of input conditions, and the system tended to return to this state when perturbed. We saw that several movement coordinations were possible on the treadmill but that alternating stepping was increasingly preferred.

Thelen and Ulrich conclude their monograph by describing how Dynamic Systems Theory can account for "long-standing puzzles" of child development that have historically eluded traditional theories like Piaget's constructivism and mainstream nativism. A main strength is that Dynamic Systems Theory can explain the origin of new abilities and competencies without resorting to black-box explanations like "it's in the genes," or "it's in the brain;" which, as we have already seen, aren't really explanations at all. The theory also gives considerable explanatory power to the environment, especially as specific environmental parameters can provide for the emergence of abilities and competencies that scientists heretofore didn't know were possible. Of course, the fact that the environment is as it is tends to produce uniformity among behaviors across vastly different individuals. It's not till we start playing around with the parameters of the standard environment that we can start seeing new abilities. So the question about whether new psychological abilities are *in* the child can easily be answered. They are not. But nor are they in the environment. They emerge at the dynamic intersection of the relevant subsystems in the child *and* the relevant subsystems in the environment.

CONCLUSIONS

You may have recognized some overlap between the perspectives and attitudes of Dynamic Systems Theory and those from other chapters in this book. Vygotsky (Chapter 4) was a staunch advocate of the belief that removing the child from its natural environment in order to study it under controlled laboratory conditions would fatally flaw the research and therefore undermine any generalized conclusions that might be drawn. Vygotsky's sentiments are very much captured by Dynamic Systems Theory. On the other hand, Dynamic Systems Theory would add that new and emergent abilities could be demonstrated under controlled laboratory conditions that would never have occurred in children's natural environments.

Dynamic Systems Theory also shares a perspective with Bronfenbrenner (Chapter 14). You may be aware that Bronfenbrenner focused on the impact of mutually interacting levels of environmental influence; pointing out that because there are multiple degrees of generality of the environment, both proximal and distal environmental effects on the child can be observed. But whereas Bronfenbrenner's approach appears to privilege environmental impacts, Dynamic Systems Theory gives "causative equality" to biological and environmental systems. Neither the biological systems nor the environmental systems play a larger role than the other, they make equivalent contributions. Still, just as there are biological subsystems to be accounted for in explaining children's psychological development, there are also environmental subsystems. I suspect that dynamic systems theorists would pay considerable homage to Bronfenbrenner for helping to work those out.

While reading in preparation for this chapter, I became enamored with Dynamic Systems Theory. The ideas it presents are provocative and generative. They are also eminently testable, which is the *sine qua non* of any useful scientific theory. The dynamic systems perspective is unique because it can explain the emergence of the extremely complicated characteristics of children's natural systems of behavior that flummox other major theories of child psychology. Stage theories like Piaget's (Chapter 3) have problems explaining why children who've achieved a particular stage, show an inability to master all the tasks theoretically linked to that stage. Nativist theories like Baillargeon's (Chapter 5) have problems explaining how advanced knowledge like object permanence can be encoded in the genes. And finally, information processing theories may be very good at simulating the outcomes of development, but they are notoriously poor in explaining the actual mechanisms underlying development.

Dynamic Systems Theory is also built to have very broad applicability across all manner of biological, chemical, and physical systems, and so provides a bridge between psychology and the rest of the natural sciences. Dynamic Systems Theory can explain very complex behaviors, using relatively simple mathematical principles. From this perspective, phenomena of interest can be explained as emerging from the culmination of individually contributing subsystems. A particularly elegant aspect of Dynamic Systems Theory is how it accommodates "discontinuous, nonlinear" development.

Yet, it says something about its popularity in the field of child psychology that I only became enamored with the theory just now, despite knowing about it for 20 years. And I am not alone. Looking to my peers and colleagues, and in browsing conference poster presentations and journal articles, I find that the theory hasn't yet gained traction in many circles of child psychological research. In a special issue of the journal *Child Development Perspectives*, dedicated to evaluating the state of Dynamic Systems Theory in modern child psychology, Marc Lewis has suggested that Dynamic Systems Theory is probably "'cool' enough to attract attention but not 'hot' enough to penetrate the empirical habits of our field." Perhaps part of the problem is that most of the theory's adherents have been motor developmentalists. As I mentioned in my opening, I've never been especially intrigued by motor development, and so I haven't spent much time reading research articles on how infants learn to reach and walk. If other child psychologists wear the same cognitive development blinders as me, then the problem is likely to be one of simple exposure; and if so, it's a problem that can be assuaged over time as the ideals of dynamic systems catch on with all of us.

Indeed, researchers have begun to explore dynamic systems applications to cognitive developmental "collective variables." For example, Larissa Samuelson and colleagues have recently applied Dynamic Systems Theory to children's word learning. And even Thelen herself, in collaboration with some of her colleagues, has written about dynamic systems applications to infant visual habituation behavior and infants' performance on the traditional Piagetian measure of object permanence, the A-not-B task.

Sadly, and extremely unfortunately for the field of child psychology, Dr. Esther Thelen met a premature death from tongue cancer in 2004, at the too-young age of 63. As noted by John P. Spencer and colleagues, 20 years is a long time for a scientist, but a relatively brief period for a scientific theory. But even though Thelen started her scientific career relatively late in the game, after earning a PhD in the biological sciences and raising two children, she put her 27 years of scientific rigor to excellent use in the service of child psychology. Through her relationships with many excellent collaborators, she took a sophisticated, technical theory of mathematical dynamical systems, and rendered it palatable for the rest of us soft-core, social scientists.

Bibliography

Adolph, K. E., & Vereijken, B. (2005). Esther Thelen (1941–2004): Obituary. *American Psychologist, 60,* 1032.

Lewis, M. D. (2011). Dynamic systems approaches: Cool enough? Hot enough? *Child Development Perspectives, 5,* 279–285.

Samuelson, L. K., Schutte, A. R., & Horst, J. S. (2009). The dynamic nature of knowledge: Insights from a dynamic field model of children's novel noun generalization. *Cognition, 110,* 322–345.

Schöner, G., & Thelen, E. (2006). Using dynamic field theory to rethink infant habituation. *Psychological Review, 113,* 273–299.

Spencer, J. P., Perone, S. P., & Buss, A. T. (2011). Twenty years and going strong: A dynamic systems revolution in motor and cognitive development. *Child Development Perspectives, 5,* 260–266.

Thelen, E. (1986). Treadmill-elicited stepping in seven-month-old infants. *Child Development, 57,* 1498–1506.

Thelen, E., & Smith, L. B. (1994). A dynamic systems approach to the development of *cognition and action.* Cambridge, MA: MIT Press.

Thelen, E., Ulrich, B. D., & Niles, D. (1987). Bilateral coordination in human infants: Stepping on a split-belt treadmill. *Journal of Experimental Psychology: Human Perception and Performance, 13,* 405–410.

Questions for Discussion

1. One aspect of the physical environment that we take for granted is gravity. Suppose humans established a colony on Mars, which has only about one-third the gravity of Earth. According to Dynamic Systems Theory, how might the emergence of walking in babies be impacted by locomotion under such low-gravity conditions?

2. In Dynamic Systems Theory, an attractor represents the preferred state of a collective variable under some set of prespecified conditions. If speech were the collective variable of interest, what might be the attractor states for speech under conditions of relaxation versus conditions of intense distress?

3. One of the greatest criticisms of Piaget's research has been that his tasks often made it too hard for children to demonstrate their true abilities. Specifically, he has been criticized for equating competence (what children "know") with performance (whether children can show what they "know"). What would a dynamic systems theorist say about this competence–performance distinction?

4. In my conversation with her, Dr. Ulrich suggested that Dynamic Systems Theory is extremely applicable to the lives of young people as they navigate their way through early adulthood. She especially encouraged young people to push themselves beyond their comfort zones, and to gather information from these new life experiences to inform their understanding of their current situations as well as possible future ones. How does this suggestion map onto Dynamic Systems Theory terminology like "attractor states," "perturbations," "system stability," and "emergent properties"?

7

What Can You Afford?

"The 'Visual Cliff'"

Gibson, E. J., & Walk, R. D. (1960). *Scientific American, 202,* 64–71.
(RANK 6)

In describing the impact of the revolutionary "Visual Cliff" study of Eleanor Gibson and Richard Walk, my friend and colleague, the famous Karen Adolph, described it as possessing all three earmarks of a classic paradigm in science. First, its findings were robust and highly replicable. This means that whomever conducted the study would get the same results, and would do so again, and again, and again. Second, the findings were sensational and memorable. How can anything else be said of the cute little images presented in the classic Gibson and Walk article, showing a kitten, a baby goat, and a baby human, each balancing precipitously over the apparent "cliff" that was not a cliff? Third, the experimental design was "simple yet elegant." If you want simple, it doesn't get much simpler than how Eleanor Gibson described construction of the visual cliff apparatus,

> Our research assistant, Thomas Tighe, and I hurriedly put together a contraption made from material we could find around the lab—a large sheet of glass, mounted with clamps, on some upright metal standards. Under half of the glass we placed a patterned surface (some checked wallpaper); about 4 feet below the other side was the same wallpaper on the floor. We put a narrow strip of wood across the middle . . .

Yet, for all the stir this study caused in the annals of child psychology, it is really only a snapshot in a very long and highly productive life of a revolutionary thinker, who was herself married to another highly productive and revolutionary thinker (her husband, the world renowned J. J. Gibson). Together, the two of them constructed an entirely new way of thinking about psychology. James Gibson's part, which E. Gibson describes as the source and motivation for her own work, focused primarily an adult perception. E. Gibson's part mainly focused on applying many of those same ideas to child psychology. Their "Ecological Theory" turned the world of psychology on its head throughout the 1950s and beyond. The Gibsons, and their very many productive and successful students, spent the next half-century developing and disseminating the major tenets of their new ecological theory throughout the global psychology community. The 1960 Gibson and Walk visual cliff study was just one step along the way.

Perhaps it is not too much of a stretch to describe the visual cliff experiment as somewhat of a "crossover" study. I mean this in the same way that musical artists sometimes achieve crossover celebrity status. In the music industry, a crossover hit catapults a popular artist from one musical genre, to popularity within an entirely different musical genre, usually because something about the musical product appeals to audiences of both genres. In the United States, country music stars Taylor Swift and Carrie Underwood are crossovers; as are hip hop artists Eminem and Drake.

The visual cliff study achieved similarly widespread audience appeal, though the audience in this case was child psychologists. What kinds of genres can there be in the field of child psychology? Lots. In other chapters of this book we've talked about how behaviorists ruled most all of American psychology, how Freud's psychodynamic theory proved insufficient for Bowlby's attachment theory, how ethological theory was relevant for Meltzoff's model of imitation, and how the temperamentalists accounted for individual differences and the emergence of child psychopathologies. As with most things, you can divide up the child psychology pie in lots of ways. But in this case I am referring to the fact that a study emerging out from under the umbrella of an early version of ecological psychology, a theoretical orientation held by relatively few scientists, had mass appeal to the lion's share of everybody else.

At this point it's useful to say something about the Gibsonian version of ecological psychology. I say "Gibsonian version" because another major theory of child psychology also claims title to *an* ecological theory (i.e., see Bronfenbrenner's, in Chapter 14). Yet, the Gibsons were thinking of something altogether different in their ecological worldview. For this reason, I will refer here on out to their brand of ecological theory as Gibsonian theory. Besides, it only seems fitting that a new, revolutionary psychological theory, heralded by the professional lifetime commitments of a husband and wife team of theoreticians, should be permanently endowed with the names of its creators.

SO WHAT'S SO SPECIAL ABOUT GIBSONIAN PSYCHOLOGY?

I believe it is fair to say, based on E. Gibson's self-disclosures in both her autobiography and her interview with Agnes Szokolszky, that the Gibsons' development of their ecological theory was a lifetime endeavor. She references numerous periods in their lives when they improved their thinking on this or that idea, or revised their opinion on one thing or another. In describing the history of specific studies, she would recount that one or another construct hadn't occurred to her or James yet, but that the findings of an individual study would later provide evidence for an idea. Under the assumption that by the end of their productive lives they got their ecological theory as close as they could to how they wanted it, my comments will be informed by their end product; and I will look through the lens of their end product to describe their findings from the interim.

The foundational premise of Gibsonian theory, and why the Gibsons conceptualized it as an ecological one, was that organisms are optimally suited, through evolution and natural selection, to survive in and adapt to their environments. Accordingly, organisms are built to engage in activity that maximally ensures their survival. A core concept of Gibsonian theory is the idea of "affordances," which J. J. Gibson described in his 1979 masterpiece. In a 1993 paper authored by E. Gibson and two of her last preretirement graduate students, Karen Adolph and Marion Eppler, an **affordance** was defined as the "fit between an animal's capabilities and the environmental supports that enable a given action to be performed." According to this definition, the "perception of affordances allows animals to guide activity adaptively, and to parse the environment into functionally meaningful units."

That's about it. These two propositions—that environments *afford* actions by organisms and that organisms *detect and act on* environmental affordances—more or less represents the essence of Gibsonian theory. Of course, this doesn't simplify child psychology any more than saying "gravity exists" simplifies physics. There is still all the hard work of specifying all the parameters of the theory. For example, what affordances are there? How do organisms' perceptual systems develop to detect affordances, and how do motor systems develop to act on them? How do motor systems and environmental affordances change over the developmental time of the organism?

Because the physical environment is invariant over time, the potential affordances offered up by the environment are always there; it's just a matter of the organism developing to the point of perceiving and acting on them. Let's consider the affordances offered by something we're all familiar with, a cliff. If we're at the foot of a cliff, then it becomes something that we can climb up. If we're on the brink of a cliff, it becomes something we can fall over, especially if we get too close and lose our footing. So in other words, according to Gibsonian theory, we can say that a cliff *affords* climbing up or falling over. It just depends on where we are, and what we are trying to do at the time. But for a cliff to have either of these affordances, we must be mobile. We must be capable of self-ambulatory behavior. A cliff doesn't provide the affordance of falling and getting hurt if we aren't sufficiently ambulatory to bring ourselves to the brink of the cliff in the first place. In the case of a very young, premobile baby, a cliff doesn't afford falling and getting hurt, either. At most, if the baby has a sufficiently developed visual system, she might see the edge of the cliff, if you pointed her in the right direction and she had sufficient visual acuity. At that point, you could say that the cliff affords edge detection for the baby, but that's about all.

The overarching focus of the Gibsonian research mission, then, was the combined study of perception and action in the developing and adult organism. Perception is needed to detect what can be done in the environment, and action is needed in order to do. And so, the Gibsons and their progenitors spent their careers designing and conducting experiments that would reveal how affordances and actions helped the organism survive, and they revised their ecological theory as the evidence from their studies permitted.

Now, I didn't want to start this chapter by talking about perception and action, because to me, well, those topics just sound boring. So I tricked you into thinking this was a chapter about people falling off cliffs and the like, which is much more exciting. So it was for the world when E. Gibson and R. Walk published their now famous visual cliff study. At the time of its publication, the concept of visual-motor affordances hadn't yet been developed. But the basic findings regarding animal depth perception were appealing to a mass audience, maybe especially because of those cute baby animal pictures. Still it was surely the case that the visual cliff methodology produced data that promoted the understanding of perceptual phenomena, and so supported the continued development of Gibsonian theory. So let's turn now to that revolutionary work, and follow it up with consideration of the scientific work that emerged from it.

GIBSON & WALK (1960)

Unlike many other studies reviewed in this book, the Gibson and Walk study appeared to the world in a popular press format, in an issue of *Scientific American*. You may recall that Robert Fantz's revolutionary findings (Chapter 8) were also revealed to the world through this medium. As a periodical dedicated to informing the general public about scientific findings, *Scientific American* has a rather different purpose than traditional scientific journals. In particular, its articles are not subject to rigorous peer review, although its authors have usually published previous versions of their work in the scientifically peer-reviewed literature. In the case of Gibson and Walk, the research findings were published initially in the journal *Science*, in 1957; with Thomas Tighe, the research assistant who helped them construct the visual cliff. It's interesting that the *Scientific American* version of the work achieved fame, whereas the harder-core *Science* version of the article, where the work was first published, seems neglected in the memories of today's child psychologists. Cute little babies and kittens, just sayin'.

INTRODUCTION

In the article's introduction, Gibson and Walk describe their research question as one about the origins of depth perception. Do children *learn* about depths, and specifically the potential hazards of cliffs? Or are they born with such knowledge? It's the old nature–nurture question. What about human depth perception versus that of other animals, are they of a kind? Or do humans differ from other animals in the availability and emergence of depth perception?

METHOD

Participants

The main sample of interest included 36 human babies, who ranged in age from 6 to 14 months. But Gibson and Walk used all sorts of other animals as well, including "chicks, turtles, rats, lambs, kids [in the goat sense of the word], pigs, kittens and dogs."

Materials

Basically, the visual cliff apparatus was the same as described previously, only bigger. A narrow centerboard was laid across the middle of a sheet of glass, and the sheet of glass was supported at least 1' off the floor by metal stands and clamps; although in most of their experiments the glass was about 53" above the floor. The shallow side was created by affixing a "patterned material" directly against the underside of the glass. The deep side was created by affixing the same material onto the floor, instead of directly onto the glass. In this way, the same pattern elements appeared on both sides of the board, but on one side they were further away.

Procedure

The visual cliff procedure is pretty simple. You just place an animal on the centerboard, and note which side of the glass it climbs down onto. For the human babies, Gibson and Walk also had mothers call to them; first from the deep side and then from the shallow side. Adolph and Kretch wrote that this procedural modification with human babies was necessary because "infants would not budge off the centerboard without their mothers serving as the lure."

An infant on the edge.

RESULTS

RATS   Rats behaved a little differently than the other animals. Whereas human, chicken, goat, cat, and lamb babies appeared to rely exclusively on visual cues for support, the rats relied on both visual and tactile clues. Initially, Gibson and Walk noticed that rats didn't prefer the shallow side over the deep side in general, so long as their whiskers could touch the glass. But rats showed a decided preference for the shallow side when the centerboard was raised high enough that the rats' whiskers couldn't touch the glass. In this case, the rats almost always walked down onto the shallow side of the cliff.

These results might lead one to think that the rats' prior visual experience contributed to their depth perception. But amazingly, the same behavior was shown for rats who were deprived of any visual experience prior to testing. Gibson and Walk compared rats raised for 90 days in complete darkness, to rats raised for 90 days normally, in the light. The specific question was whether experience seeing things would affect their depth perception, and thus their visual cliff behavior (note the similarity of this work to Hubel and Wiesel, Chapter 9). It turns out that experience seeing things did not affect rats' preferences. When presented a choice of the shallow versus the deep side of the cliff, under conditions when whiskers couldn't feel either surface, both dark-reared and light-reared rats preferred the shallow side. Apparently, depth perception was experience-independent.

CHICKS, KIDS, AND LAMBS   If visual experience wasn't needed to see depth, then maybe it was experience with locomotion that mattered. To test this possibility, Gibson and colleagues decided to test the visual cliff with "precocial" animals, that is, animals who were mobile almost immediately after birth. These included baby chickens, goats, and lambs. Chicks were tested when less than 24 hours old. Invariably, the chicks hopped down onto only the shallow side.

Baby goats and sheep were tested on the cliff as soon as they could stand, also usually within the first day. Like the chicks, no goat or lamb baby ventured onto the deep side of the cliff. Gibson and Walk even placed a kid directly onto the deep side. Despite the tactile cues for support, the baby goat refused to get up and walk. Instead, it took a defensive posture, straightened its front legs, and let its rear legs go limp. They even pushed the goat across the glass in this posture, but it didn't get up and start walking until they pushed it all the way across to the centerboard.

HUMAN   Although Gibson and colleagues tested other animals on the visual cliff first, it was their testing of human babies which caught everyone's attention. Of all the human babies tested, 27 moved off the centerboard to the shallow side of the cliff at least once. Only 3 of the 27 babies crawled onto the deep side of the visual cliff. Gibson and Walk noted that "Many of the infants crawled away from the mother when she called to them from the cliff side; others cried when she stood there, because they could not come to her without crossing the apparent chasm." Gibson and Walk concluded that human babies were capable of depth perception as soon as they could crawl.

The finding with human babies was especially intriguing since many of the babies accidentally touched the deep side of the cliff, and therefore *knew*, in some sense, that the deep side of the cliff actually afforded support, despite appearances to the contrary. Some also patted their hands on the deep side, and some accidentally touched the deep side with their bums while pivoting toward the shallow side. But they still refused to venture out onto the deep side of the cliff.

KITTENS   So what about baby cats? They are nocturnal like rats. Would they venture onto the deep side, deferring to the tactile information provided by their whiskers? Or maybe because cats are predators by nature, and rely so much more on sight than rats, they would be more dependent on the affordances provided by vision than those provided by touch. How did kittens fare? They also preferred the shallow side; and when purposefully placed onto the deep side, they acted pretty much the same as the kids. They either froze in place or circled aimlessly.

AQUATIC TURTLES   Gibson and Walk thought that aquatic turtles might be one species to show a preference for the deep side. Maybe seeing their reflections in the glass would trick them into thinking it was a pool of water, and cause them to dive right in. Yet, three-fourths of the turtles meandered down to the shallow side. Although this preference is similar to that of the other animals, the proportion is much lower. The authors concluded that either turtles have poorer visual discrimination abilities than the other animals, or turtles are less concerned about falling.

CONTROL CONDITIONS   Being the true scientists they were, Gibson and Walk implemented a number of control conditions to make sure all these preferences for the shallow side weren't due to something other than the actual perception of depth. After considering their initial findings with rats, Gibson wrote, "Impressed as we were, we worried. Could it be that one side of the room was more attractive—warmer, darker, more odiferous?" So the first control condition they employed was to attach the same patterned paper directly under the glass on both sides. With no visual cliff to be detected, the rats wandered across both sides of the glass. Another control condition was to use homogeneous gray paper on both the shallow and the deep sides, rather than a patterned one. In this control condition, rats still ventured out onto both sides equally.

WHICH AFFORDANCES?   Based on these control experiments, it appeared that visual depth perception really was the source of the animals' behaviors. But then arose the question of which visual information was most important. Vision happens when an image of something you look at it is projected onto your retina, which lines your eyeball, and your rods and cones in the retina detect the image and send neural signals to your brain through the optic nerve. But there are many signals in the visual information stream that can provide cues to depth. For example, there is the phenomenon that if you look very closely at a pattern, a checkerboard for example, the elements of the pattern as well as the spaces between them will take up more retinal space, than looking at the same pattern at a greater distance. This difference in retinal real estate used by looking at patterns close-up versus far away is part of what we use to determine depth. This cue is called **pattern density**. By definition, pattern density is defined by how many elements of a pattern are found in a particular unit of space.

Another cue to depth perception in the visual signal is **motion parallax**. Motion parallax is the name given to the feeling, when moving through space, that close-up objects appear to move faster than far away objects. You've surely experienced motion parallax if you've ever looked out the window when driving in a car or riding on a train. You would have seen nearby fence posts or telephone poles fly by, and trees in the distance move very slowly or not at all. The phenomenon results because images of nearby objects move across the retina more rapidly than images of far away objects.

Gibson and Walk were interested in determining which of these two depth perception cues, pattern density versus motion parallax, was most important in determining when animals would avoid the perceptual cliff. Because they used the same patterned paper on both sides of the cliff, with the pattern on the shallow side being nearer and the pattern on the deep side being farther away, both types of visual cues to depth were available for detection. On the shallow side, the pattern elements would be low density, but fast moving; on the deep side, they would be high density but slow moving.

To remove any effects of pattern density, Gibson and Walk changed the pattern paper so that the pattern elements on the deep side were bigger, in direct proportion to their distance from the centerboard. This change removed the effect of pattern density because it basically ensured that the pattern elements on the two sides of the cliff would occupy the same amount of retinal space in any eyeball positioned over the centerboard. But because the elements on the two sides of the cliff were still at different distances, they produced motion parallax. When reconducting the experiment under these conditions, Gibson and Walk found that both the rats and the chicks still preferred the shallow side; suggesting that pattern density wasn't a necessary depth cue, and that both species could rely on motion parallax as a cue to depth when needed.

Next, to remove any effects of motion parallax, Gibson and Walk placed the patterned paper directly under the glass on both sides of the paper; but on the shallow side they made the pattern elements bigger than on the deep side. This change had the effect of removing motion parallax because the pattern elements on both sides of the cliff were the same distance from the hypothetical eyeball, even though the elements were of different sizes. Findings from this experiment revealed that rats still preferred the shallow side (which had the larger elements), but that chicks showed no such preference. Apparently, motion parallax was a necessary depth cue for chicks; but not for rats, who could resort to using pattern density when necessary.

What did Gibson and Walk make of the finding that removing motion parallax compromised depth perception in chicks but not rats, while removing pattern density failed to compromise depth perception in either species? They concluded that the differential effectiveness of the two perceptual cues was probably due to differential experience. Whereas the chicks were tested within one day of birth, the rats weren't tested until they were 90 days old; so it seemed that motion parallax was a cue that could only be used profitably by organisms with considerable experience moving around in a visual world. This hypothesis was further confirmed when Gibson and Walk compared light-reared to dark-reared rats in this motion-parallax-controlled condition. They found that the dark-reared rats, even though they were 90 days old, behaved like the 1-day-old chicks, and were willing to walk onto either side of the visual cliff.

Discussion

Gibson and Walk don't provide much of a discussion section in their article. In fact, it amounts to only two sentences,

> *From our first few years of work with the visual cliff we are ready to venture the rather broad conclusion that a seeing animal will be able to discriminate depth when its locomotion is adequate, even when locomotion begins at birth. But many experiments remain to be done, especially on the role of different cues and on the effects of different kinds of early visual experience.*

Yet, despite its brevity, its marching orders were clear. Not only was it a cornerstone in the Gibsons' continued development of their ecological theory, it established a paradigm for testing infant and toddler development; and not just perceptual development. I used the term "affordance" in my description of the Gibson and Walk article, but it is important to remember that that idea had not yet been introduced to Gibsonian theory. But it does seem as if the shallow side of the visual cliff afforded walking on, while the deep side did not, at least for animals with experience in moving in a visual world. I might guess that E. Gibson would have applied the concept to the Gibson and Walk data had it been in her vocabulary.

BUT WHAT ABOUT THE MOM?

The Gibson's scientific work was absolutely focused on identifying environmental affordances, as well as the perceptual systems in the developing organism that can detect them. But the basic visual cliff paradigm of E. Gibson has not always been used exclusively for research on perceptual development. In fact, Adolph and Kretch describe the life of the visual cliff paradigm for purposes of perception research as "short-lived." Still, the visual cliff had certain features that appealed to researchers from other theoretical traditions. One of my favorite programs of research has used the visual cliff apparatus as a means to test the effects of maternal emotional signaling under conditions of uncertainty.

In a classic 1985 study, researchers James Sorce, Robert Emde, Joseph Campos, and Mary Klinnert put 1-year-olds on a visual cliff to see if they would use their mothers' facial expressions to decide whether the deep side of the visual cliff was safe to crawl across. Of course, we already know from the Gibson and Walk study that babies wouldn't crawl across the deep side of the cliff even when their mothers called to them. But that finding happened when the cliff was 53" high. Could babies be coaxed across the visual cliff when it was lowered some? The researchers found that a cliff depth of about 1 foot produced no avoidance on the part of the babies, although they wouldn't crawl across it on their own. In this condition, babies seemed uncertain about what to do.

Sorce and colleagues were interested in the role of **social referencing**. Social referencing happens whenever you look at someone else to see how she is reacting to something, so that you can use that information to guide your own reactions. You have surely engaged in social referencing yourself when someone in your group made a joke, and you looked at others in the group to see if they thought it was funny. In Sorce and colleagues' study, social referencing came by way of the mother's face, when babies used facial information to gauge whether their mothers thought it was ok to cross the deep side of the visual cliff. Here is how they conducted their study.

Prior to testing individual babies, Sorce and colleagues trained mothers how to put on different kinds of facial expressions. Mothers were trained to show five emotions in particular: fear, anger, interest, happiness, and sadness. After face training, infant testing began. At the start of each trial, the baby was placed on the shallow side of the cliff. The mother was positioned at the opposite side of the room, just above the deep side of the cliff, and she placed an attractive toy directly onto the Plexiglas surface. The mother then smiled at the baby, until the baby approached within 15" of the centerboard. At that point, the mother made one of the emotion faces she was trained to make.

The first of their experiments compared the effect of a happy versus a fear face. When mothers wore the fear face, none of the babies ventured across the deep side of the cliff. In fact, more than half of the babies retreated from the cliff's edge when seeing the fear expression. But when mothers wore the happy face, 14 of 19 babies ventured across.

The second experiment compared interest versus anger. This comparison still pitted a positive maternal emotional signal to a negative one, but of course the emotions were different than in Experiment 1. Still, the specifics of the emotion didn't seem to matter. Only 2 of 18 babies crossed over to the deep side when mother wore an angry face, while 11 of 15 babies crossed when mother showed interest.

The third experiment tested the effect of a sad face. Results showed that 6 of 18 babies were willing to cross when seeing their mothers portray a sad face, which is a higher rate than the other two negatively toned facial expressions, suggesting that sadness is not as strong a deterrent as showing fear. A statistical test revealed that sadness was significantly less deterring than fear.

Combining across all three experiments, then, the facial expression of fear provided the most deterring effect overall. This makes sense, especially under conditions of uncertainty when there was a small, but potentially hazardous visual cliff to fall over. In a fourth experiment, the researchers removed the visual cliff entirely by removing the apparent drop-off altogether. What would babies do when mothers displayed a fear face and there was no cliff to worry about? Sorce and colleagues found that when there was no cliff, babies didn't even look at their moms. They just crawled directly to the toy. The fear face had no effect on the babies when there wasn't any risk involved.

The work of Sorce and colleagues wasn't really focused on whether babies could perceive the depth of the visual cliff. Perception of the cliff was taken for granted. But knowing that babies could perceive the visual cliff, the researchers wanted instead to observe the effects of maternal emotional signaling, acquired as a result of infant social referencing. The conclusions are simple and straightforward. Babies social reference their mothers under conditions of uncertain risk, and the emotional signals mothers send to their babies matter.

METHODOLOGICAL INNOVATION AND THE VISUAL CLIFF TODAY

Perhaps the most direct line of descendancy between E. Gibson's early visual cliff work and modern research can be found in Karen Adolph's lab. Despite what I said previously about research on perception and action sounding boring, I find Adolph's program of research fascinating. As a direct academic descendant of E. Gibson, Adolph has continued the Gibsonian tradition, and kept ecological theory alive and well. But she has added her own spin on things, and has made the visual cliff paradigm even more ecologically valid. In fact, she even challenges the ecological validity of the deep side of the cliff altogether.

For Adolph, the main problem is that the deep side of the visual cliff produces conflicting visual and tactile clues. A fake cliff is not something that occurs naturally in the real world, and so why should we use one in research? Adolph and Kretch wrote that the visual cliff, "reveals only how infants behave when visual and tactile information conflict, not how they behave normally when visual and tactile information are complementary or redundant." To be true to the spirit of ecological theory, perception research on depth perception and the affordances provided by cliffs should be just as natural as possible.

Adolph remedied this situation in her research program by using *real* cliffs, well, laboratory versions of them anyway; as well as slopes, gaps, and bridges. Her procedure also differed by having an adult spotter follow alongside the baby to catch him in case he did venture out unsafely across those cliffs, slopes, gaps, and bridges. A very recent 2013 study makes for a nice example of the Adolphian paradigm. In this study, Adolph and her graduate student Kari Kretch tested whether infants reacted differently to a small drop-off, which they called a "step," versus an "impossibly high" drop-off, which they used for their "cliff." They also tested whether babies would respond to those two situations differently based on how much experience they had crawling or walking. Their sample consisted of 12-month-olds who were either exclusively crawling or had begun walking (called "novice walkers" in the study), and 18-month-olds who were veteran walkers.

The basic idea behind Kretch and Adolph's study was to see if babies detected affordances of drop-offs differently based on their locomotive status. Coming out the Gibsonian tradition, Kretch and Adolph were specifically interested in whether the affordances of the physical environment were different for the crawlers versus the young walkers, as well as whether the affordances were different for the young babies versus the older babies. Of course, the affordances should be different for children whose primary modalities of locomotion involve crawling versus walking. Crawlers should be scanning the environment for surfaces and features that afford crawling, while walkers should be scanning the environment for surfaces and features that afford walking. But what do novice walkers do? Do they use the lessons they learned as crawlers, or do they detect the same affordances as the seasoned walkers?

Consider the affordances of environmental features you yourself may have detected. If you are an experienced walker who has ever attempted a strenuous hiking path, you may have found it easier to get down some slopes on all fours (or your behind) than on your feet; because different surface conditions afford different locomotive modalities. But you only know this because of your walking experience. Babies with different levels of physical maturity are also confronted with a variety of surface conditions, but their abilities to navigate across those features ought to vary with the affordances they're capable of detecting. Seasoned crawlers ought to look for crawlable features, and seasoned walkers ought to look for walkable features. Novice walkers are a bit of a wildcard. For them, affordances for crawling may not be especially helpful (because they're walking now), and affordances for walking may not yet be fully detectable because they haven't had much experience walking. To test these differences, Adolph used her ecologically valid version of the cliff paradigm.

The apparatus consisted of a starting platform and a "landing platform." The two platforms were initially presented to babies at the same height, but the landing platform could be raised or lowered as needed. After babies had the chance to explore the cliff when both sides were at the same height, Kretch and Adolph began lowering the landing platform inch by inch, until they discovered the point at which each baby began either falling (and was of course caught by the adult spotter), or refusing to cross using their typical crawling or walking posture. Once this point was identified, they then raised the landing platform by ¾". This was the "affordance threshold." The affordance threshold was the point just beyond which babies would start modifying their normal locomotive posture. Once each baby's affordance threshold was established, Kretch and Adolph tested babies with several different drop-off heights, including both the step height (defined as a 2½" to 3½" drop-off) and the cliff height (defined as a 35" drop-off).

What is most amazing about Kretch and Adolph's findings is that what babies learned about drop-offs as crawlers did not seem to transfer to their experience as novice walkers. Indeed, Kretch and Adolph wrote, "The problem for [novice] walkers is that they rarely refused to walk." The authors found that crawling babies' willingness to attempt a particular drop-off was highly related to their likelihood of being successful. Crawling babies were very likely to attempt drop-offs they were good at; but not very likely to attempt drop-offs that would result in falling. But novice walkers were apparently oblivious about their chances of success. Novice walkers often walked right over the edge of the cliff, and they did so on repeated trials. Six novice walkers never refused to walk over the cliff. Only the seasoned walkers approached the riskier drop-offs with trepidation. In fact, the seasoned walkers approached the cliffs very much as the crawlers did; they avoided those they weren't likely to be successful with.

Of course, because the seasoned walkers were 6 months older than the crawlers, they were also larger; and because they were larger, they could successfully navigate larger drop-offs than their crawling peers. And this is part of Adolph's (and E. Gibson's) main point, that the affordances provided by the environment are directly linked to the characteristics of the organism doing the perceiving. The environmental affordances of the larger and seasoned walking child are necessarily going to differ from those of the smaller but equally seasoned crawling child; and they will navigate through their environments taking these different and new affordances into account.

CONCLUSION

To be sure, Gibson and Walk's visual cliff study achieved meritorious and revolutionary status. Findings from the visual cliff paradigm have inspired and fueled generations of later studies, many at the able and ingenious hands of Eleanor and James Gibson's own, much-lauded students. However, it doesn't seem as if the Gibsonian approach itself ever achieved "mainstream" status. Perhaps it is because the main goals of ecological theory are also perceived as its major limitation. The Gibsons were entirely accurate that a valid psychology should ensure an ecological match between an environment and any organism evolved to thrive within it. This makes complete sense, and is very much the same sentiment that Vygotsky strived to convey (see Chapter 4). But in developing their ecological theory, the Gibsons seemed to place all of their eggs in a perception-focused basket. By placing such heavy focus on organisms' active perception of environmental affordances, they gave short-shrift to other cognitive constructs that serve as the basis for many developmental theories that do occupy the mainstream.

One theoretical construct that Gibsonians seem to castigate globally, is the idea of mental representations. They vigorously oppose any notion that the world is usefully represented in the mind. In her interview with Szokolszky, for example, E. Gibson railed against a particular representationalist theory known as "Theory of Mind Theory" (discussed in more detail in Chapter 22). She wrote,

> The other theories are just plain wrong! [Laughs.] One reason why I think so is that the other theories base their whole notions of behavior and cognition not on perception but on representations of the world that are constructed, that are mental. They think that everything comes from representations in the head. . . . For instance, in developmental psychology a very popular topic is "what is a baby's theory of mind"? To me this is about the silliest question I have ever heard of. Babies don't have a theory of mind. It is ridiculous. But this is the kind of thing that they write papers about and talk seriously about. . . . Well, I think they are dead wrong. I think that it is a very narrow kind of psychology that will crash one day.

But there is room for many theories of child psychology, and doing the science of child psychology doesn't always require complete and total abandonment of ideas from oppositional theories. Conflict is the source of innovation, and it is through debate and disagreement that, throughout history, the greatest scientific advancements have been produced.

Theoretical differences of opinion notwithstanding, Eleanor Gibson was a living manifestation of the very theory she advocated. Over time, she developed major ideas in ecological theory, improved on some, revised others, and disposed of still others. It's as if her professional life provided her the experience to detect the affordances of ecological theory itself. There is little doubt that her lifetime of work, which began long before publication of the revolutionary visual cliff study with Richard Walk, has provided considerable evidence for the utility of her and J. Gibson's ecological theory. Student Karen Adolph has herself provided reams of data in support of very young children's detection of affordances for locomotion. Any modern-day developmental representationist theory that hopes to hold on to its mainstream status will need to take into account these perception-based, ecological, affordance-type findings. Indeed, maybe representationist theories will themselves one day detect the scientific affordances of Gibsonian theory.

Bibliography

Adolph, K. E., & Kretch, K. S. (2012). Infants on the edge: Beyond the visual cliff. In S. A. Haslam, A. M. Slater, and J. R. Smith (Series Eds.), & A. M. Slater and P. C. Quinn (Volume Eds.), *Developmental psychology: Revisiting the classic studies*. London: Sage.

Caudle, F. M. (2003). Eleanor Jack Gibson (1910–2002): Obituary. *American Psychologist, 58*, 1090–1091.

Gibson, E. J. (1987). Introductory essay: What does infant perception tell us about theories of perception. *Journal of Experimental Psychology: Human Perception and Performance, 13*, 515–523.

Gibson, E. J. (2002). *Perceiving the affordances: A portrait of two psychologists*. Mahway, NJ: Erlbaum.

Gibson, E. J., Walk, R. D., & Tighe, T. J. (1957). Behavior of light- and dark-reared rats on a visual cliff. *Science, 126*, 80–81.

Gibson, J. J. (1979). The ecological approach to visual perception. Boston: Houghton Mifflin.

Kretch, K. S., & Adolph, K. E. (2013). Cliff or step? Posture-specific learning at the edge of a drop-off. *Child Development, 84*, 226–240.

Pick, H. L. (2012). Eleanor J. Gibson: Learning to perceive, perceiving to learn. In W. E. Pickren, D. A. Dewsbury, & M. Wertheimer (Eds), *Portraits of pioneers in developmental psychology*. New York: Psychology Press.

Sorce, J. F., Emde, R. N., Campos, J., & Klinnert, M. D. (1985). "Maternal emotional signaling: Its effects on the visual cliff behavior of 1-year-olds." *Developmental Psychology, 21*, 195–200.

Szokolzky, A. (2003). An interview with Eleanor Gibson. *Ecological Psychology, 15*, 271–281.

Questions for Discussion

1. Can you identify features of your environment that you now perceive differently as an adult than you did as a child? Can you identify features of the classroom that are perceived differently by teachers versus students? What are the affordances of course content for teachers vis-à-vis students?

2. Gibsonian theory has focused primarily on perception of features of the physical environment, but might there be affordances of the social environment as well? If so, can you identify affordances of your social environment that have changed over your lifetime? How would affordances differ between two partners in a romantic relationship?

8

The Eyes Have It

"The Origin of Form Perception"

Fantz, R. L. (1961). *Scientific American, 204,* 66–72.
(RANK 11)

Elegant and beautiful. Absolute genius. And that's no hyperbole (you may need to Google *hyperbole*). If there's a single study that serves as a cornerstone for the development of the modern study of infant cognition, it's this one. And it was a cornerstone in more than one way. First of all, Robert Fantz was somewhat of a rebel in the kind of research he was doing; his research received a rather hostile reception from his fellow psychologists at the time. Do you remember back in introductory psychology when you studied about a group of psychologists called **behaviorists** who controlled the field of psychology from the early 1910s till the early 1960s? Well, if you were doing things the behaviorist way back then, it usually meant that you couldn't talk about inborn capacities for thinking. In fact, you couldn't talk about thinking at all! The hardcore behaviorists were only interested in studying behavior. Unfortunately for Fantz, the behaviorist way of doing things was firmly entrenched in American psychology in the late 1950s and early 1960s, when he came onto the scene. And more unfortunately for Fantz, the behaviorist way didn't make an exception for his own research specialty area: perception. I imagine Fantz felt a bit like an unstarred Sneetch in a community of star-bellied Sneetches (this Dr. Seuss classic was ironically published at about the same time as Fantz's work). In the end, however, the behaviorist way died out. And because he was still around, Fantz was granted the opportunity to take over the wheel and conduct research on the development of babies' internal psychological functioning.

Of course, the real importance of Fantz's work wasn't that he survived his battle with the behaviorists, it was that his work gave scientists a way to communicate with babies. And although Fantz's contributions as an innovator clearly extended far beyond his own work, Fantz the scientist was really only interested in one question: Do we have to learn to perceive? A corollary of this question, which also piqued Fantz's curiosity, was: Can babies perceive at birth?

To answer these questions, Fantz put forth an exceedingly ordinary proposition: Maybe babies can tell us about their thinking, if we simply look at their looking. Now, you might think that since human babies have been looking at things for thousands of years, and since doting adults have been watching babies look at things for just as long, we would have found out a long time ago whether infant looking can tell us about their thinking. We all know that by following the gaze of an adult, we can tell something about what the adult is looking at, and possibly even a little bit about what the adult is thinking. So why have we been so hesitant to pay attention to the gaze of babies? I suppose there are a number of legitimate reasons for such neglect. For one thing, I imagine it didn't occur to some of our ancestors that babies' looking behaviors were meaningful. And many historical cultures thought babies were unthinking, soulless reflex machines. Moreover, psychology itself is a very young discipline (less than 150 years old), so prior to the arrival of psychology, scientists didn't seem very interested in asking psychological questions. And even when psychology did hit the scene, behaviorists quickly gained control of mainstream American psychology (particularly its journals and academic departments) and dominated the field for 60 years. So, for whatever reason, it wasn't until Fantz's research was published in the late 1950s and early 1960s that his revolutionary idea took hold among the community of child psychology researchers. What exactly did Fantz do that was so cool? Let's take a look (pun intended).

The research I will be describing was originally described by Fantz in 1961, in an article titled "The Origin of Form Perception" published in *Scientific American*. Fantz actually published many related articles in other venues like *The Psychological Record* and *Perceptual and Motor Skills*, but the article I'll be describing was the one that received the most popularity (or notoriety if you were a behaviorist at the time). As I already mentioned, the overarching goal of his research was to determine whether humans come with an inborn ability to perceive "form" or whether such perceptual abilities have to be learned. Fantz knew that older children and adults could tell the difference between things that were round and square, between things that were light and dark, and between things that were large and small. But what he didn't know was when the ability to make those perceptual distinctions came to be.

One possibility, of course, was that babies learned to distinguish between shapes, colors, and sizes over time, as they became experts at seeing the world. This was sort of the default view. The bias of the behaviorists at the time led them to attribute every human ability to learning through environmental experience. However, if Fantz could demonstrate that babies could tell the difference between various forms from birth onward, then he would've made a revolutionary discovery. He would've shown that there's more to psychological development than behavioral development, and he would've shown that babies come biologically prepared, or "hardwired" to use a popular catchphrase, to respond to the world.

There was just one small problem: No one in the history of humankind had ever successfully carried on a two-way conversation with a newborn. And of course it's rather difficult to determine what newborns perceive if you can't ask them about it. Well, Fantz did get his questions answered. But to do so, he had to invent a method for communicating with babies that was in my opinion far more important for the field of child psychology than the answers he obtained. What follows is a description of Fantz's work, wherein he describes his approach through his recounting of a series of studies.

INTRODUCTION

In his introduction section, Fantz reviews previous research he and others had conducted using nonhuman animals. The findings from these animals were themselves rather fascinating. For example, he talks of one study where he tested the pecking behavior of 1,000 baby chickens that were raised in complete darkness from the time of hatching. Fantz wondered what would happen if these chicks were exposed to something they could see, what psychologists would call a visual stimulus. (A **stimulus**, the plural form of which is *stimuli*, is something psychologists present to research participants or subjects in order to see how they respond.) So Fantz and his colleagues presented some 100 objects of different shapes and sizes to the chicks under lighted conditions. Intriguingly, Fantz found that the chicks pecked 10 times more frequently at a sphere-shaped object than at a pyramid-shaped object, and they pecked more frequently at the sphere than at a two-dimensional flat disk, which was also round. Because the chicks showed this pecking behavior the very first time they experienced lighted conditions, Fantz figured that the chicks could not have *learned* to prefer spheres from previous visual experiences with food, so he concluded that chicks are born with an inborn preference for pecking at things that are likely to be edible! Of course, baby chickens are not very much like baby humans, but Fantz's findings raised the prospect that if chicks have inborn perceptual preferences, maybe human babies do too. However, the problem of how to ask *human* babies about their perceptual preferences still remained. Human babies don't engage in much pecking behavior.

A clue to a possible solution of how to converse with human babies came from some research Fantz had done with baby chimpanzees at the Yerkes Laboratories of Primate Biology in Florida. Chimpanzees don't engage in pecking behavior either, but they are like human babies in that they do look at stuff. So Fantz and his colleagues invented a "looking chamber," into which they placed baby chimps. The chamber was like a baby crib except that it had a ceiling and solid walls. Fantz attached two objects to the ceiling of the chamber, one to the chimps' right and one to the left. Fantz found that by looking through a peephole in the ceiling of the chamber, a peephole which was centered between the two objects, he could see reflections of the two objects in the chimps' eyes. The image that was centered over the pupil was a reflection of the object the chimps were looking at. Today this procedure is commonly known as the **corneal reflection technique**.

All that was left to determine was whether the chimpanzees looked longer at one of the objects than the other. If they did, two conclusions could be drawn: (1) that the chimps could tell the difference between the two objects, and (2) that, for whatever reason, the chimps preferred to look at one object more than the other. Fantz and his colleagues found that chimps did prefer to look at some objects more than others. He also found similar preferences in another chimpanzee who, like the chicks described previously, had been raised in complete darkness. So Fantz had evidence that chimps and chicks could distinguish between different visual forms, even without any prior visual experience. For Fantz, the only conclusion to be drawn was that chimps have an inborn ability to perceive form.

I want to highlight here that with his invention of the looking chamber procedure, Fantz discovered what a thousand generations before him did not. He discovered how to ask babies questions in a way they could understand, while also giving babies a way to talk to researchers in a way *they* could understand. All that was left to determine was what those babies would say. In the *Scientific American* article, Fantz describes a number of studies where he tested human babies in his looking chamber. Below are the details of the studies as summarized in the article.

Experiment 1

METHOD

Participants

Thirty infants were tested at weekly intervals from ages 1 to 15 weeks.

Materials

Four pairs of test patterns, differing in complexity, were shown to babies. From most to least complex, the pairs of test patterns were as follows:

- Pair 1 consisted of a set of horizontal stripes and a bull's-eye design.
- Pair 2 consisted of a checkerboard pattern versus a large or small plain square.
- Pair 3 contrasted a cross with a circle.
- Pair 4 juxtaposed two identical triangles.

Procedure

Babies were placed one at a time in the looking chamber and were presented with the test pattern pairs in a randomly determined order. The total amount of time babies spent looking at each member of the stimulus pair was recorded. This measure allowed Fantz to determine both the total amount of looking time to each item in the pair, as well as the proportion of looking time to one or the other pattern within the pair.

RESULTS

Fantz found that, overall, babies looked far longer at complex patterns than at simpler patterns. That is, babies looked way longer at the patterns in Pair 1 and Pair 2 than at the less complex patterns. However, a second major finding was that babies showed preferences for certain types of patterns. In Pair 2, for example, babies showed a strong preference for the checkerboard pattern over either of the plain squares. Babies also showed a strong preference for looking at one of the items in Pair 1, but interestingly, there was an age-related shift in which of the items was preferred. Early on, the striped pattern was strongly preferred, but by 2 months of age, most babies preferred to look at the bull's-eye pattern.

CONCLUSIONS

The mere detection of differences in looking times to different patterns led Fantz to a singly important conclusion: *babies could see much more than blurry blobs.* But much more than that, he also concluded that visual preferences in newborns resulted from inborn perceptual processes. Still, these discoveries didn't mean that form perception couldn't continue to develop with experience or with the maturation of visual nervous pathways. It only meant that babies seemed to be able to make some sense of the visual world right after popping out of the womb. In Fantz's next study, he set out to measure developmental differences in babies' **visual acuity**—how well they could see.

Experiment 2

METHOD

Participants

The number and ages of infant participants are not clearly specified in Experiment 2. However, the performances of 6-month-olds as well as babies less than a month old are described, so babies of at least these two ages must have been included.

Materials

Babies were shown a series of black-and-white striped patterns, each of which was paired with a gray square of equal brightness.

Procedure

As before, babies were placed one at a time in the looking chamber, and were shown the pairs of stimulus patterns; with each pair consisting of a striped pattern and a solid gray pattern. Fantz's logic here was brilliant. Since he already knew that babies preferred to look at patterned things more than plain things, Fantz realized that he could figure out how well babies could see, simply by making the stripes in the striped patterns successively thinner and thinner, until they were so thin that babies couldn't tell the difference between the striped pattern and the plain gray pattern. At that point, Fantz inferred, both patterns would have the appearance of a solid gray pattern, and it would mark the upper limit of babies' abilities to identify the detail of the striped pattern. As before, in an effort to track babies' abilities to distinguish between each pair of patterns, Fantz recorded the amount of time babies looked at each stimulus item in each pair.

RESULTS

Fantz found that 6-month-olds could see stripes as tiny as 1/64th of an inch wide, which corresponded to a visual angle of five minutes of arc. Now, adults can see stripes as thin as one minute of arc, which is equivalent to 1/60th of a full degree of arc. So even though the infant visual system was not very good by adult standards, it was only about 1/5th as good in fact, it reflected anything but a complete inability to detect patterns. In fact, even 1-month-olds demonstrated some visual competence, as reflected by their ability to distinguish stripes as thin as only ⅛th of an inch, reflecting a visual angle of a little less than one degree of arc. But the overarching point was that babies have a certain amount of visual acuity, which is possible to measure.

CONCLUSION

With this study, Fantz was able to show that babies have some amount of visual acuity that is measurable as young as 1 month of age, and that their visual acuity continues to improve over time. Experiment 1 also supported these conclusions. The finding that visual acuity continues to develop over time also supports the notion that maturation and/or experience plays a role in infants' developing visual perceptual abilities. Behaviorists would've been happy about this point. However, neither one of these preliminary studies answered the question that for Fantz was the crux of the issue: Do infants come into the world with inborn, possibly hardwired mechanisms for making "order out of chaos"? In other words, do babies come into the world seeing a "blooming, buzzing confusion," to borrow William James's oft-quoted phrase, or do they see shapes and wholes? Fantz's work with chicks suggests that at least baby chickens come into the world ready to distinguish edible things from other things. Do human infants also have some preformed categories that they can use to organize the world from chaos?

Experiment 3

In addressing this question, Fantz started out by considering what might be of utmost adaptive significance for the survival of human babies. For chicks, finding things to eat seemed to play this role. But for human babies, Fantz reasoned that social stimuli would probably be most important. Fantz gave special attention to the potential role of the human face. After all, the face is the part of the mother's body that infants spend the most time looking at, the arrangement of facial features makes it unique among other worldly objects, and the arrangement and shapes of the facial features makes one social partner recognizable and differentiable from others. Again, Fantz was able to use his newfangled methodology to translate his adult question into a language babies could understand. The question he put forth to babies was simply, "Do you like to look at faces more than other kinds of things?"

METHOD

Participants

The participants were 49 infants ranging in age from 4 days to 6 months.

Materials

The stimuli were three disk-like objects, roughly the size and shape of a head. On one object were painted black facial features arranged against a pink background in a facial pattern. On a second object were painted the same facial features, but this time arranged in a scrambled fashion so as to be nonfacial. On the third object were also painted areas of light and dark, in the same total proportions as used on each of the first two objects (in terms of total area), but on this stimulus the black was arranged in a dark patch toward the top of the object. Across all three objects, the features were made large enough so as to be detected by even the youngest babies with the poorest visual acuity.

Procedure

While in the looking chamber, babies were presented with all possible pairings of the three stimuli. As before, looking time to each pattern on each presentation trial was recorded.

RESULTS

Fantz found that babies preferred to look at the facial pattern slightly longer than at the nonfacial pattern, and they preferred the nonfacial arrangement over the pattern with a single black patch. Babies at all ages demonstrated these preferences.

CONCLUSIONS

Although the strength of the babies' preferences for the facial pattern over the nonfacial pattern wasn't altogether impressive, the slight preference that was observed was sufficient for Fantz to conclude that babies have an inborn preference for form perception. But he didn't go so far as to claim that babies are born to look specifically at human faces, at least not in the same way that chicks are born to peck at foodlike items. However, as I'll discuss shortly, he is often remembered as having made just such a claim.

Experiment 4

I'll bypass my usual outline approach in describing this last study because it was one Fantz himself described only briefly. In this study, Fantz deviated somewhat from his previous procedure and presented stimulus objects only one at a time instead of in pairs. He expected that the length of time babies spent initially looking at each item would provide meaningful information about how important each item was to the infant. Fantz showed babies a series of 6-inch-wide flat disks that differed from one another in terms of the patterns on their surfaces. Three of the disks had patterns on them, three were plain. The patterned disks consisted of a face, a bull's-eye pattern, and a patch of printed media that looked something like a piece of cut-out newspaper. The plain disk stimuli were red, fluorescent yellow, and white. Fantz recorded the length of babies' initial looks to each of the objects. As in Experiment 1, Fantz found that babies looked longer at the patterned stimuli than at the plain stimuli, even though the stimuli weren't paired with one another. And as in Experiment 3, the facial pattern was the most strongly preferred among the patterned stimuli, based on the length of the initial look. Fantz used these results as evidence that social stimuli may be extremely important to babies, perhaps to the point that babies might be biologically predisposed to begin looking for faces at birth.

CONCLUSION

Fantz's genius is striking in many regards and his trailblazing efforts should be recognized at many levels. Not only did he devise a technique that allowed researchers to "talk" and "listen to" newborns, but he single-handedly challenged behaviorist assumptions that only children's *behaviors* were studiable. Oh sure, Fantz was also studying behaviors—he was studying looking behaviors. But rather than trying to explain the development of the behaviors themselves, he explained that the behaviors were outward reflections of internal, underlying perceptual abilities. He boldly suggested that babies are more than simply the sum of their experiences. He concluded that his results required a full-out rejection of the behaviorist notion that babies—human or otherwise—start from scratch when learning to perceive visual stimuli.

Another of Fantz's contributions was that he set the research agenda for a large chunk of child psychology research for the next five decades. For example, his focus on the human face as a social stimulus with special powers in attracting and maintaining babies' attention was an issue that struck a chord with child psychology researchers throughout the 1960s and 1970s. At the core of the issue was whether babies' brains were wired, before birth, to seek out human faces, or whether babies just preferred to look at faces because they happened to have the kinds of features babies liked to look at. This issue had important ramifications for John Bowlby's theory of attachment (Chapter 17). In particular, Bowlby argued that babies and mothers were biologically prepared, through evolution, to respond to one another. Mothers responded to the signals given off by their babies; and for their part, babies responded to stimuli given off by their mothers. Thus, Fantz may have been one of Bowlby's best friends, at least in terms of providing supporting data for Bowlby's theory.

Fantz's methodology also served as a foundation for researchers studying infant intelligence. Fantz's longtime colleague Joseph Fagan even developed an infant intelligence test based on the approach (appropriately called the Fagan Test of Infant Intelligence, or FTII for short). The FTII is based on the premise that babies are capable of visually discriminating between two perceptual forms. The way the test works is that babies are first familiarized with one picture for a certain amount of time (which varies with infant age), and then are shown a pair of pictures. One picture is the old one they were just familiarized with, while the other is a completely new picture. It was found that babies who looked longer at the new picture (we call this a "novelty preference") tended to have higher IQ scores in later childhood. In contrast, babies who didn't show a novelty preference were found to be at increased risk for developmental delay later in childhood.

SUMMARY

Fantz's efforts really did open the door for hundreds of child psychology researchers who were standing in line with hundreds of questions they just couldn't wait to ask babies. Fantz more or less provided the grammar for this new way of communicating with babies. Recent developments in the field now allow us to ask babies if and when they can tell the difference between categories of things such as boys and girls, emotions such as happy or sad, or even velocities such as fast and slow. We can ask whether differences in babies' abilities to make these kinds of distinctions might be linked to their understanding of more abstract social concepts such as gender or race, to physical concepts such as time and space, or to their ability to produce and understand language. And by now we've moved beyond merely showing babies pairs of single, static objects to showing them complex, real-time visual events that are both real and fictional (as in the work of Baillargeon, Chapter 5). Since the time of Fantz, hundreds of studies have produced thousands of pages documenting an enormous profile of infants' mind-blowing intellectual capabilities. And all this came about because Fantz didn't trivialize something as simplistic as what babies like to look at. Interesting, isn't it?

Bibliography

Fagan, J. F., III. (2000, June). *Visual perception and experience in early infancy: A look at the hidden side of behavioral development.* Paper presented at the biennial meetings of the International Conference on Infant Studies, Brighton, England, UK.

Fagan, J. F., III, & Detterman, D. K. (1992). The Fagan Test of Infant Intelligence: A technical summary. *Journal of Applied Developmental Psychology, 13*, 173–193.

Questions for Discussion

1. Fantz suggested that babies might be biologically predisposed to prefer human faces. But is it possible that babies just like to look at certain things that faces happen to have? If so, does this reduce the significance of Fantz's findings? Why or why not?

2. Would Fantz have made as big a splash in child psychology had he tried to publish his findings 10 years earlier? Or 10 years later? Why or why not?

3. Some people might argue that Fantz's study of babies' looking behaviors was the result of doing little more than paying attention to the obvious. Is it fair to label Fantz a genius if he only paid attention to the obvious? Explain.

4. Why does it matter if form perception is learned or innate? That is, which constituencies, agencies, companies, industries, or groups would be especially interested in the answer to this question?

9

Developmental Lessons from Kitten Brains

Receptive Fields, Binocular Interaction and Functional Architecture in the Cat's Visual Cortex

Hubel, D. H., & Wiesel, T. N. (1962). *The Journal of Physiology, 160,* 106–154. (RANK 10)

Throughout the chapters of this book, we've been reviewing one revolutionary study after another that has made a significant contribution to our understanding of child psychology. We've talked about children's cognition, language, emotion, even their aggression. But in talking about all these psychological abilities and capacities you may have noticed that much of the talk is fairly abstract. Although the truth is that you can't really do psychology without talking about abstract psychological concepts, the problem is that you can't *see* a psychological ability or capacity; the most you can do is make inferences about it. For example, you never really see a kid thinking; all you really see is what a kid does, and you assume he's thinking. You never really see a kid's happiness; all you really see is a smile on his face or hear him laughing, and infer that he's happy. You never really see a kid's aggression; you just observe him kicking and yelling, and conclude he's aggressive. Psychology is loaded with these kinds of unobservable things, so the best a psychological scientist can hope for is to study behaviors that she thinks are driven by those unobservables.

But if there's one thing that everybody in the field of psychology knows, it's that these abstract psychological abilities and capacities, if they exist at all, ultimately are made possible by the neural circuitry of the brain. Children's thinking happens in their brains, their emotions result from what their brains do, and aggression comes from the way their brains interpret social information. So if so much of psychology really comes down to brain activity, you might ask, why aren't all psychologists doing brain science? Well, there are a couple of good reasons.

First, I suspect that most psychologists wouldn't feel comfortable with the assumption that all of human psychology can be reduced to patterns of electrical activity in the brain, at least not in our current state of technology. Human behavior is so exceedingly complicated, so unpredictable, and we know so very little about the range of possible human actions under any set of conditions, that most psychologists aren't sure what they would begin to look for. How can you look for a neurological explanation for a psychological ability, when you don't fully understand the psychological ability in the first place?

But even so, some psychologists do think of themselves as brain scientists. These people sometimes go by titles like *behavioral neuroscientist, biopsychologist, neurophysiologist,* or *psychopharmacologist*. In fact, several divisions of the American Psychological Association (APA) are dedicated to supporting brain-based research: including Division 6, Behavioral Neuroscience and Comparative Psychology; Division 28, Psychopharmacology and Substance Abuse; Division 40, Clinical Neuropsychology; Division 50, Addiction Psychology; and the second most recently created APA division, Division 55, American Society for the Advancement of Pharmacotherapy. And brain-based psychological research is more popular than ever, aided by a landslide of technological innovations allowing psychologists to take a peek at human brain functioning live and online, without requiring that the researchers get advanced medical training in brain anatomy. These new tools allow us to study how the brain reacts to all sorts of stimulation. Through functional magnetic resonance imaging, for example, we are actually able to take a three-dimensional snapshot of the parts of the brain that are most active when a person is sleeping, reading, talking, or doing math problems.

But the fact that one part of the brain "lights up" on the computer screen when a person is doing math problems, doesn't mean that that area is where math rules are stored. A highly active brain region could also indicate that a person is experiencing considerable stress while doing the math. So even brain scientists have to make some assumptions about the connections between psychological abilities and brain activity. From a scientific standpoint, one wonders if it wouldn't be a whole lot easier just to poke around in the brain to see what happens. You could electrically stimulate one section of a person's brain and then ask him what memories come to mind. Or you could remove a piece of brain and observe what a person is no longer able to do. But for some strange reason, human volunteers for these kinds of projects are in extremely short supply (and even if they did volunteer, there would be a whole bunch of ethical and legal reasons that scientists shouldn't go around removing pieces of people's brains).

This has led a lot of psychologists to turn to brain research in animals. Animals, especially mammals, have brains very similar to ours. With animal brains, you can poke, prod, stimulate, and remove stuff to your heart's (or conscience's) desire. Of course, the APA and a host of government agencies have very strict rules for how animal research subjects must be treated. But even so, we also have to come to grips with the fact that animal brains are different than human brains—animals don't talk or reason, and they can't do math problems. Still, using animal brains we can gain some excellent insight as to how brains are put together. And there are a lot of brain systems that humans and other animals have in common. One of the most thoroughly studied of these is the visual system.

The focus of this chapter is on the groundbreaking research of David Hubel and Torsten Wiesel (surnames pronounced "HUE-bul" and "VEE-zul"), on the developing visual system of the cat. Their work not only was ranked 10th most revolutionary by the child psychology community, it earned them a Nobel Prize in Physiology or Medicine in 1982. Their research was revolutionary for three major findings. First, they discovered that *individual cells* in the visual cortex of cat brains responded to specific patterns of visual input. (The cortex is the outer surface of the brain. You know, that funny-looking, squiggly, wrinkly stuff.) They found that these feline **cortical cells** mostly responded to simple patterns like edges and lines, arranged in particular orientations. But although it was based on research with kittens, this was an extremely important finding nevertheless, because it gave us some insight into how mammals are able to see. Prior to their findings, we knew that rods and cones in the eye responded to light, and we knew that incoming visual information was eventually routed to the visual cortex through the thalamus; but it was a big puzzle as to how our brains put all this visual information together to create nice, well-formed mental pictures of whatever it was we were looking at.

Think of the problem this way. Each of our eyes has about 120 million rods and about 6 million cones. Since rods and cones are both a type of nerve cell, whenever a rod or a cone detects some light coming into the eyeball, it sends a nerve impulse to the part of the brain responsible for processing visual inputs. From the nervous system's point of view, this means that at any moment in time, as many as 252 million visual nerve impulses are being processed. Of course, while you're sitting there reading these words, you don't perceive 252 million different points of light. You perceive a nice, smooth image. The puzzle that needed to be solved, then, was how the visual system could start out with 252 million different nerve impulses, and yet produce a single crisp picture in our mind's eye. Hubel and Wiesel's answer was that our cortical brain cells don't receive individual inputs from rods and cones, they only receive collections or patterns of inputs. This means that somehow, somewhere in the visual system, after the visual impulses leave the rods and cones, but before they reach the visual cortex, they are combined or *summarized* in some way.

The second discovery made by Hubel and Wiesel was that most of the cortical cells that processed visual impulses processed impulses coming in from both eyes. In other words, they discovered that cortical cells were **binocular** (from *bin*, "two," and *ocular*, "eye"). When a brain cell in the visual cortex receives binocular impulses, impulses from the eye on the same side of the body (called the **ipsilateral** side) are combined with impulses from the eye on the opposite side of the body (called the **contralateral** side). They found, moreover, that binocular cells responded most strongly when they received binocular input. What this means is that when a single binocular cell responds, it is actually responding to two images, one from the left eye and one from the right. You might think that binocularity wastes valuable brain circuitry. After all, why send the same visual information to a cortical cell twice? But binocularity is actually quite adaptive. For one thing, binocularity gives the brain the capability for perceiving depth. When we look at an object, depending on where it's located in space, the object casts slightly different images on the retinas of each eye. When cortical cells in the brain summarize this information, they have some sense of how far away in space the object is. But besides the role of binocularity in depth perception, it's probably not a bad idea to give cortical cells two chances at detecting what's in the world. If visual information is missed by one eye, the other eye has a chance to detect it. Hubel and Wiesel also found that binocular cortical cells tended to be dominated by one eye or the other. That is, a binocular cortical cell tended to respond more strongly to one eye than the other eye.

The third major discovery made by Hubel and Wiesel was that visual cortical cells were grouped together into little columns in the visual cortex. In more technical terms, we could say visual cortical cells live together in a **columnar microstructure**. These little columns of visual cortical cells are laid out perpendicular to the surface of the brain. To get a sense of what this means, imagine sticking a needle straight into the surface of an apple. The part of the needle that protrudes into the flesh of the apple corresponds roughly to how columns of cortical cells extend below the surface of the brain; that is, in a single line, one cell below another. Hubel and Wiesel also found that the cortical cells within a particular column all responded to the same types of simple patterns. This means that the cortical cells are regionally organized. Cortical cells in a column in one region of the visual cortex respond to one type of visual pattern, whereas cortical cells in columns in other regions of the visual cortex respond to other types of visual patterns.

But wait: I'm giving you the end of the story before I've even started it. Let's take a closer look at just one of their contributions to the field. In this article, published in 1963, they documented very early neural organization in the visual system of 2-week-old kittens.

INTRODUCTION

Hubel and Wiesel don't give us much by way of introduction to their study. About the only thing they tell us is that their purpose "was to learn the age at which cortical cells have normal, adult-type receptive fields, and to find out whether such fields exist even in animals that have no patterned visual stimulation." By **receptive field**, they are referring to the pattern of visual input that an individual cortical cell responds to. I mentioned earlier that individual cortical cells responded to simple visual patterns like vertical lines or horizontal edges, but to stimulate a given cortical cell, the pattern also has to be in a particular location in the visual field. For example, if you are looking at something, and there is a vertical line at the top of the image, then that vertical line will fall within the receptive fields of cortical cells that are sensitive to the top parts of images. But if you are looking at something and the vertical line is at the bottom of the image, then the vertical line will fall within the receptive fields of cortical cells that are sensitive to the bottom parts of images. Cortical cells that respond to patterns in the top parts of images do not also respond to the same patterns found in the bottom parts of images. This is because the two sets of cortical cells have different receptive fields.

METHOD

Participants

Four kittens were used in the experiment, three of which were from the same litter. The first kitten was 8 days old when the experiment began and had not yet opened its eyes. The second kitten had both its eyes covered at 9 days by "translucent contact occluders," which were basically eye covers that allowed some light to come in, but not enough to allow the kitten to see any detail. This kitten was just beginning to open its eyes at the time the occluders were put into place. The third kitten had its right eye covered by a translucent occluder at 9 days, but the left eye was allowed to open normally. The fourth kitten, the one from a different litter, was brought up normally, without anything blocking its vision. Its eyes also opened on the ninth day. To summarize, when the experiment began two kittens had no visual experience, one kitten had visual experience in only one eye, and one kitten had visual experience in both eyes.

Materials and Procedure

Hubel and Wiesel apparently had a nasty habit of describing the details of their experimental procedure by pointing their readers to earlier publications. In the method section of this article, for example, they wrote, "Procedures for stimulating and recording have for the most part been described in previous papers," and they go on to cite some of their earlier papers. I checked one of these earlier papers to get the details, and to my surprise I found that in that paper they also wrote, "Details of stimulating and recording methods are given in previous papers." I almost get the impression that they don't want their readers to know how they conducted their experiments! But their brevity was also probably due in part to the fact that journal space is usually at a premium, and editors are known to ask authors to cut down on manuscript length. Fortunately, they provided a little more detail in a 1962 publication, so I refer in part to that study in describing their methodology below.

Before being tested, each kitten underwent a short surgical procedure to create a small hole in the skull and dura mater, roughly a few millimeters wide. This hole allowed for a recording electrode to be inserted into the visual cortex. For kittens this young, surgical preparation included a very small dose of barbiturate and a local anesthetic. Hubel and Wiesel wrote, "A few minutes after injection of the local anesthetic the animal usually fell asleep and showed no signs of discomfort during the surgery or the experiment." The electrodes were inserted into the cortex at a number of locations and at a variety of depths. Most electrodes went no deeper than 3 or 4 millimeters. Because the goal was to record the neural activity of individual cortical cells, the eyes of the kittens were continually stimulated by light patterns as the electrode was advanced into the brain. This procedure made localization of individual cortical cells possible. During the electrode insertion procedure, the kittens' skulls were cemented to a special apparatus that could be clamped tightly, thus holding their heads completely still. Once the electrode was in place, and the skull was held securely, the kittens were shown patterned images on a diffusely illuminated screen. Upon completion of the experiment, the kittens' brains were subjected to **histological examination**, which means their brain tissue was extracted and examined under a microscope.

RESULTS

Hubel and Wiesel made recordings from eight or nine individual cortical cells in each of the four kittens. In general, they found these cortical cells to be much less active than those in adult cats, and some cells were too difficult to stimulate at all. Cells that did respond tended to tire out much more quickly than was typical for adult cats. But similar to those of adult cats, the kittens' cells responded most vigorously to patterned stimuli of a particular orientation (by "orientation" here, I mean the angle of the line). Hubel and Wiesel reported that finding the correct orientation of a line for a given cortical cell was often tedious. While recording from an individual cell, for example, a line or an edge had to be moved back and forth across the kittens' fields of vision, and rotated in various orientations, until the targeted cortical cell began responding vigorously.

Perhaps I can give you a sense of their procedure by invoking a little imaginary experiment. Suppose you're looking straight ahead. Imagine there is a yardstick dangling in space directly in front of you. Now, in your imagination, orient the yardstick so that it's straight up and down; and then imagine the yardstick sweeping back and forth, from left to right. Then mentally rotate the yardstick slightly until the top is at 1:00 and the bottom is at 7:00, and then imagine the yardstick sweeping back and forth across your visual field at an angle perpendicular to its orientation, from upper left to lower right. Now rotate the yardstick so that the top is at 3:00 and the bottom is at 9:00, and sweep it again across your field. If you kept on doing this, you'd get a sense of the range of visual patterns the kittens were exposed to.

Hubel and Wiesel operationally defined the receptive field for a given cortical cell as wherever the line was in the visual image and whatever orientation the line was in when the cell responded most vigorously. They wrote,

> Brief responses were consistently obtained [in one cell] when the [edge] was oriented in a 1 o'clock to 7 o'clock direction whereas there was no response when it was oriented at 90° to this [11 o'clock to 5 o'clock]. A similar kind of preference in stimulus orientation was common to all of the units isolated. Several of the cells, especially those in the 8-day-old kitten, gave responses

over a range of stimulus orientations that was unusually wide by adult standards, yet even in these cells stimulating at an orientation of 90° to the optimum evoked no response at all. Moreover, the responses to moving an optimally oriented stimulus across the receptive field were not necessarily the same for the two diametrically opposite directions of movement. As in the adult cat, this kind of directional preference varied from cell to cell; some cells responded equally well to the two opposing directions of movement, while some responded well to one direction and not at all to the other.

In other words, not only did individual cortical cells respond most vigorously to a line in a particular orientation, but the vigorous responding happened only while the line was sweeping across the visual field; and even then, sometimes the line had to be sweeping in a particular direction to produce a response.

Binocular Interaction

Hubel and Wiesel found that the great majority of the cortical cells they studied could be influenced by each eye separately. Of the 39 total cortical cells that they recorded, 26 responded vigorously to input from both eyes. Of the remaining cells, there were 4 that responded *only* to input from the contralateral (opposite-side) eye and 1 that responded *only* to input from the ipsilateral (same-side) eye. This pattern of binocular responding was pretty much the same as that found in adult cats, which led Hubel and Wiesel to conclude, "There is little to no difference in ocular-dominance distribution with age or visual experience."

Functional Architecture

Relating to the idea of the *columnar microstructure*, Hubel and Wiesel found that cortical cells contained within a single column all pretty much responded to lines of the same orientation. They found this out by first inserting the electrode into the top cell of a column and then making a recording, then pushing through to the next cell in the column and making a recording, and then pushing through to the next cell in the column and making a recording, and so on. On the other hand, when the electrode was inserted at a slight angle to a column, thus departing from cells in one column and entering cells in the next, the line orientations that produced the most vigorous responding shifted. Hubel and Wiesel diagrammed how the line orientations producing the most vigorous responsiveness shifted as the electrode advanced further and further into the brain, traversing several columns of cells: (1) cells in the first column responded most vigorously to a line orientation of 11:00 to 5:00, (2) cells from the next column over responded most vigorously to a line orientation of about 12:30 to 6:30, (3) the next cells responded best to an orientation of about 9:30 to 3:30, and finally (4) the last column of cells responded most vigorously to line orientations of about 11:00 to 5:00 again.

Cortical Differences Based on Visual Experience

In this study, Hubel and Wiesel found that there was basically no difference in the receptivity of individual cortical cells to binocular inputs coming from both eyes, even in kittens who had been deprived of visual experience. They wrote, "What can be concluded . . . is that even as late as 19 days of age a cell need not have had previous patterned stimulation from an eye in order to respond normally to it." In other words, even though some eyes were deprived of visual input from the environment, the impulses being sent by these eyes to the cortical cells were still heard "loud and clear" by the cortical cells. The connections between the temporarily blinded eyes and the cortical cells remained completely intact.

DISCUSSION

The main result of their study was to show that the basic architectural organization of the visual cortex in kittens is unaffected even in kittens deprived of visual experience. This architecture is basically in place at birth and even severe deprivation of visual experience doesn't alter it, at least not by *2-1/2* weeks of age. They wrote, "The present results make it clear that highly complex neural connections are possible without the benefit of neural experience."

CONCLUSIONS

Although Hubel and Wiesel found that depriving kittens of visual experience didn't have any significant impact on how the visual systems of those kittens were organized, it would be premature to conclude that experience plays no role in maintaining neural connections beyond the first 20 days. In fact, in a related study, published in the same journal issue, they found that serious disruptions in visual neural circuitry *would* happen if the kittens were deprived of visual experience for a much longer time. Let's take a closer look at this related study.

Related Study

In this related study, also published in 1963, but with the order of the authors reversed, Wiesel and Hubel studied kittens who had one eye closed for as long as four months. In this study, seven kittens and one adult cat were used. The blinded eye was either sewn shut, preventing any light from entering, or covered with a translucent occluder, permitting some very diffuse light to enter. The neural activity of 84 cortical cells was recorded at various points during the period of visual deprivation. They found that unlike in the earlier study, the binocular cortical cells in these kittens showed absolutely *no* receptivity to impulses coming from the visually deprived eye. If you remember from the earlier study, the cortical cells of kittens who were visually deprived for less than 20 days responded well to both eyes. Their cortical cells remained binocular. But in this second study, when visual deprivation was much longer, the same cells simply stopped responding to the eye that provided no visual input. These cortical cells lost their binocularity, maybe through something like neural atrophy. Thus, connections that were functioning quite well early on, ceased functioning in the absence of continued stimulation.

Some of the kittens in this second study were also given the opportunity to walk around with their good eye covered, but with their visually deprived eye open. Wiesel and Hubel described the kittens' behavior this way:

> As an animal walked about investigating its surroundings the gait was broad-based and hesitant, and the head moved up and down in a peculiar nodding manner. The kittens bumped into large obstacles such as table legs, and even collided with walls, which they tended to follow using their whiskers as a guide. When put onto a table the animals walked off into the air, several times falling awkwardly onto the floor. When an object was moved before the eye there was no hint that it was perceived, and no attempt was made to follow it. As soon as the cover was taken off the [good] eye the kitten would behave normally, jump gracefully from the table, skillfully avoiding objects in its way. We concluded that there was a profound, perhaps complete, impairment of vision in the deprived eye of these animals.

Taking these two studies together, the results show that kittens' visual systems are wired up properly from birth, but that portions atrophy over time through disuse. Prior to Hubel and Wiesel's research, most vision researchers thought that the visual system didn't come prewired. They thought that visual experience was necessary to cause visual cells to make connections with each other. Apparently, this wasn't the case. Instead, cells seem to start out connected, but quickly lose their functional connectivity as a result of a lack of visual experience.

So what does all this talk of cortical binocular cells, the visual system of cats, and cellular atrophy through disuse, have to do with child psychology? Actually, Hubel and Wiesel's work has quite a lot to do with child psychology. You just have to be willing to put your critical-thinking microscope on a lower power to see the bigger picture. The most direct implication of their research is that it has helped us understand how the human visual system probably works. When a cat stalks a mouse, we know that the cat has to see and to recognize the thing as a mouse. To accomplish this, the cat first has to process visual information in its eyes; the eyes then send the information to a part of the brain called the thalamus, and the thalamus sends the information to the visual cortex. The human visual system also uses eyes, a thalamus, and a visual cortex. Because the two systems resemble each other so closely, what we've learned from the visual systems of kittens may also apply to the visual systems of humans. Hubel and Wiesel's research additionally revealed that by the time visual information reaches the visual cortex, it comes in the form of a simple pattern. We know this because cells in the visual cortex respond most vigorously to lines and edges of a particular orientation. If visual information reaches the cortex in the form of a simple pattern in kittens, then it's much less of a mystery why we humans don't perceive the world as a jumble of 252 million disconnected points of light.

Of course, the next problem to address is that we don't see the world as a jumble of disconnected lines and edges either. But Hubel and Wiesel's discovery of edge-detecting cortical cells at least gives us a new way for thinking about the problem of why we don't. For one thing, the very existence of edge-detecting cortical cells raises the possibility that higher-level cells could be responsible for detecting higher-level visual patterns. A simple version of the logic goes like this. When a person looks at an edge or line, an image of the edge or line is projected onto the retinal lining along the back of the eyeball. In the lining of the eyeball are rods and cones. When the image of the edge is projected onto the retina, rods and cones that make direct contact with the image respond vigorously. The other, neighboring rods and cones remain relatively quiet. The active rods and cones then send signals, through the thalamus, to the visual cortex. Now because we know that individual visual cortical cells respond to edges and lines, and because we know that information about edges and lines is carried to the cortical cells from the rods and cones, it's easy to understand how individual cortical cells are more or less summarizing the outputs of large groups of rods and cones. But we can also take this logic a step further. If cortical cells do this with inputs from several rods and cones, why can't higher-level cells perform a similar summarizing function with inputs from several cortical cells?

As it turns out, this may very well be what happens. Hubel and Wiesel called the cortical cells they studied "simple" cells. Simple cells are those cortical cells that respond to edges and lines, which, as we've seen, represent patterns of input from groups of rods and cones. Apparently, groups of simple cortical cells can also send information to higher-level, or "complex," cortical cells. Complex cells act to summarize information from groups of simple cortical cells. Imagine, for example, that a complex cell receives input from two simple cells. Imagine that one of these simple cells responds best to a vertical line and the other responds best to a horizontal line. In this case, if both a vertical line and a horizontal line are present in the visual field, say in the form of a right angle, the two simple cells will each respond vigorously. Accordingly, the complex cell they feed into will also respond vigorously. What this means is that the complex cell summarizes the input of two simple cells, and each simple cell summarizes the input of groups of rods and cones. When there is a right angle in the visual field causing the two simple cells to respond vigorously, and when the two simple cells are responding and causing the complex cell to respond vigorously, then we can ultimately say that the complex cell is responding to the visual presence of a right angle. We might just as well call this complex cell a "90° angle detector."

But this logic can be carried further. Groups of complex cells might themselves be connected to even higher-level cells, called "hypercomplex" cells, which summarize the response patterns of the complex cells. The vigorous responding of a hypercomplex cell would indicate the presence of an even higher-level pattern in the visual field. Instead of an angle, it might be a geometric shape. As the level of responding gets higher and higher up the chain, the amount of visual summarizing and integration that goes on gets greater and greater. There might be hyper-hypercomplex cells, and hyper-hyper-hypercomplex cells. In the end, we may have very high-level cells that are responsible for our ability to detect very complicated visual pictures in the world around us. Some people have even jested that way up the cortical ladder there may even be a "grandmother cell" that responds vigorously to the visual image of your grandmother!

Admittedly, the picture I've described here is a wee bit oversimplified. And the explosion of research ignited by Hubel and Wiesel's early work has since revealed a number of shortcomings of their early findings. But it was their early work that got the train rolling to begin with, and for this they are duly recognized.

A second, far more general impact of their work was their discovery of **neural plasticity**. The term *neural plasticity* refers to the idea that neural circuits can be altered through experience (*plastic* means flexible here, rather than the type of material used to make water bottles). Neural plasticity has been a hot topic among brain researchers as well as among child psychologists because it directly addresses the nature–nurture issue. If you remember, Hubel and Wiesel found that the functioning of visual cortical cells *can* be radically altered if visual input from one eye is eliminated. But the amount of alteration depends on *when* the visual input is cut off. In cats, cutting off visual input to one eye during the first 20 days didn't seem to have much of an effect on how responsive a cortical cell would be to that eye. But if visual input is cut off for the first 2 to 4 months, then cortical cells stop responding to that eye altogether, even after vision is restored. The neural circuitry is so badly damaged that when cats are forced to use that eye to negotiate the edge of a table, they just fall off. Because the neural circuitry of the visual system can be altered through experience, it's clearly plastic.

Extending results from Hubel and Wiesel's research on the visual cortical system, raises the possibility that neural circuitry throughout the rest of the brain might also be plastic. Perhaps, the brain might be operating according to some sort of "use-it-or-lose-it" philosophy. Connections and pathways in the brain that aren't used might just atrophy, whereas connections and pathways that are used frequently will flourish. Plasticity also raises the possibility that if some cortical cells aren't used for their intended purpose, they might be co-opted by other systems that could use them to greater benefit. Some very interesting research conducted by Helen Neville has suggested that the auditory cortex (the part of the brain involved in hearing) of adults born deaf may take on some visual functions. How can this be? She suggests that at birth there may be neural connections between the visual portions of the thalamus and the auditory cortex. Normally, these connections aren't maintained because the auditory system itself takes up residence in the auditory cortex. But in people born deaf, the cells in the auditory cortex don't receive auditory input, so, as in Hubel and Wiesel's cats, these connections atrophy. This atrophia leaves intact the preexisting connections between the visual system and the auditory cortex, and because visual input keeps coming in, connections between the visual input and the auditory cortex continually strengthens. Over time, the visual system may develop quite a camaraderie with the auditory cortex.

The Joys of Good Luck

There's little doubt of the monumental significance of Hubel and Wiesel's work. But theirs is also a story of how important it is to have a good bit of luck on your side as you're struggling to make a name for yourself in a well-established scientific field. We've spent the last several pages talking about how Hubel and Wiesel made single-cell recordings of cortical responses to simple visual patterns like lines and edges. They made their career on these little recordings, and the Nobel Prize awards committee recognized them for it. But very few people outside the neuroscience research community realize how close Hubel and Wiesel came to missing out completely on their revolutionary path of discovery.

As David Hubel told the story in his Nobel Prize acceptance speech, when he and Torsten Wiesel first began trying to make recordings of individual cortical cells they met with little success. For one thing, when you insert an electrode into the surface of a brain, you can't see where it is. And when you can't see what you're doing, well, it might require a lot of trial and error before you can get it right. But they were certain there was nothing wrong with their technique, because it had been developed and used quite successfully by a previous researcher named Vernon Mountcastle to explore somatosensory cortexes in cats and monkeys. Still, for some reason, they initially found no visual stimuli they could show the kittens that would cause their visual cortical cells to respond. Since they knew their recording technique was okay, they next figured that the problem must've had something to do with how they were projecting their visual images to the kittens. Due to the fact that they had neither a lot of money, nor a lot of fancy equipment, they had to project the images onto the ceiling of the lab. Hubel wrote, "Having no other [cat] head holder, we continued for a while to use the ophthalmoscope's head holder, which posed a problem since the cat was facing directly up. To solve this we brought in some bed sheets which we slung between the pipes and cobwebs that graced the ceiling of the Wilmer [Institute's] basement, giving the setup an aura of a circus tent. One day Vernon Mountcastle walked in on this scene, and was horror-struck at the spectacle. The method was certainly inconvenient since we had to stare at the ceiling for the entire experiment." Fortunately, they eventually got their projection system worked out. They ended up projecting simple visual patterns directly onto the retinas of cats using a special contraption that allowed them to insert either a small brass plate with a hole in it, or a small glass slide with a black mark on it. The contraption would pass light through the hole in the brass plate to project a single spot of light on the cats' retinas, or it would pass light through the glass slide in order to project a shadow of the black mark onto the cats' retinas.

Although they began showering their cats' retinas with spots of light and shadows, their initial recordings were still failures. Their initial reaction was that cortical cells just didn't respond to visual images as expected. But after several hours, while recording from cell number 3004, they made their revolutionary discovery. (Well, they hadn't actually recorded from 3003 other cells. They decided to start numbering their cells at 3000 to impress Mountcastle, whose cell recordings numbered into the thousands.) At cell 3004, they got a decidedly vigorous response. What was most fascinating about this discovery was that the cell wasn't responding to a spot of light or a shadow—the anticipated targets—rather the cell was responding instead to the edge of the glass slide as it was inserted into the projection machine! Hubel and Wiesel spent the next 9 hours fiddling with the slide to reproduce the vigorous response. At the end of the day, they concluded that the cell responded most strongly to an edge with an orientation that matched the angle of the slide as it was inserted into the projection machine. When the orientation was just right, "the cell went off like a machine gun."

You can probably imagine how easy it would've been for Hubel and Wiesel to completely miss this discovery. For one thing, they apparently left the projection machine turned on as they inserted one slide after another. If they had been in the habit of turning the machine off between each projection, then the shadow of the edge of the slide would never have been cast onto the retina of the cat, and cell 3004 would never have responded. It was also a stroke of luck that they were recording from a cell whose preferred orientation matched precisely the angle of the edge of the slide. If they were recording from a cell that preferred a vertical edge, they would have failed to trigger the response altogether. But in the end, they did leave the machine on, cell 3004 was orientationally matched, and about 20 years later, the Nobel Prize awards committee called out their names.

Bibliography

Barlow, H. B. (1982). David Hubel and Torsten Wiesel: Their contributions towards understanding the primary visual cortex. *Trends in Neuroscience, 5*, 145–152.

Hubel, D. H. (1982). Evolution of ideas in the primary visual cortex, a biased historical account. *Bioscience Reports, 2*, 435–439.

Neville, H. J. (1990). Intermodal competition and compensation in development: Evidence from studies of the visual system in congenitally deaf adults. *Annals of the New York Academy of Sciences, 608*, 71–87.

Neville, H. J., & Lawson, D. (1987). Attention to central and peripheral visual space in a movement detection task: An event-related potential and behavioral study. II. Congenitally deaf adults. *Brain Research, 45*, 268–283.

Wiesel, T. N., & Hubel, D. H. (1963). Single-cell responses in striate cortex of kittens deprived of vision in one eye. *Journal of Neurophysiology, 26*, 1003–1017.

Questions for Discussion

1. Remind me. Why is a study on the visual cortex of kittens in a book on the 20 studies that revolutionized child psychology?
2. Although scientists can't ethically cut into live human brains just to play around and do research, do you think it would be okay if the brains were grown under artificial conditions in the lab?
3. Is it justifiable to do research on the brains of other animals, when the goal is just to learn about brain functioning? Is it more okay to do research on the brains of some species than others?
4. Should Hubel and Wiesel be given credit for the discovery of visual cortical cell functioning when their discovery came more or less by accident?

10

Was It Something I Said?

"Cross-Language Speech Perception: Evidence for Perceptual Reorganization During the First Year of Life"

Werker, J. F., & Tees, R. C. (1984). *Infant Behavior and Development, 7,* 49–63. **(RANK 19)**

Perhaps it is one of the coolest things ever when we reach a level of competence that allows us for the first time to outsmart our parents. Now I don't mean "outsmarting" in the sense of lying, cheating, or sneaking something by them. And I don't mean that period of time, around 18 or 19 years of age, when we *think* we know more than our parents but are really just full of ourselves. I mean the real kind of outsmarting when, matched as equals, wit to wit, we know something our parents don't know, or figure out the solution to a problem before they do. This surely represents a kind of rite of passage, and reveals a level of achievement that marks the beginning of our entry into maturity. We all get to this point at one time or another, whether our parents are willing to accept it or not; and it is normal and natural, and not especially surprising. As we get older, we get smarter, wiser, and more capable. It is the natural way of things for our current selves to be more advanced and sophisticated than our younger selves.

So it is a bit surprising that in the development of the child, there are times when the older version of a child actually acts *less* capable than the younger version, at least to all outward appearances. Developmental science has uncovered several examples of these cases. You may have heard, for example, that very young infants are shockingly competent swimmers who can remain upright and buoyant when they are tossed into a swimming pool or a lake. (**DON'T TRY THIS AT HOME!**) And yet, there are full grown adults who are unable to swim. Is the swimming baby truly the master of the nonswimming adult? Well, kind of. Although babies are born with a reflex that keeps them adaptively postured in a pool of water, it's not really swimming. These babies might *look* like they are sophisticated swimmers, but they can also swallow large amounts of water and even drown. Their demonstration of the swimming reflex needs to take place under highly controlled and closely supervised conditions. Still, the baby appears to have the sophisticated coordination of muscle movements and balance that the adult nonswimmer can only hope for.

Another illustration of the younger outperforming the older can be found in the case of the acquisition of irregular verbs. In English, most verbs are conjugated for past tense in the same way. To make the past tense of the verb *to look*, we would say "looked." To make the past tense of the verb *to laugh*, we would say "laughed." Similarly, there's want → wanted, walk → walked, sip → sipped, and so on. The rule for making the past tense of a regular verb is basically to add "ed" to the infinitive of the verb. But English also has a boatload of verbs that don't follow the regular rule, and so are called "irregular." To make the past tense of irregular verbs, we don't add "ed" to the end, rather we have to do something else. What we do depends on the verb we are conjugating. Consider for example: go → went, think → thought, sit → sat, eat → ate, grow → grew, grind → ground. Each one of these irregular verbs is marked for past tense in its own unique way.

To speak proper English, then, children have to learn not only the regular rule for making past tenses, but also all the exceptions to the regular rule. And yet—and here is the thing—when children learn to talk, there is first a period when they seem to produce all the irregular conjugations correctly, *followed* by a period when they start producing them incorrectly. In other words, they get bad at producing irregular past tenses only after they appeared good at it. On the other hand, their mistake-making only happens after gaining experience with the past-tenses of regular verbs. They make cute, but wrong, conjugations like, "goed," "sitted," and "eated." Thus, as with swimming, there is a point during language acquisition when worse performance apparently follows better performance.

In both of these cases, the younger appears to outperform the older. The younger child who produces irregular past tense forms may very well seem more advanced than the older child who makes the cute conjugation mistakes. And it's fascinating to see a swimming baby (there are numerous examples on YouTube). Yet both are also examples of normal developmental processes in which an apparently sophisticated but actually inferior ability gives way to an apparently inferior but actually sophisticated ability. Infant swimmers are simply exercising their inborn reflexes in the absence of the more sophisticated cognitive control and intentionality characteristic of the mature swimmer. Unless it is maintained through practice, the swimming reflex eventually disappears, and the older baby looks no more impressive in a pool of water than the nonswimming adult. And the toddler who produces irregular verbs accurately on first attempt simply hasn't learned the rule for producing the past tense of regular verbs yet. When she does, she'll start making the same overregularizing mistakes as the older child. But she will emerge on the other side with a far more sophisticated understanding of grammar.

In the following text, I describe a revolutionary study that revealed another apparent regression in ability. In this study, authors Janet Werker and Richard Tees discovered that younger babies, at about 6–8 months of age, could detect language sounds that older 10–12-month-old babies could not. Unlike the examples earlier in this text, however, the early abilities of the very young 6–8-month-old never reappear in a better, stronger form when the baby gets older. In fact, the abilities seem to go away forever! But it's all good, because as you'll see, it's a crucially important developmental step for babies to lose some sound discrimination abilities to make way for the sounds of the native language they'll eventually come to master.

WERKER AND TEES (1984)

The Werker and Tees (1984) paper is well known in the land of infancy science, primarily because it helped pave the foundation for our modern understanding of how babies learn to talk. Although it didn't make the cut for the 20 most revolutionary studies in my last book, it did make the cut for the top 30. Now that several other classic papers have aged out and made room, I am privileged to share just how important this paper has been for setting the agenda for the language acquisition research that has taken place since.

Especially notable about the Werker and Tees article, at least to me, is that it didn't make the grand entrance that did so many of the other pieces described in this book. It had not the acclaim that comes with publishing in internationally lauded journals like *Science* or *Nature*. Rather, it began as a humble publication in the relatively low profile journal, *Infant Behavior and Development*. By "low profile," I don't mean to demean the journal; which is one of my favorites and one that I turn to frequently for my own publications. I just mean that the journal has a relatively narrow readership, composed almost entirely of infancy scientists. In contrast, *Science* and *Nature* are read by *all* scientists. The Werker and Tees paper made it to the top despite a very humble origin.

The article begins by describing the problem confronting the language-learning baby. The authors want to know specifically, how does the child detect and parse out the sounds that are relevant for her language? Does she start from birth with the ability to detect all possible sounds in all possible human languages, and then whittle it down from there to only those that are used in her own language? Or does she have to be exposed to her native language beforehand so that she knows which of the sounds are important to detect in the first place? It's kind of a chicken and egg problem, really.

In scientific vernacular, speech sounds are called "phonemes;" and different languages use different subsets of phonemes. In English, for example, about 40 different phonemes are used to produce the more than 1.5 million or so words found in the English language. But English is only one of nearly 7000 spoken languages. Some languages have a lot fewer phonemes, others have a lot more. According to Wikipedia, the smallest number of phonemes can be found in the Rotokas language of East Papua, New Guinea, with 11; and the greatest number of phonemes, 141, are found in the !Kung language spoken in Namibia, Botswana, and Angola. However, of all the possible phonemes that there are, only a subset are relevant for any given language. The problem for the baby is to arrive somehow at the set of sounds that are relevant for the language she is setting about to learn. If she's wrong, she'll master a bunch of speech sounds that aren't helpful in learning to speak her own language.

Within the subset of phonemes that are unique to each language, there are sometimes pairs of sounds that can only be distinguished by speakers of that language, and not by speakers of other languages. It can even seem odd to speakers of a particular language when they discover that other people sometimes cannot hear the same differences. Consider a sometimes hard to distinguish contrast in English: the sounds for "l" and "r." These two sounds are technically notated with the symbols /l/ and /r/. Of course, the sounds /l/ and /r/ are easily distinguished by English speakers, as well as by speakers of other languages that use the /l/–/r/ distinction (such as Spanish, French, and German). But most famously, the /l/–/r/ difference cannot be heard very well by speakers of Japanese. To them, the sounds are more or less interchangeable. Instead of "only," for example, they might say, "onry;" or instead of "salad," they might say "sarad." These mistakes sound funny to native English speakers, but they are unavoidable by Japanese second-language-learners, because the differences between the sounds appear arbitrary. For them, differences between the two sounds never mattered when they learned to talk. The /l/–/r/ confusion apparently even carries over into written English. When my family and I visited Kyoto several years ago, where English restaurant signage was surprisingly common, we saw many portable sidewalk chalkboards describing the "Specials of the Day." The specials were often handwritten in English. One in particular caught our attention because it said: "Happy Hour, Dlinks ¥200." My daughter Sarah, who was 9 years old at the time, asked, "What's a dlink?"

Getting back to the article, Werker and Tees noted that the scientific literature of the time supported the first possibility, that babies are born with the ability to detect and discriminate between all of the world's phonemes, and only later begin focusing on the phonemes of their own language. Available evidence from the adult literature, however, also suggested that adults cannot distinguish between all of the world's phonemes. These two pieces of evidence pointed out a looming gap in the scientific literature, which Werker and Tees outlined this way,

> *If, as suggested, infant speech perception is characterized by a high degree of initial ability and adult speech perception is more restricted, it becomes of interest to ask how and when speech perception becomes modified (i.e., limited) to more precisely match only those sound units that are used phonemically in the learner's native language.*

So their research goal was to attempt to find out just when, during the lifespan, the ability to detect differences between nonnative phonemes goes away. Preliminary research from their lab had attempted to narrow down the possible time frame. In an earlier study (i.e., Werker, Gilbert, Humphrey, & Tees, 1981), for example, they asked research participants if they could tell the difference between two sound contrasts from the Hindi language. These two pairs of sounds were very similar to one another, and notated as: /t^{h}a/ versus /d^{h}a/ and /ta/ versus /ṭa/. Of course, seeing the sounds represented by letters on this page does not convey anything close to what the phonemes actually sounded like. But it apparently wouldn't matter to monolingual English speakers like me anyway, because according to Werker and Tees, I wouldn't be able to hear either of the differences. Consistent with expectations, the researchers found that 6- to 8-month-old babies, and Hindi-speaking adults, could tell the difference between each pair of sounds, but that English-speaking adults could not. Furthermore, English-speaking 12-, 8-, and 4-year-olds were just as poor as the English-speaking adults at distinguishing the two sound pairs. Based on these findings, the authors believed that they had narrowed the time frame for the disappearance of the ability to detect nonnative speech contrasts to somewhere between 6/8 months of age and 4 years of age. The purpose of the 1984 article was to narrow the time frame even further, and maybe even identify the precise time of the disappearance of this ability.

WERKER & TEES (1984)   The Werker and Tees (1984) paper describes two main experiments and a third control experiment. The first experiment was meant to be a preamble for the second. But I think it was the second experiment that really launched the authors into superstardom because that was the one that focused on establishing a timeframe for the perception of nonnative speech contrasts. However, before tackling the timeframe question, Werker and Tees felt it necessary to take one more preliminary step. Owing to the fact that their 1981 article was one of the first to demonstrate a declining sensitivity to nonnative speech contrasts, Werker and Tees were anxious to see if their Hindi findings could be generalized to other languages. Hence, in Experiment 1 they sought to replicate their 1981 study, but used speech contrasts from a different language instead. Specifically, they used speech sounds from the "Thompson language." The Thompson language, more formally known as Nlaka'pamuctsin, is only spoken by about 400 Canadian aboriginal people in south central British Colombia, Canada.

In the Thompson language there is a particular speech contrast that involves the production of "back consonants." Back consonants are called that because they are produced in the back of the mouth, kind of in the throat. English words such as "cog" and "gawk" both begin and end with back consonants, for example. In Thompson, there are a pair of speech sounds, denoted as /k̓i/–/q̓i/, which both sound like the English phoneme /k/. Differences between these two Thompson sounds are meaningful to the Thompson people, and putting one sound or the other at the beginning of a word would produce two entirely different words. However, because English does not use these two sounds differently, Werker and Tees wondered whether babies from English-speaking households, as well as English-speaking adults, could tell them apart. What follows is a description of the procedures they employed in testing this possibility.

Experiment 1

Participants

Three groups of participants were involved: a group of 10 babies ranging in age from 6–8 months, a group of 10 English-speaking adults ranging in age from 22–35 years, and a group of 5 native Thompson-speaking adults ranging in age from 30–65 years.

Stimuli

It is not as easy as you might think to produce stimuli that allow for a test of speech sound discrimination. For one thing, in the natural world speech sounds never occur in isolation. They always occur in words. If they occur at the beginning of a word, they are always followed immediately by another speech sound; and if they occur at the end of a word, they are always preceded immediately by another speech sound. In either case, the production of the target speech sound is affected somewhat by the immediately adjacent sounds. This is called a **word context effect**. Moreover, different speakers of a language can produce a target sound very differently, and even the same speaker can produce the target sound differently on different occasions. So from a technical standpoint, it's almost impossible to get perfect fidelity on the production of a target speech sound. Nevertheless, science must go on, and Werker and Tees did the best they could to collect naturally occurring samples of the /ˋki/ and /ˋqi/ sounds from native Thompson speakers, and to ensure that they were as similar as possible to one another except for the critical contrast being tested. Werker and Tees settled on the /ˋki/ sound as it occurred in the Thompson word "ˋkixm," meaning *to fry an egg*, and the /ˋqi/ sound as it occurred in the Thompson word "ˋqixm," meaning *to make one see*. They recorded these sounds as produced by one of the Thompson speakers, and then played them back to the research participants to see if the participants could hear the difference between the two sounds.

Procedure for Infants

As with most of the infant research described in this book, Werker and Tee's procedure for testing babies on these sounds was especially fascinating. They used what is known as the "head turn paradigm." The procedure went something like this. Babies were brought into a sound-attenuated chamber, and held on the mothers' lap. Mothers sat in a chair and wore headphones, so as to prevent them from listening to the speech sounds and inadvertently cueing their babies in any way. Sitting across from the mother and baby was a research assistant who was also wearing headphones, and who kept the babies' attention by manipulating small toys. While the research assistant was playing with the toys and engaging the babies' attention, a stream of speech sounds was playing simultaneously through a loudspeaker that was located to the left of and slightly behind the baby. The stream of speech sounds was composed of repetitions of first one, and then the other, of the target speech sounds.

Located near the loudspeaker was an "electrically activated toy animal inside a smoked plexiglass box." Importantly, the toy was activated and illuminated whenever the sound stream changed from one to the other of the speech sound repetitions. As you might imagine, when the toy was activated, the babies turned their heads to look at the toy. This procedure allowed babies to associate the sound change with the appearance of the exciting, shiny mechanical toy. At first, the toy was activated immediately after the sound change; but after a few trials of conditioning the babies to turn their heads, the toy wasn't activated automatically at the sound change. Instead, it was only activated *after* babies heard the sound change and turned their heads. In other words, the toy was activated only if babies made a head turn in *anticipation* of the toy coming on. Werker and Tees required babies to turn their heads toward the toy within 4½ seconds of the sound change. If a baby turned her head too soon, before there was a sound change, or if she took too long to turn her head (longer than 4 ½ seconds), the toy wasn't activated. In this way, babies learned that the toy would turn on *only* if the sound stream changed, and then *only* if they turned their heads in time. A depiction of the procedure can be found on YouTube at:

http://www.youtube.com/watch?v=Ew5-xbc1HMk

The beauty of this technique was that it allowed Werker and Tees to infer that children could detect the sound change whenever they looked toward the toy *before* it turned on. If babies didn't turn their heads to look at the toy until *after* it turned on, it could be inferred that babies were responding to the toy itself, and not to the changes in the sound stream.

Procedure for Adults

Of course, for adults, the toy activation paradigm wasn't needed. With adults, you can just tell them what you want them to do. Adults are so much more cooperative to work with than babies. For adults, the procedure was adapted to require only button presses. Specifically, adults were supposed to press a button every time they heard the sound change from /ki/ to /q̇i/, or vice versa.

REACHING CRITERION   Werker and Tees adopted a fairly strict criterion for determining when their participants distinguished between the two sounds. Specifically, they required both babies and adults to correctly identify the sound change on 8 of the 10 trials before classifying them as able to hear the difference between the sounds. Thus, participants were only allowed to make two errors before they were categorized as non-sound-distinguishers. An error could come in one of two forms. It could be a "miss," or a failure to identify a true sound change; or it could be a "false positive," or reporting a sound change when there really wasn't one.

RESULTS

The results came out exactly as expected. All of the adult Thompson speakers, most of the babies (8 of the 10), but very few of the adult English speakers (3 of 10) reached criterion. Not only did these results replicate Werker and Tees' earlier finding that babies could distinguish speech sounds in a language without having any experience in that language; but they also supported Werker and Tees' hypothesis that over time and experience within a language, adults became relatively unable to distinguish sound contrasts in other languages.

Experiment 2

Now, the purpose of the first experiment was really just to set the stage for the second one. Experiment 1 successfully demonstrated that the effects found using Hindi speech sound contrasts could be generalized to speech sounds contrasts in another language, namely Thompson. But Experiment 1 really didn't do much in the way of identifying *when* the ability to discriminate nonnative speech sound contrasts began to go away. Experiment 1 of this study, in combination with the findings of the Werker et al. (1981) study, showed that 6- to 8-month-old babies from English-speaking households could hear the difference between certain kinds of speech sounds that English-speaking adults could no longer hear. In Experiment 2, Werker and Tees narrowed down the time frame considerably. In this experiment, instead of comparing 6–8-month-olds to adults, they compared them to slightly older babies.

Participants

The participants in Experiment 2 consisted of two groups of older babies drawn from English-speaking households. The first group consisted of 26 babies (16 girls) who ranged in age from 8 to 10 months, and the second group consisted of 20 babies (10 girls) who ranged in age from 10 to 12 months. The idea here was to compare the speech-sound-detecting abilities of these older babies to the data collected from the younger babies in the two previous experiments.

Stimuli and Procedure

The speech sound contrasts that babies were exposed to came from Hindi and Thompson: Hindi (/t^ha/ vs. /d^ha/) and Thompson (/k̓i/ vs. /q̓i/). Half of the older babies in each age group were tested using the Hindi speech sound contrast, and half were tested using the Thompson speech sound contrast. The criterion for when a baby was judged able to detect the contrast was the same as in Experiment 1, namely 8 out of 10 sound changes had to be correctly identified.

RESULTS

If Werker and Tees' goal was to identify the time that humans lose the ability to hear nonnative speech sound contrasts, they nailed it with Experiment 2. The three age groups of babies performed very differently in detecting the Hindi and Thompson speech sound contrasts. I have reproduced their results in Table 10.1.

What you see in the table are the numbers of babies who reached criterion for distinguishing the non-English speech sound contrasts, paired with the number of babies who failed.

TABLE 10.1 Detection of Nonnative Speech Sound Contrasts by Baby Age

Reached Criterion in Hindi	6–8-month-olds	8–10-month-olds	10–12-month-olds
Yes	11	8	2
No	1	4	8
Reached Criterion in Thompson	**6–8-month-olds**	**8–10-month-olds**	**10–12-month-olds**
Yes	8	8	1
No	2	6	9

Looking from left to right, you'll see that the youngest babies were very good at detecting the sound differences (86% achieved criterion), the oldest babies were very bad at detecting the sound differences (only 15% achieved criterion), and the middle babies fell somewhere in between (62% achieved criterion). Based on these results, Werker and Tees concluded, "The results provide strong support for the supposition that specific linguistic experience is necessary to maintain phonetic discrimination ability. Without such experience, there is a loss in this ability by 10 to 12 months of age."

Experiment 3 (A Control Experiment)

Although Experiment 2 was clearly the most important experiment that Werker and Tees reported in the 1984 paper, they did have some loose ends to tie up and so conducted a third experiment. Something I didn't mention in my descriptions of Experiments 1 and 2 was that Werker and Tees actually employed a screening procedure. This screening procedure required that before babies could be tested using nonnative speech contrasts, they had to reach criterion using *native* speech sound contrasts. In particular, the English-speaking babies had to first demonstrate that they could detect the difference between the two *English* sounds /ba/ and /da/.

The logic of requiring English babies to reach criterion using English speech sounds was to, "ensure that [any] failure of the infant was due to an inability to readily perceive the sound difference . . . and not due to nonspecific factors such as boredom, dirty diapers, etc." Not only did babies have to detect the English sound differences *before* they were allowed to proceed to the nonnative speech contrast test, they were tested again with the English sounds if at any point they failed to reach criterion with nonnative speech sounds. In this way, if a baby failed to reach criterion using the *nonnative* speech sounds, but were successful in reaching criterion using the *native* speech sounds immediately afterward, then it was reasonable to conclude that the baby's failure must've been due to an inability to hear the difference rather than something else such as being tired or fussy.

This control procedure made a lot of sense. However, Werker and Tees found that a disproportionate number of older babies failed the screening test. Whereas 85% of the two younger age groups passed the screening test, only 60% of the oldest babies passed the screening test. Apparently, the older babies were more interested in "visiting" the toy, instead of simply turning their head to see it. Werker and Tees reasoned that the relatively poorer performance of the oldest babies on the nonnative speech sound discrimination task may have been an artifact of fewer of the older babies passing the screening test. The purpose of Experiment 3, then, was to attempt to replicate Experiment 2 using a longitudinal design instead of a cross-sectional design.

Participants

Six babies (3 girls) were tested at three ages: 6/8 months, 8/10 months, 10/12 months. The babies were selected based on being "particularly cooperative" upon first testing. At each age, babies were tested with all three contrasts: Hindi (/tʰa/ vs. /dʰa/), Thompson (/k̓i/ vs. /q̓i/), and English (/ba/ vs. /da/).

Stimuli and Procedure

Same as before.

RESULTS

Werker and Tees found that their longitudinal data pretty much mirrored their cross-sectional data from Experiment 2. Specifically, at 6–8 months of age *all* of the babies could detect both sets of nonnative speech contrasts; at 8–10 months *only three* babies could detect both sets of nonnative speech contrasts; and at 10–12 months *none* of the babies could detect either of the nonnative speech contrasts.

DISCUSSION

In sum, across the three sets of experiments, Werker and Tees found some fairly incontrovertible evidence that 1) babies can detect sound differences in languages they have never previously heard, and that 2) this ability seems to disappear by the first birthday. These findings especially make sense if babies are born with an equipotential capacity for detecting the speech sounds of any language, and are consistent with the notion that exposure to a native language serves to whittle down babies' attention to those sound contrasts that are most relevant for speaking that language. Furthermore, Werker and Tees also point out that because first words usually start appearing on the scene at about 13 months of age, it is probably no accident that babies' brains are maximally attuned to the sounds relevant for their own language at about the same time that they are first learning to talk.

GENERAL DISCUSSION

In an article that is now more than 30 years old, Werker and Tees' research accomplished much more than simply resolving questions about the course and timeframe of nonnative speech sound discrimination. It also set the research agenda for language acquisition research that was to take place in the decades that followed. But, as with many revolutionary studies, their findings also raised more questions than they answered. For example, if by 12 months of age infants can no longer discriminate certain nonnative speech sounds, where does the ability go? Does it disappear? Can it be revived? Does the baby's commitment to discriminating native speech sounds tell us that the brain has become inflexible in discriminating novel speech sound contrasts? And what about those three English-speaking adults who could detect the Thompson speech contrasts, what made them so different from the other seven?

An unexpected outcome of this research, which I learned during a phone interview with Janet Werker, was that these findings served as a sort of Rorschach inkblot test for scientists from different theoretical perspectives. Scientists saw in these findings what they wanted to see. Nativists underscored the finding that all babies were putatively born with the ability to detect speech sound contrasts from any of the world's languages. Learning theorists highlighted the finding that experience with a native language reinforced some speech sound contrasts, and extinguished nonnative ones. Maturationists could point to the gradual emergence, over the first year of life, of a preference for native speech sound contrasts.

It also seemed that some scientists didn't quite know what to make of the findings. For example, Werker described how her first research grant proposal was rejected by the National Institutes of Health because of the antagonism of two reviewers who were against the proposal for completely opposite reasons. One of the reviewers thought her hypotheses so likely to be true that they weren't interesting; while the other reviewer thought her hypotheses so likely to be false that they weren't worth the investment.

I began this chapter by describing examples of developmental phenomena in which younger children *appear* to outperform older children. Werker and Tees' findings surely fit the bill. But it is precisely on this point that Werker believes she received the most pushback and misguided criticism from the field of infancy science. In particular, she is most frequently criticized for claiming that 6–8-month-old infants have an ability that 10–12-month-old infants do not. But, ironically, this is not a position that Werker has ever taken. Indeed, the title of the revolutionary paper speaks not to evidence for the disappearance of anything, but rather to "evidence for *perceptual reorganization*" [emphasis added]. Surely, to say that a capacity is reorganized into another capacity is not to say that a capacity disappears. "In reality," she said, "we don't really know what happens. It could be that babies develop attentional biases, or maybe there are changes in brain circuitry. To say that any capacity disappears really oversimplifies the question."

A DISTRIBUTIONAL LEARNING ACCOUNT

The modern take on Werker and Tees' effects is that they are real, and play a foundational role in children's acquisition of language. But the focus these days has been more on uncovering underlying mechanisms that might explain them. In a recent article with colleagues Henny Yeung and Katherine Yoshida, Werker believes that something called "distributional learning" may be a prime candidate to explain infants' apparent expertise in native speech sound contrasts. The impetus for using distributional learning comes from the revolutionary findings of another article in this book, namely that of Saffran, Aslin, and Newport (1996; see Chapter 11). The idea behind combining these two research traditions is based on the notion that there are statistical probabilities associated with the speech sounds babies hear in a natural speech stream, and that babies' brains can detect those statistical probabilities and deduce the likelihood that those sounds come from specific phonemic categories.

Before describing how distributional learning can be used to explain the development of infants' speech perception abilities, I need to digress a moment to explain the concept of **allophonic variation**. You'll recall from my discussion earlier, that we often make the same speech sound in different ways depending on the word we are saying. As native speakers of our language, we don't really hear the difference between any two variants of a phoneme because we categorize them as belonging to a single phoneme. But the exact same sound differences made in a different language may be very meaningful, and indicate different phonemes.

Consider the phoneme /n/. You make the /n/ sound by placing your tongue against the roof of your mouth, vibrating your vocal chords (called "voicing"), and then passing air out through your nose. However, you also make the /n/ sound slightly differently depending on the words you use it in. Take, for example, the words "tenth" and "no." To make the /n/ sound in the word *tenth*, you place your tongue to the roof of your mouth very close to your teeth. But to make the /n/ sound in the word *no*, you still place our tongue to the roof of your mouth, but it is a few millimeters further back. Try it. Put your finger on the bottom of your tongue while alternately saying the two words *tenth* and *no*, paying particular attention to where your tongue is when you get to the /n/ sound.

The fact that the /n/ sound is made in different ways in the two different words means that technically they are different sounds. A computer could detect the difference, but as human English speakers we don't *hear* the difference as reflecting different sounds, because in English we only have one phoneme for both versions. So, whenever we hear any variations of the speech sound, we still categorize it as /n/. This is allophonic variation. It is when individual speech sounds are produced differently, but are still categorized as belonging to a single phoneme. Of course, the fact that English speakers may not detect different variations of a single phoneme doesn't mean speakers of other languages would not categorize those differences as reflecting different phonemes. For the Japanese speaker, there is no difference between the sounds used to make /l/ and /r/; but for us, there is a huge difference.

With this basic understanding of allophonic variation in mind, I hope you can better understand how it is possible to test a distributional learning account of infants' expertise at identifying native speech sounds. In just such a study, Werker and colleagues were interested in finding out whether babies could form different phonemic categories based on the distribution of allophonic variations they were exposed to in an artificial speech stream. To test this possibility, the authors created a "continuum" of /d/ sounds. To make a /d/ sound, you put your tongue up against the roof of your mouth, build up a little air pressure, vibrate your vocal chords, and then release the air through your mouth in a glorious burst of 'd'-ness. However, Werker and colleagues created different variations of /d/ sounds by varying the amount of time between the voice onset and the release of air. You'll note that when you produce the /d/ sound, your vocal chords start vibrating *before* you release the air. But also notice that regardless of how long you start voicing before you release the air, you will produce a /d/ sound. The extra voicing doesn't change anything. But if you wait to start your voicing until after you release the air, you won't produce a /d/ sound at all, rather, you'll make a /t/ sound instead.

So Werker and colleagues digitally created 8 different /d/ sounds. Some had early voice onset times, others had later voice onset times, but all voice onset times happened before the release of air, and all were perceived by adults as belonging to the /d/ phonemic category. They numbered the /d/ sounds from 1 (very early voice onset time) to 8 (very late onset time), with /d/ sounds numbered 4 and 5 representing something of a midpoint between 1 and 8.

Werker and colleagues then played the various /d/ sounds to two groups of babies in one of two different "distributional environments." In one distributional environment, babies were exposed to a relatively high proportion of 4s and 5s, with relatively few exposures to the more extreme /d/ sounds such as 1s and 8s. This was called a unimodal distributional environment because the highest proportion of /d/ sounds were those around the midpoint of voice onset time, and the lowest proportion of /d/ sounds came from the extremes. In the other distributional environment, babies were exposed to a relatively high proportion of 2s and 7s, but relatively few of the midpoint /d/ sounds (i.e., 4s and 5s). This was called a bimodal distributional environment because the highest proportion of /d/ sounds were those that came from the higher and lower ends of the continuum, and not near the midpoint.

For Werker and colleagues, these two distributional environments were analogous to what one might expect babies to encounter in two different languages, if those languages categorized /d/ sounds differently. In a language such as English, in which the entire range of /d/ sounds reflects a single phoneme, Werker and colleagues hypothesized that infants would be exposed to a unimodal distribution; characterized by a lot of midpoint /d/ sounds, and fewer /d/ sounds at the extremes. In another language, in which different ends of the /d/ sound continuum reflect two different phonemes, Werker and colleagues hypothesized that infants might be exposed to a bimodal distribution; characterized by few midpoint /d/ sounds, and a large number of the more extreme /d/ sounds. The bimodal distribution in this latter language, in fact, would suggest that there isn't a single phonemic category at all, but rather two distinct phonemic categories.

Werker and colleagues found that 6–8-month-old babies, who were exposed to a 2-minute speech stream of unimodally distributed /d/ sounds, became unable to distinguish the most deviant /d/ sounds from each other (1s vs. 8s). In contrast, babies who were exposed to a 2-minute speech stream of bimodally distributed /d/ sounds, remained capable of discriminating the endpoints. In other words, babies seemed to form *different* phonemic categories based on the distribution of speech sounds they heard. If babies were exposed to a unimodal distribution of /d/ sounds, they seemed to treat those allophonic variations as reflecting a single phoneme. But if babies were exposed to a bimodal distribution of /d/ sounds, they seemed to treat the variations as reflecting two different phonemes.

SUMMARY

At the beginning of this chapter I suggested that the ability of very young babies to discriminate between speech sounds in other languages, when older babies can not, is a relatively advanced ability. It is generally true that the more things a person can discriminate between, the more advanced she is. But I hope it is also clear that the disappearance, or maybe "going underground," of an ability does not necessarily imply any sort of developmental regression. Sometimes the apparent loss of an ability actually indicates developmental sophistication. Werker and Tees' babies are a case in point. For it is with those babies that we can see that infants' progressively narrower focus on and preference for native speech-sound contrasts over nonnative ones, reflects the kind of specialization that characterizes emerging expertise in speech perception.

Reference

http://www.youtube.com/watch?v=Ew5-xbc1HMk

Bibliography

Michel, J. B., Shen, Y. K., Aiden, A. P., Veres, A., Gray, M. K., Pickett, J. P., . . . & Aiden, E. L. (2011). Quantitative analysis of culture using millions of digitized books. *Science, 331*(6014), 176–182.

Miyawaki, K., Strange, W., Verbrugge, R., Liberman, A. M., Jenkins, J. J., & Fujimura, O. (1975). An effect of linguistic experience: The discrimination of [r] and [l] by native speakers of Japanese and English. *Perception & Psychophysics, 18*, 331–340.

Werker, J. F., Gilbert, J. H. V., Humphrey, K., & Tees, R. C. (1981). Developmental aspects of cross-language speech perception. *Child Development, 52*, 349–355.

Werker, J. F., Yeung, H. H., & Yoshida, K. A. (2012). How do infants become experts at native-speech perception? *Current Directions in Psychological Science, 21*, 221–226.

Questions for Discussion

1. "Minimal pairs" are pairs of speech sounds in a language that are almost exactly alike except for one critical feature. For example, /d/ and /t/ differ only as a function of voice onset time. Can you identify pairs of sounds in English that fit this description? Similarly, are there pairs of sounds in other languages that you have a hard time distinguishing between?

2. A number of methodologies for studying infant cognition have been described throughout this book. Would it be possible to use any of these other methodologies to assess infant speech perception? If so, which ones and how would you do it?

3. Does the ability to distinguish nonnative speech contrasts demonstrate a unique human preparedness to learn language? How might evidence that other animals can make the same distinctions impact the notion that language is a distinctly human endeavor?

11

Welcome to the Machine

Statistical Learning by 8-Month-Old Infants

Saffran, J. R., Aslin, R. N., & Newport, E. L. (1996). *Science, 274*, 1926–1928. (RANK 14)

Seven decades ago, the question of how children learned to talk was probably among the most challenging ones in all of child psychology. In terms of finding the ultimate answer, unfortunately, things haven't changed much since then. But it's not for lack of effort. Indeed, we have spent incalculable time and money on the topic, and we really have made considerable progress. Perhaps more than anything else, we've learned that it's an impressively complex question.

One thing we have learned is that it's probably better to describe the problem as one of children *acquiring language*, rather than one of *learning to talk*. The phrase "learning to talk," carries with it a whole bunch of additional meanings that the phrase "acquiring language" does not, and which we would wish to avoid. In particular, the verb "to learn" means *to gain from experience*; whereas, the verb "to acquire" remains silent on whether language comes from experience. You can acquire something just by letting it develop or mature—take armpit hair for example—regardless of environmental experience. In the interests of scientific neutrality then, in which we want to avoid any assertions that children necessarily learn language from experience, it may be preferable to say that children "acquire language." Why does the distinction matter? It matters because technically we don't actually know whether language develops on its own or comes from experience. Simply asserting that children *learn* language puts the cart before the horse.

Still, there is no denying that some parts of language definitely are learned through experience. For example, the reason Italians learn Italian, rather than Japanese, is because Italian is the language they are bathed in from birth onward. There is also no denying that some parts of language definitely are provided through genetic programming. For example, the reason humans are able to produce speech sounds is because of the respiro-articulatory systems they were provided by biology. No other animal can produce as many different sounds, or as rapidly, as humans. Of course, these points are relatively trivial, and not especially worth debating. The exciting topics of modern language acquisition research are to be found in those areas where the relative roles played by environment and biology are not yet fully known.

One of those areas is the subject of this chapter, fueled by the work of Jenny Saffran and her major professors Dick Aslin and Elissa Newport. Ranked 14th on the list of the most revolutionary studies published in child psychology since 1960, and published in the journal *Science*, their 1996 article "Statistical Learning by 8-Month-Old Infants" demonstrated that at least one major nontrivial aspect of language acquisition *could* be attributed to learning from experience. This finding, by itself, is pretty cool. But the essence of their article had implications for the field of child psychology that extended far beyond the domain of language acquisition proper. For one thing, it revealed the brain to be an extremely capable association-detecting device that could potentially operate on many different kinds of environmental stimuli. But it also revealed these powerful association-detecting abilities to be present in the first year of life. No wonder the article became so famous.

Before describing the very broad and powerful learning mechanism Saffran and colleagues uncovered, it is useful to consider their original research goals in the context of the broader language acquisition picture. By considering the overarching scope of the language acquisition problem, as well as how scientists have carved up the issues, it is easier to see how pursuing a relatively narrow research objective can sometimes result in a very broad and powerful scientific outcome.

Background Context

What does the science of language acquisition involve then? The short answer is "a lot." There are whole books and journals dedicated to the study of language acquisition, so I cannot hope to do service to anything approaching a full account here. But I can throw some things out there that may scratch the surface of the tip of the iceberg.

It's probably mostly true to say that researchers have framed the language acquisition problem in one of three general ways. One framing has been to focus on the biological, psychological, and social systems involved in the individual's comprehension and production of language. Within this framing, the processing of human language requires at a minimum systems for detecting linguistic information in the environment, systems for processing linguistic information as it's represented inside the person, and systems for distributing and projecting linguistic understanding back into the environment. Of particular interest here is the role that biological, psychological, and social systems play in facilitating (or inhibiting) this input → processing → output cycle. With this as the general research orientation, scientists interested in the biological aspects of language acquisition have focused on the roles of the temporal (auditory), occipital (visual), and prefrontal (associational) cortices of the brain. Scientists interested in the psychological aspects of language acquisition have focused on the roles of the motivational, attentional, memorial, and emotional systems. And scientists interested in the social aspects of language acquisition have focused on the characteristics of the speaker, the characteristics of the listener, and the characteristics of the environment. But make no mistake; every one of these topics, and many, many more, has been the subject of intensive scrutiny by hundreds of scientists, with their students and laboratories dedicated to their pet issue.

A second way of framing the problem has been to think of language as comprising various component rule systems. To study language acquisition from this perspective would be to study how children gain mastery over these rule systems. Five rule systems have received the lion's share of research attention; namely, phonology, morphology, semantics, grammar, and pragmatics. Study of the phonological rule system has emphasized how children learn the sounds and sound combinations relevant for their native language; for example, why the sound combination /t/ + /s/ can end an English word but not begin one. Study of the morphological rule system has emphasized how children combine root words with suffixes and prefixes that are meaningful in the language; for example, how verbs are marked for tense and nouns are marked for plurality. Think how important it is for the young toddler to have one *cookie* versus two *cookies*. Study of the semantic rule system has emphasized how children learn to combine words in a sentence based on meaning; for example, why the phrase "bachelor's wife" is illegal and the phrase "green ideas" is weird. Study of the grammatical rule system has emphasized how children learn the proper word order for their language; for example, acquiring the subject-verb-object structure of English instead of the subject-object-verb structure of Japanese. Finally, study of the pragmatic rule system has emphasized how children learn to use language in socially appropriate ways; for example, when they simplify speech to younger children and don't cuss in front of adults and teachers.

A third way of framing language acquisition as a research question has been to identify the challenges and barriers confronting children when entering language in the first place. This third framing seems to be what attracted the research attention of Saffran and colleagues, and a great many other scientists as well. Scientists interested in the acquisition of first words were among those first interested in the problem of language acquisition from this third perspective. Researchers in this domain all seem intrigued by the famous "conundrum" proposed by philosopher Willard van Orman Quine in 1960. Kathy Hirsch-Pasek and colleagues describe Quine's condundrum this way:

> To learn a word, infants must first segment the sound stream, discover a world of objects, actions, and events, and then map the word from the sound stream (or visual stream in sign languages) onto the referent. . . . The world provides an infinite number of possible word-to-world mappings. How is a child to learn how the word maps onto the referent?

To illustrate this logical dilemma graphically, Quine proposed a hypothetical example similar to the following. A linguist embarks upon a journey to a previously unknown land, to visit a previously unknown people, who speak a previously unknown language. The linguist is greeted at the boat by a member of the tribe, and as they walk together through the tribal lands, a distant rabbit hops into view. Upon seeing the rabbit, the tribesman points and utters "guvagai!" The linguist might assume that the word *guvagai* means "rabbit." But why would the linguist assume this, since the meaning "rabbit" is only one possibility for an otherwise unknown word? *Guvagai* could also refer to the color of the rabbit, the texture of the rabbit, a part of the rabbit (e.g., its tall ears), or the motion of the rabbit. Of course, *guvagai* might not be a single word at all, and may instead mean something like "it's time to hunt." Or if the tribesman is superstitious, it might mean "It's going to rain soon."

In sum, as Quine pointed out, it is quite impossible to learn words this way. The situation confronting the language-acquiring child is not all that much different. How is the child to make sense of all those sounds coming out of the mouths of all those people around him? How is he even to know that sound-strings have meaning let alone what those meanings are?

There is no way to overcome an impossibility of course. But impossibilities have never kept scientists from trying. In an effort to bypass Quine's conundrum, some researchers have proposed possible, but very hypothetical, "word-learning constraints" that limit the range of possible word meanings that novice word-learners have to worry about. Such constraints may at least provide children with a kind of attentional blinder that could serve to facilitate a one-to-one linking of words with real-world objects. If real, these constraints could serve a sort of bootstrapping function to help children gain a foothold into language. About a half-dozen word-learning constraints have been proposed in all, but here are a couple of examples to make the point.

The "whole object assumption" is a constraint, presumably located somewhere in the child's brain or mind, theorized to more or less force her to apply new words she hears onto whole objects in the environment. The whole object assumption would allow (or force?) the linguist above to assume that the word *guvagai* referred to the whole rabbit, rather than a limb of the rabbit, the color of the rabbit, or the texture of the rabbit.

The "principle of mutual exclusivity," also internal to the child, prevents a child from allowing an object to have two different labels. If a child already knows the word for cup, for example, then any other label would be disallowed. So if a child was holding a cup, and you said "Hey Jimmy, hand me the drosopheme," the child would know you didn't mean the cup, since he already knows the label for that object.

Word-learning constraints such as these are nice and convenient devices that have helped scientists punch their way out of Quine's brown paper bag. But there are at least three major problems with word learning constraints. First is that no one has ever seen one. Constraints are entirely hypothetical entities, proposed to solve the challenging problem of entering into language. There is evidence in support of constraints, but supporting evidence does not prove their existence.

The second problem has to do with how these constraints get "into" the child in the first place. Are children born with them, or are they learned from experience? If constraints are to be taken seriously as viable word-learning mechanisms, they must be available early enough to aid children in learning their first words. For most typically developing children, this would be around 8 months of age, when children show their first signs of word understanding.

Finally, the third problem is not so much a limitation as a question of logical priority. The usefulness of word-learning constraints is entirely dependent on the child's ability to parse the speech stream so that he knows which groups of sounds are eligible to serve as object labels in the first place. How can a child apply a novel label to a novel object unless he is able to break out the novel label from the rest of the speech stream? This is surely no small achievement for the young baby.

Consider the problem from this perspective. If someone speaks to you in English, as a native speaker, the word boundaries are obvious. The speaker doesn't pause between the English words, but you feel like he does. Because you speak the language, your mind automatically identifies the boundaries between words; but in reality, there are no pauses. When someone is speaking a foreign language, in contrast, you may know intellectually that the speaker is saying words, and that there are word boundaries, but you cannot detect any of them. And there are absolutely no pauses in the speech stream for you to use as a guide. So you can imagine the plight of the very young baby who doesn't even have the benefit of knowing there are words to be parsed. Here is where the work of scientist Jenny Saffran and colleagues comes in. It was precisely this question of infant speech segmentation that piqued their interest and provoked their now revolutionary study.

SAFFRAN, ASLIN, & NEWPORT (1996)

In the introduction of their article, Jenny Saffran, Richard Aslin, and Elissa Newport position their speech-segmentation study within the larger framework of language acquisition, much as I have done here. But they go on further to position the issue of language acquisition within the even larger framework of things organisms need to do in order to survive. In doing so, they make the point that survival in all organisms depends minimally on the ability of the individual to extract and use information from the environment to some productive end. For some organisms, survival depends on the ability to extract that information quickly, effortlessly, and accurately.

One major talking point that comes up whenever scientists discuss survival, is whether an individual's survival skills are built into the organism (known as "experience-independent") or are learned from experience (known as "experience-dependent"). And so it is for Saffran et al. But unlike with other species, a major survival skill for humans is the ability to extract meaningful *linguistic* information from the social environment. Other animals may pay attention to the auditory and visual signals given off by members of their own species, but they do not use *language* to aid in their survival as humans do. Hence, an important scientific question that applies to human survival is the extent to which the ability to extract meaningful linguistic information is experience-independent or experience-dependent.

As already noted, both experience-independent and experience-dependent elements are involved in children's extraction of linguistic information from the environment. Yet, despite the fact that linguistic information can be extracted through both experience-independent and experience-dependent mechanisms, scientific study of these two kinds of mechanisms has not been fair and balanced. Saffran et al. raise the possibility that historically too much emphasis has been placed on experience-independent mechanisms, while too little emphasis has been placed on experience-dependent factors. They wrote:

> In the domain of language acquisition, two facts have supported the interpretation that experience-independent mechanisms are both necessary and dominant. First, highly complex forms of language production develop extremely rapidly. Second, the language input available to the young child is both incomplete and sparsely represented compared to the child's eventual linguistic abilities.

In their effort to even the score, they set out to explore whether certain experience-*dependent* mechanisms could also be shown to support language acquisition; and if so, which ones.

The focus of their efforts was on whether 8-month-old babies had the skill to isolate, or separate out, individual words in the adult speech stream; and if so, how they did it. Saffran et al. wondered in particular whether there might be any cues present in the physical parameters of the speech stream that babies could use to help them demarcate boundaries between words. This was surely an important possibility because if the physical parameters of the speech stream could provide cues as to word boundaries, then scientists wouldn't have to depend on hypothetical word-learning constraints built into the child to explain children's recognition of word boundaries. Instead, the word boundary information would be contained in the speech stream itself, and it would simply be a matter of the child detecting it. Once word boundaries could be detected, it would then be just a matter of mapping those segmented words onto real-world objects.

So what kind of information in the speech stream could possibly serve to mark word boundaries for preverbal babies? Saffran and colleagues thought that the most likely candidate would be the **transitional probability** of speech sounds. How does one determine the transitional probability of sounds in a speech stream? Formally, the transitional probability is defined as the probability of one sound occurring, given that another sound just occurred. If there were only one word in a language, say that word was "baby," then the transitional probability of the sound "-by," given the sound "ba-," would be 1.00, since the sound "-by" ALWAYS follows the sound "ba-." But to my knowledge, there is no language that has only one word, and so calculating transitional probabilities for real languages is not so straightforward.

The best way I know to explain the idea of the transitional probabilities in languages with more than one word, as when explaining most complicated ideas, is to oversimplify the concept to the point of absurdity so that it's very hard to miss the point. So let's apply the concept of the transitional probability to just about the simplest possible example of a speech stream in which word boundaries can still be found, and that is to use a language with only two words.

Let's suppose the two words in this absurdly simple language were: momee & dadee. Let's suppose further in this absurdly simple language, that every possible utterance could never be longer than two words. Theoretically, you could have utterances longer than two words simply by repeating the same word over and over. I could, for example utter the following sentence: momeemomeemomeedadeemomeedadee. In this utterance I am stringing together six words, but I am only doing so because I am repeating each of the words more than once.

So if we limit the number of possible utterances to those no longer than two words, how many different possible multiword utterances could there be? The answer is, four. The four possible utterances would be:

1. Momeedadee
2. Dadeemomee
3. Momeemomee
4. Dadeedadee

Notice that I wrote these words so that the boundaries aren't depicted in any obvious way, which sort of represents the word segmenting problem faced by a baby. So if there are only two possible words, and only four possible utterances, the job of the baby is to figure out which sounds in the speech stream are involved in making up a word, and which sounds in the speech stream are involved in making up a word boundary. Again, the idea of the transitional probability comes into play when figuring out how likely it is for one sound to follow another sound.

To see how this works, let's recognize that in this made up language, there are only four possible sounds (I realize that I am equating "sound" with "syllable" here, but I am trying to simplify the explanation). The four possible sounds are: 1) mo, 2) mee, 3) da, and 4) dee. If we were to rewrite the four utterances from the paragraph above in terms of the sound sequences, we would have:

1. mo + mee + da + dee
2. da + dee + mo + mee
3. mo + mee + mo + mee
4. da + dee + da + dee

So in this absurdly oversimplified language, with absurdly few words, and absurdly few possible utterances, there are only so many ways that sounds can precede and follow each other. But nevertheless, the patterns are identifiable. For example, whenever the sound "mee" happens, it ALWAYS happens after the sound "mo." And whenever the sound "da" happens, it is ALWAYS followed by the sound "dee." But this isn't true for all other possible sound combinations is it? The sound "mo" only follows the sound "dee" 50% of the time, and the sound "mo" NEVER follows the sound "da." All in all, there are 16 possible sound combinations, and each sound combination has a particular probability associated with it. Using the four utterances above as the population of all possible utterances, the probabilities of any one sound following any other sound looks like this:

da follows da 0% of the time	mo follows da 0% of the time
da follows dee 50% of the time	mo follows dee 50% of the time
da follows mo 0% of the time	mo follows mo 0% of the time
da follows mee 50% of the time	mo follows mee 50% of the time
dee follows da 100% of the time	mee follows da 0% of the time
dee follows dee 0% of the time	mee follows dee 0% of the time
dee follows mo 0% of the time	mee follows mo 100% of the time
dee follows mee 0% of the time	mee follows mee 0% of the time

These percentages are exactly what Saffran et al. were referring to when they introduced the idea of the transitional probability, which is why they thought transitional probabilities could be useful in marking word boundaries for babies. Each probability (we can also call it a percentage) tells us something about whether a particular sound in a speech stream is part of a word, part of a word boundary, or neither. It works like this. Whenever the transitional probability is 100%, then we can infer that the second sound is part of the same word as the first sound. Whenever the transitional probability is 0%, we know that the two sounds never occur in natural speech in that order, and so they can't be part of the same word, and they can't mark a boundary between two words. But notice something interesting. Whenever the transitional probability is somewhere between 100% and 0%, that particular sound combination necessarily contains a word boundary. In the example above, there are four times when the transitional probability falls between 100% and 0%:

- when da follows dee (as in utterance #4 above),
- when da follows mee (as in utterance #1),
- when mo follows dee (as in utterance #2), and
- when mo follows mee (as in utterance #3).

If you've followed this line of reasoning, then you may appreciate the significance of three things. First, information about word boundaries really is carried within the speech stream itself. Thus, babies don't have to know any word meanings in advance, nor do they even have to know what language is being spoken. Second, knowing where one word ends and the next one begins can be learned entirely through experience, through mere exposure to the spoken language and through some sort of ability to perform statistical calculations of the transitional probabilities. Third, and finally, an organism that can detect pairings of sounds in the environment, and calculate statistical transitional probabilities (and remember them), has the skill for word segmentation.

Ok, so these were the facts that served as the starting point for Saffran et al.'s study. But even though they knew that transitional probabilities carried information about word boundaries, they had no idea whether babies could calculate transitional probabilities sufficiently so as to identify those word boundaries. To demonstrate that babies actually could engage in word segmentation would require actually testing some babies. And so, over the course of two experiments described in the same article, that is what they did.

Experiment 1

METHOD

Participants

Twenty-four babies from American-English speaking homes.

Materials

The experimenters made up an artificial language consisting of four nonsense words, *tupiro*, *bidaku*, *padoti*, *golabu*, and then programmed a speech synthesizer to produce a two-minute "speech stream" in which each word was spoken repeatedly in a random order. The speech stream was slightly more complicated than the example I gave above, but the principles are the same. Some syllables *ALWAYS* followed certain other syllables (e.g., "da" always followed "bi"), some syllables *NEVER* followed certain other syllables (e.g., "do" never followed "bi"), and some syllables *SOMETIMES* followed certain other syllables (e.g., "pa" sometimes followed "ku"). Remember it's the third case—when syllables *SOMETIMES* follow certain other syllables—where word boundaries are found.

An example of the speech stream Saffran et al. presented to babies was: *bidakupadotigolabu-bidaku*. The only rule was that no word could be presented twice in a row. The speech synthesizer generated a "female" voice that "talked" at a rate of 270 syllables per minute. There were no pauses, stress differences, or other physical cues to word boundaries available in the speech stream.

In this made-up language, the *only* cue to any word boundaries were the transitional probabilities between syllable combinations. Moreover, the only syllable combinations that could produce transitional probabilities of less than 1.00 and greater than 0.00 were those that included the final syllable of one word followed immediately by the initial syllable of a different word. Take for example the final syllable of *tupiro*, which would be "ro." Which syllables could possibly follow "ro?" There are three. Syllables following "ro" in this synthesized speech stream could be "bi," "pa," and "go." Thus, because three different syllables could possibly follow "ro," the transitional probability of any syllable pair beginning with "ro" would be 0.33. Thus, there is a 1/3 probability that "ro" would be followed by "bi," a 1/3 probability that it would be followed by "pa," and a 1/3 probability that it would be followed by "go." The point is that because the transitional probability of any syllable pair beginning with "ro" is less than 1.00 and greater than 0.00, we can conclude that any syllable pair beginning with "ro" will mark a word boundary.

Procedure

Given these speech stream parameters, the goal of Experiment 1 was to see if babies could learn the syllable sequences. It was important to establish that babies could indeed learn the syllable sequences before moving on to Experiment 2, where they actually tested infants' skills at word segmentation.

In Experiment 1, the first step was to have babies listen to the full two minutes of synthesized speech. Then babies were tested to see if they could distinguish the sound sequences they heard in the speech stream from those they didn't. Saffran et al. performed this test by having babies listen to four more "words." Two of these words were familiar sound sequences from the just-heard speech stream (e.g., *tupiro* & *golabu*). Let's call these "old test words." But two of the words were new. These "new test words" were made up of the same sounds from the just-heard speech stream, but the sounds were paired differently than what babies had just heard in the speech stream; for example, *dapiku* and *tilado*. Saffran et al. assumed that if babies had learned the four original words in the speech stream, they would show relatively little interest in the old test words (because they had just heard them in the two minute speech stream), and much interest in the new test words (because the words were made of new sound combinations).

RESULTS

Saffran et al. found that babies did indeed recognize the words in the speech stream. The babies showed significantly more interest in the new test words than in the old test words, as evidenced by how long they listened to the two kinds of words. They listened to the new test words an average of 8.85 seconds, and to the old test words an average of 7.97 seconds. This may not seem like a big difference, but it was statistically significant.

DISCUSSION

The fact that babies listened longer to the new test words than the old test words is interesting, especially since both sets of test words were made up from the same syllables contained in the just-presented, 2-minute speech stream. The only difference between the new and old test words was the order of the syllables contained within them. The old test words had old syllables arranged in the original order, while the new test words had old syllables arranged in a new order. When babies showed different levels of interest to the two kinds of words, they seemed to be saying that they noticed that the order of the syllables had changed. The babies seemed to recognize that the new test words were different from the old test words. Saffran et al. concluded, "Thus, 8-month-old infants are capable of extracting serial order information after only 2 min of listening experience."

Of course, recognizing that certain syllables go together in a certain order does not mean that the babies identified the word boundaries. Babies could have learned that "bu" always follows "la," without learning that "bu" occurs at the end of a word. So Saffran et al. conducted Experiment 2. In this second study, Saffran et al. set out to test explicitly whether babies could identify syllable combinations that differed as a function of different transitional probabilities.

Experiment 2

METHOD

Participants

Another twenty-four 8-month-old babies from American-English-speaking households.

Materials

The format of the presentation of the speech stream was the same as in Experiment 1, although different words were used. This time the words were: *pabiku, tibudo, golatu*, and *daropi*. Although these words were not exactly the same as in Experiment 1, you can see that they were very similar, and at least contained the same syllables as in Experiment 1.

What was different about Experiment 2 was how the test words were constructed. Remember from Experiment 1 that the new test words differed from the old test words based on the serial order of their syllables. Old test words contained syllables in the same order as heard in the 2-minute speech stream; new test words contained syllables in a different order than heard in the 2-minute speech stream.

In Experiment 2, however, the test words were not based on syllable order. Rather, they were based on whether or not the syllable combinations crossed a word boundary. This part gets complicated, so read slowly, attentively, and maybe even repeatedly. The four test words used in Experiment 2 were as follows:

Not Crossing Word Boundaries	Crossing Word Boundaries
pabiku, tibudo	tudaro, pigola

If you compare these four test words to the four speech stream words—which, as a reminder, were *pabiku, tibudo, golatu, and daropi*—you can see that the two test words on the left contain the exact syllable sequences as were in the 2-minute speech stream, and they are in the same order as heard in the 2-minute speech stream.

But the syllable sequences in the two test words on the right were also presented in the 2-minute speech stream, and they also occurred in the same order as originally presented in the 2-minute speech stream. It's just that the syllable sequences on the right occurred less frequently than the syllable sequences on the left. For example, the only time the syllable sequence "tudaro" happened in the speech stream, was when the word *golatu* was followed by the word *daropi*. When *golatu* was followed by *daropi*, then technically, children heard the syllable sequence "tudaro," because they heard the last syllable of the word *golatu* followed by the first two syllables of the word *daropi*: "tu" + "daro" = "tudaro." They just didn't hear it very often in the 2-minute speech stream since two other words could also follow golatu.

In sum, the only difference between the two sets of test words in Experiment 2 is that the syllables in the words on the left *did not* cross word boundaries, whereas the syllables in the words on the right *did* cross word boundaries. If you have followed well up to this point, we can move on to Saffran et al.'s expectations and findings. If not, please read through this section again because the methodological design was very important, crafty, and ingenious, but also crucial for understanding the findings.

RESULTS

As in Experiment 1, Saffran et al. hypothesized that babies would show different levels of interest in the two sets of test words. They expected babies to show little interest in the words on the left, because those words contained syllable sequences the babies had just been listening to in the 2-minute speech stream. In contrast, they expected babies to show more interest in the words on the right, because even though those words also contained syllable sequences found in the speech stream, the syllable combinations in the words on the right occurred relatively infrequently compared to the words on the left.

Saffran et al.'s data exactly confirmed their expectations. They found that babies were more interested in the words on the right (listening to them an average of 7.60 seconds) than in the words on the left (listening to them an average of 6.77 seconds). What this means is that babies could tell the difference between infrequently occurring syllable sequences and frequently occurring ones. But more importantly, precisely because infrequently occurring syllable sequences in a speech stream serve as flags for marking word boundaries, their findings showed that babies as young as 8 months of age had the skill to demarcate word boundaries based on nothing more than the transitional probability of one given syllable following another given syllable.

GENERAL DISCUSSION

Although both experiments focused on the specific question of whether babies could use information about the transitional probabilities of syllables in a speech stream to identify word boundaries, the significance of these findings potentially extends far beyond the domain of word segmentation. The fact that babies *were* able to identify word boundaries suggests that maybe they have something like a statistical probability detector in their brain. And if babies do have a capacity for detecting statistical probabilities, perhaps they can use it to detect statistical probabilities of any pair of environmental events; not just those used to mark word boundaries. Not only might babies use this statistical probability detector to identify the regularities of other aspects of language, they might even be able to extend it to entirely different areas of learning. There is nothing inherent to the concept of a statistical probability detector that would necessarily limit it to word segmentation.

If babies' statistical probability detectors have broad enough application, then child psychologists may no longer have a need for nativist accounts when explaining the many other very cool and fascinating things babies do. Scientists are trained to seek out theoretical parsimony, which basically means that all things being equal, a simpler theory is a better theory. So it is surely far simpler to theorize that babies can use one mechanism—a statistical probability detector—to quickly detect patterns of association that form the basis of most or all knowledge sets, than to say that babies must be born with all possible knowledge sets.

Let me take a moment to explain what I mean here by way of example. Take the work of the famous linguist Noam Chomsky. Beginning with his revolutionary 1957 book *Linguistic Structures* (which I featured in my previous edition), Chomsky attempted to resolve the problem of how children could acquire the grammar of their native language by suggesting that all children are simply *born with* a more or less universal grammar. He reasoned that this universal grammar—which I think of as a kind of "seed language"—must be present in children from birth, for how else could children become so proficient at picking up the grammar of their native language so quickly (by about 3 years of age), with so little exposure to all the various bits of grammar in their language? And how else could children produce grammatically creative utterances they've never heard before?

From Chomsky's perspective, an innate seed language would fit the bill perfectly because it would outfit children from birth with such grammatical basics as subject, verb, and object, that children wouldn't have to learn on their own. If children were provided a seed language innately, the only thing they *would* need to learn would be those unique elements of their specific native language. For example, English speakers, but not Russian and Japanese speakers, would have to learn that their language requires the use of articles such as "the" and "a;" while Spanish and French speakers, but not English speakers, would have to learn that their language marks nouns with grammatical gender.

Proposing an innate grammar avoided one set of theoretical problems. But arguably it introduced an even larger set. For one thing, it implied that grammatical competence must somehow be coded in the genes. And if grammar is coded in the genes, how did it get there evolutionarily; are there way-points along the evolutionary timeline in which prehistoric humanoid forms had only pieces of a grammar; wouldn't the existence of genetic deficits be possible to the extent that modern children might learn only, say, 75% of a grammar? And if grammar is uniquely genetically coded, like an elbow or a knee, shouldn't it function relatively independently of other cognitive abilities, such as perception, memory, or attention? Yet, delays in cognitive functioning are commonly associated with delays in grammatical functioning.

To some, the proposition of an innate grammar is downright supernatural, since it depends on accepting a premise on faith, in the absence of evidence. Yet if children don't have a seed language, how else can they bootstrap themselves into grammatical competence so quickly and easily? Chomsky was right that an exclusive reliance on traditional reinforcement/punishment theory is out of the question. Shaping of grammatical competence through operant conditioning would take too long, and children are well known to produce utterances they've never been reinforced for.

WELCOME TO THE MACHINE

What an ideal platform for the release of Saffran et al.'s data on statistical learning! Their construct takes advantage of the brain's well-known capacity for detecting patterns of environmental information. Moreover, because the statistical probability detector is potentially an all-purpose machine, it could be retooled as necessary for detecting statistical probabilities in all domains; not just that of word boundaries. To the extent that the statistical probability detector does excel at the specific task of word segmentation, it does so primarily because the parameters of word segmentation are well-suited to the capabilities of a statistical probability detecting machine.

In their article summary, Saffran et al. make three very important points about how their statistical probability-detecting machine ought to drive child psychological science as we move forward. They write:

> [T]he existence of computational abilities that extract structure so rapidly suggests that it is premature to assert a priori how much of the striking knowledge base of human infants is primarily a result of experience-independent mechanisms. In particular, some aspects of early development may turn out to be best characterized as resulting from innately biased statistical learning mechanisms rather than innate knowledge. If this is the case, then the massive amount of experience gathered by infants during the first postnatal year may play a far greater role in development than has previously been recognized.

The authors first suggest that we may be better off if we focus our scientific attention on how statistical learning mechanisms extract information from the environment, than on the specific kinds of knowledge structures a baby has in her possession. If we do this, we will spend much less time arguing about what babies know, and much more time discovering how babies get to know it.

Second, because we should be focusing on how statistical learning mechanisms extract information from the environment, and because in so doing we are less concerned on the specific knowledge sets that babies possess, we can spend considerably more time discovering how statistical learning has very broad-based applications that extend beyond questions of grammar acquisition and word segmentation.

Finally, they make the very interesting point that nativist stances on scientific questions—such as the assumption that children are born with grammar—are premature. Before adopting a nativist position on some scientific issue or debate, which as I have argued above is not an especially parsimonious position to take, we should rule out other simpler explanations, such as that grammar may be acquired by a general, all-purpose, statistical learning machine.

To be clear, the authors are not especially antagonistic to nativist positions, at least not entirely. Indeed, they recognize that their broad-based, all-purpose statistical learning machine must itself be innate. They also describe its functioning as being "innately biased," by which they mean that it is innately built to give preference to certain kinds of environmental information over others. One empirical test of this possibility was actually conducted with a group of French-speaking college students (as opposed to 8-month-old babies) by Bonatti and colleagues. These authors hypothesized that consonants might carry different kinds of statistical information than vowels, and probably more relevant information that could be used for the purpose of singling out unknown words from a foreign-language speech stream. They found that indeed, after being exposed to a speech-stream similar to Saffran et al., adult learners could form transitional probabilities across consonants but not vowels.

CONCLUSIONS

My goal in this chapter was to place the revolutionary work of Saffran and her colleagues against a backdrop of the very large scientific problem of explaining how children learn to talk. I stated at the outset that not much has changed in the last 65 years, and in two ways that is true. If the point of reference is that we didn't know how children learn to talk in 1957, then it is still true that we don't know how children learn to talk now. But as a field, we know so much more about the problem compared to then, and a lot of great minds have spent a lot of time thinking about and testing all manner of hypotheses aimed at addressing this problem. But there is another interesting way in which not much has changed in the last seven decades.

It has been said that what goes around comes around. So it is with great irony that seven decades ago, Chomsky shook up child psychology by challenging the dominant viewpoint of child language acquisition at the time, which was the learning-based theory of B. F. Skinner. As already noted, Chomsky vigorously opposed Skinner's claim that language is acquired like any other behavior; through a long, extended series of reinforcements and punishments. Chomsky mainly seemed to object to a theory in which learning language depended heavily on children's abilities to detect patterns of association in the environment. What could be more ironic than the fact that now, seven decades later, one of the most revolutionary articles published in child psychology since 1960, is precisely one which advocates taking into account children's abilities to detect patterns of association in the environment in explaining language acquisition?

Bibliography

Bonati, L. L., Peña, M., Nespor, M., & Mehler, J. (2005). Linguistic constraints on statistical computations: The role of consonants and vowels in continuous speech processing. *Psychological Science, 16*, 451–459.

Chomsky, N. (1957). *Syntactic structures*. The Hague: Mouton.

Hauser, M. D., Chomsky, N., & Fitch, W. T. (2002). The faculty of language: What is it, who has it, and how did it evolve? *Science, 298*, 1569–1579.

Hirsh-Pasek, K., Golinkoff, R. M., Hennon, E. A., & Maguire, M. J. (2004). Hybrid theories at the frontier of developmental psychology: The emergentist coalition model of word learning as a case in point. In D. G. Hall & S. R. Waxman (Eds.), *Weaving a lexicon*. Cambridge, MA: MIT Press.

Quine, W. V. O. (1960). *Word and object*. Cambridge, MA: MIT Press.

Skinner, B. F. (1957). *Verbal behavior*. New York: Appleton-Century-Crofts.

Questions for Discussion

1. Is a genetically transmitted statistical learning machine in the brain more parsimonious than a genetically transmitted universal grammar?
2. What other kinds of knowledge might babies be able acquire through the detection of transitional probabilities, either within the domain of language or without?
3. Is it possible to identify word boundaries in a speech stream without being consciously aware of doing so?
4. Saffran et al. demonstrated infant word-segmentation in a very simple language consisting of only four words. Does their oversimplification of the language render their results inapplicable to natural languages?

12

Monkey See, Monkey Do

Transmission of Aggression Through Imitation of Aggressive Models

Bandura, A., Ross, D., & Ross, S. (1961). *Journal of Abnormal and Social Psychology, 63, 575–582.* **(RANK 2)**

It was the middle of the evening on a blustery November day. The warmth of summer was long gone, and the dinner bell signaled the onset of darkness as reliably as it signaled the day's final meal. My wife was working her normal lunch time-to-bedtime schedule as one of the few clinical psychologists in town, and she wasn't due home for another 3 hours. My 2-year-old daughter Rachel was running around the house as part of her normal after-dinner routine, stopping just long enough to announce her presence at each of the various play stations we set up for her. And I was adjusting to my new role as evening homemaker and full-time father.

There aren't a whole lot of mid-evening recreational opportunities available to you in a small, rural, midwestern town, especially when the cold and darkness of winter set in. And when you have a 2-year-old with more go-power than the Energizer Bunny, there's little chance she'll slip into an accidental slumber. You might as well forget about catching up on your office work. So that night, I decided to do what any rational parent would do under the same circumstances. I pulled out my Sega Genesis gaming system and resumed my career as a contender in the World Heavyweight Boxing circuit.

I was making good progress in the game, working my way up the ranks—10th, 9th, 8th. The "fights" were getting harder, and I was developing a virtual reputation as a KO king. Then it happened. Right in the middle of a 10-round event, catching me completely off guard, Rachel caught me in the left ear with a strong right hook. Despite my pain, I was ROFL (MAO). It was too funny. Where on Earth did she get this inspiration? I never taught her to box. We never watched any boxing on TV (virtual boxing is the only kind I condone). And it's certainly not something she could've picked up from the street, because at age 2 years, we never let her go into the street. The only possible explanation was that she picked it up from the cartoon boxers on the TV screen. The power of video!

The question of where human aggression comes from has occupied the world's greatest thinkers for thousands of years. The popular opinion is that it's either in our genes or learned from our culture. But, hello, what other possibilities are there? These were the same answers offered two thousand years ago. Fortunately, within the last half-century, scholars have made some real progress in understanding the origins of human aggression by bringing the full arsenal of science to bear on the question.

And indeed, Albert Bandura has been at the forefront of the scientific efforts to explain the origins of aggression. In fact, his 1961 article, with coauthors Dorothea Ross and Sheila Ross, was largely responsible for starting the whole thing off. To appreciate the revolutionary character of this study, ranked 2nd overall, you really need to have a sense of the social-scientific odds Bandura was working against when he launched his search for the origins of aggression.

As I have pointed out in many other chapters, at the time of this study's publication, American psychology was pretty much dominated by behavioral psychologists who firmly disavowed the importance, and sometimes even the existence, of internal cognitive processes. Basically, these behaviorists *thought* thinking was irrelevant for psychology. Ironic, huh? Although many American psychologists had heard of Piaget, the wholesale acceptance of Piaget's theory of cognitive development in the United States was at least a decade off. The prevailing view was that learning took place not as a result of the mental construction of conceptual networks, as Piaget proposed, but as a result of behaviors that were rewarded or punished. The idea was that if you did a behavior that was rewarded by someone or something, you would be more likely to do that behavior in the future. If you exhibited a behavior that was punished by someone or something, you would be less likely to exhibit that behavior in the future. What you thought or felt about your behaviors didn't matter. The behaviorist climate didn't have room for thoughts or feelings. In short, human activity, and the psychology that addressed it, amounted to little more than an amalgam of behaviors and the rewards and punishments that molded them. For our purposes, the behaviorist view of aggression was that aggressive people became aggressive because they were rewarded for aggressive behaviors. End of story.

Now along comes Bandura. Bandura's claim to fame as a revolutionary in the field of child psychology resulted from his work on the modeling of aggression. Bandura can probably best be described as a crossover psychologist because he was a social behaviorist dabbling in the affairs of developmental child psychology. But it was his interest in children's socialization specifically that made his behaviorist presence palatable to child psychologists.

Even though Bandura may have looked like a behaviorist on the outside, on the inside he was struggling with behaviorist principles, especially the idea that behaviors were learned or eliminated *exclusively* through reward or punishment. "Would we permit an adolescent to learn to drive by trial and error?" he questioned. "Would we trust a police recruit to manage a firearm without extensive training?" he wondered. Of course not. The adolescent and the police recruit have to be trained over time—and the training has to occur through instruction and demonstration.

Bandura concluded that there had to be more to the story than learning through reward and punishment, and modeling was a particularly powerful candidate to fill the gap. In modeling a learner adjusts his own behavior so as to copy or imitate the behavior of a teacher. Modeling had the potential to be far more effective than punishment and reward systems for learning complicated behaviors. As you've probably experienced yourself, most activity classes use modeling as the primary means of instruction. The ballet teacher models the pirouette, the sensei models the roundhouse kick, and the baseball coach models batting techniques. It's not that rewards and punishment don't also mold our learning, it's just that there are other routes of learning to consider. And some of these routes may be exceptionally powerful.

INTRODUCTION

In their study, Bandura, Ross, and Ross set out to test the hypothesis that aggression was one type of behavior that could be learned through modeling. They focused on children, under the assumption that a large chunk of our adult personality is molded by our childhood experiences. Other research in the 1950s and 1960s had successfully demonstrated the effect of modeling in children, but that research had never tested whether children would carry modeled behaviors into new situations. And the behaviors that were learned didn't come close to resembling aggression.

So Bandura, Ross, and Ross set out to explore whether children who observed aggression in one situation would also behave aggressively in another situation, even when the aggressive model was no longer present. Why this carryover effect was important will become evident later on. But their expectations were clear: "According to the prediction, subjects exposed to aggressive models would reproduce aggressive acts resembling those of their models and would differ in this respect both from subjects who observed nonaggressive models and from those who had no prior exposure to any models."

Bandura, Ross, and Ross also included a couple of gender variables. Even as early as the 1950s, research was showing that parents were likely to reward "sex-appropriate" behaviors in their children. Bandura, Ross, and Ross reasoned, therefore, that because aggression is a masculine behavior, boys would be more inclined than girls to imitate an aggressive model. Further, they reasoned that children were probably used to being rewarded for imitating same-sex parents and punished for imitating opposite-sex parents. Accordingly, the researchers expected children to imitate behavior primarily from a person of the same sex. So they included both a male and a female model. Again, the expectations were clear: Boys should be more inclined to imitate aggressiveness modeled by a male, and girls should be more inclined to imitate aggressiveness modeled by a female.

METHOD

Participants

Thirty-six boys and 36 girls participated in the experiment. They ranged in age from 37 to 69 months, with an average age of 52 months (about 4.3 years old).

Two adults played the role of the model, one male and one female. These same two people played the role of the model for all 72 children. (Bandura himself played the role of the male.)

Materials

The materials used in the first part of the experiment consisted of potatoes, picture stickers, a Tinkertoy set, a mallet, and a 5-foot inflated Bobo doll. A couple of these items may need a little further explanation. The potatoes were used to create ink stamps. If you cut potatoes in half, you can make cute little designs in their flesh by carving out excess potato material. If you then dip the face of this design in ink, you can stamp out on paper a whole series of copies of the design you just created. So potatoes were used here as an art material. Tinkertoy sets aren't as popular as they used to be. In the old days they consisted of little wooden sticks, blocks, and wheels and such, and were used to build things. (These days Tinkertoys are made of plastic.) Finally, we have the Bobo doll. The Bobo doll was so central to Bandura's experiments that these days they're usually called "the Bobo doll studies." A Bobo doll was simply an inflatable plastic doll that had the likeness of Bobo the Clown printed on the surface. It also had a compartment filled with sand built into its base that kept it standing upright; so even if you knocked it over, it would pop right back up again. At 5 feet tall, it loomed larger than most of the children in the study.

Procedure

Forty-eight children were assigned to the "experimental condition" and from there to either an "aggressive" or a "nonaggressive" condition. Children in the aggressive condition saw an adult behaving aggressively; this adult was called the "aggressive model." Children in the nonaggressive condition saw a "nonaggressive model." Half of the children in each group were boys, and half were girls. Finally, half of these children saw a female model and half saw a male model. Altogether there were eight possible groups:

- Girls who saw an aggressive female model
- Girls who saw an aggressive male model
- Girls who saw a nonaggressive female model
- Girls who saw a nonaggressive male model
- Boys who saw an aggressive female model
- Boys who saw an aggressive male model
- Boys who saw a nonaggressive female model
- Boys who saw a nonaggressive male model

There was an additional group of 24 children who were assigned to the "control condition." These children saw no model at all but were otherwise treated exactly the same as the children who saw the models. These "control children" served as a comparison group, and with them Bandura, Ross, and Ross could determine what children would do if they saw no model at all.

Experimental Conditions

Each of the 48 children in the experimental conditions was taken, one at a time, to the experimental room by the experimenter. When the child and experimenter arrived at the room, a stranger would be standing in the hallway just outside the room. The experimenter invited the stranger into the room to "come and join the game." The child was then taken to a small table in one corner of the room and shown how to play with the potato prints and the stickers. The experimenter then took the stranger to the opposite corner of the room. Here was found the Tinkertoy set, the mallet, and the Bobo doll. The experimenter told the stranger that these toys were for him or her to play with, and then left the room.

NONAGGRESSIVE CONDITION   In the nonaggressive condition, the stranger assembled the Tinkertoys "in a quiet subdued manner totally ignoring the Bobo doll." At this point, we can now call the stranger a "model" because he or she was "modeling" behavior for the benefit of the child.

AGGRESSIVE CONDITION   In contrast, the model in the aggressive condition played with the Tinkertoys for only about a minute, and then began beating up the Bobo doll. The original description of the beating-up procedure is too funny not to quote in its entirety. "The model laid Bobo on its side, sat on it and punched it repeatedly in the nose. The model then raised the Bobo doll, picked up the mallet and struck the doll on the head. Following the mallet aggression, the model tossed the doll up in the air aggressively and kicked it about the room." This beating-up sequence was repeated three times, and was interspersed with verbally aggressive phrases such as: "Sock him in the nose," "Hit him down," "Throw him in the air," "Kick him," and "Pow." Two nonaggressive comments were also made: "He keeps coming back for more" and "He sure is a tough fella."

After 10 minutes, the experimenter returned to the experimental room, told the model/ stranger good-bye, and informed the child that she would be going to another room with games. The other room was located in a separate building. It was in that other room where the children were tested for their levels of aggression.

Aggression Arousal

Bandura, Ross, and Ross wanted to test the children for aggressive behavior under conditions that would allow them to express it. Bandura realized that when children were around unfamiliar, official-looking adults, they might be inclined to put on their best behavior. But if they did put on their best behavior, their efforts at politeness might override any aggressiveness they might be harboring, and Bandura's study might be foiled. For that reason, Bandura, Ross, and Ross set up an artificial situation that would more or less pull aggression out of the children. So they did something they knew would have the effect of ticking the children off. Here's what they did.

After children observed either the aggressive or the nonaggressive model, they were escorted to a second experimental room. Along the way, they had to pass through a smaller room, called an anteroom. The anteroom contained a number of highly attractive toys, including a jet fighter plane, a cable car, a colorful spinning top, and a doll set complete with wardrobe, doll carriage, and baby crib. Notice the equal representation of sex-typed toys. The experimenter told the children they could stop and play with these toys, which they proceeded to do. But after only 2 minutes, just when the children were really getting involved with the toys, she remarked that these were her "very best toys, that she did not let just anyone play with them, and that she had decided to reserve these toys for the other children." In other words, the children had just been dissed. The experimenter explained that although they weren't allowed to play with the toys in the anteroom, they were free to play with any of the toys in the main room, which they subsequently proceeded to enter.

Test for Delayed Imitation

In the experimental room, the children found a number of toys. Some of the toys were similar to those used by the aggressive model: a 3-foot-tall Bobo doll and a mallet. Others were toys not used by the aggressive model, but that still could be used for aggressive purposes: two dart guns and a tetherball suspended from the ceiling with a face painted on it. Still other toys were ones that weren't likely to be used for aggressive purposes: a tea set, crayons and coloring paper, a ball, two dolls, three bears, cars and trucks, and plastic farm animals. The play materials were arranged exactly the same way for every child that entered the room.

Response Measures

Bandura, Ross, and Ross measured aggressive behavior in several different ways. By my count, they used seven different measures, with three of the most interesting measures consisting of (1) the amount of physical aggression that was imitated, (2) the amount of verbal aggression that was imitated, and (3) the amount of verbal nonaggression that was imitated. During the process of scoring the aggression, the researchers realized that some of the imitated behaviors were only partially imitated, but they decided to count them anyway. The most common partial imitations were (4) sitting on the Bobo doll without any additional aggression and (5) using the mallet to hit other things in the room besides the Bobo doll. Finally, there were instances in which children behaved aggressively, but without imitating any of the model's behaviors. These behaviors included (6) using verbal and physical assaults invented by the children themselves (saying "Shoot the Bobo," "Cut him," or "Stupid ball" or punching the tetherball), and (7) shooting the dart gun at real or imaginary things.

RESULTS

So what were the results of the study? First of all, kids who saw the aggressive model were off the charts in imitating the aggressiveness of the aggressive models compared to kids who saw no model or who saw the nonaggressive model. The aggressive-model kids were also more likely to go around banging on stuff with the mallet than were the kids who saw the nonaggressive model. But importantly, these kids weren't aggressive across the board. They didn't run around shooting things with the dart guns any more than did the other children, for example. So to the extent that aggressive-model kids were aggressive, they were mostly aggressive in the same ways as the model they observed. You can see many YouTube depictions of children's performance in the aggressive condition, simply Google "bandura, bobo doll, video."

In terms of gender differences, boys were more likely to engage in physical aggression than were girls; but boys and girls did not differ from one another in verbal aggression. Moreover, boys were significantly more likely than girls to imitate the male model; but the reverse was not true for female models.

One interesting finding was that children who watched the male, nonaggressive model turned out to be significantly *less* aggressive than the children in the control group (who saw no model). As the authors described it, "[I]n relation to the control group, subjects exposed to the nonaggressive male model performed significantly less imitative physical aggression, less imitative verbal aggression, less mallet aggression, less non-imitative physical and verbal aggression, and they were less inclined to punch the Bobo doll." So not only did the *aggressive* model cause kids to show *more* aggression than kids in the control group, the *nonaggressive* model caused kids to show *less* aggression than kids in the control group.

DISCUSSION

The most revolutionary product of Bandura's study was the finding that children were capable of using models as a means for picking up new behaviors they otherwise wouldn't have produced. This was largely unheard of in the behaviorist-dominated scientific community at the time. Of course, laypeople were familiar with the power of imitation, as evidenced by the popularity of the phrase "monkey see, monkey do." But in old-school psychology, modeling wasn't seen as very important. Old-school scientists believed that kids only produced new behaviors by accident; and only if those new behaviors were rewarded would they continue. But the kid had to produce the behavior himself, and had to be directly rewarded for doing so. Now along came Bandura claiming that children can pick up behaviors almost magically simply by watching other people. Not only that, but they produced behaviors without being rewarded for them!

The social-political implications of these findings were **HUGE**. Not only was it clear that children could pick up aggressive behaviors simply by watching someone else, but they reproduced these newly acquired aggressive behaviors to new situations when no other aggressive people were present. Apparently, seeing aggression happen in another person was enough to bring it out in a child at a later point in time. Of course, in Bandura's study, the "later point in time" was later that same day. But an extremely important question raised by this finding was, "How long might these aggressive tendencies last? A day? A week? A lifetime?" The implications were obvious. If a child saw Bugs Bunny knock over Elmer Fudd on Saturday-morning cartoons (it was the 1960s remember), would he carry over that aggression into recess on Monday afternoon? The finding that children could delay their imitation of aggression had wide-ranging implications indeed.

But for whatever reason, all of this was predicated on the aggressive model's being male. A closer look at the results showed that the female model didn't have much success in getting kids to imitate *her* aggressive behavior. But this raised its own line of inquiry, starting with, "Why would this be?" One possible explanation for why the male model of aggression was more successful than the female model was that the male was modeling "sex-appropriate behaviors." Females weren't supposed to be aggressive. In fact, when the female modeled aggression, the children seemed shocked. They made comments like, "You should have seen what that girl did in there. She was acting like a man. I never saw a girl act like that before. She was punching and fighting but no swearing." Comments about the male model focused much less on the inappropriateness of the aggression, and much more on *how well* the aggression was carried out. One girl said, "That man is a strong fighter, he punched and punched and he could hit Bobo right down to the floor and if Bobo got up he said, 'Punch your nose.' He's a good fighter like Daddy."

Of course, all this focus on the modeling of aggression ignores the other side of the coin. Children who observed the quiet model were calmer and less aggressive than the other kids. Apparently, when quietness is modeled, quietness is the behavior exhibited. Bandura, Ross, and Ross concluded that "exposure to inhibited models not only decreases the probability of occurrence of aggressive behavior but also generally restricts the range of behavior emitted by the subjects."

CONCLUSIONS

Follow-Up Study

Before I go on to discuss the impact of Bandura's study on the rest of the world (indeed its core findings are under heated debate to this very day), I'd like to acquaint you with a follow-up experiment Bandura published in 1965. I alluded earlier to the possibility that children might imitate aggression modeled in a television cartoon. But this suggestion may have been a bit premature since Bandura's first study didn't address whether children would imitate *televised* aggressive models. However, he remedied this shortcoming with a 1965 follow-up experiment, in which he had children watch a televised model engage in aggressive behavior. He also tested what would happen if children saw the model receive a consequence for the aggressive actions. So Bandura had children view an aggressive model on TV under one of three conditions: Either the model was punished for beating up the Bobo doll, he was rewarded for beating up the Bobo doll, or he received no consequences for beating up the Bobo doll. The results revealed that children who saw the televised model rewarded for his aggression were themselves likely to behave aggressively. The take away message from this study was that it revealed television to be a powerful medium for transmitting aggressive actions to passively observing children.

Television, Video Games, and Violent Lyrics

As I already mentioned, Bandura's results were huge. I suppose on the one hand they only showed that people will copy the behavior of other people. Duh. But the overall impact was much more profound than that. His research showed that aggressive behavior can be copied, and that young children will do the copying. In the confines of Bandura's lab, these results may be relatively harmless. But beyond the confines of the lab, there's no telling the lengths that children might go to carry out imitated aggressive behavior. There's no telling the range of media that might prompt children to behave aggressively. And there's no telling the range of aggressive behavior children might respond to. Bandura's research opened a Pandora's box of possibilities.

These findings are especially scary in light of the extent that modern children are immersed in social media. Just consider the number of different social media interfaces children have at their disposal, probably on a daily basis: YouTube, Facebook, Pinterest, Twitter, Instagram, Tumblr, Vine. And every single one of them conveys a message to the recipient. Now this wouldn't be so bad if the images were always positive ones, say where Bambi risks his life to rescue Thumper from the forest fire. But the images usually aren't positive ones. They're often replete with violence, aggression, and bullying. For some communities, it appears to be a local pastime to record one child (the bully) picking on or teasing another child (the victim). In the last several years, many children have even committed suicide as a result of the bullying they received. Bandura's research underscores the very real societal damage caused by the widespread public availability of images of violence and bullying in the daily routines of our children. Aggressive models don't even have to be important figures in the children's lives; they can be complete strangers. Imagine the impact made by models whom children respect, like movie stars, sports heroes, WWF characters, or pop music icons. Consider these stories quoted from popular media sources as I write these words:

- *nj.com Web site*, 31 July, 2014: Baltimore Ravens running back Ray Rice said the altercation with his now-wife inside an Atlantic City casino was "a one-time incident" and labeled his actions that February night as "inexcusable."
- *FoxCT Web site*, 8 July 2014: Two 16-year-old Watertown High School students were arrested this week in connection with posts they made on Instagram. The teens are charged with second degree harassment after police say they created an "anonymous" Instagram account in early June, posting photos of fellow students, publicly shaming them online. Police describe the comments as "hateful" and "harassing." "Cyberbullying is like bullying on steroids," said Board of Education Chairman, Guy Buzzannco.
- *MLive Web site*, 5 August 2014: In the days after 13-year-old Michael Day was shot and killed in Kalamazoo's Edison neighborhood, rumors were flying in the hallways of Loy Norrix High School about retaliation violence. But what concerned police even more was the chatter on Facebook. According to a police report obtained by the *Kalamazoo Gazette*, two of Michael Day's friends, who reportedly had affiliation with the Washington Street Boys gang, were "saying a lot

of stuff on Facebook" that led investigators to believe retaliation plans might have been in the works.

• *Chicago Sun-Times*, 10 March 2001: Ignoring a multitude of pleas for clemency, Broward County Circuit Court Judge Joel Lazarus sentenced 14-year-old Lionel Tate to life in prison without parole Friday for killing a girl playmate while allegedly demonstrating professional wrestling techniques on her. "The acts of Lionel Tate were not acts of immaturity," Lazarus said. "The acts of Lionel Tate were cold, callous and indescribably cruel." Tate's victim, 6-year-old Tiffany Eunick, was found beaten to death July 28, 1999. Her killer, Tate, was twice his victim's age at the time and, at 170 pounds, more than three times her weight. An autopsy showed that Tiffany suffered a fractured skull, a lacerated liver, a broken rib, internal hemorrhaging and numerous cuts and bruises. She was stomped, flung against a wall and beaten while on a table.

• *Chicagotribune.com Web site*, 23 July 2014: Remember Columbine? Remember the novelty of it all? Mass shootings had occurred before, but April 20, 1999, felt unprecedented, both for the deaths and the depth with which we got to know Eric Harris and Dylan Klebold after the massacre. Fifteen years later, each mass killing seems to fade into the next for those not directly affected. Today's senselessness and loss ebb just as a new atrocity flows into our national consciousness. We have all gotten used to it. And regardless of whether you attribute this pandemic to too many guns, not enough mental health resources or something else, we all expect to get to know our mass shooters intimately after the fact. We were shown Seung-Hui Cho's videotaped messages that he sent to NBC in the hours between his two Virginia Tech attacks that killed 32 and wounded 17 in 2007. Elliot Rodger's face lit up our TV screens as anchors broke down the "Retribution" video he posted to YouTube before he killed six, injured 13, and took his own life in Isla Vista, Calif., earlier this year. We learned everything about Adam Lanza, including his guns and the tactics he used to murder 20 kids and six adults at Sandy Hook Elementary in 2012. We remember the names of the killers, but rarely the victims. But as America's massacres settle in as part of our new normal, some suggest that the way the media cover such killings gives the mass shooters the fame they were seeking, while providing a murderous template for future gunmen who feel wronged by society and want to end it all in a way that will be remembered.

In every one of these instances, media are implicated as a factor linked to the bizarre behavior patterns of the individuals involved. Of course, it's impossible to say whether or not media images necessarily promote aggression; you'd have to have a God's-eye view to know that. But based on the scientific experiments conducted by Bandura, and dozens of other scientists since, we know at least that children are highly inclined to imitate behaviors modeled by other people. Although it's the children who carry out the acts, the media may need to shoulder much of the blame.

Media Bashing

The question of who should take responsibility when children conduct criminal acts based on models observed in the media is highly controversial and emotionally charged. Most social scientists familiar with the modeling research are inclined to lay much of the blame on the media. In fact, in 1999 the American Academy of Pediatrics issued a recommendation that parents should avoid exposing their children to *any* television prior to the age of 2 years (although I've often wondered how they arrived at 2 as the magical age).

On the other hand, I can already hear the counterarguments. "Hey, whatever happened to free will? People *choose* to imitate what they observe in the media. Millions of teenage boys play violent video games and listen to the band Slayer *without* slaughtering their classmates!" You might argue further that perpetrators who inflict violence in response to media imagery are simply bad apples who *chose* to follow the path of evil, probably because something was wrong with them in the first place. As you can imagine, these are very popular sentiments which media companies are probably strongly aligned with. Indeed, media giants stand to lose a lot of money if their liberties to portray violence are removed. Violence sells.

But there are a couple of different issues intertwined here. First, blame-placing doesn't need to be an either-or, black-or-white kind of thing. Human beings are highly individualized creatures who differ from one another greatly (which you already know from your personal experiences). So why assume that everyone would have to respond to media-portrayed violence the same way? Just because you played the video game *Doom* before and didn't go out and kill someone doesn't mean the game didn't influence your behavior in some way. Perhaps you once kicked the dog afterward, or maybe you got a little snippy with your parents. And there are thousands of kids out there trying fancy and dangerous wrestling moves on their little brothers and sisters every day who *don't* kill and maim them. I remember once when I first moved into a new neighborhood, I noticed that one of the adolescent neighbor boys had a full-size wrestling ring sitting in his backyard. He and his friends were always slamming one another onto the mat and drop-kicking each other into the ropes. Apparently, no one ever got seriously injured because I never saw any EMTs rushing down the street. But I doubt he would've had a wrestling ring in the first place if the WWF hadn't had such a powerful influence on him.

So why does it seem that social science is so much at odds with popular opinion? For one thing, surely not everyone's aware of the Bobo doll studies. But even if they were, many people would probably still deny their impact. I think this stems in large part from popular misconceptions about how social science works. Social science works by describing the behaviors of large groups of people. There are bound to be exceptions to the rule. Even in the Bandura study, where we know for sure that children's aggression was enhanced by the aggressive model, not all the children performed at the same level of aggression. Some children were more aggressive than others. There was probably even one child who was the most aggressive of all. Would we be justified in concluding that the aggressive model had no influence on most of the kids simply because most of the kids failed to behave as aggressively as the most aggressive kid? Of course not. For this reason, I'm not inclined to buy the "bad apple" argument. Imitative behaviors can be extreme, and most kids don't behave extremely violently, but that doesn't mean kids are *unaffected* by the violent images in the media. They're just not all affected to the same degree.

Whether we like it or not, the balance of evidence allocates a large portion of blame on the media. Now, I don't believe the media *intend* for their violent imagery to promote violence in society. Most media sources are surely in it for the money. And to be sure, media sources would stand to gain very little by promoting a violent society, if for no other reason than that, over time, they would have fewer customers. Still, media sources are subject to scientific scrutiny, and science doesn't have a whole lot of positive things to say about the media images being distributed. Unfortunately, the media have a long history of turning a deaf ear toward scientific concerns.

Consider the following. Way back in the 1970s, Surgeon General William H. Stewart was directed to form an advisory panel to examine research on the effects of television on children. He wanted the committee to be made up of representatives from three different constituencies: the scientific community, the broadcasting industry, and the general public. To recruit scientists, he requested nominations from the American Sociological Association, the American Psychiatric Association, and the American Psychological Association. Some 200 names of prominent researchers were submitted. The surgeon general narrowed the list down to 40 and forwarded the names to the presidents of the National Association of Broadcasters, the American Broadcasting Company (ABC), the National Broadcasting Company (NBC), and the Columbia Broadcasting System (CBS). The presidents were asked to say which individuals, if any, would *not* be "appropriate for an impartial scientific investigation of this nature." Two of the corporate presidents (with the exception of CBS's) blackballed 7 scientists. Guess who was on the list. Albert Bandura! Bandura, who was at the time the most prominent expert on the effects of television on American youth, was eliminated by the television broadcasters themselves, from the most esteemed presidential advisory committee addressing the issue. What were they so afraid of?

On a Positive Note

If media have been the cause of any societal problems, they can also be the source of their solutions. What tends to be forgotten in media-blaming sessions is that the existence of media isn't at issue. We couldn't live without the media, and the diversity of media options today appeals to more people than ever. It's the content of the media that's the problem. That's what children imitate. A lot of good science has shown that children exposed to positive media are inclined to display prosocial behaviors. Indeed, for many years, Senator Joe Lieberman and former Second Lady Tipper Gore were at the forefront of a movement to pressure media to increase their positive media programming. The few prosocial media programs we've had, including children's TV shows like *Barney, Sesame Street*, and *Mr. Rogers*, have done wonders for exposing children to behaviorally positive daily routines. A 2001 monograph put out by the Society for Research in Child Development, for example, revealed that children who watched *Sesame Street* had higher grades in school, engaged in more leisure-time book use, participated more in art class, and exhibited lower levels of aggression than children who didn't watch *Sesame Street*. One can only hope that in this capitalist society, media distributors can find an attractive profit motive for exposing children to more positive media imagery.

Final Comment

Bandura revolutionized child psychology because he approached the field as an outsider. He was interested in the very general question of how people can pick up behaviors they've never been rewarded for and apply them to new situations. But the fact that he focused on the aggressive behavior of children made it all the more important to the scientific community, and to the public at large. His major finding, that children would imitate behaviors they saw modeled by other people, was elementary. Yet, because it was aggressive behavior that the children were picking up, it was at the same time of grave sociopolitical importance. To this very day, scientists and the media industry are locked in a battle over how to allocate blame for what is feared to be an unprecedented rise in social apathy and violence. The results can't yet be foreseen, because the battleground expands with every techno-media innovation that presents itself. But if there's a consensus, it's that the battle is an important one: it may be for the mental health of today's children. Now—back to my heavyweight boxing career.

Bibliography

Anderson, D. R., Huston, A. C., Schmitt, K. L., Linebarger, D. L., & Wright, J. C. (2001). Early childhood television viewing and adolescent behavior. *Monographs of the Society for Research in Child Development*, 66(Serial No. 264).

Bandura, A. (1965). Influence of models' reinforcement contingencies on the acquisition of imitative responses. *Journal of Personality & Social Psychology, 1,* 589–595.

Grusec, J. E. (1992). Social learning theory and developmental psychology: The legacies of Robert Sears and Albert Bandura. *Developmental Psychology, 28,* 776–786.

Liebert, R. M., & Sprafkin, J. (1988). *The early window.* New York: Pergamon Press.

Questions for Discussion

1. Do the media have any responsibility to the public to portray positive images? How about musical celebrities or movie stars? Athletes? Are there any classes of celebrity that should be held less accountable for their media portrayals than others?

2. Is learning aggression through imitation a new phenomenon? Or is it possible that children have been imitating aggressive models throughout history? What would be some examples of the latter?

3. Would you expect there to be age differences in children's and adult's susceptibility to aggressive models? At what age do you think children would be most susceptible to portrayals of aggression? At what age are children most susceptible to peer pressure? Are adults immune to media models of aggression?

13

The Tongue That Launched a Thousand Studies

Imitation of Facial and Manual Gestures by Human Neonates

Meltzoff, A. N., & Moore, M. K. (1977). *Science, 198*, 75–78.
(RANK 12)

When is science really science, and when is it something else? In the field of child psychology, much of what we call science is surely subject to skeptical review by people unfamiliar with our theories and goals, because so much of what we do focuses on the antics of babies and children. After all, when was the last time that a baby or young child accomplished anything especially useful?

Well, maybe not everyone would automatically be skeptical of child psychological science. Take me for instance. From my earliest nerd days, I marveled at the idea of getting paid for engaging in the science of children's play. I didn't once question the value in it. I assumed that if it was described in a textbook, and if test questions could be written about it, it was surely an important topic.

But skepticism about child psychology flashed in the pan one day early in my teaching career when I was showing an instructional video to my child psychology class. The topic had to do with children's phoneme detection, and it portrayed a 10-month-old baby, sitting on a table, looking at an adult who was examining a stuffed animal. In the background was playing a soundtrack of repeating "ba" sounds followed by repeating "da" sounds. When the audio stream changed from "ba" to "da," the child would turn in the direction of a mechanical toy, located off to the side, before the mechanical toy became activated. The narrator of the video explained that the fact that the child looked in the direction of the toy *before* the toy became activated was proof that the child could hear the difference in sounds, and had learned that the change in sounds predicted the activation of the mechanical toy. Children who did not turn in the direction of the mechanical toy until *after* it became activated, the narrative claimed, could not hear the difference in sounds. In sum, the instructional video made the very fascinating point (to me) that children lose the ability to hear differences between certain sounds that are not important to their native languages at around 8–10 months of age. (This work of Dr. Janet Werker is actually featured in Chapter 10 of this book!)

I thought this was a great demonstration of a really cool finding in child psychology. The baby was cute, the toys were colorful, and the concept was simple. But then, a youngish—albeit Grinch-like—male student heckled the video. He thought it was a joke. "What a waste," he said. "I can't believe this is serious." He was incredulous that anything like what he was watching could be called science, and he voiced his opinion loudly and unabashedly. Needless to say, he also resented having to learn anything about it for the test. That is when I first realized that just doing child psychology could rub some people the wrong way. I realized that laypeople may not understand the value of doing some parts of child psychology, and that psychologists don't always do a good job in explaining their rationale to the receivers of their science.

I use this story as a background to introduce the 12th most revolutionary study in child psychology, because if there is any study likely to raise the eyebrows, and maybe even the ire, of the lay public, it is probably this one. On the surface, this study was about babies sticking out their tongues. And as hard as you may find it to believe, the authors, Andy Meltzoff and Keith Moore, believed there was something prophetic about babies' tongue-sticking-out ability. Now, if you cannot accept on faith that the science of babies sticking out their tongues is worthwhile, I'm OK with that. A fledgling scientist really should maintain a healthy dose of skepticism. But bear with me. In the text that follows I hope to lay out a much deeper and more compelling story than you might expect about a study which became famous for its portrayal of how babies stick out their tongues.

The core finding from this 1977 work by Meltzoff and Moore was that when an adult sticks out his tongue at a baby—a near-newborn in fact—the baby will stick out her tongue right back at him. A now classic depiction of the study can be found in Figure 13.1, which is reprinted in just about every child psychology textbook out there. In this picture you see an adult—Meltzoff himself—sticking out his tongue at a baby, with the baby imitating him and sticking out her tongue right back. Science? Maybe not at first glance. But as I noted the story runs much deeper than that. For example, did you wonder how it was possible for a brand new baby, fresh out of the womb,

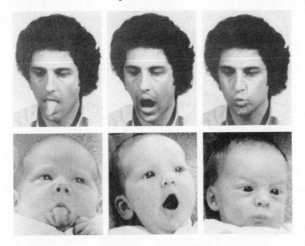

FIGURE 13.1 Infant imitating tongue protrusion.

to stick out her tongue in direct response to the tongue-sticking-out of an adult? The baby surely can't know anything about the social implications of sticking out one's tongue. And she surely has no experience seeing other people sticking out their tongues. So if the baby doesn't know anything about it, and she has never seen it done before, why would she spontaneously imitate it? What's more, and perhaps even more challengingly, if the baby really is imitating the tongue protrusion, how is it possible for her to take in a visual image and transform it into a bodily display that she herself cannot even see? Does she even know she is sticking her tongue out?

Of course, the whole point of the study was to propose some tentative answers to these questions; and as I hope to show, at least if you accept the account put forth by Meltzoff and Moore, it's possible that these answers tell a fantastic, provocative, and inspiring story of human social development. As with most studies published in the journal *Science*, this one was a very short article occupying only about three full pages. But brief as it was, the authors garnered considerable interest among the journal's readership; including, as of this writing, some 2875 Google Scholar citations by other authors throughout the scientific community. As a bonus, Meltzoff and Moore were also able to convey some tightly controlled methodologies implemented across two sequentially related experiments. The details of the two experiments are described in the text that follows.

Experiment 1

INTRODUCTION

Perhaps due to the article's brevity, the introduction does not say much about why the authors wanted to do this study. At first glance, it appears they were interested in showing that Piaget underestimated the age when children were first able to imitate. This was confirmed in a conversation I had with Dr. Meltzoff (personal communication 1/25/13), when I also learned that the main goal was to test the adequacy of Piaget's theory in the social domain, at a time when other authors were testing the adequacy of Piaget's theory in the physical domain. Although I touch on the importance of imitation for Piaget's theory in Chapter 3 of this book, suffice it to say for now that any evidence that Piaget was wrong about when imitation started could have profound implications for the rest of Piagetian theory. In addition, the fact that Meltzoff and Moore used neonates in their study suggests that they were looking to see just how early imitation could be demonstrated; with the next step being that if imitation could be observed in the very earliest days of life, then by extrapolation, maybe it was even present before birth.

METHOD
Subjects

Six babies (3 girls, 3 boys), who were 12 to 17 days old when tested.

Procedure

Each baby was tested individually. When tested, the experimenter first looked at the baby for 90 seconds and showed an "unreactive, passive face." Then, in a randomly determined order, the experimenter showed the baby each of four gestures in turn: lip protrusion (i.e., puckering the lips), mouth opening, tongue protrusion (i.e., sticking out the tongue), and sequential finger movement (i.e., "opening and closing the hand" one finger at a time). Individual gestures were repeated for 15-seconds each, up to a total of four presentations per gesture. If the baby appeared not to watch the experimenter while he delivered one of the gestures, that gesture was repeated again (and even a third time if needed). After each of the four 15-second gesture presentations, the experimenter put on a passive face for 20 seconds. It was during this passive face period that infant imitations were looked for. An additional 70-second passive face period was administered before the experimenter moved onto the next gesture.

SCORING   Video recordings were made of each session, with one camera aimed at the experimenter and one at the baby. Through these recordings, it was possible to know exactly what the baby was doing during each adult gesture. Judgments of whether babies engaged in imitation were made by two teams of undergraduate students. One team scored infant facial gestures, and one scored hand gestures. While watching the video recordings, students were asked to use the babies' own facial or hand movements to judge which adult gestures the babies were probably watching. But these judgments weren't made at random; rather, students were given a sort of multiple choice test. Each team was told the range of possible gestures each baby could be watching, and then asked to guess which gesture was actually being presented. The facial scoring team was told that babies may have been shown: 1) lip protrusion, 2) mouth opening, 3) tongue protrusion, or 4) passive face. The hand scoring team was told that babies may have been shown: 1) sequential finger movements, 2) finger protrusion, 3) hand opening, or 4) passive hand. Then for each section of videotape, the students simply had to rank order which of the four adult gestures the baby was most likely viewing.

RESULTS

As you might expect, Meltzoff and Moore found that on average babies were judged to be imitating the gesture they were actually shown, rather than any of the other possible gestures that they could have been shown. The specific statistical procedures Meltzoff and Moore used are a little more complicated than need be presented here, but the bottom line was that babies were judged to be imitating lip protrusion during the adult lip protrusion gesture (more than any other gesture, $p < .01$), they were judged to be imitating mouth opening during the adult mouth opening gesture (more than any other gesture, $p < .02$), they were judged to be imitating tongue protrusion during the adult tongue protrusion gesture (more than any other gesture, $p < .05$), and they were judged to be imitating serial finger movements during the adult serial finger movement gesture (more than any other gesture, $p < .001$).

Experiment 2

INTRODUCTION

As is usually the case in the empirical literature, the purpose of the second experiment was to control for problems that were discovered in the first experiment. In this instance, Meltzoff and Moore realized that by repeating each gesture up to three times—which they did whenever they thought babies weren't looking at the experimenter—they may have unconsciously, inadvertently, or unknowingly repeated the gestures *until* the baby demonstrated the target gesture. So they decided to redo the study in a way that would absolutely prevent them from accidently leading on their research subjects.

METHOD

Subjects

Twelve babies (6 girls, 6 boys) who were 16 to 21 days old when tested. Not that it matters necessarily, but these babies were about 25–33% older than the babies in Experiment 1.

Procedure

In this experiment, babies were shown only two gestures, and both were facial: mouth opening and tongue protrusion. Each baby saw both gestures, in a counter-balanced fashion (which means that some babies saw mouth opening first while other babies saw tongue protrusion first). One innovation of this experiment relative to Experiment 1 was that babies were given a pacifier to suck on while the experimenter presented the gestures. By using a pacifier, the experimenter could repeat each gesture as necessary until he was sure the baby had seen it, and he wouldn't have to worry that his gesture repetitions unconsciously, inadvertently, or unknowingly were influenced by the baby's own facial gestures, since the latter were theoretically prevented by the presence of the pacifier.

So here is a recap of the procedure for Experiment 2:

1. The pacifier was inserted into the baby's mouth, and the experimenter presented a passive face for 30 seconds.
2. The pacifier was removed, and a 150-second baseline period was administered (not sure what the experimenter did during this time).
3. The pacifier was reinserted, and the experimenter displayed the first gesture until he judged the baby had watched it for 15 seconds.
4. The experimenter resumed the passive face, and then removed the pacifier.
5. A 150-second response period was then observed, while the experimenter maintained a passive face.
6. The pacifier was reinserted, and the experimenter administered the second facial gesture in the same manner as the first facial gesture.

Scoring

Interestingly, Meltzoff and Moore used a different scoring technique in this experiment, relative to the first one, to measure whether babies imitated the facial gestures. Recall that in Experiment 1, teams of undergraduate coders were simply asked to judge which gesture babies were presented with. In Experiment 2, a single undergraduate coder was asked to actually count the number of times each baby stuck its tongue out or opened its mouth.

RESULTS

Again, as you might expect, Meltzoff and Moore got the results they were looking for. They found that babies were significantly more likely to stick out their tongues after they saw the adult stick out his tongue, than after they saw the adult open his mouth, or during the baseline period. Similarly, babies were more likely to open their mouths after they saw the adult open his mouth, than after they saw the adult stick out his tongue, or during the baseline period.

DISCUSSION OF BOTH EXPERIMENTS

So Meltzoff and Moore obtained their desired results, and Piaget was apparently proven wrong. OK, fine. But then how could these results have happened? That is, how could babies have accurately converted facial movements visually observed in another person, into a set of their own facial movements that they themselves could not even see? The plot thickens. Meltzoff and Moore proposed three possibilities for this previously undiscovered ability: 1) reinforcement, 2) innate releasing mechanisms, or 3) abstract supramodal representations. The first two possibilities were essentially straw-men possibilities that the authors considered temporarily just so they could knock them down with reasoning or evidence, eventually replacing them with their third and preferred explanation. I review each of these possibilities in turn.

THE REINFORCEMENT EXPLANATION   The first possibility was that reinforcement was responsible for children's production of facial gestures. For this to occur, the experimenter must have somehow rewarded babies for producing the target gestures, or at least punished them for producing any other facial gestures. For example, the experimenter could have smiled when babies stuck-out their tongues during the tongue protrusion sessions, or frowned when babies opened their mouths during the tongue protrusion sessions. Either way, babies would not have been imitating; rather, they simply would have been responding based on the reinforcements or punishments provided by the experimenter.

Meltzoff and Moore argued that they prevented this possibility through their employment of the "passive face" procedure. If the experimenter had on a passive face, he couldn't have been simultaneously reinforcing or punishing the baby by inadvertently smiling or frowning in response to the baby's gestural productions. But just to be sure, they had observers go through all the video recordings of the experimenter's face and found that "No smiles or vocalizations were noted in any trial."

THE INNATE RELEASING MECHANISM EXPLANATION   The second possible explanation for Meltzoff and Moore's findings is based on ethological theory (for more detail, see Chapter 17 on Bowlby's Theory of Attachment). In case you don't remember much of ethological theory, let's briefly review it here before we consider why it was something Meltzoff and Moore wanted to consider and then dismiss. According to ethological theory, organisms are tightly connected to their natural environments. They are so connected, that the occurrence of certain specific stimuli in the environment are thought to produce in those organisms certain predetermined, involuntary, hardwired responses. The response of the organism under these conditions is called a *fixed action pattern*, and it is automatically "released" whenever the organism encounters the appropriate releasing stimulus in the environment.

As an analogy, consider the sneezing reflex. Some of us sneeze in the bright sunlight and some of us sneeze when sniffing ground black pepper. But once the sneeze reflex is activated by the appropriate stimulus, there is nothing we can do to prevent it. The sneeze is "released" from start to finish. The ethological idea of the fixed action pattern is similar to that of the simple sneezing reflex. But whereas sneezing is a simple, single-action response, the fixed action pattern can involve relatively elaborate behavioral sequences that can be executed over relatively extended period of time (consider the "cute response" as described in Chapter 17). Ethological theory holds that the fixed action pattern is also exhibited stereotypically, which means it is delivered more or less the same way every time, and it cannot *not* be delivered when the appropriate triggering stimulus is present in the environment.

If the innate releasing mechanism idea were applied to Meltzoff and Moore's findings, then it would mean that babies didn't really imitate the adult model at all. Rather, the adult model simply provided an environmental stimulus to the baby (i.e., sticking out his tongue) which functioned to release a more or less reflexive response from the baby (i.e., sticking out her tongue). But Meltzoff and Moore argued that this possible interpretation was also a fail; for two reasons. First, they noted that the babies' behaviors were not very stereotypical; instead they were variable and inconsistently implemented. That is, babies didn't always produce the target gestures in response to the specific stimuli; and when they did, they didn't always produce them the same way. So this failed to satisfy ethological theory's stereotypical criterion. But second, Meltzoff and Moore thought it highly unlikely that babies would just happen to have a specific gesture in their repertoire of innate fixed action patterns that looked exactly like whatever gesture the adult decided to produce. To do so would mean that babies had a tongue protrusion response for the tongue protrusion stimulus, a mouth opening response for the mouth opening stimulus, and a lip protrusion response for the lip protrusion stimulus. Such one-to-one mapping didn't seem to make for a very convincing, evolutionary story. Thus, for Meltzoff and Moore, a much more reasonable explanation was an explanation based on imitation.

THE ACTIVE INTERMODAL MAPPING (AIM) EXPLANATION   So if imitation actually is involved, how would babies be capable of it? Meltzoff and Moore proposed their "Active Intermodal Matching" hypothesis to explain this ability. What does such an opaque term mean, and how does it explain Meltzoff and Moore's findings? Let's begin with their own words. They wrote, "The hypothesis we favor is that this imitation is based on the neonate's capacity to represent visually and proprioceptively perceived information in a form common to both modalities." Here they were actually making three different points. First, they were declaring their belief that the results really did happen as a result of imitation. Second, they were stating that it was a type of imitation that required babies to integrate visual information (from what they saw) with proprioceptive information (from the way their facial muscles felt when they produced the various facial gestures). Third, they were arguing that the only way babies could integrate information in the visual modality with information in the proprioceptive modality was by mentally representing both types of information in a more abstract format common to, but accessible by both modalities (which is why they called it "intermodal").

Meltzoff and Moore called this more abstract form of representation an "abstract supra-modal representation." It was considered *abstract* because it existed only in the mind, and not in the real world. That is, it was a *mental* representation. But because it was accessible to both the visual and the proprioceptive modalities, it was considered *above* each of them, which is what the prefix *supra* means. So when used to explain how babies can imitate adult facial expressions through the process of active intermodal matching, the term *abstract supramodal representation* means that babies are capable of detecting information visually, converting it to an abstract mental representation, and then, because the abstract representation is supramodal, matching it to the proprioceptive information babies perceive when they produce corresponding facial gestures. But not only do Meltzoff and Moore believe that a matching of information between the visual and proprioceptive modalities can happen, they believe babies do it *actively*. It is a behavior that babies engage in to learn not only about their social partners but also about themselves. This notion is developed further in Meltzoff's later work, which I describe next in a little more detail.

BEYOND MELTZOFF & MOORE (1977)

In my conversation with him, Meltzoff was decidedly proud of the very last sentence of his 1977 article. It read,

> The ability to act on the basis of an abstract representation of a perceptually absent stimulus becomes the starting point for psychological development in infancy and not its culmination.

On its main interpretation, this sentence conveys Meltzoff and Moore's direct challenge to Piagetian theory. As you may recall from Chapters 2 and 3, a hallmark of Piagetian theory is that the Sensorimotor Stage marks the beginning and ending of the infancy period. Of the six sub-stages that make up the Sensorimotor Stage, substage 6, emerging at around 18 to 24 months of age, is when infants were believed to enter into the social dynamic that is the basis of the first true social relationship; because it was only then that infants became capable of full-fledged imitation. In this Piagetian account, then, the starting point for infants' entry in the social world was the conclusion of the sensorimotor stage.

Meltzoff and Moore's position, in contrast, was that infants are capable of entering the social world much earlier, perhaps even in the first month. Indeed, a follow-up study by Meltzoff and Moore in 1983, using a much larger sample size of 40 babies, even revealed social imitation as early as 42 minutes of age. Based on these latter data, Meltzoff and Moore would have us believe that babies are capable of acting on an abstract representation of a perceptually absent stimulus at the very earliest beginnings of postnatal life. This was a truly revolutionary claim.

Since these two early works, Meltzoff and his colleagues have gone on to develop a sort of post-Piagetian theory of their own. As in Piagetian theory, the capacity for imitation remains a cornerstone of social development. But because Meltzoff rejects the Piagetian claim that the capacity for imitation is constructed over time, he is still left with the problem of explaining how the capacity for imitation gets *into* the baby before birth. Indeed, the burden of explanation falls on any scientist who wishes to claim that an ability or capacity is present at birth. Although to my knowledge Meltzoff has never provided a comprehensive account of the prenatal origins of social imitation, he does seem to recognize this as a challenge for child psychology in the years to come.

One assumption that Meltzoff seems to make is that imitation serves a functionally adaptive role for the baby. From the outset, he believes, imitation is pulled from the baby in recognition of a social partner from the moment she opens her eyes, as someone "Like Me." Meltzoff calls this the **Like-Me hypothesis**. The Like-Me hypothesis reflects that human babies are uniquely built to have a feeling of interpersonal connectedness, from the very earliest moments of postnatal life, whenever they gaze into their social partner's eyes. This interpersonal connectedness establishes in babies a sense that the social partner is "like me." Meltzoff argues that the perception of others as "like me" is a *social primitive*. The term *primitive* is often used by child psychologists when they believe that something that will eventually become a relatively advanced capability is present in the newborn in some rudimentary form. Meltzoff's use of the term primitive seems to convey: 1) that from birth babies recognize social partners as in some way similar to themselves, and 2) that this rudimentary recognition and understanding of human social partners will continue to evolve with experience and maturation.

Once we accept the proposition that babies are born with the primitive understanding that their social partners are like them, it is easier to understand how neonatal imitation might have come about in our evolutionary history. According to Meltzoff and colleagues, once babies have the capacity for imitation, they can use it to explore whether a social partner is somebody familiar or somebody new. In a 1999 book chapter, Meltzoff and Moore wrote:

> . . . *infants treat a person's nonverbal behavior as an identifier of who the individual is, and use imitation as a means of verifying this identity. The fundamental idea is that the distinctive behavior and special interactive games of people serve as markers of their identity. If infants are uncertain about the identity of a person, they will be motivated to test whether this person has the same behavioral properties as the old one by imitating her behavior and re-creating the previous social interaction.*

Until now, I've spent a great deal of time on the questions of *whether* neonatal social imitation exists, and to a lesser extent, *why* it might exist. But I haven't addressed perhaps the most fundamental question of all, "*who cares* if it exists?" As it turns out, the capacity for imitation is important because it is one of the most powerful learning tools that humans have at their disposal. At its core, imitation allows us to learn from the actions of another person in the absence of formal instruction. What better way to learn about the world than to imitate the actions of our seasoned and more learned fellow humans? We can imitate those who are physically near us in face-to-face interactions, as well as those who are far away, through media like Facebook or TV. We can gain social knowledge, such as which fork to use with salad at a formal dinner, or how to tell a white lie when receiving a birthday gift we don't like. We can also gain physical knowledge such as how to ride a bike or drive a car. The beauty is that no direct instruction is ever needed. We just watch and learn.

Imitation is as important for primates as it is rare throughout the rest of the animal kingdom. Chimpanzees, gorillas, and orangutans are well known imitators, and they imitate humans and conspecifics (i.e., members of the same species). Research has also shown that rhesus monkeys are excellent imitators. Ferrari and colleagues even showed that newborn rhesus monkeys can imitate the facial gestures of human models just as did the babies in Meltzoff and Moore's study.

So if Meltzoff and Moore are right, then the availability of a functional imitation system right after birth—regardless of how it got there in the first place—means that babies begin absorbing information and knowledge about the social world from the outset. There is no need to wait 18–24 months as Piaget suggested, and there is no need to wait for a fully developed perceptuo-motor system. Babies learn through imitation from the get-go. And if so, then child psychologists had better allocate more of their professional resources toward the study of the first few moments after birth if they are to further advance the science of social cognition.

An improved understanding of the imitation system would not only help us understand children's social development, it would also help us understand the nature of social development when things go awry. In one review of the scientific literature, for example, Brooke Ingersoll describes dozens of studies linking autism spectrum disorders (ASD) to deficits in imitative ability. In one of these studies, children with autism who were classified as "high imitators," verbalized significantly more frequently to the experimenter than children classified as "low imitators." In another study, this one focused on the treatment of ASD, the authors found that teaching imitation skills to children with autism improved those children's ability to produce and manipulate symbols.

In sum, social imitation is really important. It is present at birth. It provides for learning about the world. And it provides for social development. Skill in imitation accelerates learning, and deficits in imitation are associated with developmental delay.

Controversy

Not all scientists embrace the novel ideas of their peers, however, even when those ideas later turn out to be revolutionary ones. The case was no different with Meltzoff and Moore. When their findings were first published, it was very difficult for them to find a home. They didn't fit into Piagetian theory, for the very reason that they were contrary to Piagetian theory. They also didn't fit into behaviorism or ethological theory, because Meltzoff and Moore used these findings to counter behaviorism and ethological theory.

One could even make the bold assertion that these findings didn't even have a home in the natural world. After all, the findings seemed rather magical; maybe even supernatural. Meltzoff and Moore's explanations seem pretty far-fetched. On the face of it, they were trying to argue that newborns could see someone's face (despite abysmal visual acuity), actively transform those visual images into some sort of modality-free representation, and then tap into that modality-free representation to produce a matching facial gesture that they themselves could never be sure was accurate. And babies were doing this why? To see if someone was familiar or strange? Say what?

Many skeptics suggested that Meltzoff and Moore's conclusions were unnecessarily elaborate and rich. They suggested that simpler, more parsimonious explanations would do a better job than the fancy, supernatural-seeming mechanisms Meltzoff and Moore were trying to sell. Indeed, the amount of scientific pushback received by Meltzoff and Moore may explain why their study turned out not only to be one of the most revolutionary studies published since 1960, but also one of the most controversial. It's interesting that although the Meltzoff and Moore (1977) study was rated 12th most revolutionary, it was simultaneously rated 3rd most controversial. The same kind of skeptics offered the same kind of pushback against Baillargeon's work (see Chapter 5).

So what is the source of this opposition? The problem seems to be one of over-attribution. The fact that Meltzoff and Moore's babies seemed to *look like* they were imitating, didn't mean they really *were* imitating. But if they weren't imitating, then what? The answer to this question varies depending on the critic. Let's take a look at an especially strong attack leveled by Moshe Anisfeld in 1996.

ANISFELD (1996)   In his rebuttal to the Meltzoff and Moore line of work, Anisfeld begins by directing the reader to one of his own earlier articles, where he reported a total of 28 positive findings and 48 negative findings of neonatal imitation. By noting that there were nearly two failed attempts at replicating Meltzoff and Moore's findings for every successful one, he seems clearly unimpressed. But he goes even further than that, and questions whether there are any *real* positive findings at all. In doing so, he subjected nine of the "positive" studies to a "critical" statistical reanalysis. Each of these studies was chosen because it was purported to have demonstrated both a tongue protrusion imitation and another type of imitation (usually mouth opening). Of the nine studies, six were conducted by Meltzoff and Moore themselves.

Consider how Anisfeld handles the 1983 Meltzoff and Moore study, for example. He starts out by conceding that maybe babies really do stick out their tongues more frequently when they see adults sticking out their tongues. But if so, then in any experimental procedure in which a baby is sticking out her tongue in response to the adult sticking out his tongue, it must also be the case that babies spend less time doing any other gesture, such as opening their mouths, because babies cannot do both gestures at the same time. Thus, for the very same reason that the number of tongue protrusions in the tongue protrusion condition increases relative to baseline, the number of mouth openings in the tongue protrusion condition must decrease relative to baseline. You see, the decrease in mouth openings is a necessary consequence of the increase in tongue protrusions. Again, this is because there is less *opportunity* for babies to produce mouth openings, when they are spending more of their time sticking out their tongue. Okay, if you follow this point, then you're ready for the second point.

When you look at whether there are more mouth openings in the mouth opening condition, *relative* to mouth openings in the tongue protrusion condition, it appears that there are. But this difference is *not* because babies are opening their mouths more in the mouth opening condition, *it is because they are opening their mouths **less** in the tongue protrusion condition.* So any appearance of the imitation of mouth opening in the mouth opening condition is really nothing more than an artifact of an increase in tongue protrusions in the tongue protrusion condition.

Following this line of reasoning, if tongue protrusion is all that babies really do, then any argument in favor of imitation is considerably weakened. Anisfeld put it this way: "The restriction of early matching behavior to a single gesture, tongue protrusion, weakens the hypothesis that very young infants are capable of facial imitation. If [they] had this ability, why would they exhibit it in regard to only one gesture? . . . [C]laims of early imitative abilities have been too uncritically accepted."

Others critics have jumped on board Anisfeld's attack wagon and have argued that even if tongue protrusions are elicited, they're not imitations at all, but rather spontaneous oral motor movements that babies produce whenever they get excited or aroused. One proponent of this view is Susan Jones, who showed that babies increase tongue protrusions simply when listening to music. She argues that tongue protrusions are simply the way babies respond when aroused, regardless of the source of that arousal.

Rebuttal

In my conversation with Meltzoff, I asked how he felt about other scientists going after his status-quo-shattering findings so strongly. Surprisingly, he didn't seem much bothered; nor did he describe the attacks as personal. From his vantage, he saw the criticisms as stemming from different theoretical perspectives. He attributes pushback to theoretical commitments that don't allow for intermodal matching. In other words, if you believe in Theory X, and Finding Y does not fit, then you have two choices; either dispense with Theory X or reject Finding Y. Meltzoff believes that since most scientists have spent their professional lives training under their respective Theory Xs, they're not inclined to dispense with them. Instead, they're perfectly content to dispatch with Finding Y.

A fairly strong defense against critical attacks can be found in Meltzoff and Moore's 1994 study. In this study, the authors modeled two different types of tongue protrusion. For one type, they stuck out their tongue in the middle of the mouth, for the other, they stuck out their tongue in the corner of their mouth. They hoped this methodology would finally silence the critics because if babies stuck out their tongues differently in response to the two different types of adult tongue protrusion, then really there is no way to account for the findings other than imitation.

The results of this study verified Meltzoff and Moore's expectations. When babies witnessed the adult sticking his tongue out of the side of his mouth, they attempted to reproduce this side-tongue-protrusion action. They didn't get it right at first, but over repeated trials they got closer and closer to the modeled target. Meltzoff and Moore interpreted the continuously improving accuracy of their babies as fully consistent with their "AIM hypothesis." That is to say, the fact that babies don't imitate the side-tongue model accurately on the first try is not a problem. They wrote, "AIM does not rule out visual-motor mapping of elementary acts on 'first try' without the need for feedback. The crux of the hypothesis is that the adult serves as a genuine target for the infant's behavior. There may be a delimited set of primary acts ... that are achieved with little need of feedback, whereas other more complex acts involve modifications of these primitives and proportionately more proprioceptive monitoring."

CONCLUSION

The story of Meltzoff and Moore (1977) began as a test of the father of modern child psychology, Jean Piaget. Like so many other revolutionary studies covered in these pages, the gravity of this study comes from the fact that it ventured into uncharted territory. According to Meltzoff, it was the first study to challenge the social developmental aspects of Piaget's theory. At the same time, the authors were simply doing what others were doing at the time, jumping on the refutation train. But while others were testing Piaget's claims about children's understanding of the physical world, Meltzoff and Moore took the novel step of testing Piaget's claims about children's understanding of the social world.

It might be said that Meltzoff's was the tongue that launched a thousand studies. We have spent some time here talking about other tongue protrusion research spurred on by the 1977 article, but we haven't begun to scratch the tip of the iceberg of other social cognition research brought about by Meltzoff's work. Not all of it focused on imitation, but a great deal of it did; and a great deal of it was fascinating. In a 1995 study which has become a classic in its own right, for example, Meltzoff showed that infant imitation could be extended to an adults' intended behavior than an actually observed behavior. For example, after watching an adult try but fail to pull apart a Tinkertoy-like dumbbell, Meltzoff found that 18-month-olds would actually imitate the *intended* behavior (pulling apart the toy dumbbell) instead of the *actual* behavior (failing to pull apart the toy dumbbell). This study raised the possibility that very young children functioned as if their social partners had wishes and desires. This is a phenomenal ability that provides babies with a very powerful toolbox to use when deciphering the intentions of their human social partners.

Meltzoff and Moore's 1977 revolutionary study gave pause to the community of child psychological scientists because they presented it with a finding that could not be assimilated by any known or even theoretical means. Facial imitation in neonates could not be explained by behaviorism, ethology, Gestalt psychology, or contemporary Piagetian psychology; and that's saying something because Piagetianism itself represented a giant improvement over other mainstream psychological theories. As so often happens with revolutionary and controversial studies, the findings aroused the field, and instigated a mountain of follow-up research on infants' social development. Even if Meltzoff and Moore's preferred explanation eventually proves not to be true, our contemporary understanding of children's social cognition is surely the better for it. The irony is that this improved understanding can ultimately be traced to a young scientist sticking out his tongue at a baby.

Bibliography

Anisfeld, M. (1996). Only tongue protrusion modeling is matched by neonates. *Developmental Review, 16,* 149–161.

Dixon, W. E., Jr. (2014). Twenty most controversial studies in child psychology. *Developments: Newsletter of the Society for Research in Child Development, 57,* 8–9.

Ferrari, P. F., Visalberghi, E., Paukner, A., Fogassi, L., Ruggiero, A., & Suomi, S. J. (2006). Neonatal imitation in rhesus macaques. *PLoS biology, 4,* e302.

Ingersoll, B. (2008). The social role of imitation in autism: Implications for the treatment of imitation deficits. *Infants & Young Children, 21,* 107–119.

Jones, S. S. (2006). Exploration or imitation? The effect of music on 4-week-old infants' tongue protrusions. *Infant Behavior and Development, 29,* 126–130.

Meltzoff, A. N. (1995). Understanding the intentions of others: Re-enactment of intended acts by 18-month-old children. *Developmental Psychology, 31,* 838–850.

Meltzoff, A. N. (2013). Origins of social cognition: Bidirectional mapping between self and other and the "Like-Me" hypothesis. In M. Banaji & S. Gelman (Eds.), *Navigating the social world: What infants, children, and other species can teach us* (pp. 139–144). New York: Oxford University Press.

Meltzoff, A. N., & Moore, M. K. (1983). Newborn infants imitate adult facial gestures. *Child Development, 54,* 702–709.

Meltzoff, A. N., & Moore, M. K. (1997). Explaining facial imitation: A theoretical model. *Early Development and Parenting, 6,* 179–192.

Meltzoff, A. N., & Moore, M. K. (1999). Resolving the debate about early imitation. In A. Slater & D. Muir (Eds.), *The Blackwell reader in developmental psychology.* Oxford: Blackwell.

Meltzoff, A. N., & Moore, M. K. (2004). Imitation, memory, and the representation of persons. *Infant Behavior and Development, 17,* 83–99.

Questions for Discussion

1. Where do "social primitives" come from? How might they get *in* the baby?
2. Should the federal government fund child psychological research when the goal is to see whether a baby will imitate sticking out a tongue?
3. In what other ways might a young child understand the world using cross-modal perception?

14

Governments, Grade Schools, and Grocery Stores
Multiple Levels of Influence

Toward an Experimental Ecology of Human Development

Bronfenbrenner, U. (1977). *American Psychologist, 32*, 513–531.
(RANK 9)

Ever since the birth of psychology way back in the late 1800s, the field has faced a century-long struggle to be recognized as a "real" science by its more glorified sister disciplines in the "natural" sciences. Disciplines such as physics and chemistry commonly scoff at the existence of psychology and its claim to "real science" status. Even the kid sister of the natural sciences, biology, who herself has only recently been admitted to the natural science club, has taken some potshots at psychology. The criticisms of psychology are always the same: "It's way too vague," "Humans can't objectively study themselves," "Psychologists just make up stuff as they go along," "Psychology's just a collection of commonsense facts that everybody already knows," and last but not least, "Psychology is just too imprecise to be considered scientific."

On the face of it, our critics have a couple of good points. Psychology sometimes really is way too vague. And it really is true that humans can't objectively study themselves. But for that matter, neither can humans objectively study anything else, including physics and chemistry, because humans by their very nature are limited by their perceptual and cognitive belief systems. Only psychologists realize this point, apparently. Two other criticisms are simply wrong. Psychologists, at least good ones, really don't make stuff up as they go along. And psychology really isn't just a collection of commonsense facts that everybody knows. In fact, a lot of psychological research has proven many, if not most, "commonsense" beliefs to be completely false.

One of the long-term sore spots in psychology has been the criticism that psychology doesn't do a very good job of making precise predictions about human behavior. As I describe in Chapter 6, this is undeniably true, at least when it comes to predicting the specific behavior of individuals. But psychologists are actually quite good at making predictions about large groups of people. For example, I always accurately predict that 40% of my introductory psychology students will earn a D or an F on their first exam, give or take a few percentage points. This is because 40% of my introductory psychology students *always do* get a D or an F on their first exam. The precision of my group prediction is based on my past group data. But I certainly wouldn't be able to predict *which* of my students will get a D or an F. There's the rub. Psychologists are notoriously poor at predicting the behaviors of single individuals. As a case in point, psychologists are often summoned to testify at parole board hearings to predict whether a convicted arsonist is going to light more fires, or whether a convicted sex offender is going to molest more children. The most these psychologists can do is base their judgments on available data and say something like, "Based on the existing scientific literature, and the specific characteristics of this individual, it is my judgment that there is a 78.2% chance that this individual will avoid committing arson should he be released from further incarceration." This does give a fairly strong impression of scientific imprecision, doesn't it?

Now compare this level of precision with what we usually learn about in natural science classes. In physics, for example, we learn about laws of gravity, laws of motion, laws of thermodynamics, laws of quantum mechanics, and so on. Using these laws, we learn to estimate with perfect precision the outcomes of some contrived event. On one physics exam, for example, I remember calculating how fast a ping-pong ball would have to go in order to stop a moving locomotive in its tracks. The lesson I learned was that an object with very small mass has to go really, really fast to counteract the momentum of an object with a much larger mass, but moving much more slowly. It's all about plugging values for velocity and mass into certain equations, while making certain assumptions about the event. As it turns out, for a 2.5-gram ping-pong ball to completely stop a 220,000-pound locomotive moving at 45 miles per hour, it would have to be traveling at the rate of 1.8 billion miles per hour, roughly three times the speed of light.

Now, wouldn't you say physics has the flavor of a precise science? Yet the devil is in the details (and the assumptions). With the ping-pong ball event, for example, we assume that the ping-pong ball hits the locomotive head-on, and not at an angle. We also assume that the collision takes place in the absence of changing atmospheric conditions; we assume no wind, no rain, and a constant temperature. We also assume there are no bumps on the train tracks, and that the train is traveling on a level surface. These assumptions are what permit us to make highly precise predictions about physical behavior. Without these assumptions, the level of precision a physicist can muster is much closer to the level of precision a psychologist has to deal with.

My standing challenge to anyone who thinks physics is more precise than psychology is to predict with complete accuracy the outcome state of a watermelon being pushed off the roof of a five-story building. (I got this idea from watching the old David Letterman show back in the 1980s.) Now, it's not good enough just to say a watermelon will splatter when it smacks into the ground. I'm talking about a much more precise level of description, the kind most people think of when they think of physics, and the kind they demand when they think of psychology. Where will each of the seeds end up? Where will the rind crack, and into how many pieces will it break? What size will each of the pieces be? Where will the pieces end up? How will the flesh of the melon be distributed? Obviously, these questions can't be answered with a high degree of precision. There are simply too many variables to take into account. So much would depend on the varying wind speeds at each elevation as the watermelon descends. And the influence of the wind would depend on the orientation of the melon in space. And the rotation of the melon in space would depend on its wobble as it left the surface of the roof. Then there's the structural integrity of the watermelon rind. How it breaks apart would depend on the thickness of the portion of the rind that makes first contact with the ground. And the influence of the ground would depend on which part of the ground made first contact with the melon. Are there any cracks in the concrete? Are there any small pebbles or sticks lying around? You're probably getting the picture by now.

My point in bringing up the case of the falling watermelon is to show that in these kinds of situations, the physicist, like the psychologist, is reduced to making only the most general of predictions. She could predict, for example, that the flesh of the melon will spread out in a fan-like pattern, proportional to the angle and speed of the melon at impact. But I'm not inclined to call this a highly precise prediction. Yet these are the kinds of situations child psychologists have to contend with every day when predicting children's behavior. Children are subject to so many constantly changing internal and external influences that psychologists simply can't describe with any great degree of accuracy the outcomes of their development.

This is where the revolutionary work of Urie Bronfenbrenner comes in. In his 1977 article, ranked ninth most revolutionary overall, Bronfenbrenner proposed an "ecological theory of human development." He developed his theory to encourage psychologists to take into account as many factors as possible in explaining human development. Of course, the social-emotional-cultural factors that influence human development are no doubt very different from the physical factors that influence falling watermelons, but the level of complexity involved in the two kinds of predictions are probably comparable. If anything, children's development is harder to predict since they don't have the emotional stability of a watermelon.

Bronfenbrenner created his ecological theory because he thought too many child psychologists were spending too much time exploring developmental issues that were too narrow for most children under most conditions in most cultures. In a typical case, a child psychologist brings a toddler into the laboratory, gives him various puzzles and tests, and exposes him to unusual situations. Although the child psychologist might *think* she is measuring the toddler's intellectual ability, in reality she's measuring a great deal more. For one thing, she's measuring her own influence on the toddler. Not only is the toddler responding to questions on a test, but also to the tone and manner of the child psychologist. The strangeness of the laboratory also has an influence on the kid. When children are in a strange place, their responses are bound to be different than when in a familiar place. Bronfenbrenner's gripe is that these extra influences are foundational to children's behaviors, but they are usually ignored or assumed to be trivially important in most child psychology research.

In his ecological theory, Bronfenbrenner described four levels, or *contexts*, of environmental influence that child psychologists should take into account if they really want to advance the science of child psychology. By taking all four of these contexts into account, Bronfenbrenner believed that child psychologists not only would do better, more accurate science, but they also would do research that really mattered.

INTRODUCTION

Bronfenbrenner introduced us to the limitations of modern child psychology by pointing out that a lot of child psychology research consisted of elegantly designed, tightly controlled studies that bore little resemblance to what happened in the real world. Humorously, he summed up traditional child psychology as "the science of the strange behavior of children in strange situations with strange adults for the briefest possible periods of time." On the other hand, child psychologists who do try to make their research relevant to the real world, and who conduct their scientific studies outside of the laboratory, have a hard time making their studies rigorous and tightly controlled. In sum, child psychology researchers either focus on rigor at the expense of relevance, or focus on relevance at the expense of rigor.

But Bronfenbrenner rejected the idea that these are the only two options. He believed that naturalistic observations of children's development in the real world could be well controlled, and that observations in the lab could have real-world applications. The trick was to realize that the laboratory environment and the natural environment are both part of children's natural surroundings and that both can be expected to influence children's behavior. Similarly, the researcher who tested the child and the mother who cared for the child are both people in the child's natural surroundings who can be expected to influence the child's behavior. Bronfenbrenner's call to arms for an ecological approach to child psychology was a call to embrace *all* the contexts, including the physical and the social, in which children find themselves.

So what exactly is an ecological approach to psychology anyway? Well, let's start with the term *ecology*. In its standard use, **ecology** refers to a branch of biology that studies the relationship between organisms and their surroundings. Ecology addresses such issues as how an organism uses its surroundings to its advantage, and how changes in an organism's surroundings can influence the functioning of the organism. From an ecological perspective, organisms can't be truly understood unless you simultaneously take into account their surroundings. Consider the woodland beaver. You could bring the beaver into a laboratory setting, you could feed it some worms and some leaves, you could give it a doggy chew toy, and you could try to teach it to ride a bicycle. But by removing the beaver from its natural habitat, you would completely miss out on some of its most unique and interesting naturally occurring behaviors. For example, you would never see how beavers fell trees using their teeth, you would never see their crafty ingenuity in building their homes out of wood and mud, and you would never see how they build dams across waterways to preserve their water supply. An ecological approach would demand that you study the beaver in its natural surroundings.

By applying an ecological approach to child psychology, Bronfenbrenner was urging us to avoid thinking of the child as an isolated organism, and to begin trying to understand the child in the context of his or her own natural surroundings. By taking children's surroundings into account, child psychologists won't miss out on some of children's most unique and interesting naturally occurring behaviors.

In formal terms, Bronfenbrenner defined his ecological psychology as "the scientific study of the progressive, mutual accommodation, throughout the life span, between a growing human organism and the changing immediate environments in which it lives, as this process is affected by relations obtaining within and between these immediate settings, as well as the larger social contexts, both formal and informal, in which the settings are embedded." As usual for professional psychologists, this is a rather opaque definition. He was basically saying not only that children should be studied in their natural surroundings, but also that their natural surroundings exist at several different levels. I'll describe each of these levels in more detail shortly, but for now we can note that the levels of surroundings differ in how directly they influence children. The most direct impacts come from children's immediate environments, which are composed of the things and people children make direct contact with, including their homes and families, and their schoolrooms, classmates, and teachers. Then there are broader surroundings, which children don't make direct contact with, but which have an influence on the immediate surroundings. These broader surroundings include such environments as the neighborhood, the public school system, and the place where their parents work. Children may not make direct contact with these broader surroundings, but these broader surroundings can still have an impact on the children. For example, if the public school system has a policy that teachers can't accept gifts from students, then this policy has a direct impact on the child when she tries to give an apple to Mr. SerVass. And if one of the child's parents gets a promotion at work, then that parent comes home in a happy mood, which in turn has a positive impact on how that parent engages her child at the end of the day.

But there are even broader surroundings than these, although the term "surroundings" doesn't fit as well here. Perhaps the better word is "context." Consider the context of the American attitude toward public education, for example. The United States government enforces a federal law that requires all children in all communities to receive a formal, publicly funded education. Within this context, then, it is a policy that all local communities must provide a formal education for their children. As a result, local public school systems are formed, teachers are hired, and kids sit in classrooms and hopefully learn something. Home schooling is also permitted within these parameters, as long as the home schooling is formal, and meets the educational standards of the local community. Although the mandatory education policy of the United States doesn't have an immediate impact on a particular child, the policy still has an influence on the child as it works its way down the governmental chain of command. The federal public education policy drives the state public education policy, the state public education policy drives the local public education policy, the local public education policy drives how children in the community will be educated, and this affects how teachers teach their students.

Because children's surroundings, or contexts, can influence them at so many different levels, Bronfenbrenner helped clarify the role of each by dividing them neatly into four different categories. Listed in order of their directness of impact (from most to least), he called them (1) *the microsystem*, (2) *the mesosystem*, (3) *the exosystem*, and (4) *the macrosystem*. We'll consider each of these in turn.

THE MICROSYSTEM

In Bronfenbrenner's technical talk, the **microsystem** "is the complex of relations between the developing person and environment in an immediate setting containing that person." The setting can be the home, the school, the playground, or the candy store, just to name a few. The child also plays a specific role in each setting; which might include the role of the daughter, the student, the playmate, or the customer. In addition, there are certain objects within each setting that the child comes into contact with, and certain people the child interacts with. To understand the impact of the microsystem on the child is to understand how each of these settings directly impinges on the development of the child. As a child carries out his routine activities during the course of the day, he might, for example, find himself eating breakfast with his little sister, walking to school with his best friend, sitting in a classroom learning about math, practicing with the basketball team after school, eating dinner with his family, sitting at his desk in his bedroom doing his homework, taking a bath, eating a bedtime snack while watching *Monday Night Football*, and reading a book before going to sleep. Each of these activities represents a set of experiences common to the settings of the home, the school, and the peer group, and each activity has the potential to influence the child's development. All of these settings together comprise the microsystem. Bronfenbrenner outlined four "propositions" about the microsystem that an ecological psychology should embrace.

Proposition 1

In contrast to the traditional unidirectional research model typically employed in the laboratory, an ecological experiment must allow for reciprocal processes; that is, not only the effect of A on B, but also the effect of B on A. This is the requirement of *reciprocity*.

In other words, child psychology researchers must realize not only that the environment can have an effect on the child, but that the child can have just as strong an effect on the environment. Consider the case of the child eating breakfast with his little sister. When the child arrives at the breakfast table to find that his little sister has eaten the last bowl of Cap'n Crunch cereal, he may lash out and say something like, "You are literally the most annoying person on the planet." Obviously, the immediate environment has had an effect on the boy. But the very act of calling his little sister "annoying," also affects the environment, specifically, the role played by the sister as part of that environment. The next morning the child may arrive at the breakfast table to find a much more hostile setting. When he sits down at the breakfast table, his little sister may begin the conversation by calling him a "freak." No doubt this puts a rather antagonistic spin on the day's beginnings. The two might end up in a war of words, and the boy might then go off to school in a foul mood. But this whole situation can be traced back to the boy's own word-lashing of his sister the day before. The point is that when child psychologists do their research, they would be foolish to believe that the direction of influence goes only from the environment to the child. By ignoring the possible child-to-environment direction of influence, they're missing out on half the story.

Proposition 2

An ecological experiment requires recognition of the social system actually operative in the research setting. This system will typically involve all of the participants present, *not excluding* the experimenter. This is the requirement of recognizing the **totality of the functional social system** in the setting.

When children are invited to participate in research being conducted by a child psychologist, they are entering into a social system that includes themselves, the experimenter, and any of the experimenter's assistants. And just as the little boy caused his own foul mood by calling his sister "annoying," a child can influence his own performance in a child psychology experiment by virtue of how well he gets along with the experimenter. In my own research, I've seen many 21-month-old babies frustrate the bejeebies out of my laboratory assistants. In one of my experiments, for example, babies were asked to locate a ball. But instead of simply pointing to the ball, or handing it over to the lab assistant, some babies grabbed the ball and threw it across the room (and because it was a rubber ball, it **BOUNCED**!). Of course, each time the baby threw the ball, the lab assistant had to get up and go after the ball; and after she returned the ball to the table, many babies threw it again. Although I train my assistants to be very respectful and tolerant of infant "uniquenesses," I couldn't help noticing a look of exasperation on their faces that said they were going to end the session early. Thus, it's probably fair to say that babies who are ball throwers produce lab assistants who move briskly through experimental sessions. And, of course, if lab assistants move briskly through experimental sessions, then babies have fewer opportunities to reveal their intellectual abilities. Extrapolating this idea more generally, it should be obvious how babies in the lab can indirectly influence their own laboratory test scores, by virtue of their direct impacts on the experimenters giving the tests.

Proposition 3

In contrast to the conventional dyadic research model, which is limited to assessing the *direct* effect of two agents on each other, the design of an ecological experiment must take into account the existence in the setting of systems that include more than two persons. Such larger systems must be analyzed in terms of all possible subsystems.

What this means is that when more than two people are involved with each other in a setting, things get complicated real fast. Suppose you've recruited a young girl named Jenny to participate in a research study. Coming from an intact family, not only does Jenny have a relationship with Mom and a relationship with Dad, but Mom and Dad have a relationship with each other. Each of these two-person relationships is called a "dyad," and each dyadic system is a subsystem of a larger three-person system called a "triad." Well, Bronfenbrenner warns us that we can't understand the Jenny–Mom relationship, for example, without also understanding the other two relationships. If Jenny and Mom come into the laboratory, and we find during a free-play session that Mom seems overly strict and controlling of Jenny's behavior, our initial judgment might be that Mom is overly strict and controlling. But by jumping to this conclusion, we're ignoring the possibility that Mom's behavior during the lab session might have been influenced by Mom's relationship with Dad or by Jenny's relationship with Dad. For example, maybe Dad was the one who was supposed to bring Jenny to the lab, and maybe he decided at the last minute to back out of his obligation. In this case, Mom picked up the slack, which she may not have been happy about, and she might have expressed her frustration in her free-play behavior with Jenny. Thus, our initial belief that Mom was unusually strict and controlling is undermined by the fact that her behavior during this particular free-play session is probably not an accurate reflection of her usual, happy-go-lucky self.

Proposition 4

Ecological experiments must take into account aspects of the physical environment as possible indirect influences on social processes taking place within the setting.

Lastly, Bronfenbrenner pointed out that people aren't the only objects that exist in children's natural surroundings. There are physical objects too. And these physical objects can have powerful influences on any social activities taking place in their proximity. Bronfenbrenner described one study, for example, which suggested that nearly 80% of households reduce their level of conversation when a television program is on. No doubt, the emergence of television viewing in the household during the last half-century has radically curtailed children's opportunities for talking with their parents, as well as parents' opportunities for talking with their children. A modern version of this scenario results from the rampant availability of the smartphone. During recent holiday gatherings, for example, I have witnessed whole rooms of (nonsleeping) family members so quiet you could literally hear a pin drop, not because they weren't socially engaged, but because they weren't socially engaged *with one another*. They were completely submerged in their social media sites via their smartphones! Some were even messaging each other. In the same room! So before child psychology researchers jump to the conclusion that parents lack interest in communicating with their kids, they would do well to pay considerable attention to the prominence of the technology in the surroundings.

MESOSYSTEM

The best way to think about the next level of surroundings, the mesosystem kind, is to think of it as a collection of microsystems that all influence each other. Bronfenbrenner said that a "mesosystem comprises the interrelations among major settings containing the developing person at a particular point in his or her life. Thus, for an American 12-year-old, the mesosystem typically encompasses interactions among family, school, and peer group; for some children, it might also include church, camp, or workplace." The idea here is that influences that take place in one setting can spill over to influence what happens in other settings. When the influences of individual settings spill over into other settings, you have a mesosystem. Bronfenbrenner crafted three propositions that child psychology researchers should think about when studying the mesosystem.

Proposition 5

In the traditional research model, behavior and development are investigated one setting at a time without regard to possible interdependencies between settings. An ecological approach invites consideration of the joint impact of two or more settings on their elements. This is the requirement, wherever possible, of analyzing *interactions between settings*.

For example, a child might stop by the candy store on the way to school to buy a pack of Twizzlers. Already you can see the immediate influence of the candy store microsystem on the child because it provided him with a supply of chewy, cherry-flavored licorice. When the child gets to school, he might start eating the Twizzlers during a math test, causing his teacher to scold him for breaking school rules. In this case, as you might already have noticed, there is a *bidirectional* influence between the child and teacher within the classroom microsystem. The child's candy eating influences the teacher, and the teacher's scolding influences the child. But notice that there is also an indirect influence of the candy store microsystem on the classroom microsystem. The scolding arises out of the *joint* contributions of two microsystems that are brought into relation with one another by the child's actions. Without the schoolteacher the scolding wouldn't have happened, and without the candy the scolding wouldn't have happened. It's only through the joint combination of schoolteacher + candy, coupled with the child's willingness to eat the candy during the test that the scolding happened.

Now the child might go home at the end of the day and tell his mom that he got into trouble for eating candy during the math test. At this point, the mother might ground the boy, both for his willingness to waste his money on candy and for his willingness to break school rules. This represents another joint contribution of microsystems. If the child hadn't bought candy at the store, and if he hadn't broken school rules, and if he hadn't gotten scolded by the teacher, and if he hadn't told his mom anything, he wouldn't have been grounded. In the end, having a good understanding of why the child was grounded requires a good understanding of how all the microsystems interacted with each other to produce the grounding. This is what Bronfenbrenner meant by understanding at the mesosystem level. Child psychology researchers who consider the behavior of children at only one point in time are destined to miss out on the much richer sources of influence that are affecting the children's behavior.

Proposition 6

The design of an ecological experiment involving the same person in more than one setting should take into account the possible subsystems that exist, or could exist, across settings.

When a child plays different roles in different settings, such as candy buyer, student, and son, not only can the settings have different individual and joint influences on the child, but people from the different settings can also form systems of relationships with one another. For example, when the mother of our candy eater goes in for the semiannual parent–teacher conference, she meets, greets, and establishes a relationship with the teacher. She may send notes to the teacher on occasion, and the teacher may send notes back to the mother. The mother–teacher relationship that forms is an example of a subsystem that exists across settings. If the child ever decides to eat candy in the classroom again, then the teacher's scolding of the child may in part depend on her relationship with the child's mother. If the teacher thinks fondly of the mother, she may soften the scolding. But if she thinks the mother's a nasty old witch, she may not scold the child at all, under the belief that the child has it hard enough at home. Instead, she may just quietly take the candy from the child, without causing unnecessary embarrassment. The point, of course, is that children are not only a product of their own beliefs, desires, and abilities, but also a product of how their own beliefs, desires, and abilities interact with their surroundings. And the surroundings themselves both influence the child and are influenced by each other.

Proposition 7

A fruitful context for developmental research is provided by the **ecological transitions** that periodically occur in a person's life. These transitions include changes in role and setting as a function of the person's maturation or of events in the life cycle of others responsible for his or her care and development. Such shifts are to be conceived and analyzed as changes in ecological systems rather than solely within individuals.

The idea behind this proposition is that child psychologists should realize not only that individual children change and develop, but that their ecological surroundings change and develop as well. We tend to think of the home setting, for example, as just one stable, permanent, unchanging setting. But the home setting can change quite a bit, especially if the child and his family move to a new home. He might have a basketball court at his new home, providing him with an opportunity to improve his athletic skills. And the new home may have a much larger yard for him to mow, resulting in his allowance being bumped up to match.

EXOSYSTEM

In the two types of surroundings we've just talked about—the microsystem and the mesosystem—the child was a direct participant in the goings-on. It's easy to think of them as surroundings because the child is directly involved. But there are broader, more remote kinds of surroundings that affect children even when children don't actually make physical contact with them. The first of these is what Bronfenbrenner called the **exosystem**. He defined it as "an extension of the mesosystem embracing other specific social structures, both formal and informal, that do not themselves contain the developing person but impinge upon or encompass the immediate settings in which that person is found, and thereby influence, delimit, or even determine what goes on there." Typical exosystems you're probably familiar with include the work world, the media, the local government, commerce and industry, and the social community. Bronfenbrenner suggests one proposition that pertains to the exosystem, but it only implores child psychologists to take the exosystem into account, without giving any specific dictates about how to do so.

Proposition 8

Research on the ecology of human development requires investigations that go beyond the immediate setting containing the person to examine the larger contexts, both formal and informal, that affect events within the immediate setting.

I wrote the first edition of this book when I lived in a northwestern Ohio community. At that time, the local public school system had decided to set aside some of its funds to support special programming aimed at meeting the needs of the community's "gifted" children. "Gifted children" were defined as kids who score exceedingly high on standardized tests of intelligence or achievement. To satisfy the needs of these children, the local school system created a one-day-a-week "pull-out" program. On Thursdays, all the gifted elementary-school kids in the community were pulled out of their regular school classrooms and bused to a special classroom located at one of the elementary schools. There, a teacher certified to work with gifted children ran a gifted classroom with curricular goals specifically matched to the advanced intellectual needs of those children. This is a perfect example of the influence of the exosystem on children's development. The "larger context" here was the decision of the school system to offer extra services to gifted children. Although the kids didn't actually make direct contact with the policy, they did make direct contact with a gifted classroom and teacher that were created as a result of the policy.

Let's consider how the exosystem might influence the results of a child psychology research study. Suppose a child psychologist is interested in doing research on the graduation rates of gifted students. Suppose she travels to a dozen counties in her area and collects graduation data from school systems in those counties. After analyzing her data, suppose she concludes that in general, across a number of different school systems, gifted children are no more likely to graduate than other children. Could her conclusions be wrong? Why, yes they could. The accuracy of this finding is in jeopardy without considering exosystem influences. The chances that a gifted child will graduate from high school might depend in no small way on the policies of the local school systems toward providing services for gifted children. Gifted children who attend school systems that don't provide a gifted curriculum might get bored with their regular curriculum. As a result, they might actually be more inclined to drop out than other children. But gifted children coming from school systems that *do* meet their needs might be less inclined to drop out, compared with other children. The child psychologist has no way of recognizing any differences between these two groups without considering exosystem influences that affect whether or not school systems provide services for gifted children.

MACROSYSTEM

The largest, most global, most omnipresent, and most remote influences on children's development come from the **macrosystem**. Bronfenbrenner defined the macrosystem as "the overarching institutional patterns of the culture or subculture, such as the economic, social, educational, legal, and political systems, of which micro-, meso-, and exosystems are the concrete manifestations. Macrosystems are conceived and examined not only in structural terms but as carriers of information and ideology that, both explicitly and implicitly, endow meaning and motivation to particular agencies, social networks, roles, activities, and their interrelations."

Yet another hefty, obscure psychological definition. The point is only that in any society there are some cultural and subcultural values that are so central to the fabric of that society that members of that society may not even realize other values are possible. In metaphorical terms, Marshall McLuhan (*War and Peace in the Global Village*) once wrote, "One thing about which fish know exactly nothing is water, since they have no anti-environment which would enable them to perceive the element they live in." In the United States, for example, the value of education is taken as a given. These days, even a college education is expected of most people. As children develop in American culture, they're developing within the context of this cultural expectation. This is not to say that most Americans seek out college educations, but those Americans who don't often feel that they should. Education is a core fiber of the "American way."

But not all cultures place such a high value on education. In some Middle Eastern cultures, for example, it's forbidden for women to seek out a college education. And in other cultures, especially economically disadvantaged ones, it may be unusual for girls to get any education at all. Bronfenbrenner warns us that in child psychology research, we have to be aware not only that child development takes place within the context of major cultural values, but also that as scientists we ourselves espouse certain cultural values, and we need to be sensitive to the effects these values have on how we do science. These realizations provide the fodder for Bronfenbrenner's last proposition.

Proposition 9

Research on the ecology of human development should include experiments involving the innovative restructuring of prevailing ecological systems in ways that depart from existing institutional ideologies and structures by redefining goals, roles, and activities and providing interconnections between systems previously isolated from each other.

Precisely because the macrosystem is so all-pervasive, it's very difficult to see how research could do much to uncover influences of the macrosystem on children's development. You could do cross-cultural research to compare children from one culture to children from another. But since cultures are different, and since macrosystem influences affect the micro-, meso-, and exosystems so totally, you couldn't be sure if children from different cultures are different because of the macrosystem or because of the subsidiary systems. In response to this dilemma, Bronfenbrenner recommends conducting **transforming experiments**. Transforming experiments take children espousing one set of cultural values and expectations and expose them to radical departures from those values and expectations. Of course, the next question is, how do you do this?

The best example of a transforming macrosystem experiment, according to Bronfenbrenner, is the famous "Robbers Cave experiment," conducted by Muzafer Sherif in the 1950s. The setting for that study was the Robbers Cave campground. Twenty-four lower-middle-class boys, roughly 12 years old, were brought to the campground and exposed to a number of community- and friendship-building exercises typical of summer camps. Just as the boys were getting to know each other, though, they were separated into two smaller groups. Boys within each of the smaller groups lived, worked, and played with one another, and many new friendships blossomed. The sense of intra-group cohesion became very strong. Then the experimenters set up various competitions between the two groups. As a result of the competitions, within-group loyalty increased even more, and group members adopted team names and mascots (i.e., the "Eagles" and the "Rattlers"). But between-group rivalry also emerged, eventually becoming so pronounced that boys in each group developed a severe dislike for children in the other group (many of whom had recently been their friends).

Of course, the within-group connectedness and between-group mistrust that emerged in the Robbers Cave study happens throughout American culture. It's not a situation that we're especially proud of, but one that exists nonetheless. People frequently define themselves in terms of the positive qualities of their own group, and distance themselves from what they perceive to be the negative qualities of other groups. Our discomfort with the unfamiliar occasionally even rises to the level of loathing and bigotry. Anyway, after Sherif established this microcosm of American cultural intolerance among the two groups of boys, he then tried to change it. He set up a number of "emergency" problems that required the cooperation of both groups to overcome. For example, the water supply was cut off and boys from both groups were recruited to work together to help find the source of a presumed water leak. The method he chose proved highly successful. The "transforming" result was that in the end, boys from both groups put aside their differences and worked cooperatively toward the common good. Harmony replaced distrust. The macrosystem lesson learned was that nothing works so well to bring two enemies together than the sudden emergence of a third, more threatening, common enemy.

CONCLUSIONS

Since the early days, Bronfenbrenner's ecological approach has undergone continual refinement and improvement. Although some of the names have changed, most of the central ideas and issues have remained intact. Bronfenbrenner now calls his theoretical approach a "Bioecological Paradigm," and child psychology research that incorporates the bioecological perspective is described as adhering to a "process-person-context-time" (PPCT) model. As in the original formulation, the new model focuses on psychological development in children, the impact of the immediate setting, and the pervasive influences of more remote social and cultural ideologies. But the revised model gives more explicit attention to the role of *time* in children's development (called the *chronosystem*). A comprehensive description of the current state of Bronfenbrenner's ecological theory can be found in an article he published in 1994 in the journal *Psychological Bulletin* with coauthor Stephen Ceci.

Urie Bronfenbrenner's goals in bringing forward his ecological psychology were to get child psychologists to think more clearly about the multifaceted influences of children's surroundings on their psychological development, to consider how children simultaneously influence their own surroundings, and to prompt child psychologists to conduct studies designed to reveal how these influences operate. Although child psychologists had for a long time recognized the importance of the environment in children's development, "environment" had usually been a poorly defined, loosely conceptualized collection of everything that existed outside the child's head. Bronfenbrenner's ecological theory was revolutionary because it broke down the "environment" and identified a number of levels of generality of environmental influence, all operating simultaneously and interactively to influence children's lives. Bronfenbrenner also gave us a common vocabulary to use in referring to each of the levels of environmental operation.

Despite its logical appeal and comprehensiveness, Bronfenbrenner's ecological theory isn't particularly easy to use. It's hard enough to run a single experiment in a single laboratory setting, let alone extend the research to a multitude of other microsystem settings, while simultaneously taking into account the relationships of the people in each of those settings with other people in those and other settings. Perhaps for this reason, the vast majority of child psychology researchers still haven't adopted Bronfenbrenner's approach, at least not in its full-blown version. Still, Bronfenbrenner's admonitions resonate strongly with the spirit of most child psychology researchers, who usually recognize the importance of considering multiple contexts in understanding the psychological development of the child. You can typically find these declarations in the sections of their published research articles where they talk about directions for future research. Although most researchers don't explicitly acknowledge Bronfenbrenner's theory, I imagine that Bronfenbrenner is at least pleased to see so much of the contemporary child psychology community recognizing the need for considering the ecology of the child. There's no telling what the state of child psychology would look like today were it not for Bronfenbrenner's revolutionary reconceptualization of the nature of children's environments.

Bibliography

Bronfenbrenner, U., & Ceci, S. J. (1994). Nature-nurture reconceptualized in developmental perspective: A bioecological model. *Psychological Review, 101*, 568–586.

Moen, P., Elder, G. H., Jr., & Lüscher, K. (1995). *Examining lives in context: Perspectives on the ecology of human development*. Washington, DC: American Psychological Association.

Sherif, M., Harvey, O. J., White, B. J., Hood, W. R, & Sherif, C. N. (1961). *Intergroup conflict and cooperation: The Robbers Cave experiment*. Norman, OK: University of Oklahoma Book Exchange.

Questions for Discussion

1. Can you identify factors from each of Bronfenbrenner's four contexts that are influencing your behavior at this exact moment in time? Can you identify factors from each of Bronfenbrenner's four contexts that are influencing your best friend's behavior at this moment? How do they compare to yours?

2. One of Bronfenbrenner's claims is that it's impossible for the experimenter to remove herself from the experimental situation, since her very existence impacts children's responses to her. Is it possible for the physicist to remove herself from her own experimental situation? Does the physicist's existence impact on the physical environment she is investigating? Does the physicist's humanness impact on her interpretation of the results she obtains from her physical experiments?

3. To the best of your knowledge, how are macrosystem influences similar and different for the citizens of Israel versus those of Palestinians living in territories occupied by Israel? What macrosystem influences might explain why these two groups appear to hate each other so much?

15

Patience Makes the Heart Grow Fonder

Delay of Gratification in Children

Mischel, W., Shoda, Y., & Rodriguez, M. I. (1989). *Science, 244*, **933–938.**
(RANK 13)

Have you ever noticed that much of the wisdom we steer toward our children comes from brief, self-encapsulated maxims handed down through the generations? We provide these witty gems of insight as rules for children to live by, to serve as guides through rough and unfamiliar terrain. They come from old proverbs, political speeches, or great pieces of literature; and from individuals like Confucius, Benjamin Franklin, or Shakespeare.

Many comprise a common theme. When counseling children to *avoid delay*, for example, we might say:

> *Here today, gone tomorrow.*
> *He who hesitates is lost.*
> *The early bird catches the worm.*
> *Never put off till tomorrow what you can do today.*
> *Life is what happens to you when you're busy making other plans.*

Now this is a theme I can relate to. I live in the minute and for the minute. I would rather ask for forgiveness than for permission. After all, *there is no better time than the present.* But notice that other sayings comprise an opposing theme, ones we use to counsel children to *embrace patience.* In this case, we might say:

> *Haste makes waste.*
> *Look before you leap.*

A stitch in time saves nine.
All good things come to those who wait.
He who laughs last laughs longest.

Ugh, I'd rather poke myself in the eye with a Sharpie than sit around twiddling my thumbs waiting for something. But in all these sayings are embedded two time-tested principles that, for all their metaphorical sensibility, take us in completely opposite directions. Each theme makes sense individually; at least we can think of times when each theme leads to the best course of action. But side by side they make for a head-on collision. What then to teach our children? Should we caution against delay, or in favor of patience? Both? Neither?

As it turns out, much of the life's work of the famous personality theorist Walter Mischel was to show that one tenet really is better than the other, even if it is not the one I would have hoped for. For Mischel, "haste makes waste" wins. In his 1989 *Science* article, ranked 13th most revolutionary overall, with graduate students Yuichi Shoda and Monica Rodriguez, Mischel provides a compelling argument that it's best to instill patience in children, and to teach them the virtues of postponing the immediate gratification of their wants and desires. In fact, their data showed that children's abilities to delay gratification were perhaps the single best indicator of their later life success; and that the lack of the ability to delay gratification placed children at risk for bad things, including social ostracism and psychopathology.

This is a profoundly important discovery, and no doubt the main reason that Mischel and colleagues' article became so revolutionary. But the procedures Mischel and colleagues used were also very interesting, and perhaps, owing to their simplicity, may have contributed a little to the article's revolutionary impact. Hence, in this chapter I'll talk about Mischel et al.'s important findings, but I'll talk first about the procedures they used to produce them. This way, I can not only talk about how a set of procedural innovations changed the field of child psychology, but also about how these famous procedures were later misdescribed and misunderstood. After taking a look at the early research where Mischel honed and refined his "Delay of Gratification Paradigm," I will return to the bigger picture of how the capacity for delaying gratification has become such an important predictor of lifelong success.

The "Marshmallow Test"

Maybe only a child psychology nerd would praise the virtues of procedural innovations, but Mischel's delay of gratification paradigm, sometimes endearingly dubbed the "Marshmallow Test," may be one of the most famous products of the child psychology literature of the era. Several fascinating depictions of it can be found on YouTube, with my personal favorite being the one called "Kids Marshmallow Experiment:"

https://www.youtube.com/watch?v=QX_oy9614HQ.

I'll wait here patiently while you take a look.

As you just observed, the idea of the procedure is to give children a choice between eating a single marshmallow immediately, or two marshmallows after a 15-minute delay. It turns out that only a minority of children—roughly one in three—have the willpower to endure the delay. But kids with that willpower get to engorge themselves on twice as many marshmallows as kids who fail.

Now this description of the marshmallow test is dead-on, at least as portrayed by the media. YouTube, TV, magazines, and newspapers have all depicted the marshmallow test in just this way. But the funny thing about history, and the frailty of human memory, is that this public understanding of the marshmallow test is not exactly the way it happened. If we look a little closer, we can see that Mischel implemented his delay of gratification paradigm a little differently.

The two articles representing the leading edge of Mischel's work on children's delay of gratification, and that showcased his procedures, were published in the early 1970s. First was a 1970 article, authored by Mischel and his graduate student, Ebbe Ebbesen. This article was important because it's where Mischel first introduced his delay of gratification paradigm to the psychology community. But there were no marshmallows involved. Marshmallows weren't involved until a 1972 follow-up article published by Mischel, Ebbesen, and a second graduate student, Antonette Zeiss. But even then, the details were rather different than what modern, popular descriptions of the marshmallow test would lead us to believe. As for Mischel, he didn't seem to appreciate this public commandeering of his procedure. He recollected in a 2007 autobiography that his "delay of immediate gratification for the sake of delayed but more valued rewards paradigm" was also the paradigm "that the media later called more simply, albeit incorrectly, 'the marshmallow test.'" Nevertheless, marshmallows notwithstanding, Mischel's innovative delay of gratification paradigm became a cornerstone for the research that would later form the core of Mischel's revolutionary 1989 article.

The casting of Mischel's early-1970s work into national prominence was aided by the politics of late 1960s psychology. He was developing his paradigm at a time when the discipline was looking forward to the shiny new promises of cognitivism, and leaving behind the old, worn-out values of behaviorism and psychoanalytic theory. The study of individual differences was also gaining credibility, in direct proportion to the expanding scientific interest in temperament and attachment theories. So Mischel had no need to resort to factors outside the child's conscious control—such as reinforcement contingencies or pleasure drives—to explain delay of gratification. Instead, he could test the much more interesting possibility that delay of gratification might derive from something internal to the child, something controllable; and if so, he could test whether it might be improved upon through training, intervention, or practice.

Accordingly, Mischel's goal was to identify consciously-controllable, internal factors that might affect children's abilities to delay gratification. Two candidate factors were children's representational and attentional abilities. These were both constructs at the center of the fledgling cognitivist movement. Mischel's argument went this way: If children could represent the problem of waiting for a reward as if it didn't really involve waiting for a reward, for example, or if they could distract themselves by focusing their attention on something besides getting the reward, maybe they could significantly improve their performance in a delay task. Unfortunately, the impact of "mental representations" and "attention" on children's delay abilities was pretty much unknown because such renegade concepts were disallowed by old school psychology. But these were changing times for psychology. Besides, as a Jewish refugee from Nazi-occupied Austria, Mischel was experienced in disregarding dominant party viewpoints, and so took it as a challenge to test the relevance of "disallowable" psychological concepts.

INTRODUCTION TO MISCHEL AND EBBESEN (1970)

In the introduction to their 1970 article, Mischel and Ebbesen wrote that their purpose was to explore the role that self-regulation played in helping children delay their gratification. They seemed particularly interested in developing a theory of the mechanisms underlying self-regulation. They noted, "the mechanisms that maintain goal-directed delay seem especially important, considering the fact that the ability to sustain self-imposed delay for the sake of larger but delayed consequences appears to be a chief component of most complex higher order human behavior." But despite the fact that scientists at the time had ample reason to explore mechanisms underlying self-control, relatively little research had actually done so.

Without a lot of past research to go on, Mischel and Ebbesen turned their attention to possible cognitive mechanisms, reasoning that "any cues that make the delayed gratification salient—that help the person to make deferred consequences more psychologically vivid or immediate—should facilitate waiting behavior." Yet, by turning toward a cognitive explanation such as attentional saliency, they were swimming upstream against behaviorism and psychoanalytic theory. Their rationale for turning toward attentional saliency as an explanatory mechanism seems to be that, since we usually have a good reason for waiting for something, we can withstand any delay simply by keeping that good reason in mind. In other words, Mischel and Ebbesen hypothesized that the most important mechanism was children's ability to keep their eyes on the delayed gratification prize.

METHODS

Because of their new way of thinking about delay of gratification, which was to use cognition-based explanations, Mischel and Ebbesen developed a correspondingly new paradigm, which they described as "one of the chief goals of the project."

Subjects

Sixteen boys and 16 girls attending the (recently constructed) Bing Nursery School at Stanford University. Children ranged in age from 3 years 6 months to 5 years 8 months. Eight subjects (4 boys and 4 girls) were assigned to each of four experimental conditions.

Procedure

As it turns out, the procedure for Mischel's delay of gratification paradigm is far more complex than one is led to believe by media portrayals of the marshmallow test. In fact, it's tempting to wonder why Mischel made his paradigm so unnecessarily complicated, when all he had to do was give a kid a marshmallow and see how well the kid could withstand the 15 minute wait. But this would be an unfair criticism since hindsight is 20/20. The fact that he created the paradigm at all is what allowed the modern characterization of the marshmallow test to emerge in the first place. In any event, I describe the procedure in some detail here so that you can glean a sense of the complexity of the paradigm.

The basic delay of gratification procedure involved the following steps.

First, children were individually escorted by the experimenter into an experimental room, which had a table, some chairs, a box of toys, some ½" pretzels, and a cake tin.

Each child was then shown the box of toys, and informed that she and the experimenter would play with the toys later in the session. "These references to the toys were designed to help relax the children . . . "

Children were next taught about the waiting period, terminating the waiting period, and summoning the experimenter. The experimenter explained that he sometimes had to leave the room for a period of time, but that if the child needed or wanted him to return, she could simply eat one of the little ½" pretzels. The experimenter then demonstrated how the waiting termination and experimenter summoning worked. He left the room and immediately began watching the child through a small peephole in the wall. As soon as he saw the child put a pretzel in her mouth, he reentered the experimental room. This departure-summoning loop was repeated three more times, until there was only one ½" pretzel left on the table.

The experimenter next lifted the cake tin, to reveal two sets of reward items: two cookies versus five 2" pretzels. The child was asked which of the item types she liked better. After she chose her preferred item type, let's say she chose the cookies, the experimenter spoke to her at length about how he was going to leave the room, and if she could wait until the experimenter returned, she could eat all of the cookies (the more desired reward). But if she wanted the experimenter to return sooner, she could simply eat the ½" pretzel to summon the experimenter—as happened in training—and then he would let her eat all five of the 2" pretzels (the less desired reward), but not the cookies.

After all of these contingencies were described, and the child insisted she understood the instructions, a laboratory assistant informed the experimenter which of four possible experimental conditions the child was assigned to. "This method assured that the experimenter remained unaware of the subjects' experimental condition until the last possible moment in the procedure." The experimenter then left the room under one of four possible conditions:

- The experimenter left both rewards on the table in front of the child
- The experimenter left no rewards in front of the child
- The experimenter left the more preferred reward in front of the child
- The experimenter left the less preferred reward in front of the child

RESULTS

Mischel and Ebbesen hypothesized that children would be able to delay longer if they had the desired reward in front of them, because this was the condition that kept their eyes on the prize. Keeping their eyes on the prize was expected to fortify children's resolve, and let them hold out as long as necessary. But quite the opposite actually happened. The children who had *no* reward objects in front of them waited about twice as long (~11.5 minutes on average) to summon the experimenter as did children who had only one reward object in front of them (~5 minutes), and more than 10 times longer than children who had both rewards in front of them (~1 minute).

DISCUSSION

So how did Mischel and Ebbesen explain these results in light of the fact that they were contrary to expectations? They derived an explanation, at least in part, by looking more closely at what children were actually doing during the delay period, and taking note of the behaviors exhibited by successful children. What was most striking was that successful children "devised elaborate self-distraction techniques through which they spent their time psychologically doing something (almost anything) other than waiting." So in direct contrast to the expectation that keeping your eyes on the prize could promote gratification delaying behavior, Mischel and Ebbesen found that it was better to keep your eyes **off** the prize. They concluded that "learning *not* to think about what one is awaiting may enhance delay of gratification, much more than does ideating about the outcomes" (emphasis in original).

Ok, but if so, how does self-distraction work to promote delaying behavior? According to Mischel and Ebbesen, the answer to this question lies in "frustrative nonreward theory." According to frustrative nonreward theory, the presence of a highly desirable but unattainable reward causes frustration, which, in turn, renders the delay period aversive. The more aversive the delay period, the more the child will take action to avoid or discontinue the delay period. As a result, anything that increases the amount of the frustration, whether it is the increased desirability of the reward or the decreased attainability of it, should produce efforts aimed at discontinuing the delay. In contrast, factors that decrease the frustration, including any distractions resulting in not thinking of the target rewards, whether generated by the self or others, ought to promote a willingness to tolerate delay. Mischel and Ebbesen concluded the point this way:

> The overall findings tentatively suggest that learning to inhibit frustrative ideation, and to divert attention away from temptations by focusing, externally and internally, on competing and less frustrating stimuli, may be essential steps for mastery of delay of gratification.

INTRODUCTION TO MISCHEL, EBBESEN, AND ZEISS (1972)

So now you have been introduced to the famous delay of gratification task. But notice what you have not seen—a single marshmallow. Indeed, it wasn't until the 1972 article that the iconic marshmallow made its first appearance. In this second article, Mischel and his students continued the line of inquiry they began in the previous article. They began by pointing out that the concept of attention had long been linked to self-control processes, tracing the connection back to the first great American psychologist William James, who wrote about it in his classic 1890 psychology textbook. They also had evidence from the first study that young children's resistance to temptation could be traced to how they allocated attention to the task.

In the 1972 article, Mischel and colleagues took a step beyond the 1970 article, to test more specific hypotheses that emanated from the earlier work. One priority was to further test their pet *frustrative nonreward theory*, which suggested that children's delay of gratification should be improved whenever the aversion from waiting is made less aversive, or better yet, is made neutral or positive. In the 1972 article, they employed their delay of gratification paradigm under several different conditions of "covert or overt" activities which they thought might distract the children. They implemented these various conditions over the course of three separate experiments, which I will review for you here in rapid succession.

Experiment 1

Subjects

Fifty children (25 boys and 25 girls) from the Bing Nursery School, ranging in age from 3.6 to 5.6 years. Ten (5 of each gender) were randomly assigned to each of five conditions. One man and one woman served as experimenters.

Procedure

The set-up was the same as in the 1970 study, except that in this study a barrier was added. Behind the barrier was a Slinky (you know, the spring toy from Wham-O!) and a cake tin. Under the cake tin was a marshmallow (**FINALLY!**) and a stick pretzel.

Children were taught to play the experimenter summoning game as in the 1970 study, except that instead of eating a ½" pretzel to summon the experimenter, children were taught to ring a bell. Mischel changed this part of the procedure because he didn't like how the summoning item—the ½" pretzel—was the same kind of thing as one of the reward items (the 2" pretzels).

This experiment actually had two independent variables. For the first independent variable, children were given one of two types of instructions believed to help children distract themselves. In the *Distraction through Overt Activity Instructions*, children were invited to play with the Slinky while they waited for the experimenter to return. In the *Distraction through Cognition-Inducing Instructions*, children were advised to simply "think of anything that's fun to think of."

For the second independent variable, Mischel et al. were interested in seeing whether waiting for a treat actually caused children to terminate the waiting period faster than if they weren't waiting for a treat. So they designed this experiment in such a way that having the experimenter return meant different things to different children. In the delay of gratification condition, having the experimenter return after the delay meant that children could eat their preferred reward. But in the nondelay of gratification condition, children were not told about the rewards at all. Instead, they were just told that the experimenter had to leave the room for a while and would return when he could. In this case, summoning the experimenter with the bell would not result in the child getting a food reward, nonpreferred or otherwise.

So all together, five groups of children were tested. The first three were given the delay of gratification instructions. They were told they could eat the preferred treat if they waited for the experimenter to return, or they could eat the less preferred treat if they ended the waiting period earlier. Groups 4 and 5 weren't told about the rewards at all. They were just told the experimenter would return later and that they could summon him sooner if they wished. Thus the five groups represented various combinations of the two independent variables. Across the five groups, the question was whether children would end the waiting period at different times, depending on 1) whether eating a treat was at stake, and 2) whether children distracted themselves in some way. So the five groups looked like this:

- Group 1: Children were invited to play with the Slinky while waiting for the food reward.
- Group 2: Children were invited to think of fun things to do, such as singing songs or playing with toys, while waiting for the food reward.
- Group 3: Children were not given either distraction suggestion (the toy or thinking of fun things to do) while waiting for the food reward.
- Group 4: Children were not told about any rewards, but they were invited to play with the Slinky.
- Group 5: Children were not told about any rewards, but they were invited to think of fun things to do.

RESULTS

The results showed some pretty strong effects of the distractions on children's ability to wait. When children were given the opportunity to use distraction of either kind, they were able to wait 20 times longer than when they used no distraction. Children in Group 1 waited 8 minutes on average, and children in Group 2 waited 12 minutes on average. But children in Group 3 waited only about 30 seconds. Neither type of distraction helped children endure the waiting when there were no treats, however. Children in Groups 4 and 5 could only wait about a minute before summoning the experimenter.

Experiment 2

Mischel and colleagues were intrigued by their finding that simply having children think of fun things allowed them to endure more waiting and tolerate longer delays. So in Experiment 2, they tested whether having children think negative thoughts would produce the opposite effect.

Subjects

Twenty-six children (genders not identified) from the Bing Nursery School, ranging in age from 3.9 to 5.3 were assigned to one of three experimental groups. Although the three groups did not have the same number of children overall, Mischel et al. indicated that the gender ratio was equalized across groups.

Procedure

All three groups were offered the marshmallow and stick pretzel as rewards, and told that to get the preferred reward they had to wait for the experimenter to return on his own. But the three groups differed in the distraction instructions they were given. Group 1 was told to think of fun things, just like before. Group 2 was told to think of sad things, such as "falling down and getting a bloody knee which hurts a lot . . . or crying with no one to help." Group 3 was told to think of the food rewards themselves, "while I'm gone you can think of the marshmallow and the pretzel for as long as you want to, if you want to."

RESULTS

Just as expected, Mischel and colleagues found that thinking about sad things significantly reduced the amount of time children were able or willing to wait for their preferred rewards. In the "think fun" condition, children waited 13 minutes on average. But in the "think sad" condition, children only waited 5 minutes on average. However, the children in the "think rewards" condition waited about 4 minutes on average. This is interesting because the wait times in these latter two conditions, although not as long as in the "think fun" condition, are still about 10 times longer than the wait times in the nondistraction condition of Experiment 1. Apparently, directed thinking of any kind serves as a better distraction than not being directed to think of anything.

Experiment 3

On the other hand, this conclusion is limited by the fact that children had the food rewards available to their senses in all three of the Experiment 2 conditions; which means that in all three conditions children could have been thinking about the food rewards in addition to any directed thoughts. In Experiment 3, Mischel et al. physically removed the rewards, and observed whether directed thinking would still serve as a distraction.

Subjects

Sixteen subjects (11 boys, 5 girls), aged from 3.5 to 5.6. There was one experimental group and two control groups, consisting of 8, 4, and 4 subjects, respectively. Ratios of boys to girls was kept "similar" across the three groups.

Procedure

As before, children were shown a marshmallow treat and a stick pretzel treat. They were asked to choose their favorite one, and told they could either eat their favorite treat if they waited for the experimenter to return, or eat the other treat if they terminated the delay period by ringing the bell. The main difference in this experiment was that the experimenter placed the treats back under the cake tin before he left, so that children could not see the treats during the delay period.

Before leaving the room, the experimenter gave each child a suggestion of what to think about, depending on which group she was assigned to. Group 1 children were not told anything, and so were able to think about whatever they wanted. This was called the "no ideation" group. Group 2 children were in the "think fun" condition, and encouraged to think of fun things. Group 3 children were in the "think rewards" condition, and encouraged to think about the two treats.

RESULTS

The results showed that children in the "think rewards" groups were significantly less able to tolerate waiting than children in either of the other two conditions. On average, children who were instructed to think about the rewards waited only about 1 minute before ringing the bell. In contrast, children who were instructed to think of fun things waited 14 minutes on average, and children who were not instructed to think about anything waited 13 minutes on average. Clearly, thinking about the rewards, while waiting to eat one of the rewards, was not helpful in extending the waiting period. But thinking about fun things, as before, or thinking about nothing in particular, appeared to be very helpful in supporting children's waiting efforts.

Grand Conclusions across All Three Experiments

After three quick experiments, Mischel and his students demonstrated 1) that on average children are not very good at tolerating 15-minute delays of gratification unless they are given something to distract themselves, 2) that distractions can help children delay their gratification, 3) that those distractions can either be overt, as in the form of playing with a Slinky, or covert, as in thinking certain kinds of thoughts, and 4) that when distractions are covert, positive thoughts about something other than food rewards work best. These findings provided considerable support for the idea that waiting is aversive, and that anything that can reduce the aversion can produce longer waiting periods. In sum, some distraction is better than none, and positive distraction is better than negative.

As well, thinking about the treats promotes waiting when the treats are viewable, yet it inhibits or interferes with waiting when they are out of sight. I want you to think about this, so let me repeat it. Thinking about the treats promotes waiting when the treats are viewable, but interferes with waiting when they are out of sight. These opposing outcomes would become especially important in Mischel's later work, because they reflected the fact that a single distraction could have opposite effects depending on the kinds of stimuli that are available in the child's environment. Mischel would later describe this difference as between the "hot" and the "cool" qualities of the stimulus. Hot qualities are those that cause you to get excited or aroused. Cool qualities are those you *can* think about, intellectually at least, but that don't cause you to get especially excited or aroused. In his distraction experiments, Mischel and his students directed children either to think about the treats when the treats were present, or to think about the treats when the treats were absent. Mischel believed that the act of thinking about the treats when the treats were present, caused children to think about their cool qualities—their color, their size, their location—and this intellectualization of the treats facilitated their ability to wait for longer periods of time. But the act of thinking about the treats when the treats were absent caused children to desire the treats, and to focus their thinking instead on the treats' hot qualities, such as their yummy taste and their sugary goodness. In this case, children couldn't stand the waiting, and so ended the waiting period early.

THERE AND BACK AGAIN

So there you have it; the birth of the delay of gratification paradigm, and the introduction of the marshmallow. These are the experiments that started it all. But you can also see that they bear only a partial resemblance to modern portrayals of the marshmallow test. Together these articles form the substrate from which the 1989 article by Mischel, Shoda, and Rodriguez gained its revolutionary impact. What we learned from those and other studies, as Mischel later summarized, was that children's abilities to delay gratification came not from the relative strengths of the rewards or the demands of the situation, but from what was "in their heads." In his autobiography, he wrote, "This now seems evident, but at the time, when behaviorism prevailed and the cognitive revolution was in its infancy, it was startling, and it quickly made me at least as interested in self-control as in stimulus control."

Yet these early studies are probably best regarded as only Phase 1 of Mischel's ideas about self-control. Phase 2 was to begin in 1981. You will remember that the boys and girls who participated in the early experiments hailed from Stanford University's brand new Bing Nursery School. As it turns out, the fact that the school was part of Stanford became profoundly important. You see, Mischel was a professor at Stanford University, and his own kids attended Bing Nursery School. Over the course of many casual conversations with them, taking place during dinners and car rides, that kind of thing, Mischel would hear stories his daughters told of their friends and peers. As he described in an interview in *New Yorker* magazine, he would ask his daughters, "How's Jane? How's Eric?" He would also ask them to rate their friends' school performance on a scale of zero to five. "That's when I realized I had to do this seriously," he was quoted as saying.

The results of this second phase of research first appeared in the scientific literature in a 1988 article by Mischel, Shoda, and Peake. In this article, Mischel and colleagues chose some kids who participated in the early work, looked up their contact information, and sent their parents some follow-up questionnaires. By this time the children would have been in their mid-teens. The parents were asked questions about four of their children's competencies (all on a 1 to 7 scale):

1. How is your child doing academically, compared to his or her peers?
2. How skilled is your son or daughter at maintaining friendships and getting along with his or her peers?
3. What is your impression of the frequency of problems, both large and small, in your son's (daughter's) life, as compared to his (her) peers?
4. How well has he or she coped, compared to peers, with the problems that were of some importance?

Findings reported in this 1988 study revealed that children's delay tolerance in nursery school predicted better academic performance, advanced social competence, and greater ability to cope with problems in adolescence. This was a marvelous finding. Given how hard it is to show correlations between two variables at the same time, it's absolutely amazing that Mischel and colleagues found correlations between two measures of the same person across a whole decade.

So what do the results mean? We are still trying to figure that one out. But more and more resources are being spent on this fascinating topic every day. At a minimum it means that 3- to 5-year-old children already give us a great deal of information about their likelihood for later success or failure. It also means that maybe we should spend more time looking at delay of gratification behaviors to see exactly *how* they may be contributing to later successes and failures.

MISCHEL, SHODA, AND RODRIGUEZ (1989)

Now we are in a much better position to take a more profitable look at why Mischel, Shoda, and Rodriguez (1989) was ranked the 13th most revolutionary child psychology article published since 1960. As we already noted, the article was published in the journal *Science*, which has the potential to catapult any article into the stratosphere of international reputation; and indeed, as of this writing, the article shows 1766 Google Scholar citations. But not all articles published in *Science* are so highly regarded. What makes this one different? I think there are three main reasons why this article had such a strong impact on the field.

First, the article reviews Mischel's own earlier delay of gratification work, but it does so much more extensively. There were a number of studies in the early 1970s besides the two we reviewed here. So in the 1989 piece, Mischel and colleagues traced the history of the development of the delay of gratification procedure, and document the sequence of studies that introduced first one and then another factor found to impact on children's abilities to delay. Although articles published in *Science* are generally only two or three pages long, this one stands out conspicuously at 5.2 or so pages.

Second, the article traces the history of the longitudinal work linking early delay ability to later cognitive, social, and emotional functioning. They reviewed not only the 1988 article above, but they also presented new data pertaining to SAT outcomes not heretofore published. As you probably know, SAT scores are meant to indicate readiness for college, and are used by colleges to make admissions decisions. High school students pay a good chunk of change to take the test, and colleges are interested in using those scores to recruit the best and brightest applicants. For colleges, standardized test scores such as the SAT and the ACT are sometimes the most important metric for determining a student's likelihood for success. So it must have been a shocker indeed to find that the number of seconds of delay at age 4 reliably predicted the number of SAT points in mid to late adolescence. On the other hand, Mischel et al. only had SAT score data for a small sample of the total (about 35 children), so these latter results were regarded as needing replication.

Third, Mischel and colleagues made the very important point that the factor that contributes more than any other to children's abilities to delay gratification, is their ability to use strategies. Their 1970s work had shown that experimenters could manipulate children's abilities to delay gratification just by suggesting what to think about. But this finding raised two important follow-up questions. First, to what extent are children able to generate their own strategies to help them engage in delay behavior? Second, to what extent are children susceptible to interventions designed to improve their gratification delay skills. If children can voluntarily use strategies to delay gratification, and if such strategies can be taught to children through training or therapy, and if gratification delay makes children better, smarter, and friendlier, then we may have a huge self-improvement industry in the making. Whole companies could develop products whose purpose would be to teach children delay of gratification strategies. Purchasers of the product could expect higher SAT scores, stronger friendships, and better overall coping skills in adolescence and adulthood.

BEYOND MISCHEL, SHODA, AND RODRIGUEZ (1989)

In modern day child psychology parlance, the construct of *Delay of Gratification* has been absorbed into the very popular and overarching super-construct of Executive Function (EF). I use the term super-construct in part because EF is one of the hottest subjects of research throughout all of child psychology, if not all of psychology more generally; but also because it is conceptualized as a higher-level ability that coordinates and integrates several lower-level component abilities. EF is theorized to coordinate and integrate about five component abilities. Depending on the specific scientist you ask, these component abilities typically include 1) choosing to pay attention to something, 2) keeping things in mind, 3) planning, sequencing, and organizing, 4) inhibiting dominant/preferred behaviors when subdominant/nonpreferred behaviors are called for, and 5) initiating, monitoring, and correcting speech and nonspeech behaviors.

EF has also been associated with outcomes as disparate as obesity, aggression, racism, ADHD, and emotional and behavior disorders. This is a broader class of outcomes than delay of gratification performance itself has been shown to predict, but that may be because EF is usually considered a slightly different and higher-order ability than delay of gratification. Indeed, the difference between EF and delay of gratification has been the subject of interest for some researchers.

Still, many of the abilities children use to succeed in any version of the delay of gratification task, including Mischel's misnamed marshmallow test, are clearly reflected in EF more generally. For example, the key component needed for succeeding in Mischel's marshmallow test requires that the child **NOT** eat the marshmallow. But think about all the component abilities that go into a child's choice to **NOT** eat the marshmallow. For one thing, she must inhibit the dominant/preferred action of eating the marshmallow, in favor of initiating any subdominant/nonpreferred action that does not involve eating the marshmallow. The child must hold back on what is otherwise a very natural desire to eat something sweet. At the same time, the child might intentionally try to think of something to get her mind off the marshmallow, and onto something else that will serve as a distraction. This latter effort reflects the child's ability to voluntarily initiate the action of reallocating her attention from something "hot" and interesting, to something "cool" and uninteresting. The successful child must also keep in mind that it is her short-term goal to **NOT** eat the marshmallow, because there will be a better outcome if she can just wait the necessary length of time. Finally, she will need to monitor how well her chosen distraction strategy is working throughout the waiting period, as well as to start planning an alternative distraction strategy if she finds her current one ceasing to be effective. Probably the best way to think of delay of gratification performance is to think of it as just one way to measure EF. There are other ways, but these other ways draw on components of EF differently than does delay of gratification.

CONCLUSION

The Mischel, Shoda, and Rodriguez (1989) article is a new addition to the family of revolutionary articles in child psychology. I suspect its movement up the list, at least in part, reflects the field's exploding interest in children's EF. Even though a great deal is already known about EF in adults, especially in the elderly, we still know very little about EF in toddlers and infants. For this reason, child psychology researchers have ramped up their scientific investigations significantly, aiming to discover both what EF looks like in infants and children, and what outcomes in later life it predicts or contributes to. We know from Mischel's work that at least one manifestation of EF, namely delay of gratification performance, reliably and strongly predicts many important outcome measures in later childhood and adulthood. Now it is up to other researchers to identify additional manifestations of EF that are similarly predictive of long-term life outcomes. But this is because Mischel and his students have helped show them the way.

Reference

https://www.youtube.com/watch?v=QX_oy9614HQ

Bibliography

Lehrer, J. (2009, May 18). Don't!: The secret of self-control. *The New Yorker*.

Mischel, W. (2007). Walter Mischel. In G. Lindzey & W. M. Runyan (Eds.), *A history of psychology in autobiography, Volume IX*. (pp. 229–267). Washington, DC: American Psychological Association.

Mischel, W., & Ebbesen, E. G. (1970). Attention in delay of gratification. *Journal of Personality and Social Psychology, 16*, 329–337.

Mischel, W., Ebbesen, E. B., & Zeiss, A. R. (1972). Cognitive and attentional mechanism in delay of gratification. *Journal of Personality and Social Psychology, 21*, 204–218.

Mischel, W., Shoda, Y., & Peake, P. K. (1988). The nature of adolescent competencies predicted by preschool delay of gratification. *Journal of Personality and Social Psychology, 54*, 687–696.

Questions for Discussion

1. Do you fall into the "Haste Makes Waste" camp, or the "Early Bird Gets the Worm" camp? Which is better for your personal lifestyle, and what is your justification? Is this a false dichotomy?
2. Can you identify a time or event in your life when delaying gratification produced better outcomes than not delaying it? And vice versa?
3. Does the principle of delaying gratification apply equally well in the cognitive, social, emotional, and physical domains of life?

16

She Loves Me, but *She* Loves Me Not

The Affectional Systems. In A. Schrier, H. F. Harlow, & F. Stollnitz (Eds.), *Behavior of Nonhuman Primates: Modern Research Trends*

Harlow, H. F., & Harlow, M. K. (1965). New York: Academic Press.
(RANK 4)

"What's the deal with these monkeys? What've they got to do with psychology anyway? Psychology is about people." These questions erupted from a fellow student whose name I no longer recall, in an undergraduate class I took some 30 years ago. For whatever reason, the student was genuinely puzzled about how investigating monkeys could inform psychology about anything remotely human. I suppose I remember his astonishment so well because in my mind he seemed so clueless. I may have responded in excited disbelief, at least in my own head, with something like, "You're kidding, right? Why, everybody knows that on the evolutionary ladder humans are only a couple of rungs higher than monkeys. How can anybody not see the similarities?" Well, maybe I wasn't so articulate at the time, but I do remember being incredulous that someone could fail to see the parallels.

Back in those days, I wasn't especially tolerant of what I judged to be the ignorance of some of my fellow psychology majors. Now in my more forgiving years, I realize it's not always obvious how the behaviors of "lower" animals can inform an understanding of people. I realize that students' religious beliefs may sometimes obscure their view of the evolutionary similarities between higher and lower primates. And as much as I want to get on my soapbox and shout that evolution is right, I realize that what's most vital is not that apes and monkeys are like humans, but that apes and monkeys give psychologists something to look for when studying humans.

The work I'll be describing in this chapter, by Harry and Margaret Harlow, is Exhibit A in the case of the usefulness of studying monkey behavior for illuminating the secrets of human behavior. Especially through the work of John Bowlby and Mary Ainsworth, in Chapters 17 and 18, respectively, you'll learn that much of what the Harlows discovered about the emotional lives of monkey mothers and babies, is also true for human mothers and babies. The title of the revolutionary Harlow and Harlow work, which ranked 4th among the 20 most revolutionary studies in child psychology, is simply, "The Affectional Systems." But unless you've already had a course in abnormal psychology, I suspect that such a title doesn't send up firework displays of excitement. In fact, it's possible you've never even heard the word *affect* used as a noun before. So before I launch into a detailed description of the Harlows' work, let me suggest that whenever you see the word *affect*, you replace it with the word *emotion*; and if you see the word *affectional* you replace it with the word *emotional*. *Affect*, which, when used as a noun, begins with the same sound as the word *apple*, more or less means emotion. But when we get right down to it, we're really just talking about "love." Thus, one way to interpret the question addressed by the Harlows is, "How does infant–mother love develop?" And now, on with the show.

INTRODUCTION

The Harlows achieved two objectives in writing their chapter. First, they outlined what they thought were the five most important affectional systems of nonhuman primates. Although the term *nonhuman primate* refers to a wide range of species, including the great apes, the Harlows spent most of their time with a lower-level "Old World" monkey species called *Macaca mulatta*, or more commonly, the rhesus monkey. Rhesus monkeys are primarily ground dwellers native to various parts of Asia; however, more than 70,000 rhesus monkeys can be found in research labs throughout North America and Europe.

Second, the Harlows brought together in one place the results of a whole series of experiments on the emotional development of these monkeys. In the course of their exposition, they present dozens of research findings from a variety of previously published experiments. They use these findings to support their own theoretical notions, but also to generate additional research ideas.

They begin with a brief description of the affectional systems. All told, there are five of them: "(1) the infant-mother affectional system, which binds the infant to the mother; (2) the mother-infant or maternal affectional system [which ensures the mother develops a sense of protectiveness over the infant]; (3) the infant-infant, age-mate, or peer affectional system through which infants and children interrelate with each other and develop persisting affection for each other; (4) the sexual and heterosexual affectional system, culminating in adolescent sexuality and finally in those adult behaviors leading to procreation; and (5) the paternal affectional system, broadly defined in terms of positive responsiveness of adult males toward infants, juveniles, and other members of their particular social groups."

Do you notice a parallel between the affectional systems of monkeys and those of humans? You should. Modern psychology invests a great deal of effort in it, and government funding agencies have granted millions of dollars to developmental, clinical, and social psychologists who are studying precisely these same relationships between family members in *Homo sapiens* (human) families.

The system that's most relevant for this chapter is the first one: the infant-mother affectional system. Harry Harlow, in collaboration with a number of other colleagues who were also researching the development of infant bonding and security, achieved the greatest and most widespread attention with regard to this topic. Consequently, my focus will be on describing the Harlows' take on the emotional development of infant rhesus monkeys, as it pertains to the development of the **infant-mother affectional system.**

The Infant-Mother Affectional System

At the very beginning of their discussion of the infant-mother affectional system, the Harlows point out that this particular system is probably the least variable and least flexible of all the systems. They say so because they believe it's probably the most important one for the survival of baby monkeys, and therefore the one most firmly rooted in monkey biology. This system, in which baby monkeys emotionally attach themselves to their mothers, is even more important than the complementary mother-infant affectional system (system number 2) through which mother monkeys attach to their babies. In some ways, this sounds rather backward. How can a baby's emotional attachment to its mother be more important than a mother's protective attachment to her baby? If a mother doesn't develop an emotional attachment to her baby, how could the baby possibly survive? According to the Harlows, the infant-to-mother attachment is more important because "many infants can survive relatively ineffective mothering, and the system will even continue with great strength in the face of strong and protracted punishment by unfeeling mothers." So even if some mother monkeys don't think too highly of their babies, the babies will increase their chances of survival if they develop a strong attachment to their mothers anyway.

The Harlows describe four normal stages in the development of the infant-mother affectional system: (1) a reflex stage, (2) a comfort and attachment stage, (3) a security stage, and (4) a separation stage. But although they separate the emotional system into four stages, they also point out that there is some overlap between them. The stages also don't necessarily begin and end at the same time, since a lot depends on the specific characteristics of the mother and the baby, as well as on the specific environment in which the baby is being raised. But under relatively normal circumstances, babies progress through these four stages in order to survive to maturity, and to successfully separate from the mother when the time is right.

REFLEX STAGE   The reflex stage of the infant-mother affectional system, which lasts for about the first 15 to 20 days, is a lot like the reflex substage (Substage 1) of Piaget's sensorimotor period (which we talked about in Chapter 3). It's made up primarily of the basic reflexes needed to ensure the baby's survival. The reflexes are of two types: those pertaining to nursing and those pertaining to maintaining close physical contact with the mother. One of the nursing-related reflexes is the rooting reflex. The rooting reflex first gets activated when the baby monkey detects some stimulation on her face, especially near the mouth. This stimulation causes the baby to move her head up and down or side to side until her mouth makes contact with the nipple. Once contact is made with the nipple, the mouth engulfs it and the sucking reflex starts up (which is a second nursing-related reflex). A third reflex that might also be related to nursing is the climbing reflex. This reflex is apparently useful when the baby monkey is situated near the feet of the mother, and tries to climb up the mother until the rooting reflex gets stimulated. This climbing-up thing seems to be a reflex rather than something a baby monkey does intentionally, because according to the Harlows, "If a neonatal monkey is placed on a wire ramp, it will climb up the ramp and even climb over the end of the ramp and fall to the floor unless it is restrained." Clearly, this is a reflex that separates human babies from monkey babies. Human babies don't gain any climbing capabilities until well into childhood.

Another reflex that isn't seen in human babies is the clinging reflex, although remnants of the clinging reflex can be seen in the palmar "grasping" reflex of human babies. The clinging reflex occurs when baby monkeys cling with both their hands and their feet to the underside of their mothers' bodies. This reflex also promotes survival. Without it, monkey mothers would have to use their hands and arms to hold onto their babies most of the time, which, since monkey groups may migrate several miles per day and since monkeys need both their hands and feet to walk, would make it difficult for the mother to keep up.

THE STAGE OF COMFORT AND ATTACHMENT   As the reflex stage starts to go away, it is slowly replaced by the second stage, in which the baby's primary goals are to maintain closeness to the mother and to feel belongingness. The Harlows mention that although this stage lasts until 2 to 2½ months of age in monkeys, it probably lasts until about the 8th month in humans. The mother is highly protective at this stage. The baby achieves her sense of comfort and attachment primarily through two routes: nursing and physical contact. But based on experiments conducted by the Harlows, some of which I'll describe below, these two routes aren't equally important. Even though the baby must nurse to get the necessary nutrition in order to survive, physical contact seems far more important for the baby's "mental" health. Then, as long as the baby is allowed to maintain close physical contact with the mother, the baby will slowly and gradually begin to explore her surrounding environments—first exploring the mother's body, and eventually exploring the nearby things that were otherwise out of reach.

THE STAGE OF SECURITY   Baby monkeys who have bonded normally with their mothers, and who develop a sense of comfort and attachment, will next begin exploring the more remote outreaches of their environments. However, for monkey babies to engage in such exploratory behavior, the mother at least has to be accessible. When the mother is available, it's as if the baby has the courage to venture out into uncharted territory. But when the mother's unavailable, bad things happen. The Harlows wrote, "The behavior of infants change[s] radically in the absence of the mother. Emotional indices such as vocalization, crouching, rocking, and sucking increase sharply. Typical response patterns [are] either freezing in a crouched position or running around the room on the hind feet, clutching themselves with their arms." This presents a rather disconcerting image, doesn't it?

One interesting caveat is that how far away baby monkeys go to explore their environments depends partially on their mothers' social status in the monkey group. Monkeys whose mothers are highly dominant in the group can strut around freely with little fear of being assaulted or harassed by other monkeys. They can act like little monkey snobs. But the story is quite different for monkeys born to mothers who are low on the social totem pole. These babies have to maintain a high level of vigilance and constantly be on the lookout for bullying by their peers, and even other mothers.

THE SEPARATION STAGE   The very last stage of the infant-mother affectional system emerges when baby monkeys have matured to the point that they can leave the tightly knit bonds previously established with their mothers. In part, this impending separation results from the monkey youths' natural interest in venturing out on their own to explore the world. But it also partially results from the mother's sort of "booting the kid out of the house." In fact, Stage 2 of the mother-infant affectional system, which we haven't been discussing here, is a stage the Harlows called the "Transitional or Ambivalence Stage." During this stage, the mother starts acting more and more indifferent to the presence of her child. She also starts using harsher and harsher punishments. In general, separation of the child from the mother seems to correspond with a relative increase of negative responsiveness of the mother to her offspring. Eventually, it's simply in everyone's best interest if the child decreases the frequency of contact with Mother. When separation happens, the household negativity goes away.

The Harlow Studies

The Harlows developed their theory of affectional systems after a long series of experiments conducted primarily by Harry Harlow and his colleagues. And as also happened with Hubel and Wiesel (Chapter 9), an important discovery happened early on largely by accident. Harry Harlow and his colleagues were initially interested in the outcomes of social isolation, and so proceeded to intentionally separate baby monkeys from their mothers at birth. Unexpectedly, however, they found that the baby monkeys developed strong attachments to the cheesecloth blankets used as flooring in their cages. In fact, with colleague Robert Zimmerman, Harry Harlow reported in 1959 that baby monkeys exhibited extreme emotional reactions when attempts were made to remove the cloth flooring.

It was this very serendipitous discovery that first raised the possibility that contact with something soft and cuddly could be extremely important in the emotional development of babies. Up to that point, it was common knowledge in psychology that babies became attached to their mothers either through some form of conditioning, wherein mothers were deemed attractive because they provided babies with the rewarding properties of eating, or through some form of oral satisfaction of the type Sigmund Freud talked about. Harry Harlow's exciting discovery suggested instead that feeding might have nothing to do with infants' emotional attachments with their mothers. Rather, it might have something to do with skin-to-skin contact.

Because the revolutionary Harlow and Harlow book chapter summarizes so many studies that were conducted and published, it would be impossible to review them all. What I'll do instead is review the general procedures used by the Harlows, and review the major findings of some of the most prominent studies. Just as their work serves as a summary presentation, I'll do my best to extract the most interesting and important results and present a summary of their summary.

METHOD

As with other research reports covered in this book, detailed information about Harlow's subjects isn't readily available from the authors' own description. However, to at least give you a sense of the scope of the projects, I'll cheat a little bit and borrow the information from the report published by Harry Harlow and Zimmerman in the journal *Science* in 1959.

Participants

Sixty infant macaque (rhesus) monkeys were separated from their mothers within the first half-day after their births. Surrogate care for the monkeys proved successful as evidenced by the fact that these monkeys gained even more weight than the infants who were raised by their own mothers.

Materials

Two artificial surrogate mothers were constructed. The "cloth mother. . . was a cylinder of wood covered with a sheath of terry cloth, and the wire mother was a [cylinder commonly used to store hardware cloth]. . . . The two mothers were attached at a 45-degree angle to aluminum bases and were given different faces to assure uniqueness in the various test situations." In Figure 16.1, you can get a sense of what these surrogate mothers actually looked like. Given this arrangement,

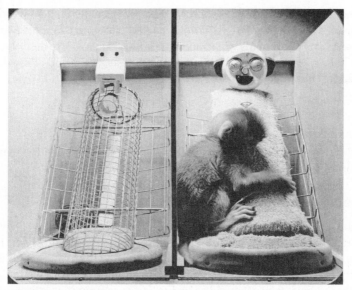

FIGURE 16.1 One of Harlow's monkeys gaining comfort from the cloth 'mother'.

both mothers were constructed so that they could provide food for the babies, but only one of the surrogates could provide contact comfort. With this arrangement, babies raised with both types of surrogate mothers gained normal weight from the food they received. For some reason, however, Harlow also reported that the monkeys raised by the wire mothers had softer stools.

Procedure

The exact procedures used by Harlow and his colleagues differed depending on the specific experiments that were conducted, but there were many commonalities across the experiments. In a typical procedure, 4 newborn monkeys would be "raised" in one condition, and 4 others raised in a different condition. Also, they were usually raised in a particular condition for a minimum of 165 days.

For example, in one arrangement, each of 4 newborns would be raised in isolation from other monkeys and would have both surrogate mothers present; but the cloth mother would provide the milk. In a corresponding condition, everything would be the same except that the wire mother would provide the milk. In a different setup, each of the infants might be raised in the presence of only a single surrogate mother. But again, 4 would be raised with the cloth mother and 4 with the wire one. In one particular version of this latter experiment, for example, 4 newborns were raised with a lactating (milk-providing) wire mother, whereas the other 4 newborns were raised with a nonlactating cloth mother (but were hand-fed through other means).

An important issue persisting throughout all these "family arrangements" was how the infants would deal with anxiety-producing situations. The anxiety-producing situations themselves differed in how the anxiety was produced. In some cases, a moving toy bear or dog was introduced to a chamber very near the infants' own living quarters. In other cases, the infants were introduced to a completely unfamiliar room containing a number of "stimuli known to elicit curiosity-manipulatory responses in baby monkeys." On some occasions a surrogate mother would be present during the time of the anxiety-provoking situations (and in this case it would sometimes be the wire mother and sometimes the cloth one), and on other occasions the surrogate mother would be absent.

I think you can see that the number of ways these experiments could be conducted is mind-boggling. And indeed, one of the reasons Harlow and his colleagues had some two dozen publications from this series of experiments was simply that it took that many to describe all the different kinds of studies they conducted. But throughout all the tests, at the end of the day, the question always amounted to, "How does infant-mother love develop?"

RESULTS

Because there were so many findings reported by the Harlows, I've divided them into separate sections based on which conditions were manipulated.

Infants Raised by Both Surrogate Mothers

In this condition, half of the infants were raised with the wire mother providing the milk and half were raised with the cloth mother providing the milk. But for all the babies, both surrogates were always present. The most interesting finding here was that all the babies spent the vast majority of their time in contact with the cloth mother. Even when babies had to go to the wire mother to feed, they often did so by leaning over from the cloth mother. From 25 to 165 days of age, both sets of babies spent anywhere from 15 to 18 hours per day in contact with the cloth mother. In contrast, they spent only about 1 to 2 hours per day in contact with the wire mother.

Now there are at least two interpretations of these results. On the one hand, you could argue that the reason the infants spent so much more time clinging to the cloth mother was because the cloth mother was more comfortable to be around. Who wants to lie around on something made of wire? On the other hand, it could be that the cloth mothers provided a better sense of security to the babies than did the wire mother. If this latter possibility were true, then we would expect to see the baby infants flee to the cloth mother under times of fear or distress. To test such a possibility, Harlow and his colleagues introduced the fear-provoking stimulus.

Infants Raised by Both Surrogate Mothers and Who Were Exposed to a Fear-Provoking Toy

In this condition, as before, the infants were raised with both surrogate mothers, but for half of the infants the wire mother provided milk, and for the other half the cloth mother provided milk. Then the fear-producing stimulus was introduced. In about 80% of the cases, the monkeys preferred to run to the cloth mother, regardless of which mother provided the milk. But shortly after seeking the security of the cloth mother, they would begin to venture back out into the open to explore the fear-producing toy. Harlow and Zimmerman described it graphically: "In spite of their abject terror, the infant monkeys, after reaching the cloth mother and rubbing their bodies about hers, rapidly came to lose their fear of the frightening stimuli. Indeed, within a minute or two most of the babies were visually exploring the very thing which so shortly before had seemed to be an object of evil. The bravest of the babies would actually leave the mother and approach the fearful monsters, under, of course, the protective gaze of their mothers."

Apparently, then, the babies were not spending all their time on the cloth mothers simply because those mothers were more comfortable. Based on the fact that the babies would also run to the cloth mother in times of extreme fear, it seems that the cloth mother provided a sense of security in addition to being comfortable to the touch.

Infants Raised by a Single Surrogate Mother and Exposed to a Strange Room

The next question Harlow and his colleagues investigated was what would happen if the monkeys never had a chance to develop a "relationship" with a cloth mother in the first place. To explore this possibility, a number of babies were raised with *either* the cloth mother or the wire mother, but not both. What's more, the cloth mother in this experiment was not a feeding mother, whereas the wire mother was a feeding mother. Then twice a week for 8 weeks, they were introduced to the strange room, which contained lots of unfamiliar objects. Each week, the appropriate surrogate mother was present for one of the visits but not for the other. In this experiment, a control group of infants was used where infants weren't even raised by a surrogate mother, but instead were only given a cheesecloth blanket for the first 14 days.

When placed in the strange room, infants who were raised by the cloth mother "rushed to their mother surrogate when she was present and clutched her tenaciously, a response so strong that it can only be adequately depicted by motion pictures. Then, as had been observed in the fear tests in the home cage, they rapidly relaxed, showed no sign of apprehension, and began to demonstrate unequivocal positive responses of manipulating and climbing on the mother. After several sessions, the infants began to use the mother surrogate as a base of operations, leaving her to explore and handle a stimulus object and then returning to her before going to a new plaything."

In sharp contrast, infants who were raised by the wire mother didn't seem to be affected by whether or not she was in the strange room, even though the wire mother had been the primary source of food for these babies. Sometimes the babies would go to the wire mother, but their contact with her was qualitatively different from the monkeys who had access to the cloth mother. Here is another graphic description of infants' behaviors in the strange room in the presence of their lactating wire mothers: "they sat on her lap and clutched themselves, or held their heads and bodies in their arms and engaged in convulsive jerking and rocking movements similar to the autistic behavior of deprived and institutionalized human children."

DISCUSSION

The series of experiments described by the Harlows lead to the unmistakable conclusion that one of the most important factors in the establishment of a healthy mother-infant bond is physical contact. Moreover, not just any physical contact will do. The contact has to provide comfort to the touch. In these studies, the feel of cold, hard metal on the skin just wasn't good enough to enable the close emotional connection needed between infant monkeys and their wire surrogates. Without this emotional connection, a secure sense of belongingness and security never quite seemed to develop in these babies.

All this is not to say that an inanimate, unresponsive conglomeration of wood and cloth is good enough for the emotional needs of the infant, at least not to the point that it replaces a real, live, biological mother. For all we know, from the point of view of wild monkeys in their natural monkey habitat, the babies in Harlow's studies could have grown up to be dysfunctional, neurotic wrecks, even though they were raised with cloth surrogates. This is something we don't know, since Harlow never released the babies back into the wild. But at least when baby monkeys were raised by cloth surrogates, they showed two behaviors that are typical of baby monkeys raised with real, biological mothers.

First, cloth surrogates served as a secure base for the baby monkeys. When they were frightened, babies ran to their cloth mothers and maintained close physical contact. Babies raised by biological mothers also behave this way. Second, after frightened babies ran to their cloth surrogates, they felt comfortable enough to venture out and explore the fear-provoking toy and the strange room. Again, these are behaviors exhibited by monkeys raised by real mothers.

In its entirety, the Harlow work took a strong stand against the prevailing views of infant-mother affectional systems in vogue at the time. One of the most popular theories back then came from the behavioral psychologists. Although behavioral psychologists may have had their idiosyncratic differences from one another, they would have shared the common belief that infant-mother connectedness comes from conditioned associations. They would have argued, for example, that an infant develops an attraction to his mother, not because of feelings of love, but because she provides food. As a result of repeated pairings between the food and the mother's presence, infants couldn't help but learn an association between the food and the mother, and ultimately become attracted to the mother simply because of her association with the food. Obviously, the Harlow work provided a significant challenge to this notion. The baby Harlow monkeys preferred the cloth mother over the wire mother, even when the wire mother was the one who provided the food.

The Harlow findings also flew in the face of some of the prevailing Freudian views of the time. As you may recall from your introductory psychology course, Freud argued that a significant motivating influence on infant behavior was the drive to seek oral satisfaction. Because nursing was one way that babies could meet their oral needs, they would seek out their mothers primarily to nurse. Thus, according to the Freudian view, the drive to nurse, and not love of the mother, is what drew babies and mothers together. But again, this explanation fails to account for the Harlow findings. Any oral needs that might have driven the baby Harlow monkeys were apparently insufficient to overcome their desires to maintain physical closeness to the cloth surrogate mother.

CONCLUSIONS

The Harlow work revolutionized child psychology because it was the first to underscore, under experimentally controlled conditions, the importance of physical contact in establishing the infant-mother affectional bond. As you might imagine, this approach paved the way for Bowlby's attachment theory (discussed in Chapter 17), which arrived on the scene a few years later.

The Harlow work also anticipated and informed what were to become intense, emotion-laden debates on the nature of mother-infant bonding. In one such debate, especially in the late 1970s and early 1980s, there was considerable concern in the child-rearing literature about whether human mothers needed to make skin-to-skin contact with their babies immediately after birth. Many high profile, and vociferous, child-rearing experts, including John Kennell and Marshall Klaus, took the position that skin-to-skin contact was essential because it jump-started the instinctual caregiving drives that were built into mothers by hundreds of thousands of years of evolution.

Yet this perspective frightened many new mothers. It implied, for example, that in the absence of immediate skin-to-skin contact, babies might be at risk for abnormal emotional functioning. It also injected women with heavy doses of guilt, since they were ultimately responsible for ensuring the skin-to-skin contact. Such a caregiving standard meant that on top of having to give birth to the baby, the new mother would also have to ensure immediate postnatal skin-to-skin contact as well. If she failed at the skin contact thing, she would be responsible for any emotional problems that the baby may later develop. Yet, many events during childbirth fall outside the mother's locus of control. A baby born premature or with complications, for example, might have to be whisked away for emergency medical attention. Or an exceptionally strenuous labor might incapacitate a mother for several hours after the birth. In sum, pregnancy-induced stress took on a whole new psychological dimension in the '70s and '80s, in response to the skin-to-skin contact movement.

Fortunately, the skin-to-skin contact claim was soon found to be a bit of an exaggeration. Beginning in the early 1990s, researchers like Diane Eyer found that babies turned out just fine even without immediate skin-to-skin contact. These researchers found that the problem wasn't the lack of skin contact per se; rather, it had more to do with whether mothers *believed* skin-to-skin contact was essential. It was only when mothers *believed* that skin contact was essential, that problems emerged when the skin contact didn't happen. Why? Well, it may have been a sort of self-fulfilling prophecy. If a mother believed that healthy emotional development depended on immediate skin-to-skin contact after birth, and if that skin-to-skin contact was prevented for some reason, then the mother may have *expected* to see emotional problems in her child. As a result of such expectations, the mother may have started treating her child as if he already had those emotional problems. Arguably, it was *this* behavior that may have brought about children's emotional problems, not the lack of skin contact per se. Funny how the mind works, isn't it?

Bibliography

Eyer, D. E. (1992). *Mother-infant bonding: A scientific fiction*. New Haven, CT: Yale University Press.

Harlow, H. F., & Zimmerman, R. R. (1959). Affectional responses in the infant monkey. *Science, 130*, 421–432.

Kennell, J. H., & Klaus, M. H. (1979). Early mother-infant contact: Effects on the mother and the infant. *Bulletin of the Menninger Clinic, 43*, 69–78.

Kennell, J. H., & Klaus, M. H. (1984). Mother-infant bonding: Weighing the evidence. *Developmental Review, 4*, 275–282.

Questions for Discussion

1. Is there much of a difference between infant-mother love in humans and infant-mother love in other primates? What specific behaviors do human infants and mothers engage in that indicate they're in love? How does this differ from the sorts of behaviors exhibited by the nonhuman primates in Harlow's studies?

2. From an evolutionary point of view, what survival value might infant-mother love provide? Isn't it risky for a mother to expend all her energy caring for a baby?

3. Is it ethical to intentionally raise baby monkeys without their mothers? Can you think of any situations in which human babies would be raised in environments like those of Harlows' monkeys?

4. We know that the exploratory behaviors of rhesus monkeys depend in part on the social status of their parents in the group. Do human children experience the effects of the social status of their parents similarly?

17

The Invisible Bungee Cord

Attachment and Loss

Bowlby, J. (1969) Vol. 1. *Attachment.* New York: Basic Books.
(RANK 7)

Have you ever observed a spontaneous game of bungee-baby? Well, maybe you've never heard it called "bungee-baby" per se, but I'm sure you've seen it played. The game has many features in common with the extreme sport of bungee jumping. In bungee jumping, a crazed individual ties a long, hopefully strong bungee cord to his ankles and proceeds to jump off a tall building or bridge. The hope is that moments before crashing face first into the Earth, the bungee cord's elasticity will slow down the person's descent and snap him back up from the depths of gravity and doom.

The game of bungee-baby is also a game of risk and daring, and also involves a stationary platform, but in this case the bungee cord links a mother to her toddler. But no real jumping takes place, and the bungee cord is invisible. You can see bungee-baby played in public venues the world over, wherever mothers and toddlers are found. The mother, playing the role of "home base," starts the game by taking a relatively stationary position in a waiting room or playground. The child begins in a position very near the mother. The goal of the game is for the child to wander as far away from the mother as possible before the invisible bungee cord of anxiety and fear snaps the child back toward the mother. However, if the child isn't paying attention or wanders too far from home base, the bungee cord snaps the mother toward the child. Bungee-baby is played all the time in public places. Next time you go to a playground, an airport, or a restaurant, just sit back and watch. You'll see mothers and toddlers moving to and fro, back and forth, coming and going. You'll never actually see the bungee cord, but you'll know its there because it always keeps the mom and the baby within a well-defined distance.

John Bowlby was an enormous figure in the field of children's mental health, especially because he discovered the rules for bungee-baby. Well, okay, probably nobody else calls it bungee-baby. That's my name for it. And it's not necessarily a game either. It's just something that happens between mothers and young children under normal circumstances. Bowlby called it "attachment." But you'll have a clearer picture of what Bowlby was talking about if you think about his attachment idea as if it were a game of bungee-baby.

Bowlby and his colleague Mary Ainsworth (see Chapter 18) were responsible for arguably the single most important theoretical achievement in the scientific investigation of mother-child love relationships ever, let alone the last 50 years. Jointly, the two of them established a huge ideological umbrella known throughout psychology as attachment theory. Using the PsycINFO database, I conducted a search to see exactly how many articles were published on the topic of attachment. Over 16,000 pieces of work emerged. Fortunately for me, I at least have the luxury of two chapters to scrape the surface of the contributions of these two attachment icons. In the current chapter we'll be focusing on the efforts of Bowlby (who came in 7th among the 20 most revolutionary authors published since 1960). In Chapter 18, we'll take a closer look at Mary Ainsworth's contributions (which ranked #1).

Bowlby was trained as a medical doctor, with a specialization in psychiatry. As was typical for psychiatrists educated in the early part of the twentieth century, Bowlby's clinical training was steeped in the philosophical traditions of psychoanalysis, a form of psychotherapy rooted in Freudian theory. Due to space limitations, I can't delve much into Freud's extensive psychosexual theory of personality development. But to place Bowlby's work in context, it helps to briefly review the approaches espoused by Freud and his intellectual descendants.

Freud derived his method of psychotherapy, as well as his overarching theory of personality development, from his experiences with adult patients. These patients were usually women, and often came to him with unusual, sometimes downright bizarre, psychological symptoms. One reason the symptoms were so odd was that they seemed to have no physical basis, as if coming from nowhere. A typical disorder might be something like "hysterical paralysis," in which a patient reported limited movement or sensation in one of her limbs. The term *hysterical* was often applied to conditions like these because they had no underlying neurological explanation. But the term *hysterical* may also be preferred because it was women who usually had these symptoms, and the word *hysterical* comes from the Greek *hystéra*, meaning uterus or womb.

Fascinatingly, Freud found that the severity of his patients' bizarre symptoms could often be reduced or even eliminated just by talking with patients about their personal histories. And indeed, this was how psychoanalysis generally proceeded. By talking with patients about their personal histories, it became possible to look back through time and identify a particularly noteworthy event or experience that might have served as the source of the pathology. Freud often found that the source of a disorder could be traced to a patient's childhood relationships with her parents. But Freud's focus wasn't on whether parents provided the child the usual amount of love and compassion; rather, he was intently interested in whether parents satisfied a child's fundamental pleasure needs. Children who received too much or too little pleasure during early childhood, Freud thought, were doomed to an adult life of "neuroses."

Because Bowlby was trained as a Freudian psychoanalyst, he was keenly sensitive to the role of mother-child relationships in forming children's personalities. But Bowlby was a little bummed out by the fact that psychoanalytic theory generally focused on parent-child relationships **retrospectively**. For him, it was unfortunate that somebody had to have a psychological problem on display *before* the dynamics of her relationship with her parents could be worked out (i.e., psychoanalyzed). Bowlby thought this was a fairly backward approach. He thought it would be far more beneficial to the field of psychology were we to start with an understanding of *normal* parent-child relationships, and only then work on understanding deviations from the typical. Once the basic nature of mother-child relationships was understood, he believed, scientists could focus on the role these relationships play in contributing to psychological development later in life.

Since no one had yet fully developed such a forward-looking approach, Bowlby was pretty much on his own. One goal of his book, then, was to draw up a set of blueprints for the methodology of a **prospective** (forward-looking) psychoanalytic psychology. Not only would a prospective psychology be immensely useful for the field, but a prospective approach would increase the scientific credibility of psychoanalysis. In this case, expectations about a kid's future emotional functioning could be based on the quality of his relationship with his parents *as he's currently experiencing it*. Scientifically, this would be a lot better than the traditional Freudian method of explaining everything after the fact, because a prospective approach would allow psychoanalytic theories to be testable. Testability is a fundamental tenet of science. Ideas that aren't testable aren't scientific. Unfortunately, much of psychoanalysis before Bowlby's time depended on probing patients' personal histories, including their own recollections of what happened to them when they were very young children. Personal recollections after they've happened simply aren't all that reliable. With his prospective approach, Bowlby was clearly on his way to revolutionizing psychoanalytic theory, because his version would allow scientists to make testable predictions about what would happen in the future based on parent-child relationships in the present.

Now, it's not as if Bowlby was contemplating these ideas in the abstract while sitting in a rocking chair sipping his afternoon tea. Rather, Bowlby was compelled to confront these broader theoretical issues when he was faced with a large number of very young children who, for one reason or another, were separated from their mothers and were being raised institutionally, often amid serious social isolation. Bowlby himself had experienced several emotional separations from important caregiving figures. For example, Minnie, his favorite nursemaid and primary caregiver, and who was in many ways like a mother to him, left his household when he was only 4 years old. Thus, in sum, no one really knew the prognosis for very young children being raised in relative states of maternal separation, because no prospective science had yet been undertaken. Bowlby set out to change all that.

INTRODUCTION

In his book, Bowlby's efforts to lay out his vision for a prospective psychoanalytic psychology begins with his presentation of the "Observations to Be Explained," which is also the title of his second chapter. In laying out the observations to be explained, Bowlby gives us a sense that he wants to avoid starting out with a presupposed set of theoretical beliefs. He acknowledges that his training was in psychoanalysis, but he also acknowledges the scientific shortcomings of that approach. Instead, he gives us the sense that he wants to develop his new theory *inductively*. In other words, his plan is to start out with observations of what happens when children are separated from their mothers, and only then begin developing a theory to account for these observations.

METHOD

Participants

Bowlby credits his colleague James Robertson for providing the brunt of the observations used to build Bowlby's Attachment Theory. Specific characteristics of the children filmed by Robertson aren't provided, but the children were all filmed during stays at institutions in or around London in the mid-twentieth century. The basic data from the films consist of recordings of the day-to-day behaviors of toddler- and preschool-aged children who were required to stay in residential nurseries or hospitals for extended periods of time. As a result, the children were no longer cared for by their mothers, and were "cared for instead in a strange place by a succession of unfamiliar people."

Materials

No special equipment or materials were used here since the research was pretty much based on filmed recordings of children's naturally occurring behaviors during periods of separation from their parents.

Procedure

Similarly, nothing that could be called a formal research procedure was really used. At best, the procedure for data collection might be called "naturalistic observation." However, the recordings weren't raw, disconnected video clips; they were pieced together in true filmmaking style to tell a narrative story. Indeed, Robertson turned out to be such a gifted filmmaker that his filming methods were subsequently adopted as standard protocol whenever the filming of separated children was necessary. Robertson's films were eventually distributed widely throughout Europe and the United States, and frequently resulted in hospitals' changing their visitation policies.

RESULTS

In his films, Robertson outlined what appeared to be a three-phase progression of separation behaviors that children exhibited when they were forced into prolonged separations from their primary caregivers. This progression appeared to be an equal opportunity employer, and was observed in all children equally, regardless of how strong their relationships with their parents were prior to the separation. The three phases of separation behaviors described by Robertson included (1) protest, (2) despair, and (3) detachment. Bowlby notes that the children didn't necessarily experience these phases one right after the other. And the children could differ quite a bit from one another in terms of how long they spent in each phase. But the apparent universality of these phases made a significant impression on Bowlby. Here are some examples of what happened during each of the three phases.

PROTEST   The "Protest" phase is so-called because when children were first separated from their mothers, they underwent an intense period of protest. For some children, the protesting started immediately; while for others it sometimes took awhile. Similarly, some children protested for only a few hours, while other children protested for more than a week. What contributed to these differences apparently had to do with the quality of children's relationships with their mother. Thus, although all children went through a protesting phase, the quality of their initial relationships with their mothers affected the length and intensity of protesting.

As Bowlby described it, while protesting, "the young child appears acutely distressed at having lost his mother and seeks to recapture her by the full exercise of his limited resources. He will often cry loudly, shake his cot, throw himself about, and look eagerly towards any sight or sound which might prove to be his missing mother. All the behavior suggests strong expectation that she will return. Meantime he is apt to reject all alternative figures who offer to do things for him, though some children will cling desperately to a nurse."

DESPAIR   After the protesting phase, which, from the child's point of view, obviously didn't work, children gradually begin accepting the idea that their mother isn't going to return. During this "Despair" phase, children develop an increasing sense of hopelessness. The energy and vigor displayed during the protesting stage goes away, and children become increasingly withdrawn and nonresponsive. Bowlby describes it as a state of deep mourning.

DETACHMENT   After despairing, and upon entering the "Detachment" phase, children just sort of give up. Ironically, at least from a purely behavioral standpoint, they actually seem to improve. It may even appear to the naive observer during this third phase that a child's stress has gone away, and that he has finally come face to face with his fate. It's as if he's gotten over his mother's leaving. For one thing, he begins accepting the caregiving efforts of the nurses rather than continually rejecting them. And he may even show signs of happiness and sociability. However, as Bowlby noted, when the mother visits, all is not well. Instead of showing normal attachment behavior, the child may act if he doesn't know his mother; instead of clinging he may exhibit apathy; instead of crying he may simply turn away.

Although the films were based on video records of children who had gone to hospitals or who had undergone extended stays at residential children's nurseries, similar kinds of observations can sometimes be made under less extreme circumstances. Lesser amounts of protest can be observed in children attending their first day of school, for example. Similarly, I recall vividly how my nephew Matthew, who was 2 at the time, completely rejected his mother when she returned home after a week-long excursion. In his case, Matthew never showed any outward signs of protest or despair, probably because he remained with his father in his mother's absence. But when his mom returned, I was struck by how little interest he showed in being hugged or even approached by her. Instead of the joyful embrace of a long-awaited mother-child reunion, I witnessed what appeared to be a complete, albeit temporary, detachment.

DISCUSSION

So there Bowlby was, a scientist in possession of all those filmed observations, with little besides psychoanalytic theory to guide his interpretations. Thus, he began inventing a whole new theory. He was guided in large part by a rapidly growing literature emerging from the field of **animal ethology**. As a scientific discipline, ethology is based on Charles Darwin's evolutionary notion of adaptation through natural selection. Ethologists study the behaviors of individual species to see whether specific behaviors might help individual species better survive in their environments. Behaviors that help members of a species adapt, bestow upon those members greater opportunities for survival. And if a behavior increases the likelihood for survival, then any genes responsible for producing that behavior may be transmitted to the next generation, thus increasing the likelihood of those offspring engaging in the same adaptive behavior.

Bowlby thought that the human mother-child relationship was a type of adaptive behavior. He believed it was so strong and so important to the developing child as to be built into the child by evolution in order to help the human species survive. And why not? The Harlows (Chapter 16) had recently shown how important the infant-mother relationship was for the well-being of infant rhesus monkeys. Why couldn't the same be true for humans?

Borrowing from Ethology

Ethology had a heyday during Bowlby's time. Ethologists all over the world were publishing articles that documented all kinds of animal behaviors, many of which proved to be absolutely fascinating. The behaviors were often unusual and exotic, but they were almost always clearly adaptive for the species exhibiting them. Bowlby thought that maybe ethology could provide some insight into why human mothers and their very young children remained in such close proximity, as if bound by an invisible bungee cord. Throughout much of the rest of his book, Bowlby presents ideas from animal ethology that he believed were probably responsible for contributing to the formation of the strong mother-infant bond in humans.

THE ENVIRONMENT OF ADAPTEDNESS   One central ethological idea that Bowlby latched onto was something he called the **environment of adaptedness**. The environment of adaptedness refers to the specific environment that a particular system, through natural selection, was "built" to work best in. A "system" can be any number of things. For example, we can imagine a whole species as a system. Take for example, *Oncorhynchus mykiss*, the rainbow trout. As a system, the rainbow trout species functions best in freshwater environments, where water temperatures range somewhere between 44 and 75°F. Should members of this trout species be displaced into deviant environments, such as warm tropical freshwater ponds, or saltwater environments of any temperature, they would function poorly. And of course, rainbow trout function *extremely poorly* in hot, waterless environments, such as those found in cast iron frying pans hovering over open campfires.

We can also imagine a biological process as a system. Consider the human cardiopulmonary system. For the most part, the human cardiopulmonary system functions to extract oxygen from the immediate surroundings and pump it into the bloodstream. Human cardiopulmonary systems were built to work best under atmospheric conditions such as you might find at sea level. It works less well under other atmospheric conditions. This is one reason so many teams in the National Football League dread playing games against the Denver Broncos. Players on opposing teams find themselves huffing and puffing up and down the field, slapping oxygen masks over their faces as much as possible. And these athletes are otherwise extremely physically fit. Breathing is simply more challenging at 1 mile above sea level because there is relatively little oxygen available in the atmosphere.

Although all systems function best in their environments of adaptedness, over time the environment of adaptedness for a particular system can change. This change can challenge the adaptability of the system in question. Sometimes the environment changes only temporarily, such as when a goose's favorite lake bed dries up as a result of a long summer drought. However, sometimes the environment changes permanently, and it can do so as a result of a species' own intentional actions. Humans are probably most notorious for permanently changing their own environments. The environments that humans live in now are dramatically deviant from the original environments they evolved to fit into. No human system was built to survive in a world of planes, trains, and automobiles, for example. Rather, the behavioral and biological systems we now have in place actually evolved to help our ancient ancestors survive in a world that by today's standards we would consider extremely primitive. So right off the bat you can appreciate the great mismatch between the current evolutionary state of humans, which evolved to fit a primeval environment, and humans' current industrialized environment, which is anything but primeval.

From an ethological point of view, it's also pretty easy to see that human babies born today are relatively ill prepared for survival in modern society. Human babies were built to survive in a time and place where there were no planes, trains, and automobiles; where there were no institutions like hospitals and orphanages; and where children wouldn't ordinarily experience extended separations from their mothers. Bowlby was very clear that if we are to understand the mother-child relationship, we can't do so from the point of view of modern society. Rather, we have to do so from the point of view of their original environment of adaptedness. Bowlby wrote, "the only relevant criterion by which to consider the natural adaptedness of any particular part of present-day man's behavioral equipment is the degree to which and the way in which it might contribute to population survival in man's primeval environment." Accordingly, to really understand the survival value of the modern mother-child relationship, we have to understand it against the backdrop of the conditions under which it evolved; which, unfortunately, hasn't existed for many hundreds of thousands of years. Understood this way, the protest, despair, and detachment phases experienced by children who are separated from their mothers, come from the mismatch between the actual biological adaptedness of babies and mothers and the reality of the modern environments in which these babies and mothers actually find themselves.

Bowlby was interested in the idea of systems to the extent that it could be applied to collections of children's behaviors. At this level, we could refer to children's behaviors as part of one or more *behavioral systems*. Bowlby had reason to believe that children had inside of them a particular system that served to keep them physically close to their mothers. At least it would appear that such a system might exist, based on the separation behaviors children exhibited in institutional settings. In its full complexity, he labeled this system the **attachment system**.

With this idea in mind, Bowlby tried to accumulate additional evidence in support of his notion of a primeval attachment system that might exist within humans. Not only would such evidence support the idea that an attachment system was "built into" prehistoric human babies and mothers, hence giving them, and the human species as a whole, an evolutionary edge for survival, but it might also help explain babies' protesting, despairing, and detaching behaviors during periods of separation. Since there are two parts to the equation of the mother-child relationship, we should ask two questions: (1) What factors, if any, contribute to a baby's inborn, overwhelming desire to be near its mother? (2) What factors, if any, contribute to a mother's natural urge to be near her baby? Again, Bowlby saw potential answers to these questions in the ethological research being conducted with nonhuman species.

IMPRINTING   As to whether human babies have a special inborn attraction to their mothers, one of Bowlby's favorite ethological ideas was **imprinting**. Imprinting is probably best known from ethologist Konrad Lorenz's research with baby geese and ducks. Lorenz found that when baby geese and ducks hatched, they developed a preference for the nearest moving object they saw. Hatchlings soon began following that object around, and they did their best to stay as close as possible to it. If the object went away, the hatchlings tried to find it, or they gave off distress calls to beckon the object back. Because this is the process of imprinting, we might loosely say that the object of desire has been imprinted on the "minds" or brains of the baby geese and ducks.

Now, in a natural environment, the imprinted object is almost always the mother goose or duck. And the imprinting system more or less ensures that the hatchlings will remain near their mother. But the conniving hands of experimental ethologists have shown that the mother bird is not the only object that can be imprinted. The imprinted object can also be a ball, a dog, or even a pair of orange socks worn by the ethologist himself. Although the specific object doesn't seem to matter much, a number of naturally occurring factors does help narrow the range of potentially imprintable objects. For one thing, the imprinted object needs to be of a particular size. Objects that are too big or too small don't trigger imprinting. Also, auditory calls given off by the object, like quacking, can enhance the strength of imprinting. But once an object is imprinted upon, it's very difficult for imprinting to happen with any other objects. And objects that aren't imprinted can sometimes even produce fear responses should they venture too close to the recently imprinted hatchlings.

The adaptive value of imprinting is obvious. In natural environments, it virtually guarantees that babies will stay close to their mother. Near lakes or streams you may have even witnessed the familiar trail of ducklings or goslings following their mothers around in a sort of little waterfowl train. Remaining close to the mother is adaptive because it gives the babies all the protection from predators and intruders the mother can provide. And as I can testify firsthand, the ire of the brooding mother is not to be messed with. My errant short game when trying to play golf has brought me all too close to gaggles of hissing mother geese who've just watched my ball dribble into a nearby pond.

Bowlby believed that imprinting had obvious implications for the human mother-child relationship. Perhaps human babies imprint on their mothers too. Of course, there are obvious differences between birds and mammals, especially higher-level mammals like people. For one thing, human newborns can't totter around after their mothers right after birth. So any application of the idea of imprinting to human babies will have to take place over a much longer course of time, say several months. But adhering to a less rigid definition, there are a few parallels between the behaviors of chicks and human babies. For example, after human babies are a few months old, they begin showing a strong preference for some objects over others. Usually, the preferred object is the mother. Human babies also show fear responses in the absence of the mother, and they can appear incredibly frightened at the unwelcome advances of strangers. Human babies who are mobile also show a strong tendency to remain close to the mother when she's around, and to follow her as she moves about (bungee-baby!).

Bowlby wrote, "We may conclude, therefore, that, so far as is at present known, the way in which attachment behavior develops in the human infant and becomes focused on a discriminated figure is sufficiently like the way in which it develops in other mammals, and in birds, for it to be included, legitimately, under the heading of imprinting—so long as that term is used in its . . . generic sense. Indeed, to do otherwise would be to create a wholly unwarranted gap between the human case and that of other species." You can see that it was important for Bowlby to remain in keeping with the spirit of Darwin's theory of evolution in explaining human attachment. Bowlby's theory was based on potential ethological parallels between human behaviors and those found in subhuman species.

INSTINCTS   Although imprinting may help explain babies' natural interests in maintaining closeness with their mothers, it doesn't account for any natural tendencies of mothers to stay near and care for their babies. So Bowlby borrowed another idea from ethology, that of the so-called maternal **instinct**. The question of whether any human behavior can be regarded as instinctual causes quite a bit of controversy these days. Many modern psychologists would probably argue that no human behaviors are truly instinctual. However, Bowlby thought otherwise. For him, maternal caregiving behavior met the criteria for being labeled instinctual. According to his criteria, maternal caregiving is instinctual because (1) it follows a similar and predictable pattern in most members of the species, (2) it is not a simple response to a single stimulus, but a sequence of behavior that runs a predictable course, (3) the consequences of the behavior are valuable for ensuring the survival of the individual or the species, and (4) the behavior develops even when there are no opportunities for learning it.

Now, because modern human society no longer reflects the original environment of adaptedness, we have to rely significantly on observations of other animals to best understand the maternal instinct. We can learn especially well from what other "ground-living primates" do. One remarkable characteristic of other ground-dwelling primates is that they are highly social. They have their own little primate societies with their own little primate pecking orders. Different members of the group have different statuses within the group, and each member dares not try to live at a more privileged level than her or his status allows, else the higher-level group members will put them back in their place (just like in American culture). But one benefit of living in a highly role-differentiated society is that everyone knows what she or he is supposed to do. When the group is threatened by a predator, for example, the males all gather together to fend off the beast. In contrast, the females gather up their young and run off to safety. By the definition we've just outlined, these role-governed behaviors are instinctual. One reason that human mothers might be so protective over their babies, then, could be because the prehistoric baby-grabbing and baby-hiding behaviors during times of threat have helped the human species survive as a whole. In turn, the survival of the species has selected for genes that initiate maternal grabbing and hiding behaviors, making them behaviors that have survived alongside human societies to this very day.

Another ethological factor may also be partially responsible for arousing a desire in moms to hold and care for their babies. And that is that babies give off signals that mothers feel obligated to respond to. For example, babies inevitably cry when they need something. Infant crying has the effect of more or less forcing mothers to seek out and relieve the source of their babies' distress. But babies also smile, and smiling can bring about the most rewarding of emotions in the mother. Bowlby wrote about the mother, "When she is tired and irritated with her infant, his smile disarms her; when she is feeding or otherwise caring for him, his smile is a reward and encouragement to her . . . her infant's smile so affects a mother that the future likelihood of her responding to his signals promptly and in a way favoring his survival is increased."

Finally, it's probably no small matter that babies are so dang cute! In fact, the natural cuteness of babies may bring out caregiving behaviors in all of us, not just mothers. Have you ever experienced an overwhelming desire to go up and hug a really cute little baby? And they don't have to be human babies either. Puppies, kittens, baby monkeys, and even baby birds seem to bring out smiles of adoration and hugging impulses from adult humans around the world. Is it an accident that baby members of many species are so cute? Konrad Lorenz (the imprinting guy) noted a long time ago that baby members of many animal species have a number of anatomical characteristics that humans perceive as cute. Relative to adult members of their species, babies all tend to have an unusually large, rounded head, rounded cheeks, large eyes, and a large forehead. Such characteristics of babyness may be found by adult members of the species to be powerfully appealing, and may even "pull" caregiving behaviors right out of the adult providers. These caregiving efforts in response to the cuteness of the baby have even been given a name: the **cute response**. Anyway, although Bowlby didn't talk about the cute response himself, it may very well be another evolutionary item built into mothers to guarantee a willingness to care for their babies.

Mother and Baby: A Mutual Attraction

Drawing on the ethology literature to establish an evolutionary, biological basis for the mutual attraction experienced by mothers and children was a stroke of genius. No one before, or possibly ever since, has drawn together such vastly different disciplines to articulate such a well-defined position about mother-baby relationships. But Bowlby also points out that the mother-child relationship is not biological destiny. It's not like moms and babies are computerized machines running on software programs. Evolution might have *nudged* moms and babies toward a mutual attractiveness, but additional work by both partners is needed to ensure a successful attachment relationship.

Mothers and babies have to be mutually responsive to one another, for example. Bowlby points out that the attachment relationship is an intensely emotional affair. If for some reason the mother is unavailable to the baby, emotionally or physically, or if the baby is unavailable to the mother, emotionally or physically, then psychological disorders can emerge. He wrote, "for proximity and affectionate interchange are appraised and felt as pleasurable by both whereas distance and expressions of rejection are appraised and felt as disagreeable or painful by both. . . . As a result, whenever during the development of some individual these standards become markedly different from the norm, as occasionally they do, all are disposed to judge the condition as pathological." And this is where we came in. As we saw in the results section, children who were separated from their mothers due to some form of institutionalization inevitably displayed signs of intense emotional trauma, either in the form of protesting, despair, or worst of all, detachment.

Finally, although mothers may be the preferred attachment objects of choice, babies can also show attachments to other key figures in their lives. Just as baby ducks might imprint and follow around Duke the dog, so might human babies imprint and attach to fathers, older siblings, nurses, and even babysitters. There have even been rare cases of nonhuman animals playing the role of attachment figure and primary caregiver. For example, the feral boy nicknamed Viktor was found in the woods near Aveyron, France in the late eighteenth century. He had apparently been raised by a pack of wolves.

The Attachment Revolution

It's notable that we've spent the last several pages discussing the theoretical ingenuity of a trained Freudian psychoanalyst, while referencing Freudian psychoanalysis only minimally. As I mentioned earlier, this is mostly because Bowlby was dissatisfied with Freudian theory. But even though Bowlby initially only intended to update Freudian theory through the infusion of new ethological ideas, he ended up producing an attachment theory that could pretty much stand on its own. It required little if any support from Freudian theory itself. In fact, some of Freud's more traditionalist followers have even called Bowlby a heretic.

Still, many psychoanalytic therapists draw heavily on Bowlby's attachment theory when treating adult patients with various psychological disorders. This post-Bowlbyan psychoanalytic approach begins the traditional way—by starting with a current psychological problem and tracing it backward into the patient's childhood. But there is a distinctly Bowlbyan flavor to such a new form of psychoanalysis. For one thing, therapy centers on the patient's current attachments with important social figures, including the spouse, the children, and any best friends. If the quality of these relationships is found to be generally poor, the next step is to explore whether the patient may have failed in childhood to establish a secure attachment with her own mother.

Although this approach is still retrospective, Bowlby's ideas about attachment are clearly central. The goal of therapy is to help the patient establish new attachment relationships through many years of intensive, hour-long therapeutic sessions. Procedurally, analysis would consist of the therapist helping the patient gain insight about how her childhood attachment with her mother may have been obstructed or otherwise compromised. Through such insight, the Bowlbyan psychoanalyst can also guide the patient toward corrective measures designed to repair any damaged attachment relationships, even though the patient has long since left childhood.

THE DEVOLUTION OF ATTACHMENT THEORY   Although it might be said that imitation is the sincerest form of flattery, some "unauthorized" applications of attachment theory would probably have Bowlby turning over in his grave. One such application, which appears to be diminishing in popularity these days, goes by the name of "rebirthing therapy." The idea behind rebirthing therapy is simple. An individual with an attachment disorder symbolically goes back in time, experiences "birth" again, and is granted a second chance at establishing a secure attachment relationship, maybe even with a primary caregiver. Probably not coincidentally, some "Rebirthing Centers" offer 9-month programs. Rebirthing centers became very popular for a time, and you could get yourself reborn for a meager $5,000–7,000. Simply Google *rebirthing* and *center* to find the clinic nearest you!

While I don't particularly oppose symbolic rebirthing, one high profile case revealed just how far this approach could be taken. Candace Newmaker was a 10-year-old girl having problems getting emotionally close to her adoptive mother. Her mother paid $7,000 to a rebirthing clinic in Evergreen, Colorado, for a 2-week program that included an episode of symbolic rebirthing. To represent being in the "womb," the child was wrapped up in a blanket. Four adults then began pushing pillows against the now-engulfed girl, which was symbolic of labor contractions. According to a *U.S. News & World Report* article, the child indicated, on seven occasions in the first 24 minutes, that she couldn't breathe. She said six times during the first 16 minutes that she felt like she was going to die. Instead of ending the session, the therapist continued on by saying, "You want to die? Okay, then die. Go ahead, die right now." One hour and 10 minutes into the session, after the failed rebirth of Candace, they unwrapped the womb to reveal an unconscious, blue child—ironically, in the fetal position. She was pronounced dead the next day.

CONCLUSIONS

John Bowlby's work provided a new perspective on the emotional development of children for health care providers around the world. His work showed that if a child is denied contact with an attachment figure for an extended period of time, significant emotional trauma and long-term damage could result. Evolution simply wouldn't permit human babies to be separated from their mothers for very long. Mothers were much more than walking breasts designed solely to serve the nutritional needs of their children, they also supplied love. Bowlby showed that if institutions were truly interested in the mental health of their child patients, they would let their mothers be available on a full-time basis. And for orphaned children, special staff people would need to step in and take over the mother role. Moreover, mothers were essential for providing a secure base from which children could venture and explore uncharted waters. So attachment was necessary not only for emotional security, but also for the kind of intellectual development that comes from learning about the surrounding world.

Mary Ainsworth, John Bowlby's longtime acquaintance, colleague, and friend, wrote in the *American Psychologist*, "John Bowlby the scientist cannot be separated from John Bowlby the human being. All those who knew him considered him a deeply warm and caring person. A good clinician, he viewed others with respect, understanding, and compassion. Some misconstrue his emphasis on parental behavior in influencing the course of a child's personality development as blaming the parents for anything that goes wrong. He knew that 'to understand all is to pardon all.' He was incapable of blame."

Bibliography

Ainsworth, M. D. S. (1992). John Bowlby (1907–1990): Obituary. *American Psychologist, 47,* 668.

Bretherton, I. (1992). The origins of attachment theory: John Bowlby and Mary Ainsworth. *Developmental Psychology, 28,* Im-lll.

van Dijken, S. (1998). John Bowlby: His early life: A biographical journey into the roots of attachment theory. London: Free Association Books.

Questions for Discussion

1. Can human babies really imprint like Konrad Lorenz's birds? In general, how are the behaviors of baby humans and baby birds similar and different when it comes to survival?
2. How can Harry Harlow's work (Chapter 16) be incorporated into Bowlby's attachment theory?
3. Based on what you know of the role of attachment relationships, what might the attachment behaviors of babies born to chronically depressed mothers look like?
4. How is modern human society different from the environment of adaptedness? Do any cultures remain that deviate very little from the environment of adaptedness? Can you think of any future societal conditions that could actually render attachment behaviors unadaptive?

18

What a Strange Situation

Patterns of Attachment: A Psychological Study of the Strange Situation

Ainsworth, M. D. S., Blehar, M. C., Waters, E., & Wall, S. (1978). Hillsdale, NJ: Erlbaum.   (RANK 1)

"Utter fear" describes my emotional state the first time I visited downtown Chicago as a grown-up. Now it's not that Chicago is especially frightening. In fact, it's not much different than any other major city with a population of several million. And now that I'm a seasoned visitor to Chicago, I'm thrilled with the cultural opportunities Chicago provides. But for some reason, I was pretty freaked out by my first visit. After many years of reflection, I think I know why. On the day that my fiancée and I arrived in Chicago, our contact person was nowhere to be found. You see we had planned on visiting our friend Sharon, who lived in downtown Chicago; we intended to surprise her because we were "in the neighborhood" (actually, we were an hour away in northern Indiana, but what's a few dozen miles?) and because we knew she wasn't away on one of her frequent business trips. We thought we would just pop in and say "Hi." We assumed that because she wasn't traveling on business, she would be holed up in her high-rise apartment. Seemed like a reasonable expectation to us. After all, what else could anyone possibly do in Chicago on a sunny Saturday afternoon, right? Well, she wasn't expecting us, and she wasn't home.

The moment it dawned on me that we were alone in that very large, noisy, towering city, a mild sense of panic washed over me. Even though I grew up in a city (a much, much smaller city), my initial reaction was to hightail it out of that urban jungle and get back to familiar territory. As I reflect back on that moment now, I am aware that the reason I felt so intimidated, so vulnerable, was that we had no home turf, "no center of operations." I knew that if Sharon would just come home and open up the safety net of her apartment, all would be well. We would be free to make plans about which sights to see and even which restaurants to try out. We could venture out safely to explore our strange new urban surroundings, with the comfort of knowing that there was a secure base awaiting us. As it turned out, Sharon came home shortly afterward, and the presence of that secure place really did make all the difference in the world. One could hear my sigh of relief as we carted our luggage up those 42 floors (on the elevator).

According to the work of Mary Ainsworth, it turns out that my need for the assurance of a secure place isn't all that unusual. In fact, needing a secure place (or "base" in Ainsworth's words) may be fundamental to being human. In her book, which was voted the number one most revolutionary work in the field of child psychology published since 1960, Ainsworth explored in great detail the developmental importance of having a secure base. To get to that point, she and her three coauthors, Mary Blehar, Everett Waters, and Sally Wall, began by reviewing Bowlby's concept of attachment (which we also visited in Chapter 17), and launched on a voyage to explore the impact of attachment on children's emotional development. Ainsworth and her colleagues were especially interested in how a child's "attachment system" worked in a familiar versus a strange environment. To cut to the chase, Ainsworth discovered that different children can have very different kinds of attachment relationships with their parents. It was her discovery of these patterns of attachment that made Dr. Ainsworth and her work so revolutionary. Indeed, she titled her book *Patterns of Attachment*.

INTRODUCTION

As I just mentioned, Ainsworth and her colleagues began their book by rehashing the central features of John Bowlby's attachment theory. Of course, we just spent a chapter on the topic, so we don't need to talk about it again here. Suffice it to say that the feature of Bowlby's theory that most interested Ainsworth and her colleagues was the attachment system Bowlby believed existed inside all human babies. Ainsworth was especially interested in understanding the conditions that activated children's attachment systems, as well as the conditions that resulted in their termination.

What's that you say? You've forgotten a bit about attachment theory? Okay, here's a brief review. Bowlby suggested that human infants have an inborn attachment system that consists of an evolutionarily adaptive set of behaviors that helps them remain close to their mothers. Just about anything a child can do to bring his mother close to him—and keep her there—is an attachment behavior. One obvious thing a child can do, for example, is follow his mother around. But this isn't really an option for children who can't crawl or walk yet. For pre-mobile children, crying or smiling will have to do. Although imperfect, these **signaling behaviors** work at a distance, and are often good enough to bring the mother close. But even they won't work very well if the mother can't detect them. But eventually children become mobile, and their collection of attachment behaviors expands to include locomotion, which permits them to move toward their mothers all by themselves. As we noted in the previous chapter, the significance of all these behaviors is that they serve the survival function of keeping the child under the protective care of the mother. This would have been an important factor in prehistoric times, when a separated child could have become a scrumptious midmorning snack to a hungry lioness and her cubs.

Ainsworth and her colleagues were also interested in how the development of children's thinking might accompany and improve their attachment behaviors. Older children, in addition to having mobility, have the ability to think and make plans about how to stay close to their mothers. Although I ran out of space in Chapter 17 to discuss it, Bowlby spent a lot of time developing his notion of a **mental model**, or "cognitive map," and argued that it probably plays an important role in children's attachment systems. What is a mental model? You can think of a mental model as a set of expectations you develop based on your experiences. Let me give you an example. When I was a kid, everyone in my neighborhood was familiar with the sound of the ice cream truck. The ice cream truck was a vehicle that drove through our neighborhood at a very slow pace, played a pleasant melody very loudly through loudspeakers attached to its roof, and supplied all the neighborhood kiddies with as much ice cream as their parents could afford or tolerate. No matter what neighborhood games we were playing, the melody of the ice cream truck grabbed our attention, and we knew that the ice cream vendor would soon be driving by. In Bowlby's words, we had formed a mental model of the ice cream truck. Our mental model included the loud sound of the melody, the sight of the truck, and the taste of the ice cream we bought, were we lucky enough to convince our parents to indulge us. Also embedded in our mental models of the ice cream truck was the time of year. We never had expectations of seeing an ice cream truck in the middle of winter, which in the Midwest is usually accompanied by several inches or feet of snow. (Actually, I do remember one cold but very sunny January day when an ice cream truck cruised through my neighborhood, the familiar tunes being absorbed by the cascading snow mounds. I don't think he made many sales.)

Anyway, both Bowlby and Ainsworth believed that children's mental models of their mothers played a fundamental role in determining when children's attachment systems would be activated, with the caveat that the nature of those models would also depend on children's unique and individual experiences with their mothers. Children with mothers who reliably remained nearby would eventually develop mental models of mothers who were reliable. In contrast, children with mothers who frequently wandered off or were otherwise inaccessible would end up developing mental models of mothers who were unpredictable. Ainsworth and her colleagues wrote, "If in the course of his experience in interaction with his mother he has built up expectations that she is generally accessible to him and responsive to his signals and communications, this provides an important 'modifier' to his proximity . . . goal under ordinary circumstances. If his experience has led him to distrust her accessibility or responsiveness, his . . . goal for proximity may well be set more narrowly."

With these ideas in mind, Ainsworth and her colleagues set out to study children's attachment systems. They thought that if they could activate children's attachment systems under controlled conditions, they would understand the attachment systems better because they would have an opportunity to scrutinize their detailed inner workings. To activate children's attachment systems, Ainsworth implemented a now famous procedure known worldwide as the **strange situation**. The source of Ainsworth's ingenuity in creating the strange situation can be traced to Harlow's work with rhesus monkeys (Chapter 16). If you recall from that chapter, Harlow placed infant rhesus monkeys in an unfamiliar room, which he called an "open-field chamber." The chamber was unfamiliar enough to cause a great deal of distress in the baby monkeys, especially when Harlow introduced a scary, drum-banging, walking toy bear. Although Ainsworth didn't want to freak out human children to the same extent that Harlow frightened his monkeys, she did want to present children with unusual and unfamiliar situations of the sort they might encounter in their real-life, day-to-day experiences.

METHOD

Participants

Quoting Ainsworth and colleagues, "The subjects come from white, middle-class, Baltimore-area families, who were originally contacted through pediatricians in private practice. They were observed in the strange situation at approximately 1 year of age. The total [sample] of 106 infants is comprised of four samples that were observed in the course of four separate projects."

Materials

THE PHYSICAL SETUP   All observations took place in one of two laboratory rooms that were connected by way of two-way mirrors. (A two-way mirror is made of a special kind of glass that looks like a real mirror when viewed from one side, but that works like a clear window when viewed from the other side.) The 9' × 9' experimental room was sparsely furnished with items such as a desk, chairs, a bookcase, and metal storage cabinets (the specifics varied from project to project). For 13 of the subjects the floor was covered with a braided rug, but for the rest of the subjects the floor was bare and marked off into 16 squares so that the observers could make more accurate observations of where and how the children moved about the room. At one end of the room was a child's chair "heaped with and surrounded by toys." Near the other end of the room were two adult chairs, one for the mother and one for a "stranger." The two-way mirrors were on the wall nearest the two adult chairs. Observers watched everything that happened through the two-way mirrors, and dictated their observations into a Stenorette reel-to-reel tape recorder.

PERSONNEL   Under ideal conditions, five different personnel were involved in carrying out the strange situation procedure: two observers, a stranger, an experimenter, and a greeter. The greeter's job was to meet the parents and show them to the experimental room. The experimenter's job was to time the episodes and to cue the mother and the stranger about when to enter and exit the experimental room. The observers' job was to observe and record a play-by-play narrative of everything that happened in the experimental room (two observers were used to help make sure nothing important was overlooked). Finally, the stranger's job was to be a stranger; but also to enter, exit, and then reenter the room on cue. I guess you could say that a sixth person was also needed: the mother. The mother's job was to be a mother, but she was also expected to exit and reenter the room on cue. At an absolute minimum the procedure could be carried out with as few as two staff people, with one person playing the role of greeter and observer and the other playing the role of experimenter and stranger.

Procedure

The strange situation procedure consists of eight separate episodes. Because this procedure is so well known, and is arguably among the most ingenious experimental methodologies invented in the last half-century for measuring parent-child relationships, I'll present a fair amount of descriptive detail for each episode. However, it's interesting to note that Ainsworth did not spend a lot of time thinking up the procedure. She and her colleague Barbara Wittig developed the episodes, as well as their order of occurrence, after chatting for only about a half-hour.

EPISODE 1: MOTHER, BABY, AND EXPERIMENTER   During this episode, Mom and Baby are introduced to the experimental room. Mom is asked to carry her baby into the room and is shown where to put her child. She is also shown where to sit afterward (one of the chairs near the two-way mirror). Observations of Baby are made during this episode, which also counts as the first introduction to an unfamiliar place.

EPISODE 2: MOTHER AND BABY   Mom places Baby down midway between her own and the empty chair. Baby is sat down so as to face the toys on the other side of the room. It is okay, even expected, that the baby will explore the room (especially the toys). For the first 2 minutes, Mom is asked not to initiate any activity with Baby, although she is allowed to respond any way she sees fit to solicitations made by Baby. If after 2 minutes Baby has not begun to explore the room and the toys, Mom is instructed to carry Baby to the toys and to try to stimulate Baby's interest in the toys. During this episode, observations are made of the amount and kind of exploration exhibited by the baby.

EPISODE 3: STRANGER, MOTHER, AND BABY   The Stranger then enters the room and says, creatively, "Hello! I'm the Stranger." The Stranger immediately sits down in the empty chair (near Mom's chair) and remains quiet for 1 minute. She doesn't look at the baby if the baby seems wary of her. After 1 minute, the Stranger strikes up a conversation with Mom. After 1 more minute, the Stranger is cued to leave her chair and begin interacting with Baby. Three minutes later, Mom is cued to leave the room, making sure to leave her purse behind. Mom tries to leave at a time when Baby isn't paying direct attention to her. During this episode, observations are made of how much and what kind of attention Baby pays to the Stranger compared to the attention he pays to Mom or to exploring the toys. Observations are also made of how accepting Baby is of the Stranger's attempts to interact with him.

EPISODE 4: STRANGER AND BABY   After Mom leaves the room, the Stranger reduces her interaction with Baby so that he has a chance to notice that Mom is gone. If Baby returns to exploring the toys, the Stranger returns to her chair and sits quietly. Observations are made of how much exploration Baby does compared to when Mom was still in the room. But if Baby starts crying, the Stranger tries to intervene by distracting him with a toy, and if this fails, by picking him up or talking to him. If her soothing efforts succeed, the Stranger tries to reengage Baby's interest in the toys. If Baby's distress isn't too severe, this episode lasts for 3 minutes. Observations during this episode are made of Baby's response to Mom's departure, as well as Baby's response to the Stranger when she tries to soothe him. After 3 minutes, Mom is cued to return to the room.

EPISODE 5: MOTHER AND BABY   Mom returns to the outside of the closed door of the experimental room and speaks loudly enough to be heard by Baby. Mom pauses, then opens the door, then pauses again. The planned pausing is designed to permit the baby to mobilize toward the door if he is going to. If Baby is upset by that point, Mom is instructed to take whatever actions are necessary to calm Baby down and to redirect his attention to the toys. Meanwhile, the Stranger leaves the room quietly. After 3 minutes, or whenever Baby has settled enough to begin the next episode, Mom is cued to leave. Mom chooses a moment when Baby seems happily engaged with the toys, walks to the door (again leaving her purse on her chair), says "bye-bye," exits, and closes the door behind her. Observations during this episode are aimed at Baby's response to Mom when she returns, as well as to her re-departure.

EPISODE 6: BABY ALONE   Three minutes are allocated to this episode when Baby is allowed to explore the room alone. If he cries, he is given a chance to calm himself down. But if the intensity of his crying is too great, the episode is cut short. Observations are made both of Baby's emotional responsiveness to Mom's leaving and how quickly he returns to exploring the toys.

EPISODE 7: STRANGER AND BABY   Now the Stranger returns to the outside of the closed door and speaks loudly enough to be heard by Baby. She pauses, opens the door, then pauses again. As before, the pauses are planned to allow Baby a chance to approach the Stranger if he is going to. If Baby is upset, the Stranger again tries to soothe him, picking him up if he permits. If the soothing succeeds, she places him near the toys and tries to interest him in them. If he engages the toys, the Stranger returns to her chair. If Baby isn't crying when the Stranger enters the room, she tries to coax him over. If Baby doesn't come, she approaches him and tries to interest him in playing. If he starts playing, as before, she retreats to her chair. Observations are made of how easily soothed Baby is by Stranger, whether he seeks or accepts her initiations, and whether he will play with her. Observations are also made of Baby's reactions to the Stranger's return as compared with Mom's return to the room as in Episode 5.

EPISODE 8: MOTHER AND BABY   After 3 minutes of Stranger and Baby alone, Mom returns to the room, beginning Episode 8. Mom opens the door and pauses a moment before greeting Baby. She then speaks to the baby and picks him up.

How Do You Know Attachment When You See It?

The observers were trained to look for a lot of different attachment-related behaviors. Six behaviors in particular were thought to be especially important. Ainsworth and colleagues labeled them this way:

1. *proximity and contact seeking*, reflected how hard a baby tried to get near another person;
2. *contact maintaining*, reflected how hard a baby worked at staying in contact with another person once contact was established;
3. *resistance*, this was sort of the opposite of proximity and contact seeking and reflected how hard a baby actively tried to stay away from another person;
4. *avoidance*, reflected not so much active resistance, as in trying to get away from another person, but rather how much babies ignored another person;
5. *search*, this was a lot like proximity and contact seeking except that it happened when the desired person wasn't in the room, a baby engaging in search behavior would tend to go to the door and try to open it or otherwise remain near it;
6. *distance interaction*, reflected babies' efforts at interacting with a desired person from a distance, that is, even though they didn't seek physical contact they displayed an interest in establishing eye contact or smiling back and forth with a desired person.

RESULTS

Although Ainsworth achieved great fame for her ingenious innovation of the strange situation procedure, her star rose even higher when she noticed that babies' attachment behaviors could be grouped into one of three patterns. She called the three patterns, mundanely, "Group A," "Group B," and "Group C." One thing I remember thinking the first time I encountered these labels was why the heck Ainsworth would use such boring names. They obviously didn't correspond to anything meaningful. As it turns out, Ainsworth chose these arbitrary labels precisely because they were nondescript. She feared that if she gave the groups labels that were more meaningful, such as "the Crying Group" or "the Happy Group," the group names themselves would end up biasing her and her colleagues into looking for certain types of behaviors and ignoring others. By choosing the arbitrary "A," "B," and "C" labels, Ainsworth hoped that the names of the groups children belonged to wouldn't influence what the observers saw. Still, Ainsworth had to distinguish between different patterns of attachment behavior somehow, and so the different group labels eventually corresponded to different patterns of attachment behaviors anyway.

Now in distinguishing among the different patterns of attachment behavior, Ainsworth was quick to point out that *all* children demonstrated attachment behaviors of some kind, and so *all* were attached to their mothers in some way. It was just that the quality of these attachments differed. But there were no unattached children. Here's a brief description of the three main patterns of attachment behaviors that children exhibited in Ainsworth's strange situation, arranged in terms of Ainsworth's three category labels.

GROUP A   The single most obvious pattern of behavior for Group A babies was that they weren't bothered by being left alone with a strange person in a strange room, but they also avoided their mothers during the reunion episodes! The general impression was that these babies didn't care whether the mother was present or not. Some of these babies even seemed more interested in being around the stranger than the mother! Ainsworth further classified these Group A babies into two subtypes. Group A_1 babies avoided or ignored their mothers altogether. Group A_2 babies, on the other hand, seemed to show a very slight interest in being near their mothers intermixed with an occasional strong desire to stay away from their mothers.

GROUP B   Babies in this group demonstrated the healthiest and most adaptive attachment behaviors with their mothers. A common characteristic of babies in this group was that they acknowledged the importance of their relationships with their mothers during the reunion episodes, by wanting to be near her. However, they differed from one another in how they expressed their attachments. Some babies became highly distressed when their mothers left them alone, whereas others weren't bothered so much. But common to all the babies in this group was that they recognized the importance of the mother as a secure base, and they appreciated her presence. Based on how Group B babies differed from one another, Ainsworth classified them into three subgroups. B_1 babies showed little distress during separation but showed definite signs of interest in the mother when she returned. However, these babies' interest in their mothers more or less took place across a distance. That is, they didn't try to get near their mothers, but they definitely greeted their mothers with smiles of approval when the mothers returned to the room. B_2 babies showed mild distress when mothers left the room, and they were more likely than B_1 babies to physically approach their mothers during the reunion episodes. B_3 babies differed from the other two B subgroups in that they were the most proximity-seeking of the three. During reunions, these babies sought out the mother most actively, and spent the most time near her. But these babies didn't necessarily show a lot of distress when their mothers left the room, and they weren't particularly clingy prior to the separation episodes.

GROUP C   These babies were most notable because their attachment behaviors seemed to contradict each other. During reunion episodes these babies showed a bizarre, zigzag pattern of actively approaching their mothers and then actively resisting them. A child might run up to the mother during the reunion episode to be held, for example, only to immediately struggle to get loose from the mother's hug. Babies in this group either acted extremely distressed and downright angry during the separation episodes (the C_1 subgroup), or they appeared noticeably passive (the C_2 subgroup). By noticeably passive, I mean they didn't *do anything*. They just sat there motionless like a wet rag.

DISCUSSION

Ainsworth's main contribution in coming up with these different attachment styles was that she gave the field of child psychology a handle on the different kinds of relationships that could exist between children and their mothers. But there was another important outcome of Ainsworth's work: Her classification system could be used to predict successes and failures in other domains of children's later development. Wouldn't it be useful, Ainsworth thought, if we knew which type of attachment relationship led to the best outcomes? If so, then we would have some reason to intervene when we saw evidence of mother-child relationships gone bad. Let's begin by taking a deeper look at the hidden implications of having an A-, B-, or C-type attachment relationship.

GROUP B IS BEST (SECURE ATTACHMENTS)   Although Ainsworth and her colleagues used nondescript labels to avoid biasing their own perceptions of babies' attachment behaviors, in the end it was all for naught because some attachment types clearly turned out better than others. The "B" kind were best. They wrote, "The typical Group B infant is more positive in his behavior toward his mother than are the infants of the other two classificatory groups. His interaction with his mother is more harmonious, and he is more cooperative and more willing to comply with his mother's requests. [Group B babies] appear to be positive and unconflicted in their response to close bodily contact with the mother." In addition, Group B babies were likely to use their mothers as a secure base to explore, and were likely to feel relatively comfortable when their moms weren't in the immediate vicinity. Ainsworth and colleagues wrote, "Even when [Mom] is out of sight, [the typical Group B baby] nevertheless usually believes she is accessible to him and would be responsive should he seek her out to signal her." The reason for their comfort level, Ainsworth believed, was that Group B babies developed mental models of their mothers which included easy access to her and reliable responsiveness from her. Even when their mothers weren't around, Group B babies felt as if their mothers could be called upon if needed. The characteristics of mothers that contributed to Group B babies developing these positive mental models, Ainsworth believed, was a consistent and reliable "sensitive responsiveness." Fortunately, about two-thirds of babies are Group B babies.

What are the long-term benefits of having a Group B, or secure, attachment? Well, there are many, and they are cascading. For one thing, these babies are more cooperative and willing to comply with their mothers' requests. Consequently, securely attached babies are easily socialized children. An easily socialized child is a socially competent child, and a socially competent child is a popular child. Second, securely attached babies are less fearful of unknown people and things. If they are generally less fearful of new things, securely attached children will be more likely to perform well in unfamiliar situations such as on the first day of school or when taking a school placement exam. Not surprisingly, securely attached Group B babies tend to score better on a variety of different kinds of tests.

GROUP C (ANXIOUS-AMBIVALENT) ATTACHMENT   There are fewer babies with a C-type attachment than babies in either Group B or A, but there are enough babies sharing these "anxious-ambivalent" behaviors to justify giving them their own group. Remember that Group C babies generally cried when their mothers left them alone in the strange situation, and they seemed uncertain about whether they should hug their mothers or avoid them when mothers returned. In fact, these babies sometimes wanted to be held by their mothers while simultaneously pushing them away. These babies seemed to have opposing feelings about the whole thing. For this reason, these babies have sometimes been called "ambivalently attached." Of course, the word *ambivalent* means having opposing feelings.

As it turns out, one characteristic common to babies in this group was that they all tended to have mothers who weren't very responsive to their signals. Not surprisingly, these Group C babies also spent a lot of time crying. This makes sense. If you were a baby, and your mother didn't readily respond to your needs, wouldn't you have something to cry about? Also, because their mothers were relatively unresponsive to their communicative signals, Group C babies never quite developed a mental model of mothers being emotionally available. Instead, they developed mental models of mothers who were mostly emotionally unavailable. And, because these babies never developed mental models of having a dependable mom, they never quite developed a sense of how to use Mom as a secure base to explore the world. Lacking a secure base in turn had the effect of diminishing how much exploration these Group C babies did. And to the extent that exploration of the world translates into having knowledge about the world, you can easily imagine how these Group C babies were generally not as cognitively advanced as Group B babies.

GROUP A (ANXIOUS-AVOIDANT) ATTACHMENT   Ainsworth and colleagues write that the "key to understanding Group A behavior seem[s] obviously to lie in their avoidance of the mother in those very episodes of the strange situation in which the attachment behavior of other babies was activated at high intensity." Whereas Group B and C babies looked to their mothers for security (Group B babies had secure mental models and Group C babies cried intensely when their mothers left), Group A babies seemed to have a take-it-or-leave-it attitude. In fact, they seemed more in favor of the leave-it part. In the strange situation, they often actively avoided their mothers, especially during the reunion episodes.

Were these babies cold and unfeeling? No. As it turns out, these babies' active efforts at avoiding their moms were probably quite adaptive. You see, they had mothers who really didn't want to be around *them*. Rather than being sensitively responsive, Group A mothers were rather rejecting, and often found close contact with their babies as something to be avoided. Such rejection probably caused a great deal of grief in the babies, who may have developed considerable anger and resentment toward their mothers as a result. But, from an ethological point of view, chronically expressing anger toward your mother is probably not a good thing. You run the risk of her giving up on you and leaving, which would be bad because she is your protector and the primary source of your sustenance. So if you can't express your anger toward her and if she doesn't like being near you, avoiding her is probably the best thing you can do. When you avoid her, you don't risk expressing anger toward her and you're also not getting in her face. Because Type A babies are pretty much in a bind here, avoidant responses are probably the most adaptive behaviors they can muster under such short notice.

However, being an avoidantly attached baby comes at some cost. The most obvious consequence is that later in life these babies may not be able to form secure, stable relationships with other important figures in their life. They run the risk of living their lives alienated from the social comforts provided by healthy attachments with other people. Accordingly, they also run the risk of not being able to get along with people very well later in life. Recent research has shown that children classified as having an avoidant attachment are more likely to get in trouble in school and are less likely to be able to get along with their friends.

NEW DIRECTIONS

Coming up with these attachment styles was a monumental achievement for Ainsworth, and her work launched a thousand more studies on attachment. Yet despite Mary Ainsworth's high profile as a revolutionary researcher, and despite her innovations of the strange situation and the three attachment classifications, she was surprisingly unsuccessful at securing grant funding in support of her research. You may not be aware of this, but at most academic research universities around the country, faculty are expected and sometimes even required to obtain funding for their research from external agencies. The United States government is the largest recipient of funding requests, with agencies such as the National Institutes of Health and the National Science Foundation supplying millions of dollars annually to child psychology researchers. Thus, there is a lot of pressure on researchers for getting money to support their own research efforts.

But for one reason or another, Ainsworth didn't get to taste much of the fruits of external funding. According to Mary Main, Ainsworth's colleague and research collaborator, Ainsworth's grant-getting failures rested largely on the fact that her work was "peculiar in its virtually clinical focus upon individuals, and that the claims she had made regarding the import of differences in the organization of infant-mother attachment involved shockingly small-sized groupings, and were very unlikely to be replicated." Despite any skepticism expressed by the various grant-funding agencies, hundreds of attachment researchers have followed in Ainsworth's footsteps, mostly extending and building upon Ainsworth's original theorizing and methodology. As with any good revolutionary study, Ainsworth's work raised a lot more questions than it answered. And so a common theme of the subsequent research was to begin to answer those questions.

Early on, one of the most central research questions was whether the mother was the only possible attachment figure. The mother would appear to be an ideal candidate, but was she destined by nature to be the only one? Or might other figures play that role as well? Based on research over the decades that followed, we now know that children can form secure attachment relationships with all kinds of people besides their mothers, including their fathers, their grandparents, their siblings, or probably just about anyone else who serves as a primary caregiver. Apparently, the mother doesn't have an exclusively important role just because she's the mother. Her importance as an attachment figure lies in the fact that she is typically the primary caregiver, and because she is in a position to be sensitively responsive to the child's needs. As you can imagine, this finding is a big relief for nontraditional families, including those with a single-father, head-of-household.

Another central research question was whether children who attended day care centers 8 hours a day were at any special risk for developing insecure attachment relationships. As you probably know, or may have directly experienced, many young children live in families where the primary caregivers have to go to work five or more days per week. With no other relatives available to help care for the children, parents often have no choice but to place their children in all-day, every-day day care facilities. For many years, there was a rampant fear that children raised in day care settings were going to develop insecure attachment relationships because they spent so much time away from their primary caregivers. Unfortunately, the research findings on this question are a lot less clear. Although some research shows that children who go to day care may be at risk for developing avoidant attachment relationships, other research fails to find such a risk. But even in studies which reveal such a risk, the number of children affected is a relatively small percentage.

One recent research movement that I think is especially interesting is the development of an interest in measuring attachment in adulthood. Using a test called the Adult Attachment Interview, parents are probed about the kinds of attachments they had with their own parents back when they were children. Using this approach, researchers have found that adults can also be classified into one of three attachment classifications, and these categories directly parallel Ainsworth's. Perhaps even more intriguingly, research has found that adults who adopted particular patterns of attachment with their parents, tended to be involved in parallel attachment relationships with their own children. I guess this is called handing down attachment across the generations. But it does raise the point that parents who had insecure attachments as children are at risk for promoting insecure attachments with their children. Attachment relationships are contagious.

CONCLUSIONS

I suppose the most important take-home message from Ainsworth's work is that the mother (or some other primary attachment figure) plays a strong and very central role in the child's formation of healthy attachment relationships. In particular, **maternal sensitive responsiveness** is crucial for the formation of those attachments. Thus, while all babies appear to develop some kind of attachment relationship with their mothers, as opposed to *no* attachment relationship at all, only babies with sensitively responsive mothers become securely attached. But consider one important fallout of this claim. It places a tremendous amount of responsibility on the shoulders of the mother (or other attachment figure) for the well-being of the child. Like Bowlby before her, Ainsworth has been accused of "mother blaming" when infant-mother relationships go astray. Yet, as others have pointed out, the mother makes up only half of the mother-child relationship.

A major limitation of attachment theory is that it doesn't pay much attention to differences in children's temperament. Temperament researchers have pointed out that some children might cry during strange-situation separation episodes, not because of an insecure attachment, but because of a biological predisposition to exhibit high anxiety under unusual circumstances. Harvard child psychologist Jerome Kagan is well known for his work documenting that some infants are just biologically predisposed to have a highly reactive sympathetic nervous system, which means that they cry at the slightest deviation from normality. When these babies cry, Kagan argues, it doesn't necessarily mean they're insecurely attached; they might simply be temperamentally inhibited. The point is that if children's own temperament can explain some of their tendencies to cry then mothers don't need to take all the blame.

Although Ainsworth's work was focused on clinical aspects of children's **normative emotional development**, her work has had far-reaching impacts extending beyond the boundaries of normative emotional development, most notably on the field of developmental psychopathology. In this research area, scientists are busy conducting longitudinal studies to see if early childhood attachment classifications are predictive of later childhood pathologies such as depression and behavioral conduct disorders. And researchers in the area of cognitive development have been considering whether children's attachment relationships with their parents factor into their own cognitive growth. These are the kinds of things that make common sense—if you have a troubled relationship with your parents at home, you may become depressed and anxious and you may not be able to perform very well in school. Of course, science can't depend on common sense alone. It needs the actual data. And early indications support these expectations exactly.

The construct of attachment lies at the center of almost all contemporary thinking about children's emotional growth. I guess you could say that attachment theory provides the scientific community itself with a secure base from which it can venture out into exploring new, uncharted territories of children's psychological development. The one-two punch provided by the theoretical developments of Bowlby and the methodological-empirical advancements by Ainsworth have clearly revolutionized the field of child psychology. It's difficult, but exciting, to imagine what the next revolution in the area of children's attachment will be.

Bibliography

Ainsworth, M. D. S., & Marvin, R. S. (1995). On the shaping of attachment theory and research: An interview with Mary D. S. Ainsworth (Fall 1994). *Monographs of the Society for Research in Child Development*, 60(Serial No. 2-3), 3–21.

Bretherton, I. (1992). The origins of attachment theory: John Bowlby and Mary Ainsworth. *Developmental Psychology, 28*, 759–774.

Fagot, B. I., & Kavanagh, K. (1990). The prediction of antisocial behavior from avoidant attachment classification. *Child Development, 61*, 864–873.

Main, M. (1999). Mary D. Salter Ainsworth: Tribute and portrait. *Psychoanalytic Inquiry, 19*, 682–736.

Questions for Discussion

1. Ainsworth has been criticized for placing too little emphasis on children's own behaviors in contributing to the quality of the mother-child relationship. How might differences in children's temperament impact favorably or negatively on their attachment relationships?

2. Ainsworth's "strange situation" was truly an experimental innovation. A limiting factor, of course, is that it's restricted to being used in the artificial conditions of the laboratory. Can you think of any naturally occurring situations that resemble the "strange situation"? Would scientists be better off using these naturally occurring situations than Ainsworth's laboratory version? Why or why not?

3. Attachment theorists view the "secure base" notion as central to healthy emotional development in childhood. However, having a secure base throughout life may also be important for good mental health. Can you come up with two or three examples from your own personal experiences in adulthood in which you benefited or didn't benefit from having some sort of secure base?

19

"If You Were Born First, I Would've Stopped"

Temperament and Behavior Disorders in Children

Thomas, A., Chess, S., & Birch, H. G. (1968). New York: New York University Press.   (RANK 15)

Several years ago at my niece's second birthday party, I overheard a longtime family friend remark that had her third child, Kristi, been born first, she probably would have stopped having children. Kristi was apparently a rather challenging child to parent. I suppose it was a good thing for the sake of Kristi's siblings that she came last in the birth order. Still, even though her mother viewed her as a difficult child, Kristi seemed to use her temperament to her advantage. She's now approaching 50, and pursues a professional career. I know her well because she is the mother of the niece whose birthday party I was attending.

The fact that brothers and sisters can be so uniquely individualistic is quite a wondrous thing. How can siblings be so different when they're raised under the same roof with the same rules and same daily routines, especially when they get their genes from the same two parents? Behavioral psychologists would no doubt say that sibling individuality comes from receiving different patterns of reinforcements and punishments. But this explanation doesn't go very far in helping parents understand why a reinforcement works so well for one child and fails miserably for the next. Developmental behavior geneticists would probably remind us that full-blooded siblings, despite their genetic similarity, are still not genetically identical.

Alexander Thomas, Stella Chess, and Herbert Birch earned their revolutionary status because they placed children's individuality at the center of their microscope. Their book, ranked fifteenth overall, proved a rather radical departure from mainstream child psychology, because the status quo at the time was to follow a nomothetic approach. Pursuing a **nomothetic approach** is just a fancy way of saying that child psychologists spent most of their time documenting universal laws of development that could be applied to all children. Piaget applied a nomothetic approach to his research on cognitive development, Bowlby applied a nomothetic approach to his research on attachment, and Bandura applied a nomothetic approach to his research on modeling. Studying universal laws is just one of those things we're trained to do when we're scientists.

However, like so many other revolutionaries we've been discussing, Thomas, Chess, and Birch were pretty displeased with the standard nomothetic approach. They were even more displeased that the only other theoretical dishes on the menu included behaviorism tartare, which developmental psychologists had been force-fed for years, and the ever-popular Freudian psychoanalysis flambé. Thomas, Chess, and Birch found both courses difficult to swallow, and found both left a bitter aftertaste. So like good little revolutionaries, they catered their own theoretical banquet. They had a lot at stake too. As child psychiatrists, their primary concern was understanding, and hopefully eliminating, the many bizarre and maladaptive behavior patterns they often observed in their child patients. So they not only had to come up with a scientific explanation for children's individuality, they also had to come up with scientifically valid ways for fixing those behavior problems that emerged at the extreme ends of the range.

INTRODUCTION

The purpose of their 1968 book was to present the results of a monstrous longitudinal study of children's individuality, which they began some 12 years earlier. A **longitudinal study** is a study of a single group of people over a certain period of time. A short-term longitudinal study might follow a group of kids from, say, age 4 to age 5, to observe what happens during the transition to kindergarten. A longer-term longitudinal study might follow a group of kids from, say, age 13 to age 18, to investigate what happens as adolescents transition into adulthood. But Thomas, Chess, and Birch's study began in 1956 and was still going strong until 1988, 20 years after their book was published. The study is so famous that it's been given its own name, "the New York Longitudinal Study."

As I said, a primary goal of their study was to document children's individuality from early infancy through later childhood. They focused not only on how the environment influences individuality, but on internal contributions as well. These internal contributions were collectively called **temperament**. The authors believed that to get a full-blown account of a child's individuality, you would need to know about that child's temperamental starting point, but also about how the rest of the world reacted to that temperamental starting point. But you wouldn't stop there. You would also need to know how the child's temperament changed as a result of the world's response to her temperamental starting point. But you wouldn't stop there either. You would next need to know how the world responded to the changed temperament, which changed as a result of the world's response to the temperamental starting point. And so on, and so forth. It's kind of like that children's song about the old lady who swallowed a fly—I think you get the picture. In sum, Thomas, Chess, and Birch argued that a child's individuality at any point in time was the result of a complex history of cyclical interplay between the child's temperament and environmental reactivity to that temperament.

However, before describing the role of temperament in the development of children's individuality, Thomas, Chess, and Birch first had to come up with a workable definition of temperament. Being pioneers, they had to be sure their definition captured the essence of what they were describing, but they also had to be sure that it would be sufficiently palatable to other scientists in the field. Since most other child psychologists in 1956 had a strong behaviorist orientation, Thomas, Chess, and Birch were painstakingly careful to describe temperament in terms of children's actual physical behaviors. They might not have been accepted into the scholarly community otherwise. Moreover, they weren't particularly interested in *what* children did, or *why* they did it, but rather in *how* it was done. They described it as a *style*.

Imagine three different boys on a baseball team going up to bat. Top of the order, nobody out. The pitcher on the opposing team is known for throwing a lot of balls and very few strikes. One by one, each boy trots up to the plate, takes four wild pitches, and gets a walk. Boy 1 seems extremely pleased with getting on base. He tosses his bat aside, and with giddy excitement, sprints to first, grinning ear to ear at the first-base coach. Boy 2 seems to have little interest in being given a walk. He sets his bat down gently, looks casually around at the fans, and walks tranquilly to first base, combing his hair along the way. Boy 3, on the other hand, is furious. He throws his bat down, makes some candid gestures to the opposing team, spits at the pitcher, and trots stridently to first. Three boys, three walks, three very different behavioral styles. This is the essence of temperament.

As you might imagine, given the behaviorist climate of the time, the study of temperament wasn't considered an especially worthy topic for psychological investigation. Indeed, it was probably viewed by many as beneath a scientist's dignity. The theories in vogue held instead to the assumption that children's behaviors were entirely products of their environment. Bad behavior was simply due to bad parenting. But Thomas, Chess, and Birch held strongly to their own convictions as well. They believed that studying temperament was essential for three reasons. First, there rarely seemed to be a one-to-one correspondence between the environmental consequences of a child's behavior and her future behaviors. Second, children seemed highly variable in how susceptible they were to environmental stressors. And third, as we saw in the beginning, children from the same family could differ dramatically in response to similar parenting practices.

So Thomas, Chess, and Birch launched their study. They had three explicit goals in mind. First, they wanted to figure out how best to study temperament. Remember, they were pioneers, so they were on their own in coming up with ways to study temperament. Second, they wanted to use their temperament classifications to identify children at risk for behavior disorders. Here you see their child psychiatry training showing through. And third, they wanted to carefully document the environmental conditions in which their participants were being raised. To accomplish this last goal, they had to carefully chart how the children were cared for, as well as the kinds of environmental stresses the children encountered in their day-to-day activities.

METHOD

Because Thomas, Chess, and Birch were dealing with the hairy subject of children's individuality, a topic they expected to be inherently "noisy" from the outset, they thought it would be a good idea to eliminate as many external sources of "noisiness" as possible. To achieve this end, they limited their study to middle and upper class families from New York City and a few surrounding suburbs. By minimizing the demographic variability of their sample in this way, the authors minimized the number of external factors that could possibly contribute to differences in children's individuality. They didn't have to worry about, for example, whether part of a child's individuality came from being raised in a small-town, since all the kids in their study were being raised in a big town (a *very* big town). The only sources of individuality that were left, then, were those that came from inside the child. These were the ones that were most interesting. At any rate, as I already mentioned, the study began enrolling families in 1956 and continued until a total of 85 families was reached. Once a family was enrolled in the study, any new children born to that family were automatically included as research participants as soon as they popped out.

Participants

A total of 136 children were included. Five children were lost during the study because they moved away. Forty-five families had 1 child, 31 had 2 children, 7 had 3 children, and 2 families had 4 children. By 1966, 10 years after the study began, they had 40 10-year-olds, 25 9-year-olds, 18 8-year-olds, 16 7-year-olds, 15 6-year-olds, 10 5-year-olds, and 12 4-year olds. About half of the children were boys (69) and half were girls (67). Seventy-eight percent of the children were Jewish, 15% were Protestant, and 7% were Catholic. At the beginning of the study, the mothers ranged in age from 20 to 41 years and the fathers ranged in age from 25 to 54 years.

A subset of the entire sample was designated the "clinical sample." These were 42 children who had symptoms of concern to their parents or their school and who were diagnosed through clinical psychiatric judgment to have a "significant degree of behavioral disturbance." Examples of behavioral disturbance were (1) significant delay in such areas as language, perceptual, or motor development; (2) self-destructive or self-endangering behaviors; (3) significant unresponsiveness to the environment; (4) flagrant flouting of social conventions such as masturbating in public; (5) significant isolation from friends; (6) persistent bullying; or (7) failure in school without having an intellectual deficiency. Although it's never a good thing when children have behavioral disturbances, it was extremely important for the study that some kids did have behavior problems, because one of the goals was to see if temperament was related to behavior disorders. Thomas, Chess, and Birch couldn't have gotten very far if all their participants were normal.

Materials

Because it was a study of such huge proportions, Thomas, Chess, and Birch used a lot of different materials to measure the psychological well-being of the children and their parents. For starters, all the children were given standard tests of cognitive functioning (in other words, IQ tests) at 3 and 6 years of age. In addition, when the children were 3 years old, the parents were interviewed about their attitudes toward child-rearing and were asked about their actual child care practices.

Children in the clinical sample sometimes needed additional testing, depending on their specific behavioral problems. The additional testing came in the form of psychiatric play interviews, for example, or neurological workups. The results of this additional testing were also included in the study.

Probably the most relevant measurement device for our consideration was the one Thomas, Chess, and Birch used to measure children's temperament. Remember, there were no temperament measurement instruments available at the time of their study, so they had to invent their own. They ended up developing a series of parent and teacher interviews, containing meticulously devised questions, in which parents and teachers were asked about very specific behaviors of the children that occurred under very specific circumstances. The interviews focused on behaviors that took place in typical daily routines such as feeding, sleeping, dressing, and playing. For example, parents might've been asked how their child responded to interruptions in feeding or bedtime routines. Or teachers might've been asked how easily a child responded to transitions from naptime to recess. Throughout the interviews, the authors gave special emphases to children's responses to new people, things, and situations. In addition, only examples of real behaviors were counted. If parents or teachers made *interpretations* of children's behaviors, such as "The baby hated his cereal," or "This child always gets angry if he doesn't get his way," an extra effort was made to press the parents to say exactly what the child did that led them to their conclusions.

In addition to the interviews, school observations were made of each child during a 1-hour free-play episode. During these episodes, an observer sat "unobtrusively in a corner of the schoolroom." According to the authors, "The observer noted the general and specific attributes of the setting and every observable verbal, motor, and gestural interaction of the child with materials, other children, and adults. All notations of behavior were made in concrete, descriptive terms. Inferences as to the meaning of the child's behavior were avoided."

Procedure

Unfortunately, Thomas, Chess, and Birch don't give us a lot of detail about the precise procedures they followed, at least not in this book. But we do know they were quite systematic in interviewing the parents and teachers. The parents were first interviewed as soon after enrolling in the study as possible. The interviews were then conducted at 3-month intervals until the child was 3 years old, at 6-month intervals until the child was 5 years old, and at yearly intervals after that.

Eighty-nine percent of the children attended nursery school, what we would call preschool today, so it was possible to begin interviewing the teachers in nursery school for the majority of the children. The first teacher interview occurred during a child's "initial adaptation to the nursery school situation, and the second took place during the latter portion of the school year." Teacher interviews appeared to continue on a yearly basis afterward, through a second year of nursery school (if it happened), through kindergarten, and then through first grade. It's not clear from the authors' descriptions whether teacher interviews continued beyond first grade, but it seems that they did.

RESULTS

Defining Temperament

As noted earlier, one of Thomas, Chess, and Birch's first goals was to come up with a way to measure temperament. Based on their interviews and classroom observations, the authors came up with a nine-dimensional definition of temperament. Whew! In other words, they thought children's temperament should be defined as a series of scores on nine different kinds of behaviors. The nine dimensions of temperament they came up with were: (1) activity level, (2) rhythmicity, (3) approach or withdrawal, (4) adaptability, (5) intensity of reaction, (6) threshold of responsiveness, (7) quality of mood, (8) distractibility, and (9) attention span and persistence. This is quite a bit to swallow in one bite, so let's look at the dimensions one at a time in a little more detail. As we pass over each one, it might be interesting for you to consider where you might've scored if you were a child, so for each dimension I'll ask you a college student-level question that might probe where you would've fallen on that dimension if you were several years younger.

ACTIVITY LEVEL   The dimension of **activity level** reflects how fast and often a child engages in some behavior, and it always includes a measure of movement. Kids who splash a lot in the bathtub, crawl all around the house, run all over the playground, or are squirmy to hold would score high on activity level. Kids who sit quietly in the bathtub, who remain in one place in the house or at the park, or who are easy to pick up and hold would score low. *(College student-level question: Do you fidget or bounce your leg when sitting still? Would you prefer the slow pace of life in a small town, or the hustle and bustle of a big city?)*

RHYTHMICITY **Rhythmicity** focuses mostly on the regularity of bodily functions. Kids who go to sleep, wake up, get hungry, and "go potty" at roughly the same time each day would score high on rhythmicity. Kids who go to sleep, wake up, get hungry, and go potty at different times each day would score low. *(College student-level question: Do you get sleepy, wake up, get hungry, and "go potty" at about the same time each day?)*

APPROACH AND WITHDRAWAL In **approach/withdrawal**, the focus is on how children deal with new things. The new things can be people, places, toys, or routines. Children who tend toward the approach end of the scale are likely to smile when they see new people, or they'll want to play with new toys. Children at the withdrawal end do just the opposite. They tend to fret in the presence of strangers, they back away from new toys, or they might cry when they go to the doctor's office for the first time. *(College student-level question: Does the idea of dining at an exotic foreign restaurant appeal to you? Would you rather pull your own teeth than travel to a foreign city like Tokyo?)*

ADAPTABILITY The **adaptability** dimension overlaps a little bit with approach/withdrawal. But whereas approach/withdrawal focused on the child's initial reaction, adaptability is focused on how easily the initial reaction can be modified or soothed in the desired direction. Examples of high adaptability given during the parental interview were things like, "He used to spit out cereal when I gave it to him, but now he takes it fairly well," "Now when we go to the doctor's he doesn't start to cry till we undress him, and he even stops then if he can hold a toy." Children low in adaptability never fully adapt to the situation in the desired direction. For example, "Every time he sees the scissors he starts to scream and pull his hand away, so now I cut his nails when he's sleeping," or, "He doesn't like eggs and makes a face and turns his head away no matter how I cook them." *(College student-level question: If you and a group of friends were on your way to see a movie you've really been wanting to see, and the rest of your friends decided they'd rather go hiking, how easy would it be for you to go along with their decision? Are you able to shake off pesky little irritants pretty easily?)*

INTENSITY OF REACTION The **intensity of reaction** dimension focuses on how much energy a child puts into her response when she responds to something. It doesn't matter if the reaction is positive or negative. Children at the high-intensity end of the scale tend to overrespond, or respond beyond what would seem normal. A baby who sees balloons at a restaurant might squeal loudly with excitement. Another baby might cry for half an hour if the sun gets in her eyes for the briefest time. Children at the low end of the scale barely respond to things at all, but they give evidence that they noticed the thing by responding a little bit. They might look at the balloon for a while, or might squint slightly at the bright sun. *(College student-level question: Do you "blow up" when something irritates you? Or do you just shrug your shoulders and let it slide?)*

THRESHOLD OF RESPONSIVENESS This measure reflects how intense something has to be before a child notices it. Children with a high **threshold of responsiveness** may not respond to the most intense stimuli, even though all their senses are working perfectly. High threshold older children may seem to ignore the wails of a fire truck speeding by the city park, while high threshold babies may tolerate wet diapers for hours. In contrast, children with a low threshold of responsiveness may look around when they hear the softest of sounds or sniff at the faintest of smells. When these children play at the city park, not only do they take notice of the fire truck, but they also pick out the song of the sparrow and the chatter of the chipmunks above all the traffic noise. Low-threshold babies might begin crying the moment they wet their diapers. *(College student-level question: When you're taking an exam in the classroom, does it bother you if somebody nearby starts tapping a pencil, or makes an inadvertent whistling sound when breathing through his nose? On your drive back from the beach or the pool, do you feel uncomfortable if you're still wearing your wet bathing suit?)*

QUALITY OF MOOD   Here the focus is on whether reactions tend to be positive or negative. Babies with a positive **quality of mood** spend a lot of their day being happy. They smile and laugh a lot, they're frequently content, and nothing seems to be particularly bothersome to them. One parent said this about her positive child, "He loves to look out of the window. He jumps up and down and laughs." Babies with a negative mood quality, on the other hand, appear stressed out by a variety of things they encounter throughout the day, and other people may find it rather difficult to tolerate them. As an example, "I've tried to teach him not to knock down little girls and sit on them in the playground, so now he knocks them down and doesn't sit on them." *(College student-level question: Would your friends and family describe you as a Happy Camper? Or would they more likely call you a Grumpy Gus?)*

DISTRACTIBILITY   Children high in **distractibility** are easily interrupted from whatever they're doing. This is a good quality to have when a child is mildly injured, because parents can easily get him to forget about his injury by redirecting his attention to the pretty yellow flower in the garden or the bluebird gliding through the air. Children low in distractibility, on the other hand, would go right back to crying despite their parents' efforts at redirecting their attention. *(College student-level question: Do your friends ever call you "ditzy" or "scatterbrained" behind your back [or in front of your back for that matter]? Can you get so absorbed in a good book that you lose track of time?)*

ATTENTION SPAN AND PERSISTENCE   This dimension is actually two different measures rolled into one. **Attention span** refers to the length of time a child stays engaged in a particular task when there's little interference. **Persistence** is more along the lines of how long a child will keep doing something despite interference. A child high in attention span, for example, might "play Barbies" for hours on end. If the child is also high in persistence, she will continue playing Barbies even when her big brother keeps coming into her room and taking her Barbies away from her. A child low in attention span doesn't stay engaged in any one thing for very long, and so might switch from playing Barbies to playing dress-up to watching a cartoon on TV. A child low in persistence will break off from playing Barbies if something interrupts her flow of activity, such as when her dog comes into her room and licks her face. *(College student-level question: Does it get under your skin if you're watching TV with someone who likes to channel-surf? Do you enjoy texting even when you're studying for an exam or writing an essay for a class?)*

Temperament and Severe Behavioral Disturbances

If you remember, one of Thomas, Chess, and Birch's goals was to see if children's temperament had anything to do with the emergence of severe behavior disorders. So they conducted a second analysis to see if the children in their clinical sample were different from the rest of the kids in terms of each of the nine dimensions of temperament. They began by dividing the clinical sample into two general groups: children with active behavior disturbances and children with passive behavior disturbances. These two groups of children were more or less at opposite extremes in terms of the types of behaviors they exhibited. The active behavior disturbance group engaged in what today would be called "acting out," or **externalizing** behavior. These were kids who generally had behavior control problems. They might bully other children, for example, or they might defiantly disobey the teacher. You can probably best understand the passive behavior disturbance group as kids who are extraordinarily shy. They didn't participate in group activities when requested, but they didn't show outward signs of anxiety or fear either. They were "wallflowers." These behaviors would be characteristic of what today we'd call **internalizing**.

Thomas, Chess, and Birch found that, indeed, a number of temperament measures predicted whether or not a child would develop a behavioral disturbance. Now this is not to say that children's temperaments *made* them have behavioral problems. Rather, children's temperamental profiles were merely *predictive* of those behavioral problems. You might think of temperament as a risk indicator. Not all the children who were in the clinical sample had deviant temperaments. And not all the children with deviant temperaments developed behavior disturbances. We're simply talking about group *tendencies*. Here is a summary of how each of the two behavior disturbance groups differed from "normal" on the various temperament dimensions. I'll also point out how the various temperament dimensions changed over time for the two clinical groups. We'll begin with the active behavioral disturbance group.

TEMPERAMENTAL PROFILE OF KIDS WITH ACTIVE BEHAVIOR DISTURBANCES   Not surprisingly, children in the active behavior disturbance group were higher in *activity level* and more *intense* in their responses to the world. You can almost picture this child from your own elementary-school days as the kid who could never sit still and who constantly made loud, rude comments to the teacher and other students. These children were also less *adaptable* and more *persistent* than normal. This means they were hard to calm down once they got on a roll, and because they were *persistent*, once they got on a roll, they stayed on it. On a few of the temperament dimensions, children with active behavior disturbances were at first indistinguishable from normal children. It was only as they got older that their temperamental profiles began deviating from normal. One temperament dimension that followed this pattern was *threshold of responsiveness*. Active behavior kids started out being no more sensitive to the sights and sounds in the surrounding environment than normal kids, but with age they became more and more sensitive to them. Similarly, at the younger ages, these kids were no more *distractible* than the normal kids, but they got more and more distractible as they got older.

TEMPERAMENTAL PROFILE OF KIDS WITH PASSIVE BEHAVIOR DISTURBANCES   As a rule, the temperamental profiles of kids in the passive behavior disorder group were far more complicated, and they changed greatly from one age to the next. However, there were a couple of across-the-board differences. For one thing, passive behaviorally disturbed children were much lower in *activity level* than normal children. They were also far more negative in *mood*. In other words, these were stationary, unhappy little children. For the rest of the dimensions, the temperaments of these children varied quite a bit depending on how old they were. In terms of *rhythmicity*, the passive kids were initially far more regular and predictable than normal children, but over time they became as unpredictable as normal children. For five other dimensions—approach/withdrawal, threshold of reactivity, intensity, distractibility, and persistence—they started out on one side of the normal children, and then as they got older they moved completely to the other side of the normal children. For example, the passive kids started out being much more likely than normal kids to be interested in new things, but later were much more likely to withdraw and shy away from new things. They started out having a low threshold of reactivity, meaning they didn't seem to notice much going on around them, but after a few years they ended up being hypersensitive. They started out being much less intense in their reactions, but eventually became much more intense. They also started out being much less persistent, but ended up being much more persistent. Finally, they started out as more distractible, and ended up being much less distractible. Of course, these age-related changes are extremely complicated and we can't really spend much time on them here. But the point is that early temperament was a predictor of children's likelihood for developing a behavior disturbance.

Temperament Clusters

If there's a single feature of Thomas, Chess, and Birch's work that made the headlines, it was their identification of *clusters* of temperament characteristics that led them to describe three general *types* of children. Through a number of highly technical statistical analyses, they found that a number of temperament dimensions tended to go together. For example, they found that children who tended to have high withdrawal (shying away) scores also tended to have biological irregularity, tended to have a negative mood, tended not to be adaptable, and tended to have high-intensity reactions. They called these children **difficult children**. Children with this temperamental profile were royal pains in their parents' keister, and were sometimes even referred to as "mother killers" by Dr. Stella Chess in her public addresses. On the other side of the coin were children who were interested in new things (high in approach), who tended to be biologically regular, who tended to have a positive mood, who tended to be high in adaptability, and who tended to have low-intensity reactions. These were labeled **easy children**. Children with this temperamental profile are the kind parents imagine having before they actually have them. Thomas, Chess, and Birch also discovered a third cluster of temperament dimensions, which they thought characterized **slow-to-warm-up children**. The slow-to-warm-up child is initially high in withdrawal and slow to adapt, but has low-intensity negative reactions. In many ways, the reactions of slow-to-warm-up children mirror the reactions of difficult children, but differ in that they eventually come around and get along just fine in new situations.

DISCUSSION

Goodness of Fit

Having identified nine dimensions of temperamental individuality among children, along with three major temperamental clusters, Thomas, Chess, and Birch laid out the blueprints for what they called "a dynamic theory of child psychiatry and development." The essential feature of their new theory was, of course, children's temperament. Now, being the major innovators of this new-fangled temperament theory, they admitted to being tempted to place temperament at the central core of their theory. But they realized that if they gave temperament an exclusive role, their theory would be no better than the "static" theories of their time which they were rebelling against: behaviorism and Freudian psychoanalysis.

What made these other theories static was the assumption that the direction of influence was always a one-way street, that the children themselves didn't play much of a role in their own individuality. Behavioral theories, for example, placed almost exclusive emphasis on environmental punishments and reinforcements in producing children's individuality. Similarly,

Freudian-type theories placed too much emphasis on unconscious motivating forces. Thomas, Chess, and Birch didn't want to fall into the same trap by placing the entire developmental burden on children's temperament. No, they thought a realistic account for the development of children's individuality would have to be much more dynamic.

The "complex dynamic" that they thought would be better at explaining the development of children's individuality was one in which factors internal to the child collaborated with factors external to the child to produce an ever-changing developmental system (note some similarity here with Thelen & Ulrich, Chapter 6). The interactional system they proposed would go something like this: A child with a certain temperamental profile would elicit characteristic responses from the environment, and these characteristic environmental responses would then feed back into the child and impact his specific temperamental characteristics. The now-changed temperamental characteristics of the child would then have additional impacts on the surrounding environment, and responses from the environment would then feed back once again into the child and have additional impacts on the child's temperament. This cycle of temperament → environment → temperament → environment conceivably goes on forever. This isn't necessarily a bad thing, especially if the child is well adjusted and mentally healthy. But if the cycle results in the emergence of behavioral disturbances, the cycle would need to be broken, either through psychotherapy or through improved parenting skills. A child who cries and whines a lot, for example, might elicit frustration and impatience from his parents. If these parents get annoyed with their child because of his constant crying and whining, they might be inclined to get angry and possibly resort to excessive punishment. The punishment given by the parents would then further increase the amount of crying and whining. The only way to break this cycle would be either to reduce the child's crying and whining (unlikely with very young children), or teach the parents to be more patient. An effective psychotherapeutic intervention here might be nothing more than providing parents with alternative strategies for dealing with their crying, whining child.

In an effort to capture the essence of this complex dynamic, Thomas, Chess, and Birch introduced the idea of **goodness of fit**. The goodness-of-fit concept, which remains popular today, reflects how well a given child's environment accommodates his unique temperamental profile, while simultaneously allowing both the child and the environment to be responsible for the child's outcome. Within this framework, good temperament-environment fits are likely to produce mentally healthy, well-adjusted children; while poor temperament-environment fits are likely to produce children who either have behavioral disturbances, or are at risk for them. Thus, for example, although children with difficult temperaments might be difficult to deal with, if they had understanding parents, they wouldn't necessarily develop behavioral disturbances because their environments could accommodate their temperamental difficulty. Similarly, although easy children might be easy to deal with, they *could* develop behavioral disturbances if their environments didn't fit them well. This latter outcome might obtain, for example, if a parent who is always on the go becomes intolerant of a child who doesn't share the enthusiasm.

CONCLUSIONS

Thomas, Chess, and Birch revolutionized child psychology because they developed a whole new temperament-based theory that launched wave after wave of research on the developmental impacts of children's individuality. Early temperament research focused on the role of temperament in the development of behavioral disturbances, following essentially the same trail blazed by the authors. But more recently, researchers have taken temperament for a ride in all manner of developmental areas. A number of researchers, for example, have investigated whether temperament might be related to the development of children's intelligence. As you may have noticed, a couple of Thomas, Chess, and Birch's temperament scales are closely related to measures of cognitive functioning. Attention span, for instance, has a long history of being drawn into measures of intelligence. On standard IQ tests like the Wechsler Intelligence Scale for Children, attention span is routinely assessed.

Some of the findings from this line of research have led to some fascinating implications. In two studies, for example, children with difficult temperaments were actually found to be cognitively advanced! This should give us cause to pause before making any overly negative generalizations about temperamentally difficult children. But why would difficult children be cognitively advanced? Well, if you think about it beyond the surface level, it does make some sense. For example, one thing that makes some children more intelligent than others is the fact that they know a lot of things and can solve problems quickly. When children know a lot of things and can solve problems quickly, it stands to reason that under certain circumstances they may become bored more quickly than less intelligent children. And if they become bored more quickly than less intelligent children, it also stands to reason that they might become cranky and discontented more quickly than less intelligent children. Being cranky and discontented is one characteristic of the temperamentally difficult child. So being temperamentally difficult isn't necessarily a bad thing. It could be an indication of better intellectual functioning.

On the other hand, temperamental difficulty has also been associated with slower language development. This also makes some sense. Language development proceeds most rapidly when children have people to talk to; and if a child is temperamentally difficult, she may not be the most pleasant conversational partner. Temperamentally difficult children simply may not get as many opportunities to engage in long, extended conversations with other people. Temperamentally easy children, in contrast, make for delightful conversational partners.

Finally, researchers have also been exploring the biological underpinnings of temperament. Thomas, Chess, and Birch's goal of maintaining a strict behavioral definition is laudable, especially since they wanted to make sure parents and teachers weren't reading too much into children's behaviors. But still, the behaviors have to come from somewhere, and the most likely candidate would probably be underlying brain activity. These days, modern temperament researchers have been exploring which parts of the brain might be most responsible for temperament-related behaviors. In a wonderfully thorough review article, Mary Rothbart and John Bates highlighted a number of neurological factors that might be responsible for producing a variety of temperamental characteristics. (If you're interested in knowing, most of these are located in the brain's limbic system.) Once the brain parts responsible for extremely maladaptive temperamental characteristics have been identified, it may eventually be possible to develop medications for their treatment.

Measurement Issues

It should be noted that Thomas, Chess, and Birch received a lot of criticism for basing their temperament research on parent and teacher interviews. Consequently, a number of researchers have been developing alternative techniques for measuring temperament. At least a half-dozen different checklists have been invented for measuring temperament, but they usually still depend on parents' perceptions in filling them out. Other techniques have been invented to measure temperament directly, through laboratory observations. But the problem with laboratory observations is that they reflect children's behaviors in only a single situation. Because temperament is believed to wind its way through *all* of children's day-to-day experiences, laboratory observations simply have to be supplemented with observations in a variety of alternative settings. Whether we should employ parent-reported temperament or laboratory-observed temperament is actually the source of quite a bit of controversy these days. But then again, revolutionaries are known to kick up a little dust in their path.

As with any other scientific topic, additional refinement of what temperament is, what it means, and how it's measured will only take place one study at a time. And it may not take all that much longer. At its current pace, temperament researchers are pumping out scientific studies at the rate of over 180 investigations per year. We can only hope that a continued focus on children's individuality will continue sharpening our understanding of the psychological development and well-being of our children. Once the temperament concept loses its effectiveness, we'll have to brace ourselves for another revolution.

Bibliography

Dixon, W. E., Jr., & Smith, P. H. (2000). Links between early temperament and language acquisition. *Merrill-Palmer Quarterly, 46*, 417–440.

Rothbart, M. K., & Bates, J. (2006). Temperament. In N. Eisenberg, W. Damon, & R. M. Lerner (Eds.), *Handbook of child psychology, vol. 3, social, emotional, and personality development* (6th ed). Hoboken, NJ: Wiley.

Smith, P. H., Dixon, W. E., Jr., Jankowski, J. J., Sanscrainte, M. M., Davidson, B. K., & Loboschefski, T. (1997). Longitudinal relationships between habituation and temperament in infancy. *Merrill-Palmer Quarterly, 43*, 291–304.

Questions for Discussion

1. Although it's hard to raise temperamentally difficult children, is it possible that temperamental difficulty would give any children an adaptive advantage? Why? Who gets more attention from parents, difficult or easy children? How might this attention-getting differential influence children's later development?
2. What kinds of parenting strategies would work best with temperamentally easy versus temperamentally difficult children?
3. Temperament researchers have shown that mothers and fathers show only moderate agreement when it comes to judging the temperament of their children. Why might mothers and fathers rate their children differently when it comes to temperament? What are some specific examples of how mothers and fathers might perceive their children's temperament differently?

20

"This Is Gonna Hurt You a Lot More Than It's Gonna Hurt Me"

Current Patterns of Parental Authority

Baumrind, D. (1971). *Developmental Psychology Monographs,*
4 (1, part 2). (RANK 16)

There once was a family, blue collar.
Dad worked so hard for a dollar.
Mom watched the kid,
Blowing her lid.
Dad came home only to holler.

This is a story about parenting. It's a story we're all familiar with, whether we were raised by biological parents, stepparents, foster parents, adoptive parents, robotic parents, or maybe even a pack of wolves. And we all have something to say about it (unless we were raised by wolves, in which case we wouldn't have language). We often defend our parents' disciplinary strategies, while at other times we vow never to raise our children the way our parents raised us. One of the quickest ways I can get a rise out of my students is to challenge them about how they were raised. In my most authoritative voice, I'll say something like, *"Studies show that frequent spanking produces long-term negative consequences."* No sooner than I finish my sentence, a largish male athlete type speaks up, "Hey, my parents spanked me, and I turned out just fine!" Coyly, I usually follow up with, "How exactly *did* you turn out?" It's about then that some classmates start giggling.

We all have opinions on the topic of parenting. But we can't always distinguish fiction from fact. For this reason, the psychology instructor often takes a lot of grief from her students when she suggests their beliefs about parenting might be wrong. It's interesting that other sciences don't have to carry around this same kind of baggage. When our physics teacher tells us atoms are composed of electrons, neutrons, and protons, we say, "Yeah, okay." We don't challenge the physicist. How could we? We've had no experience with the insides of an atom, and many of us probably wouldn't know a proton from a protein. It may have something to do with not being able to get ourselves small enough.

But we've all been parented. And when the child psychology teacher tells us that spanking is associated with long-term negative consequences, she's hitting very close to home on a topic that is up close and personal. But just as we listen to what the physicist has to say in a course on physical science, I think it's a pretty good idea in a class on human science to put our own stereotypes and biases aside and listen to what the child psychologist has to say. As budding scientists, students owe it to themselves to review the evidence on the matter, especially when the evidence has the effect of revolutionizing the field of child psychology.

In the 16th most revolutionary study published since 1960, Diana Baumrind focused on the outcomes of different styles of parenting. Among her most important findings was that some ways of parenting really are better than others, although it depends in part on what you mean by "better." And she didn't rely on her own opinions in classifying parenting styles as good or bad. Rather, she examined how the children themselves turned out. "Good" parenting styles were defined as those which best prepared children to adapt to the adult world or were socially adaptive. "Bad" parenting styles, in contrast, were defined as those which produced children with poor survival skills. Her research was revolutionary because it scientifically documented a standard of good parenting that remains in place to this day, at least for mainstream, educated, middle- and upper-income families.

INTRODUCTION

In the introduction to her 1971 article, Baumrind doesn't give us much of a history of parenting research. She simply points out that she was conducting her study to answer a few questions raised by a couple of her earlier studies. In those earlier studies, she had already identified three different styles of parenting, which she called *authoritative*, *authoritarian*, and *permissive*. But they were based on children's behaviors, not on how the parents themselves actually parented. So one goal of her 1971 study was to explore parents' *actual* parenting behaviors, and to see if the same three parenting styles emerged.

Another limitation of the earlier work was that Baumrind didn't consider whether different parenting styles affected boys and girls differently. The question of male-female differences was quite an important social issue at the time. In the early 1970s the women's movement was just getting underway. Women were "burning their bras" under the banner of "women's lib." Ratification of the Equal Rights Amendment to the United States Constitution was making headlines in all the papers. And social scientists throughout the country were clamoring to explore the origins of gender differences and gender equality. So a key issue for the 1971 study was whether parenting styles worked differently for boys versus girls.

METHOD

Participants

The children in the study were all enrolled in one of the 13 Berkeley, California, area nursery schools (roughly similar to today's preschools). Baumrind required the children to be at least

3 years, 9 months of age with an IQ score of at least 95 (in the normal range). In addition, the parents had to allow Baumrind into their homes for the "home visit phase" of the study. Sixteen black children and their families were excluded from the study because in other work Baumrind found that black parents parented differently than white parents. Although she indicated that a separate article on the parenting styles of black parents was in preparation, it's important to keep in mind that Baumrind's results, as described in this monograph, may apply only to white families, and then possibly only to high-IQ, upper-income, white families from the Berkeley, California area. The final sample consisted of 60 white girls and 74 white boys, with an average IQ of 125 (placing them in the above-average range) and an average age of slightly over 4 years.

Materials and Procedure

As a revolutionary, Baumrind's interests in measuring parenting styles and child outcome quality meant that she was dabbling in a new area. And as a dabbler, she would have to figure out a way to measure both parenting style and quality of child behavior. What she ended up with was a very complicated set of data points taken from a very complicated series of measurement instruments that she administered to both parents and children. On top of that, she used a very complicated series of statistical techniques to analyze her very complicated set of data. To give you an idea of how complicated the whole thing was, she spent 46 pages of her article describing her measurement instruments and procedures. Of course, I'll do *my* best to summarize these 46 pages in the next couple of paragraphs.

CHILD MEASURES   As mentioned earlier, because Baumrind was interested in figuring out which parenting styles were better than others, she had to invent a way to measure "better." She was ultimately guided by the logic that a better parenting style would have to be one that produced socially adaptive behaviors in children. After all, what is the purpose of parenting if not to raise your kids to be successful on their own? So one of her first objectives was to measure socially adaptive behaviors in children. She started with a method known as **naturalistic observation**. In naturalistic observation, an observer simply watches a child in some sort of naturally occurring situation and records instances of behaviors believed to be important. In Baumrind's study, the children were observed in two situations: in their nursery school class and while taking a Stanford-Binet intelligence test.

Baumrind used seven different observers in her study, but each child was assigned only to one observer. She also used a lot of reliability checks to make sure the observers were in agreement about how to record the behaviors. The observers were trained to look for seven different types of behavior. Each type of behavior was anchored at one end with a developmentally adaptive characteristic (in other words, a behavior that was viewed as relatively good) and at the other end with a developmentally unadaptive characteristic (a behavior that was viewed as relatively bad). Again, keep in mind that a behavior was defined as adaptive or unadaptive relative to the goals of a white, well-to-do, high-IQ culture. Carla Bradley, who studies African American parenting strategies, would be quick to remind us that what's adaptive for European American kids may not be adaptive for African American kids. In any case, here's a list of the seven behavior types Baumrind recorded, along with a couple of examples of behaviors at each end of the "good" and "bad" range.

Behavior Type	Examples of Adaptive Behavior	Examples of Unadaptive Behavior
Hostile-Friendly	Nurturant or sympathetic toward other children. Helps other children carry out their plans.	Insulting. Bullies other children.
Resistive-Cooperative	Obedient. Can be trusted.	Tries to evade adult authority. Provocative with adults.
Domineering-Tractable	Nonintrusive. Concerned about adult disapproval.	Manipulates other children.
Dominant-Submissive	Peer leader. Resists domination of other children.	Suggestible.
Purposive-Aimless	Confident. Self-starting and self-propelled.	Spectator. Disoriented in environment.
Achievement Oriented-Not Achievement Oriented	Likes to learn new skill. Gives his best to work and play.	Does not persevere when encountering obstacles. Does not become pleasurably involved in tasks.
Independent-Suggestible	Individualistic.	Stereotyped in thinking. Does not question adult authority.

Although I've listed only a couple of examples of each category of behavior, each child was actually observed for many more specific behaviors. In fact, each child was rated on 72 different behaviors!

PARENTING MEASURES   Measures of parenting quality were also taken from naturalistic observation. But for the parents, the observations were done in the home. Baumrind described the structure of the home visits this way: "In order to achieve a standardized situation, the home visit was structured identically for each family and occurred for all families during a period commencing from shortly before the dinner hour and lasting until just after the child's bedtime. This period is commonly known to produce instances of parent-child divergence and was selected for observation in order to elicit a wide range of critical interactions under maximum stress." In other words, the observers camped out in these people's homes during one of the most stressful times of the day—the time when parents battle their children to get them into bed.

Baumrind's development of the parenting measure is a bit trickier to describe. It had two phases. In the first phase, she came up with 15 different parenting behaviors she thought would *likely* describe how parents parented. In the second phase, she conducted a sophisticated statistical analysis to reduce these 15 practices down to a more reasonable number (like 5 or 6). In addition, she also conducted the statistical analyses separately for mothers and fathers to see if the most important parenting practices for mothers differed from the most important parenting practices for fathers. I'll start out by listing the 15 parenting behaviors Baumrind initially looked for, and follow with the reduced set of parenting behaviors as they turned up for mothers and fathers separately.

First, here are the 15 original parenting behaviors. Keep in mind that for each parenting behavior, as with the child measures, Baumrind identified a number of specific behaviors that observers were to look for. For each behavior, I'll list two examples that observers were trained to detect. You might find it instructive to rate your own parents on each of these scales as well (think back to when you were about 4 years old).

1. Expects versus Does Not Expect Participation in Household Chores. Examples: Parent demands child put toys away; parent demands child dress self.
2. Provides Enriched versus Impoverished Environment for Child. Examples: Parent provides an intellectually stimulating environment; parent makes demands upon child that have educational value.
3. Directive versus Nondirective. Examples: Parent has many rules and regulations; parent assigns child fixed bedtime hour.
4. Discourages versus Encourages Emotional Dependency on Parents. Examples: Parent encourages child to make contact with other adults; parent isn't overprotective of child.
5. Discourages versus Encourages Infantile Behavior. Examples: Parent discourages child from exhibiting babyish speech and mannerisms; parent demands mature table behavior at mealtime.
6. Provides Flexibility and Clarity versus Inflexibility and Lack of Clarity in Parental Role. Examples: Parent can specify aims and methods for how child should do stuff; parent has stable, firm views about things.
7. Provides Firm versus Lax Enforcement Policy. Examples: Parent uses negative sanctions when defied by child; parent requires child to pay attention.
8. Treats Obedience as an Important Positive Value versus Treats Obedience as an Unimportant or Negative Value. Examples: Parent forces confrontation with child when child disobeys; parent willingly exercises power to obtain obedience from child.
9. Promotes Respect for Established Authority versus Seeks to Develop a Cooperative Working Relationship with Child. Examples: Parent believes parents should take precedence; parent does not share decision-making power with child.
10. Shows Confidence versus Lack of Confidence in Self as a Parent. Examples: Parent regards self as competent person; parent believes child must defer to parental expertise.
11. Encourages or Discourages Independence. Examples: Parent encourages independent actions; parent asks for child's opinions.
12. Encourages versus Discourages Verbal Exchange and the Use of Reason. Examples: Child disobedience results in parent giving additional explanation; parent encourages verbal give and take.
13. Reluctant versus Willing to Express Anger or Displeasure to Child. Examples: Parent feels shameful and embarrassed after expressing anger; parent hides annoyance or impatience when child disobeys.
14. Promotes Individuality versus Social Acceptability. Examples: Parent promotes individuality in child; parent expresses own individuality.
15. Expresses Punitive versus Nurturant Behavior. Examples: Parent becomes inaccessible when displeased; parent disciplines harshly.

Whew! That's a bunch to handle. You better learn it too, because there's going to be a pop quiz during the next class period. Anyway, from these initial 15 practices of parenting, Baumrind's statistical procedure found the following reduced sets of parenting behaviors to be most important for mothers and fathers, respectively. Baumrind used slightly different names here because some of the dimensions of parenting in the reduced sets arose out of certain combinations of items from the larger set. But the main point, as you can see, is that the reduced set of the most important parent practices that turned up for mothers was very similar to the reduced set that turned up for fathers, with only a couple of exceptions.

Important Parenting Practices for Mothers	Important Parenting Practices for Fathers
1. Firm Enforcement	1. Firm Enforcement
2. Encourages Independence and Individuality	2. Encourages Independence and Individuality
3. Passively Acceptant	3. Passively Acceptant
4. Rejecting	4. Rejecting
5. Self-Confident, Secure, Potent Parental Behavior	5. Promotes Nonconformity
	6. Authoritarianism

Most of these aspects of parenting are self-explanatory. But I think a couple need a little further explanation. First, *passively acceptant* means that parents were almost always outwardly accepting of the child, even when she disobeyed. They might get angry at the child, but if they did they hid their anger from her. And if they didn't hide their anger, then afterward they felt embarrassed about not doing so. Also, passively acceptant parents tended to avoid using negative sanctions when the child disobeyed. Second, *promoting nonconformity*, which was important only for fathers, means that some fathers tended to express their own individuality by deviating from cultural norms, and encouraged their children to do the same. Third, *authoritarianism*, which again was important only for fathers, means that some fathers tended not to listen to their children and tended to take a very strict, inflexible stance whenever interacting with them.

Baumrind also discovered a third subset of parenting measures. She called this third subset "Joint Parenting Behaviors" because they didn't so much reflect the behaviors of one of the parents as much as they reflected the *climate of expectation* established by both parents together in combination with how they structured the child's environment. These 5 joint parenting behaviors are reflected in the original set of 15 parenting behaviors Baumrind started with, so they share the same names here. They include:

Important Joint Parenting Aspects

1. Expects Participation in Household Chores
2. Provides Enriched Environment
3. Is Directive
4. Discourages Emotional Dependency
5. Discourages Infantile Behavior

RESULTS

Baumrind's first goal in the study was to identify valid patterns of parenting that could then be used to achieve the second goal of the study, which was to see if parenting styles were related to child outcomes. She was most interested in the three parenting patterns she had identified in her previous research (namely, the authoritarian, authoritative, and permissive parenting styles); but remember, those patterns were developed by observing the behaviors of children. So an important first question was whether or not the same parenting styles would emerge when observing the parents' actual parenting behaviors. It turns out that by and large they did, but there were a couple of subtypes of parenting styles that emerged in this study that didn't come up in the earlier research. We'll take a look at these styles and substyles one at a time. But let me warn you. These styles were established through some complicated scoring procedures. I don't expect you to memorize the definitions of each style and substyle, but I present them here anyway so you can get a good sense of the level of parenting complexity Baumrind was dealing with. What most child psychologists remember from the Baumrind study is her main three parenting styles.

Parenting Styles

THE AUTHORITARIAN PARENT   The goal of the **authoritarian parent** is complete obedience. She favors forceful, **punitive** discipline when the child's will conflicts with her own. She doesn't believe in give and take, but does believe her word is always final. Baumrind found two subtypes of the authoritarian parenting style: *authoritarian-not rejecting* and *authoritarian-rejecting/neglecting*.

The *authoritarian-not rejecting* parenting style was said to describe the household when (1) both parents scored above the midpoint on Firm Enforcement, (2) both parents scored below the midpoint on Encourages Independence and Individuality, (3) both parents scored below the midpoint on Passive Acceptant, and (4) the father scored in the bottom third of Nonconformity or in the top third on Authoritarianism. Stated in less technical terms, these parents enforced rules very firmly, they discouraged independence and individuality, they didn't hide their anger or frustration, and the father demanded conformity. Ten families had this parenting style.

The *authoritarian-rejecting/neglecting* parenting style was defined as **all** of the above plus (1) both parents scored above the midpoint on Rejecting and (2) the family scored below the midpoint on Provides Enriched Environment. So in other words, not only were these parents as authoritarian as the first group, they were additionally rejecting of their children and they expended little effort in trying to stimulate their children's minds. Sixteen families had this parenting style.

THE AUTHORITATIVE PARENT   The primary goal of the **authoritative parent** is the personal growth of her child. She sets rules firmly but is willing to change them in cooperation with the child. She values her child's individuality and opinions. She also believes that when rules are set, they should be accompanied by an explanation the child can understand. Baumrind also found two subtypes of this style of parenting: *authoritative-not nonconforming* and *authoritative-nonconforming*.

The *authoritative-not nonconforming* parenting style, despite its awkward name, was similar to the authoritarian styles in two respects. It was defined as (1) having both parents score above the midpoint on Firm Enforcement or having one parent score in the upper third and (2) having both parents score below the midpoint on Passive Acceptant. But the authoritative-not nonconforming parenting style was additionally defined as having (3) both parents score above the midpoint on Encourages Independence and Individuality. In other words, these parents had firm rules and they tended to express their anger and frustration openly when they experienced it, but they also placed a very high value on promoting the emotional growth of their children as separate and autonomous people. Nineteen families had this style.

The *authoritative-nonconforming* parenting style was the same as authoritative-not nonconforming except that (1) one of the parents scored in the upper third on Firm Enforcement and one of the parents scored below the midpoint on Firm Enforcement, (2) the father scored below the midpoint on Rejecting and Authoritarianism, and (3) the father scored in the top third on Promotes Nonconformity. In other words, these parents were basically the same as the authoritative-not nonconforming group except that the father was extremely responsive to his child and encouraged the child to question authority. Only six families had this style.

THE PERMISSIVE PARENT   The primary goal of the **permissive parent** is to serve as a resource for her child to use as he wishes. She is nonpunitive, completely accepting, and always positive toward the general whims of her child. She places few demands on her child for helping with the housework and behaving socially appropriately, believing that her child should regulate his own activities. In Baumrind's classification of the subtypes of permissive parenting, she points out that no parents fit the perfect stereotype of the completely permissive parent. Rather, they differed by degrees in one way or another from what we might normally think of as a parent who was really, really permissive.

For example, the *nonconforming (not permissive and not authoritative)* parenting style had many features of the prototypical permissive parent. This style was defined as having (1) at least one parent scoring below the midpoint on Firm Enforcement, (2) at least one parent scoring above midpoint on Encourages Independence and Individuality, (3) the father scoring below the midpoint on Rejecting, (4) both parents scoring in the top third on Encourages Independence and Individuality *or* the father scoring in the top third on Promotes Nonconformity, and (5) the father scoring below the midpoint on Authoritarianism. What this means in normal English is that although the parents didn't exactly enforce any household rules, they at least tried to encourage their children to be independent, and at least one of the parents tried not to be rejecting. And if both parents didn't encourage independence, the father at least tried to promote nonconformity and to encourage his children to question authority. This style characterized the parents of 15 children.

In the *permissive (not nonconforming)* style, a more truly permissive style of parenting emerged. This parenting style was diagnosed if (1) both parents were below the midpoint on Firm Enforcement, and (2) at least one parent was in the top third of Passive-Acceptant, and (3) at least one parent was in the bottom third of Rejecting. In addition, households with this parenting style showed two out of the following three criteria: (a) at least one parent scored below midpoint on Expects Participation in Household Chores, (b) at least one parent scored below the midpoint on being Directive, and (c) at least one parent scored in the bottom third on Discourages Infantile Behavior. In other words, these parents didn't enforce rules firmly and tended not to expect children to participate in household duties. Moreover, they showed an across-the-board acceptance of their children, and even tolerated when their 4-year-olds acted like little babies. Are you getting the picture? Fourteen families had this parenting style.

REJECTING-NEGLECTING   Finally, there was a group of parents who had a rather disturbing style of parenting. Baumrind used the label "rejecting-neglecting" to describe the habits of these parents, who scored (1) below the midpoint for Encourages Independence and Individuality and (2) above the midpoint for Rejecting. If both parents didn't score above the midpoint for Rejecting, then they were still defined as rejecting-neglecting if either (a) one parent scored in the top third on Rejecting, or (b) the household was scored in the bottom third on Enrichment of the Child's Environment and in the top third on Discourages Emotional Dependency. In other words, not only did these parents *not* provide very much structure for their children in the form of providing rules, but they were in fact quite rejecting of their children and provided little guidance for nurturing their independence. Eleven sets of parents had this parenting style.

Relationships between Parenting Styles and Child Outcome Measures

After Baumrind established that it was possible to identify different parenting styles from the parents' own behaviors, she next examined whether these styles led to desirable or undesirable qualities in the children. Remember, a desirable quality was one that would help the child adapt to human society. Although she measured seven general child behavior characteristics, she combined these seven characteristics to form two even more general characteristics that she believed really got to the heart of the most important, most societally adaptive outcome measures. The first she called social responsibility; the second she called independence. Social responsibility is highly valued in most (if not all) cultures, and more or less reflects how much children respect and show concern for the well-being of other people. She created her measure of social responsibility by combining children's scores on three of the seven behavior types we talked about earlier. Specifically, she combined scores from the behavior types of *hostile-friendly, resistive-cooperative,* and *achievement oriented-not achievement oriented.* Children with the highest social responsibility scores were those who were rated as friendly, cooperative, and achievement oriented. And, of course, children with the lowest social responsibility scores were rated as hostile, resistive, and not achievement oriented.

Working independently is also highly valued in many cultures, especially mainstream Western cultures. So she reasoned that children with high levels of independence would also be well prepared for entry into mainstream Western culture. Her measure of independence was created by combining children's scores on the remaining four of the original seven behavior types; specifically, *domineering-tractable, dominant-submissive, purposive-aimless,* and *independent-suggestible.* Children high in independence would score high on tractable, dominant, purposive, and independent; whereas children low in independence would score high on domineering, submissive, aimless, and suggestible.

So now, let's take a look at how the children turned out as a result of the types of parents they had, in light of Baumrind's original hypotheses.

HYPOTHESIS **1**   *Baumrind thought that children of authoritarian parents, relative to other children, would be lacking in independence, but not in social responsibility. In terms of social responsibility, Baumrind expected children of authoritarian parents to be no different than other children.* Baumrind found that girls of authoritarian parents were, in fact, significantly less independent than the girls of authoritative parents. Boys of authoritarian parents were also less independent than boys of authoritative parents, but not to the same degree as girls. Boys of authoritarian parents were also less socially responsible than boys of authoritative parents, not because the authoritarian boys were especially low in social responsibility, but because the boys from the authoritative households were exceptionally high in it. In addition, she found that girls with authoritarian parents were less achievement oriented than girls with authoritative parents.

HYPOTHESIS **2**   *Baumrind expected the children of authoritative parents, relative to children of all other parents but authoritarian parents, to be socially responsible, and relative to children of all other parents but nonconforming parents, to be independent.* As it turned out, boys of authoritative parents were significantly more socially responsible than boys with authoritarian or permissive parents. They were also friendlier than boys with nonconforming parents. Girls with authoritative parents were slightly more achievement oriented than girls with authoritarian parents. But not all authoritative parents produced children with desirable behaviors. Children from authoritative-nonconforming parents were actually rather hostile to their friends and disrespectful of adult authority!

HYPOTHESIS **3**   *Baumrind expected the children of permissive parents, relative to the children of authoritarian and authoritative but not to the children of nonconforming parents, to be lacking in social responsibility. These children were also expected to score low in independence.* As she predicted, Baumrind found that boys of permissive parents were lower in social responsibility than boys from other parenting styles. Specifically, they were lower in social responsibility than boys with authoritative parents. But they weren't lower in social responsibility when compared to boys with authoritarian parents. Girls with permissive parents, on the other hand, were not especially lacking in social responsibility. However, girls with permissive parents were lacking in independence compared to girls with authoritative parents. Girls with permissive parents were no lower in independence than girls with authoritarian parents. Finally, boys with permissive parents were somewhat less **purposive** (that is, interested in obtaining goals) than boys with authoritative parents, and they were far less independent than boys with nonconforming parents.

HYPOTHESIS 4   *Baumrind believed the children of nonconforming parents, relative to the children of authoritarian and authoritative parents, but not to the children of permissive parents, would be lacking in social responsibility. She also expected that, relative to the children of authoritarian and permissive parents, but not to the children of authoritative parents, children of nonconforming parents would be more independent.* Contrary to Baumrind's expectation, children of nonconforming parents were not lacking in social responsibility compared with children of any other parenting style. Moreover, boys with nonconforming parents were way more achievement oriented and way more independent than boys with permissive parents. Still, girls with nonconforming parents were less independent than girls with authoritative parents.

DISCUSSION

As you can see, the patterns of findings are very complicated. It's even more complicated when you consider that different parenting styles sometimes influence boys and girls differently. But here are some general conclusions that Baumrind made about the different socialization practices for boys and girls, and their impacts on the two global types of socially desirable behaviors that children might express.

Social Responsibility

If you want your kids to be socially responsible, then your best bet is to adopt an authoritative approach to parenting. Prior to Baumrind's research, authorities on parenting believed that having a strict style of parenting would almost automatically result in aggressive and delinquent behavior. But this is obviously not the case. The strict parents in Baumrind's study produced socially responsible children so long as they accompanied their strictness with positive acceptance of their children and provided their children with explanations for their rules. But it's important that the authoritative parenting style you adopt not be of the nonconforming type. Authoritative-nonconforming parents produced children lacking in social responsibility.

Independence

If you want your kids to be independent as they grow up, then your best bet is also to choose an authoritative approach to parenting. Prior to Baumrind's research, authorities on parenting also believed that having a strict parenting style would lead to passivity and dependence. But Baumrind found quite the opposite. She wrote, "It appears that children are not that easily cowed by parental pressure." Authoritative parents tended to have a lot of characteristics that were likely to promote independence in their children. For one thing, they provided environments that were stimulating to their children. Stimulating environments are likely to promote interest and exploration on the part of the children, which, of course, is part of the definition of being independent. Authoritative parents also rewarded individuality and self-expression in their children, even when the children displayed what we might call "willfulness," so long as the willfulness didn't cause harm of some kind. Authoritarian parents, on the other hand, were more likely to punish willful children whether or not their willfulness would cause any harm. From the perspective of the authoritarian parent, disobedience of any kind was not tolerated. In contrast to authoritative and authoritarian parents, permissive parents really didn't reward children differently for displaying either a tolerable or an intolerable kind of willfulness. As Baumrind put it, "Permissive parents instead would accede to the child's demands until their patience was exhausted and then punish the child, sometimes very harshly."

In sum, it seems that strictness by itself isn't so bad, it's *how* the parent is strict that makes all the difference. If strictness is accompanied by good reasons, reasons that children can understand, then the outcome is good. Children will understand why the rules are in place, and they'll further understand when it's permissible to break a rule. Consequently, authoritative parents will understand why children are breaking the rule, and they'll tolerate a violation of it. And then when children see their parents accepting violations of the rule when there is good reason, the parents are serving as a nice model for the children themselves to emulate when they make their own transition to parenthood.

CONCLUSIONS

Baumrind revolutionized child psychology because she showed that different styles of parenting can be identified, and that different parenting styles can lead to better or worse outcomes in children. She also showed that socialization practices could affect boys and girls differently. Perhaps the single most important finding her work produced was that an authoritative style of parenting produced the best outcomes. And it should come as no surprise that once her work started getting published and circulating throughout the child development community, many parents around the country began employing parenting techniques associated with an authoritative parenting style. And why shouldn't they? Doesn't everyone want to have competent, well-adapted, successful children?

However, at the risk of sounding like a scratched CD, remember that Baumrind's parenting scheme came from a sample of white, high-IQ, highly educated, middle- and upper-class American families from the Berkeley, California, community. Although her findings have pretty much held up over the decades for white, educated, middle- and upper-class families in other parts of the United States, a number of researchers have questioned the value of an authoritative parenting style for other cultural groups. As noted before, the problem is that what counts as a "good" and adaptive outcome behavior can vary considerably from culture to culture. In the United States, for example, we value independence very highly. We all strive to "be the best we can be." We're encouraged to question authority, and to think for ourselves. In elementary school classrooms, children who know the right answers and say them aloud (provided they raise their hands first) are praised and encouraged. But this kind of independence-fostering isn't seen as a valuable socialization goal in other cultures. In many Asian classrooms, for example, children might get into trouble if they do something to distinguish themselves from their peers. In these Asian cultures, collaboration and cooperation are seen as "better" outcome measures than independence. Consequently, the same authoritative parenting style that serves many European American children well for fostering independence may serve many Asian and Asian American children poorly for the same reason. Parents from different cultures have different goals in their parenting. An Asian parenting goal includes producing children who will contribute to the cooperative efforts of the society, rather than finding ways to personally benefit from it.

But even in European American households, there are some environments where children may not be best served by authoritative parenting styles. Consider households located in high-crime neighborhoods or neighborhoods high in gang activity. Kids raised in these kinds of conditions may not benefit much from having parents who are warm and fuzzy. Rather, a parenting style that nurtures toughness and aggressiveness may be far more adaptive. And so a style of parenting that shares many characteristics of an authoritarian style of parenting may be called for.

Since Baumrind's original work, there has been a great deal of additional refinement of the basic parenting-style concepts, much of it done by Baumrind herself. These days, researchers point to two dimensions of parenting that are especially crucial in identifying four basic parenting styles. One dimension is *responsiveness*. A responsive parent is one who acknowledges, accepts, and tries to satisfy his children's needs. The other dimension is *demandingness*. A demanding parent has high expectations about the level of maturity his children display, as well as how much responsibility they take for caring for themselves and following household rules. By crossing these two dimensions, you get four parenting styles that have much in common with Baumrind's original parenting types. In tabular form, they look like this:

	High in Demandingness	Low in Demandingness
High in Responsiveness	Authoritative	Permissive-Indulgent
Low in Responsiveness	Authoritarian	Permissive-Indifferent

The recent work also continues to show that parenting styles influence children's outcome behaviors into adolescence and beyond. Now that Baumrind's original sample of children has had a chance to grow older, it's possible to look at longer-term influences on parenting style. In a 1991 study, for example, Baumrind reported that her "authoritative parents who were highly demanding and highly responsive were remarkably successful in protecting their adolescents from problem drug use and in generating competence."

We haven't spent much time talking about how authoritarian parents discipline their children, but given their high demandingness and low responsiveness, it's not surprising that their disciplinary tactics rely heavily on power-assertive techniques like spanking. Authoritarian parents, by definition, *make* their children obey, through sheer power if necessary. But based on Baumrind's research, we know that you may not have to cause pain in your children in order to socialize them. Except for the adaptive advantages that authoritarian parenting provides for some children in some cultures, in mainstream American culture, authoritarian parenting generally works against children's successful transition to adulthood. Authoritative parents rarely resort to spanking as a means of discipline, and their children turn out to be the happiest, most outgoing, most successful, most independent, and most socially responsible children. And authoritative parents are just as high in demandingness as authoritarian parents. If there is a moral to this story, it might be something like, "You don't have to spank your kids to get them to turn out okay." To my largish, male athlete student who says he turned out fine despite being spanked, I still can't help wondering how he might have turned out otherwise.

Bibliography

Baumrind, D. (1991). The influence of parenting style on adolescent competence and substance use. *Journal of Early Adolescence, 11*, 56–95.

Bradley, C. R. (1998). Child rearing practices in African American families: A study of the disciplinary practices of African American parents. *Journal of Multicultural Counseling and Development, 26*, 273–281.

Questions for Discussion

1. There's a lot of effort among parenting researchers not to make assumptions that parenting styles for one group, culture, or ethnicity are equally appropriate for other groups, cultures, or ethnicities. Is it possible that there is any single parenting practice or behavior that would be good for all people?
2. Do you think Baumrind's findings from 40+ years ago would still be applicable today? If not, why not?
3. Choose three of your favorite TV families and see if you can classify the parents in those families according to Baumrind's classifications. Do the children in the TV families resemble the children in Baumrind's study, in terms of the parents' styles of parenting?
4. Would the effectiveness of a parenting style differ in a single-parent versus a two-parent household? In what ways might parenting in the former setting be more or less efficient than parenting in the latter?

21

Voices from Another Mother

Of Human Bonding: Newborns Prefer Their Mothers' Voices

DeCasper, A. J., & Fifer, W. P. (1980). *Science, 208,* 1174–1176.
(RANK 17)

When I was in college, I had a professor who specialized in infant psychology. I took at least three courses from him, as well as several "independent studies" under his direction. I began volunteering in his lab as an undergraduate research assistant, and eventually he liked me enough to hire me. At one point I even served as his undergraduate laboratory coordinator. If there is one thing I remember about Professor Bob Haaf, it's that he was reliable. The same themes would appear in class after class; the same stories, at the beginning of his courses, the same content, and even the same jokes. I remember thinking I could probably skip the first three weeks without missing test material, since I had covered it so many times before.

Ironically, as I was preparing for this chapter, two of Bob's famous quotes suddenly popped into mind. These were quotes Bob always proffered, on the first day usually, and I was reminded of them when initially reading the abstract of DeCasper and Fifer's revolutionary article. The quotes were:

And one man in his time plays many parts, his acts being seven ages. At first the infant, mewling and puking in the nurse's arms.

—SHAKESPEARE, *from As You Like It*

and,

> *The baby, assailed by eyes, ears, nose, skin, and entrails at once, feels it all as one great blooming, buzzing confusion.*

—WILLIAM JAMES, *from Principles of Psychology* (1890)

These quotes stood out because of the visual images they generated, or at least that they generated in my mind. The Shakespeare quote makes you think of a baby, all messy and smelly, perhaps staining the caregiver's apron with bodily residue. But the underlying message is that the human infant is completely unable to regulate his own bodily functions, and entirely dependent on caregivers for his well-being. The James quote makes you think of what it must be like to perceive the world in the complete absence of organizing principles. The sights, sounds, smells, and touches are all mixed together, with none of the sensations having meaning. When Bob used the James quote, I often thought of a psychedelic Todd Rungren-like visual display, Pink Floyd music, and psilocybin mushrooms (hey, it was right after the 1970s).

I believe Bob's goal was to generate these kinds of images precisely so that his students could appreciate the challenges confronting anyone interested in the psychological development of babies. Over the next several weeks Bob would then impose order on chaos by reviewing ingenious methodologies that infant researchers developed to overcome the mewling and puking of those bloomingly and buzzingly confused babies. One of those ingenious methodologies, the nonnutritive sucking technique, is featured in DeCasper and Fifer's revolutionary article.

A LITTLE BACKGROUND CONTEXT

As I've mentioned throughout, studying the psychological world of the human baby is totally different than studying the psychological world of the older child or adult. Older children and adults can read and write (at least in industrialized societies), and so they can complete surveys, diaries, questionnaires, and self-reports. Preschoolers have language, and so you can at least interview them or ask them questions. But babies don't have either. They can't read, and they can't even talk. Pretty much the only scientifically instrumental thing babies have going for them is their physiological reactivity. Show babies a picture and they look at it. Make a loud, sudden noise, and they startle. Give them a vaccination and they cry.

With only this to go on, it's no wonder that the scientific study of baby psychology has been so neglected for so long. It's only relatively recently (the last 60 years or so) that child psychologists figured out how to study babies, they just had to learn to ask babies questions in ways babies could understand. Other revolutionary studies described in this text have focused primarily on using babies' visual reactivity. Both Fantz's (Chapter 8) and Baillargeon's (Chapter 5) studies, for example, involved showing babies visual pictures of various forms, and then recording how babies looked at the pictures.

Things are a little different with DeCasper and Fifer's study; however, for they relied upon an entirely different modality. They were studying brand new babies, and so couldn't depend much on infant eyesight. Infant visual acuity at birth is horrible. Adults who have the eyesight of a newborn baby, usually characterized as the equivalent of a Snelling chart score of 20/200 or worse, are regarded as legally blind by all 50 states and the Social Security Administration. Instead, DeCasper and Fifer turned to a sensory system that is far better developed at birth: audition.

DeCASPER AND FIFER (1980)

DeCasper and Fifer produced their revolutionary work at the end of the 1970s, and published it in the journal *Science* in 1980. Ostensibly, they were interested in mother-infant bonding. But in reality, I think they were really interested in something else altogether, and just used mother-infant bonding as a cover story for their research on neonatal perceptual acuity. The 1970s was a very important period for the emergence of scientific interest in mother-child bonding. Close on the heels of the fall of the behaviorist empire in American psychology, and spurred on by the triumvirate of revolutionary studies by Harlow, Bowlby, and Ainsworth (see Chapters 16, 17, and 18, respectively), it seemed as if everybody was talking about the role of the mother-child relationship in promoting children's healthy development. Harlow, for example, discovered the primary role that physical contact played in facilitating mother-infant bonding. Two controversial pediatricians, John Kennell and Marshall Klaus, even radicalized this position to the point of claiming that an absence of skin-to-skin contact in the first few minutes (or hours) after birth would prevent mother-infant bonding, and with it any chance for healthy development (a position later refuted by Diane Eyer in her famous book, *Mother-Infant Bonding: A Scientific Fiction*).

But DeCasper and Fifer took a different tack. Instead of focusing on skin-to-skin contact, they investigated infant voice-discrimination ability. Their primary focus on the perceptual-discriminative capacities present at birth is why I wonder whether they were really interested in bonding at all. But they linked infant voice-discrimination to mother-infant bonding, nevertheless, under the logic that an infant's preferences for its own mother's voice would set the stage for an endearing, intimate, and connected mother-child relationship.

In any case, DeCasper and Fifer's objective was to see if babies showed a preference, at birth, for their own mother's voice over other mothers' voices. To achieve this goal, DeCasper and Fifer had to demonstrate two things; first, that babies could *distinguish* their own mother's voice from another mother's voice, and second, and only then, that babies *showed a preference* for their own mother's voice over another mother's voice. Perhaps there was a third requirement; they had to demonstrate that these abilities were present at birth. If babies weren't capable of discriminating and preferring their own mother's voice right after birth, then what possible role could maternal voice preference play in facilitating mother-baby bonding?

This is where DeCasper and Fifer's methodological and scientific ingenuity comes in. As I already pointed out, infants don't have an especially large response repertoire. All they can do is react to environmental stimuli, which they do primarily through their reflexes. Toward this end, DeCasper and Fifer turned their attention to one of the most basic, life-succoring capacities found in human infants, their ability to suck. It's not often that one thinks of attributing meaning to infant sucking; but DeCasper and Fifer did, which is why they produced one of the most revolutionary studies in child psychology published since 1960.

INTRODUCTION

DeCasper and Fifer do not provide us much by way of an introduction section. In fact, they spend only one paragraph setting up their study. They note that fetuses were known to respond to sound prenatally, by the third trimester of pregnancy, and suggest that this prenatal responsiveness to sound "probably" subserves the development of mother-baby bonding. But as I just noted, for it to subserve mother-infant bonding, babies would have to show evidence of discriminating and preferring their mother's voice over other things. Other studies had demonstrated these two abilities in older babies, babies whose bonding with their mothers would have already been established, but no researchers had yet explored the topic in newborns. DeCasper and Fifer set out to be the first.

Experiment 1

METHOD

Participants

Ten white newborns (5 girls), tested within the first 24 hours of birth.

Materials

Audio recordings of mothers reading from the Dr. Seuss book, *And to Think That I Saw it on Mulberry Street.*

Procedure

Mothers were asked to read the Dr. Seuss book shortly after giving birth. All recordings were edited to provide 25 total minutes of speech from each mother. Testing involved placing each baby on its back in a bassinet, placing headphones over its ears, and placing a "nonnutritive" pacifier-type nipple in its mouth. The pacifier was held in place by a research assistant who was unaware of the specific research condition, and who could not hear the recording nor be seen by the baby. Inside the pacifier was a pressure transducer, which sent a signal to a computer every time the baby implemented a suck.

For the next 2 minutes, the baby was allowed to adjust to the novelty of the situation, and no sound was played through the headphones. The following 5 minutes were used to determine a baseline sucking rate for the baby. During this baseline period, the computer tabulated the baby's sucking rate, which served as a point of comparison for later analyses. DeCasper and Fifer found that during the baseline period, newborns did not suck continuously or even systematically. Rather, they engaged in sporadic bursts of sucking activity. For example, they might've sucked 6 times in rapid succession, paused 4 seconds, sucked 5 more times in rapid succession, then paused 3 more seconds. DeCasper and Fifer used the term "interburst interval" to describe the period of time between bursts of sucking. They also required the interburst interval to be at least 2 seconds long, otherwise sucks would be counted as part of a single sucking burst.

Summarizing across the entire 5-minute baseline period, DeCasper and Fifer calculated the median interburst interval for each baby; and used this measure as an index of how frequently each baby sucked when nothing interesting was going on. Not surprisingly, they found that babies differed from one another in their sucking frequencies, so different babies had different median interburst intervals. Testing for voice discrimination and preference took place next, immediately after the 5 minute baseline period.

The goal of the testing phase was to see if babies would change their rate of sucking in response to the voices they heard through the headphones. DeCasper and Fifer reasoned that if babies could learn the association between their sucking rate and the voices they were hearing, they should modify their sucking rate to maximize their exposure to the preferred voice. The procedure was fairly straightforward. First, babies were randomly assigned to one of two groups. The only difference between the two groups was which voices were paired with which sucking rates. In Group 1, babies heard their own mother's voices whenever their interburst intervals fell below the baseline rate; and they heard a different mother's voice whenever their interburst intervals rose above the baseline rate. The reverse was true for Group 2 babies. The question of interest was whether babies would shorten or lengthen their interburst intervals in the direction that would produce more frequent and longer exposure to their own mother's voices. Would

Group 1 babies suck *more* frequently to hear their own mothers' voices? Would Group 2 babies suck *less* frequently to hear their own mothers' voices?

In case this abstract description is difficult to follow, let's make the matter a bit more concrete. Let's assume that a particular baby was assigned to Group 1. Babies in this group could make their own mother's voice come on by sucking *more* frequently than during baseline. Suppose this baby's median interburst interval during baseline was 14 seconds. Essentially, this means that on average that baby engaged in a burst of sucking activity every 14 seconds. Now suppose that during testing, the baby engaged in one burst of sucking and then followed that 10 seconds later with a second burst of sucking. Because this interburst interval was only 10 seconds long, and because it was shorter than the baseline median of 14 seconds, he would have heard the recording of his own mother's voice. But suppose a third burst of sucking happened 18 seconds after the second. This time, his mother's voice would have been turned off, and another mother's voice would have been played through the headphones.

RESULTS

Based on this procedure, DeCasper and Fifer expected that if babies preferred their own mothers' voices over other mothers' voices, the interburst interval for Group 1 babies would *decrease* over time, while the interburst interval for Group 2 babies would *increase* over time. This is exactly what they found. The interburst intervals for 8 of the 10 babies shifted away from the baseline rate, and *toward* the direction that produced their own mothers' voices. Group 1 babies began producing shorter and shorter interburst intervals, while Group 2 babies began producing longer and longer interburst intervals. This difference was statistically significant. Of the 2 babies that failed to shift in the expected direction, one shifted in the direction of preferring the stranger's voice, and the other made no shift at all.

This in itself was evidence that babies could distinguish between their own and another mother's voice, and that babies preferred their own mother's voice. But DeCasper and Fifer next wondered what would happen if they reversed the response requirements. Would babies switch their sucking frequencies in the other direction, if the response contingencies were reversed? To test this possibility, they tested 4 of the babies a second time 24 hours later, only they reversed the sucking requirements that would produce their own mothers' voices. They found that all four babies shifted toward the new requirements, and shifted away from the sucking rates that generated their own mothers' voices the day before.

There were, of course, some limitations to this study. DeCasper and Fifer recognized that their sample size was small. They also wanted to see if their findings would hold up in a different discrimination procedure. So they conducted a second experiment which had a larger sample and a different procedure.

Experiment 2

Participants

Sixteen female newborns.

Materials

Audio recordings of mothers reading from the Dr. Seuss' book, *And to Think That I Saw it on Mulberry Street.*

Procedure

This procedure was a little more complicated than Experiment 1, but was designed to see just how discriminating the babies could be. As before, infants were placed on their backs in a bassinet, were outfitted with the headphones, and were given the pressure sensitive pacifier. The 2-minute adjustment period was also employed. However, unlike in Experiment 1, testing began immediately after the adjustment period; so no baseline sucking rate was needed. This was because DeCasper and Fifer were interested in seeing not whether babies would increase or decrease their sucking rates relative to their own baseline sucking rates, but whether babies could learn an association between the presentation of their mothers' voice and a relatively arbitrary sound pattern.

During testing, babies heard an alternating tone-silence sequence. The tone-silence sequence was comprised of a 4-second, 400 Hz tone, followed by a 4-second period of silence. To the baby it would sound like a series of beeps, maybe not that different from the sound of a garbage truck backing up in slow motion, with each beep separated from the next by a period of silence. This tone-silence sequence was played to babies whenever they were not sucking (i.e., it only played during the interburst interval). What happened next depended on the timing of the babies' sucks. For Group 1 babies, if they started a sucking burst during the tone, the tone would turn off and the recording of the mother's voice reading the Dr. Seuss book would turn on. If they sucked during the silent period, another mother's voice would turn on. In contrast, Group 2 babies would hear their own mother's voice if they started sucking during the silent period, and another mother's voice if they started sucking during the tone.

When the baby stopped sucking, whatever voice they were hearing was turned off, and the tone-silence sequence was turned back on. The testing phase lasted 20 minutes. The research question, of course, was whether babies would learn that their sucking bursts only triggered their mother's voice when they started sucking at a particular time during the tone-silence sequence.

RESULTS

DeCasper and Fifer compared babies' sucking performance during the first third of the testing session to the last third of the testing session. They found that during the first third of the testing session, babies seemed not to notice that the timing of their sucking bursts had anything to do with hearing their own mother's voice. But that changed by the last third of the testing session. By then, babies had begun changing the timing of their sucking bursts so as to synchronize with the portion of the tone-silence sequence that generated their own mothers' voice. DeCasper and Fifer reported that by the end of the testing session, newborns showed a 24% preference for initiating their sucking bursts at the time that would produce their own mothers' voice, relative to the time that would produce another mother's voice. Again, this preference was statistically significant.

DISCUSSION

In sum DeCasper and Fifer produced proof that all three of the prerequisites needed to support the proposition that maternal voice preferences may play a role in mother-baby bonding were in place. Data from both experiments showed that babies were capable of discriminating their own mother's voice from another mother's voice, that babies preferred to listen to their own mother's voice compared with another mother's voice, and that they could do both of these things within 24 hours of being born.

Amazingly, babies demonstrated these preferences in the relative absence of experience with their own mothers, in a facility which allowed minimal contact between mother and child. DeCasper and Fifer reported that all babies were cared for in a group nursery, and that general care and night feedings were handled by "female nursing personnel." Mothers only fed their babies at 9:30 A.M., and 1:30, 5:00, and 8:30 P.M. DeCasper and Fifer estimated total postnatal contact prior to testing to be only 12 hours. They conclude by noting, "The neonate's capacity to rapidly acquire a stimulus discrimination that controls behavior could provide the means by which limited post-natal experience with the mother results in preference for her voice." This voice preference, in turn, could set the stage for the communion between mother and child that results in bonding.

A Phenomenal Next Step

Given its purported focus on mother-baby bonding, one might expect a treatise at the end of the article on how an infant perceptual-discriminative apparatus which privileges the mother's voice over others, would then promote the bonding of the baby to the mother. Yet, this connection is conspicuously absent. But it's still "all good," as they say, because DeCasper and Fifer's findings are no less cool because of how they were marketed. It's really pretty phenomenal that babies identify, distinguish, and prefer their mother's voice from birth, regardless of whether that preference can be used to support mother-infant bonding. It's so cool, in fact, that it leads to even more provocative questions. If babies identify, distinguish, and prefer their own mother's voice at birth, when might they acquire these abilities? Might they acquire them before birth? If so, what other kinds of things can babies learn prenatally? Although addressing these questions wasn't DeCasper and Fifer's deal in 1980, their results raised the issue as something that needed to be addressed by someone. Perhaps it is not surprising then, that a follow-up study spearheaded by DeCasper, in collaboration with colleague Melanie Spence, served exactly that purpose. Because of the complete coolness of this follow-up study, it is also worthy of some consideration.

DeCASPER AND SPENCE (1986)

Although not published in as prestigious a journal as *Science*, the DeCasper and Spence study still gained considerable notoriety. Google Scholar lists it presently as cited 811 times (none too shabby, but maybe a pittance compared to the 2,002 citations of DeCasper & Fifer). There is no hand-waving in the direction of mother-baby bonding here; just pure, unadulterated perceptual science. The article begins by demonstrating for the reader why it is a good idea to see whether babies can learn things prenatally. Past research had demonstrated that sound enters the womb, and that babies can hear prenatally. Research had also demonstrated that some mammalian species can perceive auditory stimuli before birth, and be influenced by it after birth. So from DeCasper and Spence's perspective, there was no reason to believe that human babies couldn't hear and remember auditory information as well. Someone just had to step up to the plate and take a swing.

They were interested in testing the hypothesis that babies developed the preference for their mothers' voices prenatally; however, there was no way to ethically test this possibility experimentally. To do so would require random assignment, such that, for example, a control group of babies would hear their mothers' voices in-utero like normal, while an experimental group of babies would be deprived of their mother's voice in-utero. Obviously, it would be unethical, even impossible, to conduct this kind of study just to see if it could identify the origin of infant voice preferences.

So DeCasper and Spence pursued an alternative. They opted to experiment with the *kinds* of speech sounds presented to babies prenatally. They hypothesized that "newborns (would) prefer the acoustic properties of a particular speech passage if their mothers repeatedly recite(d) that passage while they (were) pregnant." They tested this hypothesis by having pregnant women tape-record three different prose passages, and had them recite only one of those passages to their unborn babies once each day, for the last 6 weeks of their pregnancies. Then, using the same procedures described earlier, they tested babies after birth, to see if they recognized and showed a preference for the one passage they were exposed to prenatally, relative to the other passages.

METHOD

Participants

Sixteen healthy women, approximately 7½ months pregnant.

Prenatal Procedures

Each woman was audio-recorded reading each of three short stories. The three stories were taken from: *The King, the Mice and the Cheese*; *The Cat in the Hat*; and a retooled version of the *The Cat in the Hat*, called *Dog in the Fog*. DeCasper and Spence indicate that the *Dog in the Fog* was basically the same story as *The Cat in the Hat*, with the "salient nouns changed." The three stories were about the same length, and had the same level and variety of words. However, the cadences across the three stories were different. DeCasper and Spence noted that the stories, "differed in the acoustic properties of individual words as well as in prosody."

Postnatal Procedures

Before the babies were born, mothers read their assigned stories an average of 67 times, which totaled an average of 3½ hours. Testing was similar to that in DeCasper and Fifer. However, instead of a recording of one mother's voice being pitted against a recording of another mother's voice, a recording of the target story (heard prenatally) was pitted against a recording of a novel story (one of the other two).

But there was an additional twist. Because in this experiment DeCasper and Spence weren't especially interested in seeing if babies preferred their own mothers' voices over other mothers' voices, babies were either assigned to an own-mother condition or an other-mother condition. If they were assigned to the own-mother condition, then they heard their own mothers reading both the target and the novel passages. But if they were assigned to the other-mother condition, they heard one of the other mothers reading both the target and novel passages.

The testing procedures for this experiment were much the same as in Experiment 1 above. Babies were laid down in a bassinet, headphones were placed over the ears, and a nonnutritive pacifier was inserted. They were given two minutes to adjust, and then a 5-minute baseline period followed. As in Experiment 1 from DeCasper and Fifer, baseline sucking rates for all the babies were determined. And as in Experiment 1, the baseline interburst interval was used as the point of comparison. Group 1 babies heard the target story if they sucked *more* frequently than baseline, and the novel story if they sucked *less* frequently; whereas Group 2 babies heard the target story if they sucked *less* frequently than baseline, and the novel story if they sucked *more* frequently.

RESULTS

The results were as you surely expect. The vast majority of babies' sucking rates changed *in the direction of* producing the target story—the one they had heard prenatally—and *away from* producing the novel story. Remember, the target story was the particular story that the mother recited to her unborn baby every day, during the entire last 6 weeks of pregnancy. So babies heard the target story prenatally a great deal. In contrast, babies never heard the novel story prenatally. So given the choice between the two, they preferred the story they were familiar with, and they modified their sucking rates to bring it about. Moreover, it didn't seem to matter to the babies whether the headphones played each story in their own mother's voice or the other mother's voice. Either way, they preferred the familiar story over the unfamiliar story.

GENERAL DISCUSSION

Although DeCasper and Spence really didn't discuss it much, implicit in their findings was that infants were capable of forming memories prenatally. In fact, to me, the idea of prenatal memory formation is their coolest finding of all. Obviously, there is no way to explain why babies preferred the target story, other than the fact that they formed a memory of certain aspects of the story at the time they heard it. If you think about it, this is not just a cute little finding. Rather, there are profound implications for fetal/newborn mental health if babies are capable of forming memories prenatally. More and more, empirical research is suggesting that what happens to babies in infancy, can have lasting impacts for the rest of their lives. This would be fine if only good things happened to babies, but babies are also exposed to lots of bad things. Even relatively typical environmental stressors do not escape the notice of babies.

Consider for example, a very recent study by Alice Graham and colleagues. I heard a description of it on National Public Radio just this morning while driving to work. The authors were interested in whether babies were affected by negatively toned speech expressed to them while sleeping. There is a lot of research to suggest that exposing babies and children to parental bickering and arguing can have negative impacts on their health. What is not known is whether babies have to be awake to hear it. So Graham and colleagues used an fMRI machine to scan the brains of sleeping babies while emotionally charged speech was piped to them via headphones. Of course speech is not only emotionally toned, it has meaning. To separate out the impact of the emotional tone of speech from the meaning of its words, the authors constructed nonsense utterances that were recorded in different emotional valences. An example of a nonsense utterance was, "I pulimented a mopar." This utterance was then produced in a very angry tone, an angry tone, a neutral tone, a happy tone, or a very happy tone. Graham and colleagues found that the brains of babies whose parents argued a lot showed significantly higher responsiveness to the angry nonsense utterances than to the neutral ones. Moreover, the parts of the baby's brains that showed this heightened sensitivity were those parts most highly connected with emotional processing and emotional regulation (specifically, the limbic system, including the rostral anterior cingulate cortex and the hypothalamus). Of course, it's not exactly clear what these results mean in the long run, but it seems clear that even sleeping babies are capable of processing emotional stimuli. Connecting these results with those of DeCasper and colleagues—babies can differentiate emotional stimuli while sleeping, fetuses can process and remember auditory stimuli prenatally—is it just possible that fetuses can differentiate, and remember, emotional stimuli prenatally? If so, and to be sure there is no evidence in support of this possibility just yet, then we may very well need to rethink how we characterize the condition of pregnancy.

CONCLUSION

It is difficult to overstate the legacy of Anthony DeCasper and his colleague's work. As did many other scientists in this book, they transformed what amounts to a primordial infant reflex into a looking glass to the workings of the infant mind. Nonnutritive sucking behaviors were not new to the scientific community in the 1980s. They were the focus of an extensive study by H. M. Halverson as far back as 1938. Indeed, they weren't even new as a tool for measuring babies' cognitive abilities. Einar Siqueland and his colleagues used nonnutritive sucking to index infant perceptual discriminatory capacity in two *Science* articles of their own just 10 years earlier. One of these (Eimas et al.) was even considered for inclusion in this book, having been ranked 28th overall, and cited nearly 2,181 times in the professional literature. But to my knowledge DeCasper and colleagues were the first to use nonnutritive sucking as an index of perceptual functioning right at birth, let alone before. Perhaps the mewling, puking, blooming, and buzzing world of the infant envisioned by Shakespeare and James was a bit of an embellishment. But then Bill and Bill weren't informed by modern infancy science.

Bibliography

DeCasper, A. J., & Spence, M. J. (1986). Prenatal maternal speech influences newborns' perception of speech sounds. *Infant Behavior and Development, 9,* 133–150.

Eimas, P. D., Siqueland, E. R., Jusczyk, P., & Vigorito, J. (1971). Speech perception in infants. *Science, 171,* 303–306.

Eyer, D. E. (1993). *Mother-infant bonding: A scientific fiction.* New Haven, CT: Yale University Press.

Graham, A. M., Fisher, P. A., & Pfeifer, J. H. (published online, 28 March, 2013). What sleeping babies hear: A functional MRI study of interparental conflict and infants' emotional processing. *Psychological Science.*

Halverson, H. M. (1938). Infant sucking and tensional behavior. *The Pedagogical Seminary and Journal of Genetic Psychology, 53,* 365–430.

Klaus, M. H., & Kennell, J. H. (1976). *Maternal-infant bonding: The impact of early separation or loss on family development.* St. Louis, MO: Mosby.

Siqueland, E. R., & DeLucia, C. A. (1969). Visual reinforcement of nonnutritive sucking in human infants. *Science, 165,* 1144–1146.

Questions for Discussion

1. In what specific ways might infants' preferences for their own mothers' voices contribute to mother-baby bonding?

2. DeCasper and colleague's work seems to show beyond a shadow of a doubt that babies recognize and prefer certain kinds of speech sounds. Do you think they are consciously aware of their recognitions and preferences, and if not, how might their abilities impact later social, emotional, and cognitive development?

3. If babies can *learn* prenatally, what obligations, if any, do mothers have toward facilitating that learning? What about governmental agencies? If not obligations, then what about responsibilities?

22

Mind over Matter

Does the Autistic Child Have a "Theory of Mind"?

Baron-Cohen, S., Leslie, A. M., & Frith, U. (1985). *Cognition, 21*, 37–46.
(RANK 20)

Autism is arguably one of the earliest and most challenging psychological disorders confronting families today. Even just describing autism is challenging. In general, the disorder is characterized by two very different, seemingly unrelated collections of symptoms. First are difficulties with social interaction, including both verbal and nonverbal communication. But autism is also characterized by an excessive focus on objects, a preference for sameness, and a tendency toward behavioral repetition. These symptoms can also vary substantially within individuals, in both variety and severity, such that some children with autism are so profoundly affected that they can't be left alone, while others may appear so "normal" you may not know anything was out of order.

As with any psychological disorder, child psychologists are interested in finding out what causes autism and how to treat it. But they've also been interested in understanding what the disorder is like for the children who have it. Sadly, because of their difficulties with communication, children with the severest forms of autism can't provide us with much insight. Many may not even know that they have autism. However, Ellen Notbohm, herself a mother of a child with autism, has provided us with a starting point. Through careful observation, she has compiled a list of *Ten Things Every Child with Autism Wishes You Knew*. Here's an abbreviated, largely paraphrased version of Notbohm's list of what a child with autism would tell you if he could:

1. I am a child. I have autism. I am not "autistic." My autism is only one part of who I am.
   [*Author's note: For this reason, I use the phrase "child with autism" rather than "autistic child."*]

2. My sensory perceptions are disordered. The ordinary sights, sounds, smells, tastes, and touches of everyday life that you may not even notice can be painful to me.

3. Please distinguish between "won't" and "can't." It's not that I *won't* listen to your instructions. It's that I *can't* understand you. When you call to me, all I hear is "blah-blah-blah-blah, Billy."

4. I am a concrete thinker. I interpret words literally. It's very confusing for me when you say, "Hold your horses, cowboy!" And please don't tell me something is a "piece of cake," because I might get upset when there's nothing sweet to eat.

5. Please be patient with my limited vocabulary. It's hard for me to tell you what I know and what I need when I don't have the right words. I sometimes memorize scripts from the world around me (TV, books, movies, radio) to compensate for my vocabulary deficits. Pay attention to my body language.

6. Don't just tell me how to do something, show me. And please show me many times, repetition helps me learn.

7. Please don't criticize me when I fail. Focus on my strengths and what I *can* do.

8. Help me be sociable. I can't read facial expressions and body language, and I don't understand the emotions of others. Sometimes I want to play with my friends, but I don't know how to start a conversation or enter a playgroup. Please coach me when I don't know the appropriate social response, instead of scolding me or laughing at me.

9. Try to figure out what triggers my tantrums. It's usually because one of my senses has been overloaded. If you write down when it happens, you might see a pattern, and maybe you can prevent it in the future. Sometimes tantrums speak for me when words cannot.

10. Love me unconditionally. I did not choose to have autism; and it is happening to me, not you. But without you, my chances to be successful and self-reliant are slim.

A moment ago, we noted children with severe autism can't convey these feelings themselves because of their communication difficulties. But this begs the question. As a society, we have usually assumed that children with autism don't communicate because they can't. But has anyone considered the possibility that children with autism don't communicate because they don't want to? Maybe children with autism don't talk to people simply because they don't know, or don't realize, that people have minds. In other words, maybe children with autism don't have a *theory of mind*.

This was the very question posed by graduate student Simon Baron-Cohen, and his mentors Alan Leslie and Uta Frith in the 1980s. They were interested in the theory of mind question because they thought it might help complete the autistic puzzle. They speculated that children with autism have communication difficulties not because of their communication skills per se, but because they don't believe the people around them are things to communicate with. I mean, have you ever spoken to a toaster or a candle? Probably not, unless you were very young and just finished watching Disney's *Beauty and the Beast*. We don't speak to inanimate objects because we don't believe they have minds, and so wouldn't understand or appreciate our communications. Might such a perspective be shared by people who don't have an understanding of minds? Before considering this logic further, let's take a closer look at both the concept of theory of mind and the nature of autism. Then we can better appreciate their interconnections, and how they inspired Baron-Cohen and colleagues' revolutionary work.

A BRIEF PRIMER ON THEORY OF MIND

In the 1980s, child psychologists became increasingly interested in children's understanding of mental states. By "mental states," I mean things like believing, knowing, wanting, and thinking. We all have mental states, and we attribute mental states to one another. We talk about mental states using mental state words. When I say something like, "I *believe* you," I'm using the word *believe* to describe the internal mental state I have about something you said. The phrase, "I believe you" means that I accept what you say to be true. However, I could also say, "I don't believe you," meaning that my internal mental state is one of disbelief, and that I don't take what you say to be true. Either way, you would have the mental state of knowing that I have the mental state of believing or disbelieving because I used a mental state word to tell you so. The basic idea that one person has knowledge about another person's mental state, is described in the psychological literature using terms like *Theory of Mind* and *Mind-Reading*.

Now, the capacity for theory of mind is associated with some pretty serious advantages, both phylogenetically (i.e., development of the species as a whole) and ontogenetically (i.e., development of the individual person). In terms of phylogenetic impact, knowing that other people have minds probably gave humans a survival advantage over many other species. As mind-minded individuals, for example, prehistoric humans could have anticipated many of the behaviors of their conspecifics without the need for continuous communication. To the extent that constant communication among members of a species requires resources, our ancestors may have bested their competitors simply because they needed fewer resources to function collaboratively in their ecological niche. It is notable that humans, among all the world's creatures, are the only ones who seem to have an understanding of minds. Perhaps this uniqueness even explains why humans have cornered the market on all the planet's resources; but that is the subject for a different book.

We can only speculate about the role of theory of mind in our phylogenetic development, but a great deal of effort has been expended in learning about its ontogenetic impact. Under normal circumstances, an understanding of minds emerges around 3 to 5 years of age; and with it comes a capacity to understand and anticipate the moods and feelings of peers and social partners. This advanced knowledge allows children to predict what their peers and social partners will likely do or think as a result of those moods and feelings. The main advantage of having a theory of mind is that it gives children a kind of "insider" mind knowledge they can use to their advantage. If Jack falls down and breaks his crown, a mind-minded Jill could reason that Jack might appreciate some loving companionship. Comforting Jack in his time of need, in turn, might give Jill some bonus friendship points that, in the long run, could increase the likelihood that Jack will share his pail of water.

As a result of its ontogenetic role in the emergence of children's social competence, it's not surprising that theory of mind research has come to occupy the center of attention of child psychologists. One of the earliest articles on the topic was a famous 1978 paper by Premack and Woodruff, which found that not even our closest cousin the chimpanzee has a theory of mind. In fact, it was the title of that paper, "*Does the Chimpanzee Have a Theory of Mind?*", that served as the inspiration for the title of Baron-Cohen et al.'s paper, "*Does the Autistic Child Have a Theory of Mind?*"

A BRIEF PRIMER ON AUTISM

Before 2013, children diagnosed with autism were actually classified as having one of four different subtypes of autism. The subtypes included full-blown "autistic disorder," "childhood disintegrative disorder," "pervasive developmental disorder not otherwise specified," and "Asperger syndrome." But in 2013, everything changed as a result of the *Diagnostic and Statistical Manual of Mental Disorders, Fifth Edition* (DSM-5). The DSM-5, published by the American Psychiatric Association, has long been the go-to reference for mental health diagnoses; so when it redefined autism in 2013, its declarations were widely accepted.

The main practical change was that all of the subtypes of autism were grouped into a single overarching diagnostic category known as "Autism Spectrum Disorder" (ASD). By including the term "spectrum" in its classification, the DSM-5 recognized that children with autism vary along a multidimensional continuum of autism symptoms, in some cases ranging from very severe to very mild, while still being considered as having the same overarching diagnosis. According to the DSM-5, the technical criteria required for an ASD diagnosis include the following (they may be technical but they are interesting):

A.   Persistent deficits in social communication and social interaction across multiple contexts, as manifested by all three of the following:
  1. Deficits in social-emotional reciprocity, ranging from abnormal social approach and failure of normal back-and-forth conversation; to reduced sharing of interests, emotions, or affect; to failure to initiate or respond to social interactions.
  2. Deficits in nonverbal communicative behaviors used for social interaction, ranging from poorly integrated verbal and nonverbal communication; to abnormalities in eye contact and body language or deficits in understanding and use of gestures; to a total lack of facial expressions and nonverbal communication.
  3. Deficits in developing, maintaining, and understanding relationships, ranging from difficulties adjusting behavior to suit various social contexts, to difficulties in sharing imaginative play or in making friends, to absence of interest in peers.

B.   Restricted, repetitive patterns of behavior, interests, or activities, as manifested by at least two of the following:
  1. Stereotyped or repetitive motor movements, use of objects, or speech.
  2. Insistence on sameness, inflexible adherence to routines, or ritualized patterns of verbal or nonverbal behavior.
  3. Highly restricted, fixated interests that are abnormal in intensity or focus.
  4. Hyper- or hyporeactivity to sensory input or unusual interest in sensory aspects of the environment.

C.   Symptoms must be present in the early developmental period.

D.   Symptoms cause clinically significant impairment in social, occupational, or other important areas of current functioning.

E.   These disturbances are not better explained by intellectual disability or global developmental delay. Intellectual disability and autism spectrum disorder frequently co-occur; to make comorbid diagnoses of autism spectrum disorder and intellectual disability, social communication should be below that expected for general developmental level.

Although practitioners are expected to take all five of these criteria into account when diagnosing an ASD, notice that the symptoms are really only addressed in the first two categories. To distinguish between the two kinds of symptoms, let's call them "Category A" and "Category B." Category A symptoms are the ones that reflect the quality of communication and social interaction. They include absent or unusual eye contact, unusual or poorly timed facial expressions, and speech intonation that doesn't match the context. But the most ubiquitous Category A symptom is probably language delay, with children having the greatest ASD severity manifesting the fewest words in their vocabularies.

While Category A symptoms reflect deficiencies in communication, Category B symptoms mainly reflect unusual or maladaptive behavior patterns that, on the surface, seem to have little to do with communication deficiencies. Nevertheless, Category B symptoms are strikingly conspicuous, and often form the basis for media portrayals of autism. These symptoms may manifest, for example, in an obsessive-like passion for lining up objects (as in the 1999 film *Molly*) and detecting patterns (as in the 1998 film *Mercury Rising*); or in compulsive schedule-following (as in the 1988 film *Rain Man*) and repetitive motor activities such as hand flapping, spinning, or rocking (as in the 2004 film *Miracle Run*).

But although symptoms from both categories are found in children with ASD, not all children exhibit all symptoms with the same frequency and severity. To accommodate these differences, the DSM-5 identifies three levels of ASD severity. These severity levels indicate how much help and support children with autism will probably need for a maximally productive life.

Children with Level 1 severity require *some* support, and come closest to exhibiting what used to be called Asperger's syndrome (although children previously diagnosed with Asperger's syndrome would not necessarily be diagnosed with ASD under the new system). Children at this level exhibit noticeable but not completely debilitating impairments in their social interactions. They have language, can speak in full sentences, and by and large function well in their everyday social settings. If you were to meet someone at a party with Level 1 severity, you wouldn't necessarily realize she had ASD, but you might detect slightly odd behavior patterns. An adult with Level 1 severity may even be highly functioning and professionally successful.

An excellent case in point is the noted author Temple Grandin. Dr. Grandin earned her PhD in Animal Science and currently serves as a professor of Animal Sciences at Colorado State University. Her website identifies her as the most accomplished adult with autism in the world. She has written two *New York Times* best-selling books on her experience with autism, and her story is featured in an HBO movie starring Claire Danes. In 2010, *Time Magazine* identified Grandin among the top 100 Most Influential People. You can see Grandin tell her own story in a TED talk, available at:

http://www.ted.com/speakers/temple_grandin.

Children with Level 2 severity require *substantial* support. They may have especially odd reactions to others, or none at all, and when they do interact with social partners, they may be preoccupied with a specific topic of interest. A child may be interested in dinosaurs, for example, and may only choose to interact with others when the topic involves exchanging information about dinosaurs or playing with toy dinosaurs. Level 2 children are often inflexible, and have a very hard time transitioning between activities.

Children with Level 3 severity require *very substantial* support in their day-to-day functioning. They may be unintelligible when they speak, or have no language at all. They may be so focused on a particular activity, such as the circular motion of ceiling fan blades, that they are unable to do anything else. For these children, even the slightest deviation in routine, or transitioning between activities, may result in severe emotional outbursts and distress.

Judging levels of severity depends on a number of factors, including the symptoms that are most predominant, how disruptive those symptoms are, and in which environments they are most disruptive. Thus, even children within a given level of severity may differ considerably in the kinds of symptoms they express. Some may express impairment in the area of social relationships, while others may express more dysfunction in the area of repetitive behavior patterns. Of course, there may also be differences in the skill and experience of the clinician making the diagnosis, and in the reliability/validity of the diagnostic tools they employ.

An accurate ASD diagnosis is further complicated by the fact that some children with ASD may also have an intellectual disability. This situation is known as *comorbidity*, which means having two different diagnoses at the same time. If you look back at Criterion E of the DSM-5, you'll see that an ASD diagnosis is only supposed to be made if the Category A and B symptoms are *not clearly* the result of an intellectual or global developmental delay. It's possible, for example, to have language delay for reasons other than autism. Yet, ASD often co-occurs with intellectual or global developmental delay, and so it becomes crucial with ASD diagnoses to ensure that the identified deficiencies are not solely attributable to intellectual or developmental delay.

One problem in addressing Criterion E, however, as you might imagine, is that children with autism are predisposed not to do well on standardized intelligence tests. Often the reason that children with autism perform poorly on IQ tests is not because of the challenge of the test, but simply because they don't respond well to the social cues of the examiner. Remember, children with ASD have impaired social skills. To the extent that IQ tests are administered by people, the performance of test-takers who are disposed to avoid social interactions is bound to be compromised. When children with autism earn low IQ scores then, those scores are not necessarily because of an intellectual disability; rather, they could be the result of other impairments common to children with autism.

THE REVOLUTIONARY STUDY

INTRODUCTION

We're now in a much better position to consider the revolutionary significance of the Baron-Cohen, Leslie, and Frith article. Remember that their research objective was to test whether lacking a theory of mind, or being "mind-blind" could explain the social impairments of children with autism. In introducing the topic, they pointed out (as we have also just done) that although the majority of children with autism demonstrate intellectual delay, their intellectual impairments are not necessarily the cause of their social impairments. Consider one of the main differences between children with autism and children with Down syndrome. As noted by Baron-Cohen et al., "there are autistic children with IQ's in the normal range" but there are also "mentally retarded non-autistic children, such as Down's syndrome (sic), [who] are socially competent relative to their mental age." In sum, having a low IQ cannot be the reason that children with autism are socially impaired. If it *were* the reason, then children with Down syndrome would also be socially impaired, but they aren't.

Accordingly, Baron-Cohen et al. hypothesized that social impairment in children with autism must come from something other than IQ, and something not found in children with Down syndrome. That thing was theory of mind. They anticipated that children with autism had a social deficit *because* they had a theory of mind deficit. So they set out to test whether children with autism had theories of mind. Simultaneously, they also tested whether children with Down syndrome had theories of mind. Discovering theories of mind in the latter, but not the former, would serve as prima facie evidence for the hypothesis that the source of social impairment in children with autism was the absence of a theory of mind.

METHOD

Participants

The research participants consisted of 20 children with autism, 14 children with Down syndrome, and 27 "clinically normal preschool children." Because they were dealing with such differing clinical diagnoses, the authors took into account both the children's chronological ages and their mental ages. Making a distinction between mental and chronological age is important when dealing with intellectual impairments, because by definition, the mental ages of intellectually impaired children are significantly lower than their chronological ages. It wouldn't be fair, for example, to compare the social skills of 4-year-old Down syndrome patients to those of 4-year-old typically developing children, because the mental age of Down syndrome patients would be considerably lower than that of the typically developing children of the same chronological age. By assessing children's mental ages, Baron-Cohen et al. could look for group differences in theory of mind while equating for mental age, regardless of chronological age.

TABLE 22.1 Mean Chronological, Nonverbal Mental, and Verbal Mental Age of Children as Function of Diagnostic Group

Group	Chronological Age	Nonverbal Mental Age	Verbal Mental Age
Typically Developing	4;5	4;5 (assumed)	4;5 (assumed)
With Down Syndrome	10;11	5;11 (as tested)	2;11 (as tested)
With Autism	11;11	9;3 (as tested)	5;5 (as tested)

They also measured children's verbal and nonverbal intelligence. Verbal tests of intelligence measure things like vocabulary size, the ability to understand complex sentences, and the ability to follow verbal directions. Nonverbal tests of intelligence, in contrast, measure nonlinguistic abilities, including short-term memory, puzzle-solving, and pattern completion. Differences between these two kinds of intelligence were important for Baron-Cohen and colleagues, because the primary intellectual impairment of children with autism involves their verbal intelligence, *not* their nonverbal intelligence. It is possible, for example, that a child with autism has a very small vocabulary, but is especially good at solving puzzles and completing patterns. Children with Down syndrome, in contrast, are impaired in *both* verbal and nonverbal intelligence.

The average chronological and mental ages of the children in Baron-Cohen et al.'s sample are presented in Table 22.1 (expressed in years;months). The typically developing children were not actually tested for their intelligence, so their verbal and nonverbal intelligence levels were assumed to be the same as their chronological ages. But the remaining children were administered actual intelligence tests to determine both their verbal and their nonverbal mental ages.

Take a moment to scan the chronological and mental ages of the children in Baron-Cohen et al.'s sample. The relationships among them are fairly complex, but take special notice of the following:

1. The typically developing children (about 4½ years old) were less than half the chronological ages of the intellectually impaired children (about 11 and 12 years old).
2. The children with autism had about the same verbal intelligence as the typical children, but had much higher nonverbal intelligence.
3. The children with Down syndrome had slightly higher nonverbal intelligence than the typical children, but slightly lower verbal intelligence.
4. Both of the intellectually impaired groups had much higher nonverbal intelligence scores than verbal intelligence scores.
5. The children with autism were intellectually superior to the children with Down syndrome across the board, on both nonverbal and verbal intelligence.

Materials

THE SALLY-ANNE TEST (AKA "THE FALSE BELIEF" TEST) The key innovation of the study was in using a procedure known as the "Sally-Anne Test" with children who had autism. At the time, the Sally-Anne Test was a recent innovation designed to measure typically developing children's theory of mind. The test was based on the logic that if Person A knows that Person B has a belief—whether that belief is true or false—then Person A must also know that Person B has a mind. The Sally-Anne Test simply employs this logic in the form of a kind of puppet show appropriate for young children. You can see a

FIGURE 22.1 Schematic Depiction of the Sally-Anne Procedure.

schematic depiction of the Sally-Anne Test in Figure 22.1. A number of intriguing real-life administrations of the Sally-Anne Test can also be found on YouTube (search terms: Sally Anne Test).

PROPS   In the Sally-Anne Test, children are presented with two dolls ("Sally" and "Anne"), two scale-size storage containers (a basket and a box), and a marble.

NARRATIVE   Children are then told a short story about the two characters, Sally and Anne. While the story is being told, the experimenter acts out the events using the props. The narrative portion of the drama goes something like this:

> *This is Sally and this is Anne. Sally has a basket, and Anne has a box. Sally also has a marble. Sally puts her marble into the basket, and then goes out to play. While Sally is outside, Anne takes the marble out of the basket and puts it into the box. Later Sally comes back and wants to play with her marble.* <u>*Where will Sally look for the marble?*</u>

If you followed along, and if you understand that other people have minds, you should quickly realize that when Sally comes back from her walk, she will think her marble is still in the basket. Obviously, since Sally didn't see Anne move the marble to the box, there is no way for her to know that the marble has been moved from the basket. So Sally should *believe* the marble is still in the basket.

DEPENDENT VARIABLES   Now, the child who has a theory of mind should believe that Sally should believe that the marble is still in the basket. So the child is simply asked, *Where will Sally look for the marble?* This is called the "Belief Question." If the child answers the Belief Question correctly, by saying that Sally will look in the basket—even though the marble is really not in the basket—then the child has "passed" the Sally-Anne test, and can be said to have a theory of mind. Well, almost. Two alternative explanations have to be ruled out first.

Admittedly, it's possible that the child didn't pay attention to the story at all, and so just *guessed* where Sally would look for the marble. It's also possible that the child had a bad memory, and simply *forgot* where Sally would look for the marble. In both of these cases, it's possible for a child to answer the Belief Question correctly without actually having a theory of mind. To make sure that children aren't just guessing at their answers, the Sally-Anne Test includes two additional "control questions." First is the "Reality Question," *Where is the marble really?* If the child had been paying attention, she should be able to say where the marble is *really* located, regardless of where Sally *believes* the marble is located. Second is the "Memory Question," *Where was the marble in the beginning?* If the child's memory is intact, she should be able to say that the marble was initially in the basket, even if later the marble had been moved to the box. If a child answers the two control questions correctly, while also answering the Belief Question correctly, it's safe to conclude that the child has a theory of mind, and wasn't just a lucky guesser.

RESULTS

Every single child, across all three diagnostic groups, answered the two control questions correctly. Thus, all children were paying attention, and had decent memories. Their answers to the Belief Question can be found in Table 22.2. Note that the vast majority of typically developing children, as well as those with Down syndrome, passed the Sally-Anne Test. In contrast, the vast majority of children with autism failed the Sally-Anne Test. These results are especially fascinating because, as you'll recall, the children with autism were the oldest, and had the highest nonverbal intelligence of any group. Children with autism also had nearly twice the *verbal mental age* of the children with Down syndrome, yet they performed terribly in comparison on the Belief Question. Whatever was going on with the children with autism, their failure on the Sally-Anne Test was clearly not the result of any inferior intellectual capabilities. A much better explanation, at least if you ask Baron-Cohen, is that their performance resulted from an inability to understand that Sally had a mind, and so failed to appreciate that Sally could have a false belief.

TABLE 22.2 Performance on the Belief Question of the Sally-Anne Test as a Function of Diagnostic Group

Answer	Typically Developing	Down Syndrome	Autism
Correct	27	12	4
Incorrect	4	2	16

DISCUSSION

These results confirmed Baron-Cohen and colleagues' suspicions that children with autism have a special deficiency in understanding the mental states of others. With this deficiency, they wrote, children with autism are "at a grave disadvantage when having to predict the behavior of other people." But surprisingly, the *mental-state* perspective-taking deficiencies of children with autism didn't carry over into perspective-taking more generally. A 1984 study by Peter Hobson revealed that children with autism seemed to do just fine on perspective-taking tasks that didn't involve "reading" the minds of others. Using Piaget's classic "three-mountain task," in which children are asked whether a doll positioned on one side of a three-dimensional model of a mountain ridge could "see" what was on the opposite side of the mountain ridge, Hobson found that children with autism performed at a level appropriate for their mental age. In other words, children with autism understood that the doll could not see through the mountains. Hobson concluded that "the cognitive abilities required in taking different points of view in perceptual situations are not the same as those that underlie the autistic child's social disability."

SO WHAT?

It would be difficult to overstate the impact of Baron-Cohen et al.'s findings on our modern understanding of ASD. Theirs was among the first scientific studies to highlight a very specific cognitive deficit, perhaps unique to children with autism, that was not also associated with intellectual deficiency more generally. The specific deficit involved children's understanding of minds. Whereas most children are mind-minded, children with autism seem to be mind-blinded. This finding charted a new path to understanding ASD.

Along with this new way of thinking came some new attempts at a treatment approach. The goal of these attempts, not surprisingly, was to improve children's understanding of minds. One specific technique that evolved from this approach was "thought-bubble training." In thought-bubble training, children are first shown a manikin (or doll), with a photograph inserted into a slot in the head. Children are then trained to think of the contents of the photograph as representing the contents of the character's mind. After training, children learn that thoughts and ideas can be visualized as if in a picture. And indeed, in a pretest/post-test experiment, Henry Wellman, Simon Baron-Cohen, and associates found that thought-bubble training significantly improved Sally-Anne reasoning among children with autism.

But does thought-bubble training cause children to construct theories of mind, where none existed before? Probably not. Although interventions aimed at improving children's theories of mind have proven effective, and have improved the quality of children's interactions with others, they don't work with all ASD children. Even when they do work, they don't raise ASD children's theories of mind to a level comparable to that of typically developing children. Much of the treatment's success depends on children's level of functioning to begin with. Children with the least severe ASD benefit the most from thought-bubble training. Wellman et al. interpreted their findings this way:

> We want to emphasize that in our minds a picture-in-the-head intervention strategy does <u>not</u> attempt to target a normal developmental conception that children of autism fail to develop; nor do we claim that this understanding would somehow result in a normal theory of mind being acquired by individuals with autism. Instead … pictures in the head can serve as an analogy based on phenomena individuals with autism understand well—physical photographs and pictures—to help reason about phenomena that they understand poorly—mental states and mental representations.

But even if thought-bubble training worked flawlessly, and children's social-communicative functions could be restored to normal, it's difficult to see how the theory of mind approach to treating autism would address the other symptoms of ASD. For example, having a theory of mind would seem to do little to reduce other ASD symptoms like obsessive repetition of behaviors and rigid insistence on sameness. In summary, it's probably fair to say that despite its recognition as one of the 20 most revolutionary articles in child psychology, Baron-Cohen et al. didn't take the autism intervention community by storm. In fact, based on the sheer number of evidence-based interventions developed to treat autism, Baron-Cohen et al.'s approach may represent little more than one drop in a bucket of intervention efforts. On the other hand, for the glass-half-full people out there, at least it's one more drop than we had before.

EMPATHIZING-SYSTEMATIZING THEORY

How do Baron-Cohen et al.'s findings fit into the big ASD picture? In a concise little book that summarizes the lion's share of what we know about ASD, Baron-Cohen reviews several major psychological theories. The "best one," he notes, is his own, called "Empathizing-Systematizing Theory." This theory not only accommodates the theory of mind aspect of ASD, but many other aspects of ASD as well, including savantism. As the name implies, Empathizing-Systematizing Theory has two parts. Each part maps onto one of the categories of symptoms we identified previously.

First is the empathizing part, which addresses limitations in both cognitive empathy and affective empathy. Whereas cognitive empathy includes the understanding and knowledge that other people have minds, affective empathy involves knowing what to do with that knowledge. Children with ASD are deficient in both types of empathizing, which is why, according to the theory, Category A symptoms are so pervasive. But the deficiency in both types of empathizing skills may also explain the limited impact of thought-bubble training. Thought-bubble training may improve children's mind-mindedness, and with it their cognitive empathy, but the technique itself sidesteps affective empathy because it provides little guidance about what children should do with their mind-mindedness. Still, having a deficiency in cognitive empathy is consistent with having a deficiency in language. After all, what's the point of having a language if there are no minds to communicate with?

The Sally-Anne results have direct relevance for the empathizing portion of the theory, but they have much less to do with the systematizing part. The systematizing part of the theory has to do with the "drive to analyze or construct systems." Broadly speaking, a "system" is anything that follows a set of rules. When children are "systematizing," they're working on identifying the rules that govern a particular system. As it turns out, systematizing requires a skill set that children with autism are actually pretty good at; so good that their expression may result in the pervasiveness of the Category B symptoms we talked about before. According to Baron-Cohen, systems that are especially interesting to children with ASD include the mechanical (such as a bicycle or window lock), the numerical (such as an airport timetable or a calendar), the abstract (such as musical notation or mathematics), the natural (such as tidal wave patterns or plant growth), and even, ironically, the social (such as dance choreography with a partner). Their interest in systematizing may cause children with autism to exhibit an intensive, even obsessive, focus on objects, especially their movements through space and their mechanical underpinnings.

The fact that children with ASD show prowess in systematizing may also explain why an occasional few show evidence of savantism. Savantism happens when individuals with profound intellectual deficiencies, such as found in ASD, paradoxically exhibit a small number of exceptional capabilities or talents far in excess of what would normally be expected. Savantism is exceedingly rare, despite its portrayal in the media. But when cases are discovered, they are fascinating. At 14 years of age, for example, Leslie Lemke didn't walk or talk. Yet one day he walked over to a piano, sat down, and flawlessly played Tchaikovsky's Piano Concerto No. 1, after hearing it only once on TV (see: http://www.youtube.com/watch?v=ZWtZA-ZmOAM). He eventually added operatic singing to his repertoire, even though he otherwise continued to show profound language deficiencies. Similarly, Stephen Wiltshire developed a passion for drawing while in a school for special needs children. To this day, he sketches accurate and highly detailed panoramic renderings of major cities after only a single aerial flyover (see: http://www.youtube.com/watch?v=95L-zmIBGd4).

A REMAINING CHALLENGE

One of the greatest remaining questions regarding autism is its origin. Increasing evidence points to the role of genetics, but the genetics are proving exceedingly complicated. Hundreds of genes have been implicated. *Yale News* science writer Bill Hathaway even suggested that, "The task of searching for a cause for [autism] is the scientific equivalent of trying to reach an unknown town in Maine knowing only that you started from a street in San Diego."

Unfortunately, the absence of a scientifically informed account of autism's origins hasn't prevented the void from being filled with whack-a-doodle conspiracy theories. One of the most infamous campaigns of misinformation has been the myth that autism is caused by immunization vaccinations. This "theory," despite being soundly debunked in the scientific literature, seems to have established a prominent foothold in American folk medicine. Hundreds of thousands of earnest, yet frightened parents refuse to immunize their children every year. As a result, previously eradicated diseases have reappeared. According to the Centers for Disease Control, for example, the incidence of whooping cough in the United States nearly tripled from 2000 to 2012 for children under 1 year of age, and a 2010 outbreak in California resulted in more than 9,000 bona fide cases—including 10 deaths—all directly linked to vaccination refusal. The financial burden on the American health care system has been incalculable.

Overcoming this kind of misunderstanding may be among the most manageable of the remaining challenges for experts in the study and treatment of autism. Accordingly, it may be instructional to consider how such an insidious myth gets its legs in this modern age of medical science. The bogus claim that immunizations cause autism started with a 1998 article published in the journal *Lancet*, by scientist A. J. Wakefield and 12 coauthors. *Lancet*, it should be noted, is one of the most prestigious medical science journals in the world. Relying on parental testimony, Wakefield et al. reported that 9 of 12 children in his study began showing signs of "regressive autism" (and in some cases, bowel disease) shortly after receiving MMR vaccines (i.e., a "triple" vaccine that simultaneously targets measles, mumps, and rubella). The obvious solution to the problem, according to Wakefield and colleagues, was to make sure that children were no longer given triple vaccines such as the MMR, and given instead only traditional, time-tested, single-purpose vaccines.

There was no reason to question these findings, at least initially, and so they were widely accepted. And as you might imagine, they also led to widespread panic and public outcry. How could we have been so easily duped by medical science as to expose our children to such a dangerous medical practice as administering triple immunizations? However, red flags about Wakefield's research were soon raised. The first thing that happened was that other laboratories failed to replicate his findings. Both a study in Finland involving 2 million children, and a study in the United States involving 3 million children, reported that *no* relationship existed between triple immunizations and the development of autism.

Then Wakefield's scientific objectivity itself was called into question. An investigative journalist named Brian Deer, working for the British newspaper, *Sunday Times*, discovered that some of the children who participated in Wakefield's study were actually recruited by the very law firm that was in the process of suing the manufacturer of the MMR vaccines used in the study. Could the children have been recruited into the study *because* they were showing symptoms of autism? It gets worse. Deer reported that at the time of the 1998 article, Wakefield himself was developing a single vaccine, and had even applied for a patent. Did Wakefield stand to gain financially if other rival vaccines were pulled from the market? Deer believed so.

As a result of the growing body of counterevidence, amid a swirling crescendo of controversy, 10 of Wakefield's original 12 coauthors eventually retracted their position that vaccines were linked to autism. And in 2010, the article itself was retracted by the journal *Lancet*. Today, no legitimate expert or scientific authority believes that autism is caused by, or is in any way linked to, immunization vaccines. Still, sadly the legend lives on, and a few high profile kooks with media access continue to spread the insidious nonsense to anyone who will listen.

Although it is tempting to point fingers at the "bad parents" who persistently refuse to immunize their children, the fact that so many of them remain steadfast in their opposition to vaccines is testament to just how frightening the prospect of ASD has become. Some parents would rather expose their children to known life-threatening infections, than risk a chance at "catching" ASD from the very vaccines that protect against those infections. In the face of this scientific counterinsurgency, and others like it, the burden on scientists and an educated public to ensure a calm, reasoned, empirically-informed triumph over fear-inspired insecurity and panic has never been greater. Perhaps even incremental advances in our understanding of ASD should be taken as cause for celebration. Maybe this is why the Baron-Cohen results were voted among the top 20 most revolutionary results published since 1960.

LIGHT AT THE END OF THE TUNNEL

At present, there is no cure for autism. However, there are many scientifically informed and effective treatments that make living with ASD less challenging. The problem for parents is sorting out the good ones from the ineffective ones, or worse, the ones that do damage. The single most accessible and comprehensive source of information on the treatment of autism is the website *Research Autism*

(http://www.researchautism.net/).

The website lists every known treatment methodology for autism, more than 1100 in all, and marks the best proven therapies with up to three green checks, and the worst proven therapies with up to three red x's. Most of the differences between the therapies result from differences in the aspects of ASD they are designed to target. Some target the core symptoms of ASD, while others target comorbid side-issues that result from the core symptoms.

Medication-based treatments tend to focus on the side-issues. According to *Research Autism*, for example, there is scientific evidence supporting the use of Risperidone to treat symptoms of irritability and hyperactivity that may impact some individuals with ASD. Similarly, melatonin therapy has been shown to help manage some of the sleep problems that may accompany ASD. But while medication-based therapies have focused on treating some of the symptoms, other therapies have larger-scale applications.

One of the most effective therapies with large-scale application comes from the field of Applied Behavior Analysis (ABA). Ironically, despite being the most effective, ABA-based therapies are also among the simplest. ABA-based therapies can be used in isolation, such as when working on a specific behavior problem, or in combination with a comprehensive treatment approach that involves working with the whole person in the context of a variety of treatment settings.

ABA-based therapies are founded on positive reinforcement principles, which you may have read about in your Introduction to Psychology course when you covered B. F. Skinner and operant conditioning. In positive reinforcement, a child is given a valuable reward of some sort after exhibiting a desired behavior. When the desired behavior is rewarded, it tends to increase in frequency. In children with ASD, the desired behaviors are usually those they are deficient in, and tend to be represented among the Category A symptoms. Remember that Category A symptoms are those that contribute to children's social isolation and their inability to communicate effectively with others. By increasing the frequency of effective communication skills, like making eye contact, or verbalizing needs or wants, appropriately credentialed therapists can make living with ASD far less difficult than it otherwise might be.

But it also turns out that when desirable behaviors increase, many undesirable and maladaptive behaviors go away. In fact, many of the maladaptive behaviors common to children with ASD, like self-injury and biting and hitting others, may actually result from children's inability to communicate with those around them. By improving children's communication behaviors, ABA therapists may simultaneously remove incentives children have for the maladaptive behaviors.

In a very recent study, Elizabeth Fulton and colleagues demonstrated just this finding. The specific ABA-based intervention they used was called the *Early Start Denver Model* (ESDM). The therapy involves certified ESDM therapists combining ABA principles with teaching children how to engage in specific communicative activities in the course of their play and everyday routines. The authors noted that, "The main focus is on teaching imitation; developing awareness of social interactions and reciprocity; teaching the power of communication; teaching more flexible, conventional, and creative play skills; [and] making the social world as understandable as the world of objects." After an 11-month training program, Fulton found that children with ASD exhibited significantly fewer maladaptive behaviors, suggesting that the presence of the newly trained communication skills rendered the socially maladaptive behaviors no longer necessary.

CONCLUSION

In this chapter I've perhaps drifted away from the main topic of interest—Baron-Cohen and colleagues' revolutionary 1985 study—more so than I have in other chapters. My reason for doing so is that autism has become a highly visible, even polarizing disorder that has attracted the interests of people from widely divergent political interests. Yet, there is so much more to be learned about autism. ASD remains shrouded in mysteries. Only through continued and persistent scientific research will we begin to unravel some of those mysteries. According to the *Autism Speaks* website (http://www.autismspeaks.org/), although autism now affects 1 in 68 children or 1.4% of all children, funding for autism research by the U.S. National Institutes for Health (NIH) amounts to only 0.55% of the total NIH budget. This represents a problem-to-expenditure ratio mismatch of almost 3:1. Fortunately, not all scientific research needs to be funded by a government or private agency. Sometimes what is most needed are creative scientists, some provocative ideas, and some children with ASD eager to participate in the research. Then revolutionary things can happen. The work by Baron-Cohen, Leslie, and Frith fits this bill perfectly.

Reference

http://www.youtube.com/watch?v=ZWtZA-ZmOAM
http://www.youtube.com/watch?v=95L-zmIBGd4

Bibliography

American Psychiatric Association. (2013). *Diagnostic and statistical manual of mental disorders* (5th ed.). Arlington, VA: American Psychiatric Publishing.

Baron-Cohen, S. (2008). *Autism and Asperger syndrome*. Oxford University Press.

Fulton, E., Eapen, V., Črnčec, R., Walter, A., & Rogers, S. (2014). *Reducing maladaptive behaviors* in preschool-aged children with autism spectrum disorder using the Early Start Denver Model. *Frontiers in Pediatrics, 2*, 1–10.

Hathaway, B. (2013, November 21). Follow the genes: Yale team finds clues to origin of autism. *Yale News*.

Hobson, R. P. (1984). Early childhood autism and the question of egocentrism. *Journal of Autism & Developmental Disorders, 14*, 85–104.

Notbohm, E. (2012). *Ten things every child with autism wishes you knew*. Arlington, TX: Future Horizons.

Premack, D., & Woodruff, G. (1978). Does the chimpanzee have a theory of mind? *Behavioral and Brain Sciences, 1*, 515–526.

Wakefield, A. J., Murch, S. H., Anthony, A., Linnell, J., Casson, D. M., Malik, M., . . . & Walker-Smith, J. A. (1998). RETRACTED: Ileal-lymphoid-nodular hyperplasia, non-specific colitis, and pervasive developmental disorder in children. *The Lancet, 351*, 637–641.

Wellman, H. M., Baron-Cohen, S., Caswell, R., Gomez, J. C., Swettenham, J., Toye, E., & Lagattuta, K. (2002). Thought-bubbles help children with autism acquire an alternative to a theory of mind. *Autism, 6*, 343–363.

Questions for Discussion

1. In addition to the example already provided, how might having a theory of mind provide humans with a selective survival advantage over other species?

2. Considering that "Autism Spectrum Disorder" is the new DSM-5 diagnosis given to children who otherwise differ vastly from one another in symptoms, abilities, and challenges, is there any value in applying a single diagnostic label to all of them? What benefits and costs might result from such labeling? From the lack of such labeling?

3. *Research Autism* is a charity designed to help stakeholders identify resources for working with people with autism. On their website, they list more than 1000 interventions used in working with autistic populations (see: http://researchautism.net/autism-interventions). Besides thought-bubble training, can you identify any interventions, treatments, and therapies that would be consistent with a theory of mind approach?

GLOSSARY

Accommodation: (from Piaget's theory) the process that explains how existing schemas adjust themselves to allow for new information.

Activity level: one of Thomas, Chess, and Birch's temperament dimensions, characterizing the speed and frequency of a child's movement.

Adaptability: one of Thomas, Chess, and Birch's temperament dimensions, reflecting that children can be soothed when distressed.

Affordance: the fit between an animal's capabilities and the environmental supports that enable a given action to be performed. The perception of affordances allows animals to guide activity adaptively, and to parse the environment into functionally meaningful units.

Allophonic variation: when individual speech sounds are produced differently, but are still categorized as belonging to a single phoneme within a language.

Animal ethology: the scientific study of animal behavior, especially as it relates to an individual's or a species' current environmental conditions.

Approach/withdrawal: one of Thomas, Chess, and Birch's temperament dimensions, focusing on the extent that children are comfortable with new things and people.

Assimilation: (from Piaget's theory) the process of fitting new information into existing schemas.

Attachment system: a system, selected by thousands of years of evolution, that ensures mothers and babies are attracted to one another, thereby increasing the likelihood of babies' surviving to maturity.

Attractor (or attractor state): the preferred pattern of behavior of a complex system (including humans) that results from the cooperation of the participating elements of the system, in a particular context.

Authoritarian parenting: one of Baumrind's major parenting styles, characterized by an emphasis on strict obedience and high expectations.

Behavioral psychologist (or behaviorist): a psychologist who believes that all behaviors are learned through experience through some form of classical or instrumental conditioning.

Binocular cells: cortical cells in the visual cortex that receive input from both eyes.

Collective variable: from Dynamic Systems Theory, a relatively simple variable or system that represents the collective functioning of multiple other variables or systems; such as when *walking* represents the collective contributions of all of the systems that are involved in walking.

Columnar microstructure: reported by Hubel and Wiesel, a type of organization found in the visual cortex in which groups of cells that respond to highly similar visual stimuli are arranged in columns.

Contralateral: coming from the opposite side.

Corneal reflection technique: a technique whereby it's possible to tell what an organism is looking at simply by observing the reflection centered over the organism's pupil.

Cortical cells: cells that make up the cerebral cortex.

Cute response: a proposed biologically built-in system ensuring that babies will be perceived as "cute" by adults, thereby increasing the likelihood that adults will want to care for babies.

Ecological transitions: according to Bronfenbrenner, fruitful contexts for developmental research. These transitions include changes in role and setting as the person matures.

Ecology: the branch of biology that studies the relationship between organisms and their surroundings.

Environment of adaptedness: the specific environment that a species was built, through evolution, to best fit into.

Epistemology: a branch of philosophy that deals with the meaning and origins of knowledge.

Exosystem: from Bronfenbrenner's ecological theory, the set of social structures that influence the developing person's immediate surroundings, but that do not contain the person.

Functionally invariant: this notion was used by Piaget to suggest that even though the contents of thought and knowledge might change and develop over time, the processes that lead to the development of thought and knowledge always function the same way. In other words, they become *functionally invariant*.

Higher psychological process: in Vygotsky's theory, the abilities to use language and tools.

Histological examination: a type of examination in which slices of brain tissue are examined under a microscope for neuroanatomical organization.

Imprinting: a biological process through which a baby *attaches* to an adult member of the species.

Information processing theory: a theory of cognitive development that uses the computer as a metaphor for thinking about babies' thinking abilities. Just like a computer, babies have inputs (the senses) and outputs (behaviors), and presumably there's some important stuff that goes on in between.

Inner voice: in Vygotsky's theory, the running inner dialog we carry on with ourselves, when we're attempting to solve problems.

Instinct: in Bowlby's theory, any system of behaviors that (1) follows a similar and predictable pattern in most members of the species, (2) is not a simple response to a single stimulus, but a sequence of behaviors that runs a predictable course, (3) has consequences that are valuable for ensuring the survival of the individual or the species, and (4) develops even when there are no opportunities for learning it.

Intellectual adaptation: the more general process that subsumes *accommodation* and *assimilation*.

Intensity of reaction: one of Thomas, Chess, and Birch's temperament dimensions, reflecting the amount of energy children put into their responses to the world.

Interpersonal function of speech: Vygotsky's notion that sometimes speech between two people is needed to solve a problem.

Intrapersonal function of speech: Vygotsky's notion that children eventually become capable of more or less talking to themselves when solving a problem. They have an *inner voice*.

Ipsilateral: coming from the same side.

Like-Me hypothesis: the possibility that human babies are uniquely built to have a feeling of interpersonal connectedness, from the earliest moments after birth, whenever they gaze into the eyes of a social partner.

Long-habituators: usually refers to babies who take a relatively long time to habituate.

Longitudinal study: a study of a single group of people over a certain period of time.

Macrosystem: from Bronfenbrenner's ecological theory, the overarching institutional patterns of the culture or subculture, including the educational, legal, and political systems.

Maternal sensitive responsiveness: the extent to which mothers respond to the behavioral cues and signals of their children reliably and appropriately.

Mental model: as used in attachment theory, a set of expectations held by a baby, based on experience, about the reliability and responsiveness of the mother.

Microsystem: from Bronfenbrenner's ecological theory, the complex of relations between the developing person and environment in an immediate setting containing that person.

Motion parallax: the perception that when we are moving through space, close-up objects appear to be moving by us faster than objects that are farther away.

Naturalistic observation: a research design in which the researcher observes behavior in a naturally occurring environment.

Nomothetic approach: a scientific approach that aims to discover universal, underlying laws.

Ontogeny: the developmental course of an individual member of a species.

Operational definition: when psychologists measure abstract psychological traits, characteristics, or abilities, they describe the specific operations or procedures they use to measure them. Whatever operation or procedure they settle on to measure a trait, characteristic, or ability makes up their *operational definition* of that trait, characteristic, or ability. An IQ test score is a typical operational definition of intelligence.

Pattern density: the number of elements of a pattern found in a particular unit of space. Patterns appear to become less dense as they drawer nearer to us, so pattern density can be used as a cue to how far away something is.

Phylogeny: the developmental course of a species as a whole.

Primary circular reactions: Piaget's second substage of sensorimotor development. A baby does something interesting with or on his own body, and attempts to reproduce it. In this sense, *primary* means "own body" and *circular* refers to "repetition of the act."

Principle of parsimony: a practice adopted widely throughout all of the sciences dictating that the simplest possible explanation for a phenomenon be assumed until evidence to the contrary is uncovered. *Parsimony* basically means "simple."

Prospective science: an approach to doing psychological science in which the goal is to observe behaviors at an early point in time and observe how they change and develop over time. It's a forward-looking approach.

Punitive behavior: behavior aimed at punishing.

Receptive field: the field of vision for a particular set of retinal cells that is most responsive.

Reflexes: in Piaget's theory, the basic knowledge structures that babies start out with, and therefore the very first schemas.

Rhythmicity: one of Thomas, Chess, and Birch's temperament dimensions, focusing on the regularity and predictability of bodily functions.

Schemas: basic structures that underlie all knowledge; a schema is our internal representation or understanding of an object, a concept, an event, a fact, or anything else that we know.

Secondary circular reactions: Piaget's third substage of sensorimotor development. A baby does something interesting with or on an external object, and attempts to reproduce it. In this sense, *secondary* means "external object" and *circular* refers to "repetition of the act."

Short-habituators: usually refers to babies who habituate relatively quickly.

Signaling behaviors: from attachment theory, a biologically prepared and evolutionarily significant set of signals given off by babies to inform their mothers of some need or state. Includes crying and smiling.

Social referencing: looking at another person and using his or her reaction to guide our own reaction to a stimulus or event.

Stimulus: any object or event that is detected and/or responded to by an organism.

Strange situation: an extremely popular methodology developed by Ainsworth to measure the quality of mother-child attachment.

Temperament: a set of biological and behavioral predispositions to respond in a certain way to sources of stimulation in the environment.

Tertiary circular reactions: Piaget's fifth substage of sensorimotor development. A baby does something interesting, and attempts to reproduce it while varying the details of the event each time to "see what will happen."

Totality of the functional social system: Bronfenbrenner's dictate that any decent theory of child development must take into account the fact that experiments involving humans are themselves a social system, and that children's behavior in these experiments will inevitably reflect that social system.

Transforming experiment: a type of experiment in which children are exposed to radical departures from the existing belief systems of their own culture.

Transitional probability: in the context of Saffran's work on infant statistical learning, defined as the probability of one sound occurring given that another sound has just occurred.

Visual acuity: how well you can see. "Normal" visual acuity is 20/20.

Word context effect: when the production of a target speech sound is affected by the immediately adjacent sounds in the speech stream.

Zone of proximal development: this extremely popular notion refers to the fact that children can perform at higher levels when they are guided by a more mature or more experienced person. The zone is technically defined as the difference in ability when performing alone and when performing with the more experienced person.

CREDITS

Text

Page 25: Yogi Berra. (2009). *You can observe a lot by watching: What I've learned about teamwork from the Yankees and life.* John Wiley & Sons.

Pages 27, 29: Piaget, J. (1962). *Play, dreams and imitation.* New York: W.W. Norton & Company. (pp. 7, 18–20).

Pages 27, 28, 29, 30, 31, 32: Piaget, J. (1945). *La formation du symbole chez l'enfant: imitation, jeu et rêve, image et représentation.* Neuchâtel: Delachaux & Niestlé.

Pages 32, 33, 34: Piaget, J. (1962). *Play, dreams and imitation.* New York: W.W. Norton & Company.

Pages 39, 40, 41, 42, 43, 45: Vygotsky, L. S. (1978). *Mind in society: The development of higher psychological processes.* Harvard University Press.

Page 53: Baillargeon, R. (2000). Reply to Bogartz, Shinskey, and Schilling; Schilling; and Cashon and Cohen. *Infancy,* 1, 447–462.

Page 54: Baillargeon, R. Object permanence in 3 1/2- and 4 1/2-month-old infants. *Developmental Psychology,* 23, 655–664. Copyright 1987 by the American Psychological Association, Inc.

Page 57: Bates, E. (1999). Nativism versus development: Comments on Baillargeon and Smith. *Developmental Science,* 2, 148–149.

Page 57: Smith, L. (1999). Do infants possess innate knowledge structures? The con side. *Developmental Science,* 2, 133–144.

Pages 63, 65, 66, 69, 71: Thelen, E., & Ulrich, B. D. (1991). Hidden skills: A dynamic systems analysis of treadmill stepping during the first year. *Monographs of the Society for Research in Child Development,* 56, (1, Serial No. 223). (pp. 11, 37, 41, 44, 48, 52, 81, 83).

Pages 69–70: Based on http://plus.maths.org/content/walk-trot-gallop.

Page 72: Lewis, M. D. (2011). Dynamic systems approaches: Cool enough? Hot enough? *Child Development Perspectives,* 5, 279–285. (p. 282).

Pages 74, 78, 79, 80: Gibson, E. J., & Walk, R. D. (1960). The "visual cliff." *Scientific American,* 202, 64–71.

Page 76: Adolph, K. E., Eppler, M. A., & Gibson, E. J. (1993). Crawling versus walking infants' perception of affordances for locomotion over sloping surfaces. *Child Development,* 64, 1158–1174.

Pages 77, 82: Adolph, K. E., & Kretch, K. S. (2012). Infants on the edge: Beyond the visual cliff. In S. A. Haslam, A. M. Slater, and J. R. Smith (Series Eds.), & A. M. Slater and P. C. Quinn (Volume Eds.), *Developmental psychology: Revisiting the classic studies.* London: Sage.

Page 83: Adolph, K. S., & Adolph, K. E. (2013). Cliff or step? Posture-specific learning at the edge of a drop-off. *Child Development,* 84, 226–240.

Page 84: Szokolzky, A. (2003). An interview with Eleanor Gibson. *Ecological Psychology,* 15, 271–281.

Pages 97, 98, 99, 100: Wiesel, T. N., & Hubel, D. H. (1963). Receptive fields of cells in striate cortex of very young, visually inexperienced kittens. *Journal of Neurophysiology.*

Page 100: Wiesel, T. N., & Hubel, D. H. (1963). Single-cell responses in striate cortex of kittens deprived of vision in one eye. *Journal of Neurophysiology,* 26, 1003–1017.

Pages 103, 104: Hubel, D. H. (1982). Evolution of ideas in the primary visual cortex, a biased historical account. *Bioscience Reports,* 2, 435–439.

Pages 108, 110, 112, 114: Werker, J. F., & Tees, R. C. (1984). Cross-language speech perception: Evidence for perceptual reorganization during the first year of life. *Infant Behavior and Development,* 7, 49–63. (pp. 50, 52, 55, 59).

Page 119: Hirsh-Pasek, K., Golinkoff, R. M., Hennon, E. A., & Maguire, M. J. (2004). Hybrid theories at the frontier of developmental psychology: The emergentist coalition model of word learning as a case in point. In D. G. Hall & S. R. Waxman (Eds.), *Weaving a lexicon.* Cambridge, MA: MIT Press. (p. 175).

Pages 121, 125, 128: Saffran, J. R., Aslin, R. N., & Newport, E. L. (1996). Statistical learning by 8-month-old infants. *Science,* 274, 1926–1928. (pp. 1926, 1927, 1928).

Pages 132, 133, 134, 136: Bandura, A., Ross, D., & Ross, S. (1961). Transmission of aggression through imitation of aggressive models. *Journal of Abnormal and Social Psychology,* 63, 575–582.

Page 137: Perez, A. J. Ray Rice won't say what happened in the casino elevator, but admits abuse by saying it was 'the first time'. *nj.com,* 31 July 2014.

Page 137: Buzzannco, G. Watertown teens arrested for instagram bullying. *FoxCT,* 8 July 2014.

Pages 137–138: Mueller, A. From Facebook to the streets: How social media is fueling youth violence in Kalamazoo. *Mlive,* 5 August 2014.

Page 138: Chicago Sun-Times, 10 March 2001.

Pages 147, 148: Meltzoff, A. N., & Moore, M. K. (1977). Imitation of facial and manual gestures by human neonates. *Science,* 198, 75–78. (pp. 77, 78).

Page 149: Meltzoff, A. N., & Moore, M. K. (1999). Resolving the debate about early imitation. In A. Slater & D. Muir (Eds.), *The Blackwell reader in developmental psychology.* Oxford: Blackwell.

Pages 151–152: Anisfeld, M. (1996). Only tongue protrusion modeling is matched by neonates. *Developmental Review,* 16, 149–161. (p. 160).

Page 152: Meltzoff, A. N., & Moore, M. K. (1994). Imitation, memory, and the representation of persons. *Infant Behavior and Development,* 17, 39–61. (p. 54).

Pages 158, 159, 161–162, 163, 164: Bronfenbrenner, U. (1977). Toward an experimental ecology of human development. *American Psychologist,* 32, 513–531.

Page 164: McLuhan, M. (1968). *War and peace in the global village: An inventory of some of the current spastic situations that could be eliminated by more feedforward.* McGraw-Hill.

Pages 170, 176: Mischel, W. (2007). Walter Mischel. In G. Lindzey & W. M. Runyan (Eds.), *A history of psychology in autobiography.* Vol. IX. (pp. 229–267). Washington, DC: American Psychological Association. (p. 246).

Pages 170, 171, 172: Mischel, W., & Ebbesen, E. G. (1970). Attention in delay of gratification. *Journal of Personality and Social Psychology,* 16, 329–337. (pp. 330, 332, 333, 335, 337).

Page 175: Mischel, W., Ebbesen, E. B., & Zeiss, A. R. (1972). Cognitive and attentional mechanism in delay of gratification. *Journal of Personality and Social Psychology,* 21, 204–218. (p. 211).

Page 177: Mischel in DON'T!, The secret of self-control by Jonah Lehrer. *The Newyorker,* 18 May 2009.

Page 177: Mischel, W., Shoda, Y., & Peake, P. K. (1988).The nature of adolescent competencies predicted by preschool delay of gratification. *Journal of Personality and Social Psychology,* 54, 687–696.

Pages 181, 193, 196, 197, 198, 199: Bowlby, J. (1969). *Attachment and loss Vol. 1. Attachment.* New York: Basic Books.

Pages 182, 183, 184, 186, 187: Harlow, H. F., & Zimmerman, R. R. (1959). Affectional responses in the infant monkey. *Science,* 130, 421–432.

Pages 200, 204, 205, 209, 210: Ainsworth, M. D. S. (1992). John Bowlby (1907–1990): Obituary. *American Psychologist,* 47, 668.

Page 211: Main, M. (1999). Mary D. Salter Ainsworth: Tribute and portrait. *Psychoanalytic Inquiry,* 19, 682–776.

Pages 218, 219, 220: Thomas, A., Chess, S., & Birch, H. G. (1968). *Temperament and behavior disorders in children.* New York: New York University Press.

Pages 229, 230, 235–236: Baumrind, D. (1971). Current patterns of parental authority. *Developmental Psychology Monographs*, 4 (1, part 2).

Page 237: Baumrind, D. (1991). The influence of parenting style on adolescent competence and substance use. *Journal of Early Adolescence*, 11, 56–95.

Page 239: Shakespeare, W. (1632). *You like it.* London: Printed by Theodore Cotes.

Page 240: James, W. (1890). *Principles of psychology.* By H. Holt. (p. 488).

Page 245: DeCasper, A. J., & Fifer, W. P. (1980). Of human bonding: Newborns prefer their mothers' voices. *Science*, 208, 1174–1176. (p. 1176).

Pages 245, 246: DeCasper, A. J., & Spence, M. J. (1986). Prenatal maternal speech influences newborns' perception of speech sounds. *Infant Behavior and Development*, 9, 133–150. (pp. 134, 136).

Pages 249–250: Notbohm, E. (2012). *Ten things every child with autism wishes you knew.* Arlington, TX: Future Horizons.

Page 252: American Psychiatric Association. (2013). *Diagnostic and statistical manual of mental disorders* (5th ed.). Arlington, VA: American Psychiatric Publishing.

Pages 254, 255, 258: Baron-Cohen, S., Leslie, A., & Frith, U. (1985). Does the autistic child have a "theory of mind"? *Cognition*, 21, 37–46. (pp. 38, 43).

Page 256: With kind permission from the artist, Axel Scheffler.

Page 256: Frith, U. (2001). Mind blindness and the brain in autism. *Neuron*, 32(6), 969–979.

Page 258: Hobson, R. P. (1984). Early childhood autism and the question of egocentrism. *Journal of Autism & Developmental Disorders*, 14, 85–104.

Page 258: Wellman, H. M., Baron-Cohen, S., Caswell, R., Gomez, J. C., Swettenham, J., Toye, E., & Lagattuta, K. (2002). Thought-bubbles help children with autism acquire an alternative to a theory of mind. *Autism*, 6(4), 343–363. (pp. 361–362).

Page 260: Hathaway, B. Follow the genes: Yale team finds clues to origin of autism. *Yale News*, 21 November 2013.

Page 262: Fulton, E., Eapen, V., Crncec, R., Walter, A., & Rogers, S. (2014). Reducing maladaptive behaviors in preschool-aged children with autism spectrum disorder using the early start denver model. *Frontiers in Pediatrics*, 2, 1–10.

Photos

Page abbreviations are as follows: (L) left, (C) center, and (R) right.

Page 22: AP Photo; *p. 36:* Courtesy of Dr. Michael Cole; *p. 48:* Courtesy of Dr. Renee Baillargeon; *p. 61:* (L) Pearson Education, (R) Photo provided courtesy of the University of Michigan; *p. 74:* (L) Courtesy of Karen Adolf, (R) Pearson Education; *p. 78:* Science Source; *p. 86:* Pearson Education; *p. 94:* AP Photo; *p. 105:* Courtesy of Dr. Janet Werker; *p. 117:* (L) Photo by Jeff Miller/University of Wisconsin-Madison, (C) Dick Aslin/Courtesy of the University of Rochester, (R) Courtesy of Lloyd Wolff Photography/Dr. Elissa Newport; *p. 130:* With Courtesy from Albert Bandura; *p. 142:* Courtesy of Dr. Andrew Meltzoff; *p. 143:* A. N. Meltzoff & M. K. Moore "Imitation of Facial and Manual Gestures by Human Neonates" *Science* 1977, 198, 75–78; *p. 155:* AP Photo; *p. 168:* (L) Photo Courtesy of Dr. Walter Mischel/Michele Meyers, (C) Courtesy of Yuichi Shoda, (R) Courtesy of Dr. Monica I. Rodriguez; *p. 180:* (L) Courtesy of Harlow Primate Laboratory/University of Wisconsin, (R) Courtesy of Harlow Primate Laboratory/University of Wisconsin; *p. 185:* Photo Researchers, Inc/Science Source; *p. 190:* Courtesy of Richard Bowlby; *p. 202:* Courtesy of Dr. Patricia Crittenden; *p. 214:* (L) Pearson Education, (C) Pearson Education, (R) Pearson Education; *p. 226:* Courtesy of Dr. Diana Baumrind, Institute of Human Development, University of California, Berkeley; *p. 239:* (L) Courtesy of Anthony J. DeCasper, (R) Courtesy of William P. Fifer; *p. 249:* (L) Courtesy of Simon Baron-Cohen, (C) Courtesy of Alan M. Leslie, (R) Courtesy of Uta Frithe.

INDEX